MY CAGE

Year One

Written by Ed Power

Illustrated by Melissa DeJesus

My Cage Year One

Distributed by King Features Syndicate.

King Features Syndicate
300 W 57th Street
New York, NY 10019

YEAR ONE

Containing daily strips from May 6, 2007 to May 5, 2008

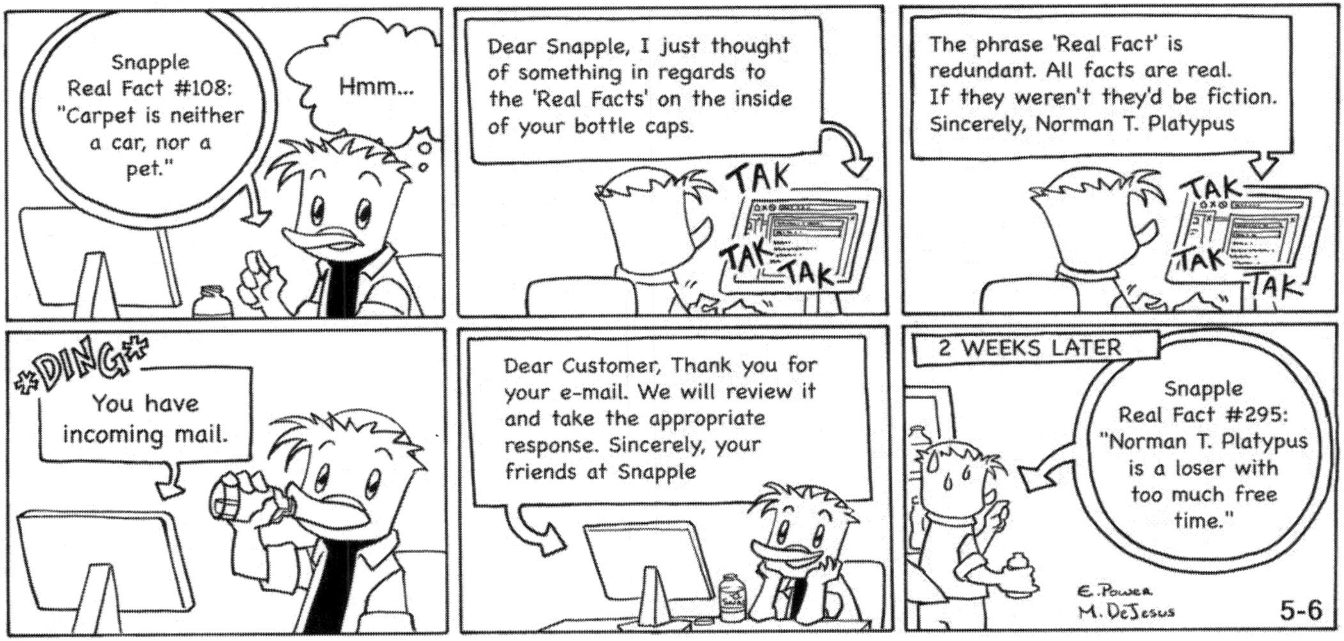
Snapple Real Fact #108: "Carpet is neither a car, nor a pet."
Hmm...
Dear Snapple, I just thought of something in regards to the 'Real Facts' on the inside of your bottle caps.
TAK
TAK
TAK
The phrase 'Real Fact' is redundant. All facts are real. If they weren't they'd be fiction. Sincerely, Norman T. Platypus
TAK
TAK
TAK
DING
You have incoming mail.
Dear Customer, Thank you for your e-mail. We will review it and take the appropriate response. Sincerely, your friends at Snapple
2 WEEKS LATER
Snapple Real Fact #295: "Norman T. Platypus is a loser with too much free time."
E. Power
M. DeJesus
5-6

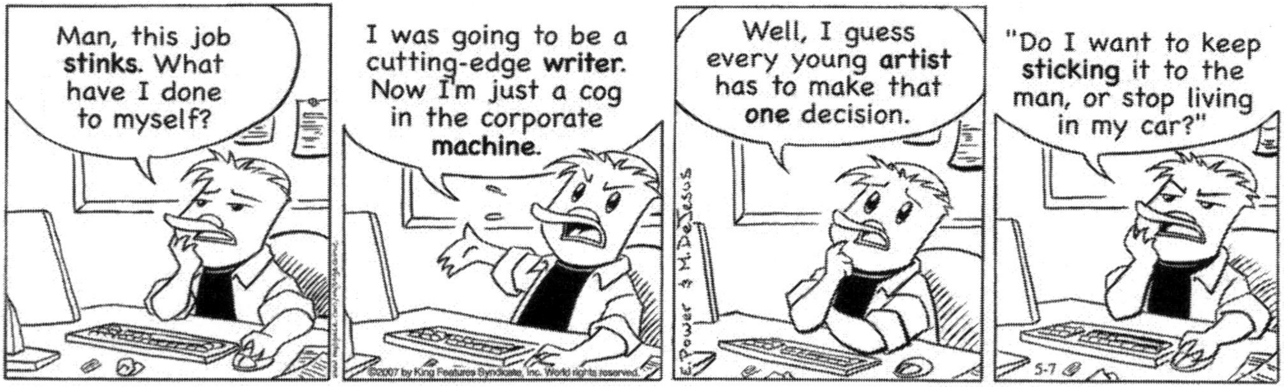
Man, this job **stinks.** What have I done to myself?
I was going to be a cutting-edge **writer.** Now I'm just a cog in the corporate **machine.**
Well, I guess every young **artist** has to make that **one** decision.
"Do I want to keep **sticking** it to the man, or stop living in my car?"
E. Power & M. DeJesus
©2007 by King Features Syndicate, Inc. World rights reserved.
5-7

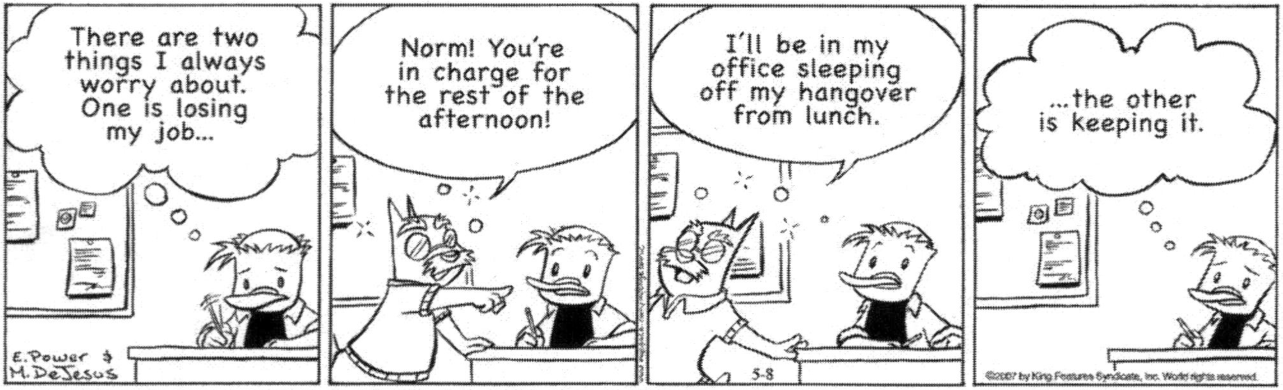
There are two things I always worry about. One is losing my job...
Norm! You're in charge for the rest of the afternoon!
I'll be in my office sleeping off my hangover from lunch.
...the other is keeping it.
E. Power & M. DeJesus
5-8
©2007 by King Features Syndicate, Inc. World rights reserved.

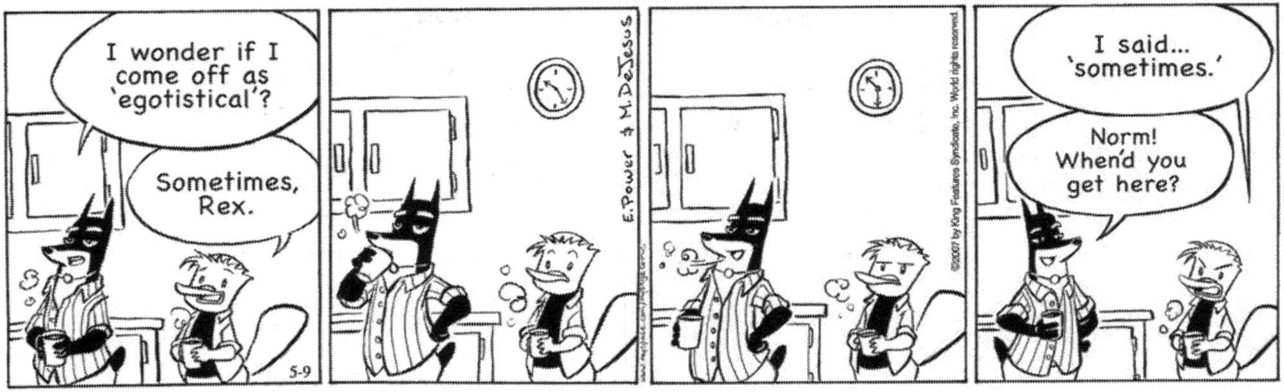
I wonder if I come off as 'egotistical'?
Sometimes, Rex.
5-9
E. Power & M. DeJesus
I said... 'sometimes.'
Norm! When'd you get here?

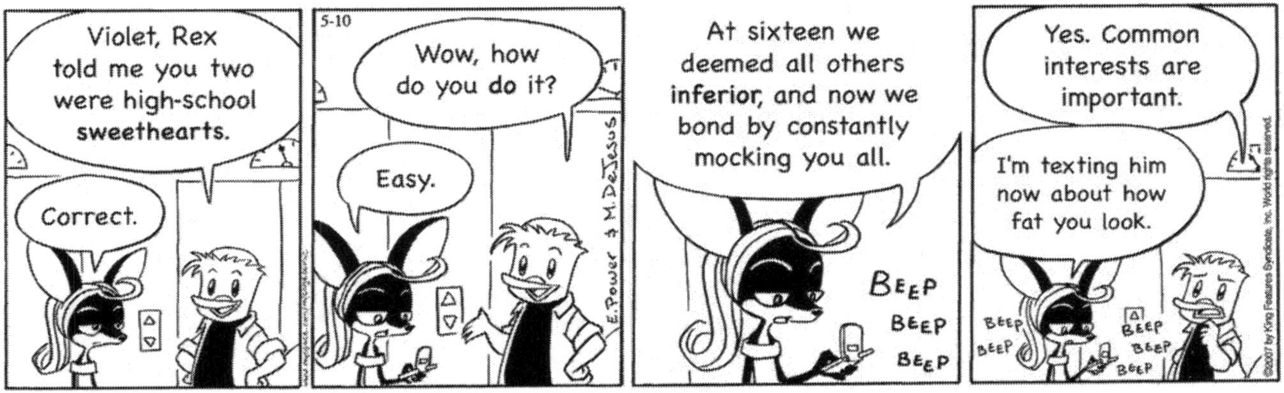
Violet, Rex told me you two were high-school **sweethearts.**
Correct.
5-10
Wow, how do you **do** it?
Easy.
E. Power & M. DeJesus
At sixteen we deemed all others **inferior**, and now we bond by constantly mocking you all.
BEEP
BEEP
BEEP
Yes. Common interests are important.
I'm texting him now about how fat you look.
BEEP
BEEP
BEEP
BEEP
BEEP

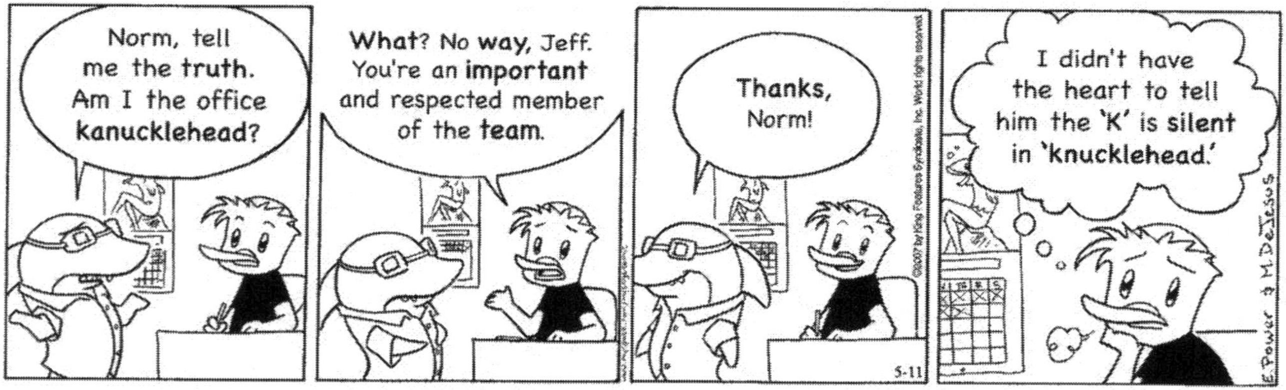
Norm, tell me the **truth.** Am I the office **kanucklehead?**
What? No **way,** Jeff. You're an **important** and respected member of the **team.**
Thanks, Norm!
©2007 by King Features Syndicate, Inc. World rights reserved.
5-11
I didn't have the heart to tell him the **'K'** is **silent** in **'knucklehead.'**
E. Power & M. DeJesus

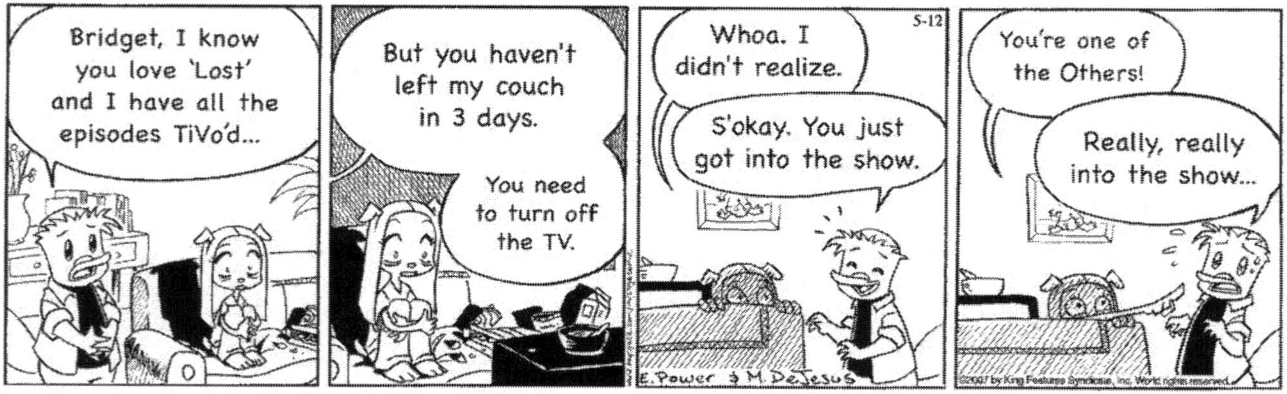
Bridget, I know you love 'Lost' and I have all the episodes TiVo'd...
But you haven't left my couch in 3 days.
You need to turn off the TV.
5-12
Whoa. I didn't realize.
S'okay. You just got into the show.
E. Power & M. DeJesus
You're one of the Others!
Really, really into the show...
©2007 by King Features Syndicate, Inc. World rights reserved.

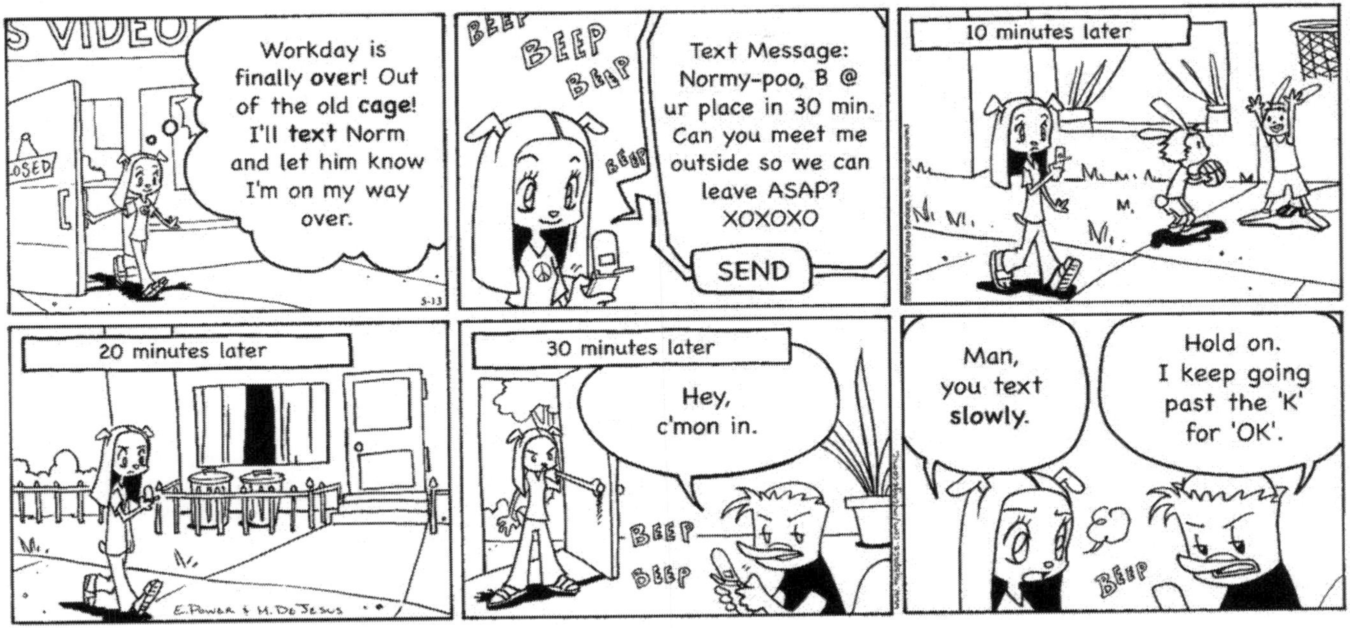
S VIDEO
OSED
Workday is finally over! Out of the old cage! I'll text Norm and let him know I'm on my way over.
5-13
BEEP
BEEP
BEEP
BEEP
Text Message: Normy-poo, B @ ur place in 30 min. Can you meet me outside so we can leave ASAP? XOXOXO
SEND
10 minutes later
20 minutes later
E. Power & M. DeJesus
30 minutes later
Hey, c'mon in.
BEEP
BEEP
Man, you text slowly.
Hold on. I keep going past the 'K' for 'OK'.
BEEP

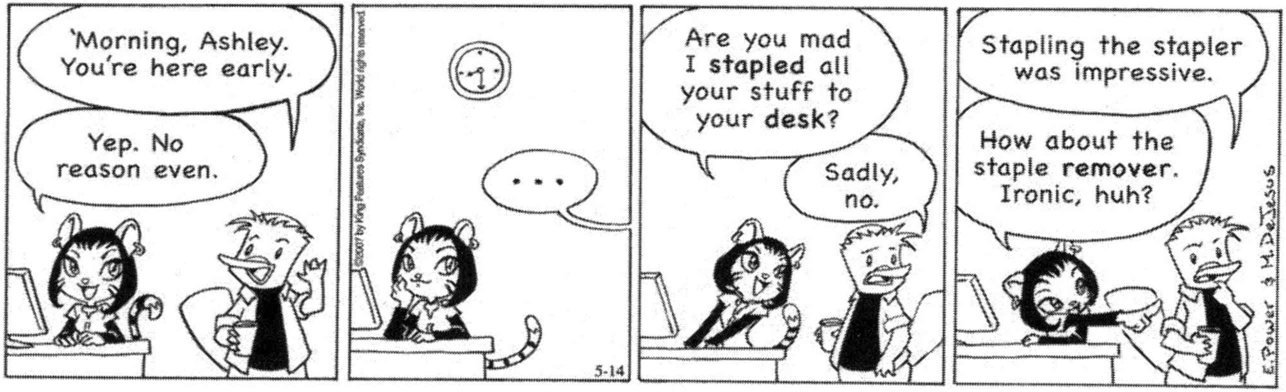
'Morning, Ashley. You're here early.
Yep. No reason even.
. . .
Are you mad I stapled all your stuff to your desk?
Sadly, no.
Stapling the stapler was impressive.
How about the staple remover. Ironic, huh?
E. Power & M. DeJesus
5-14

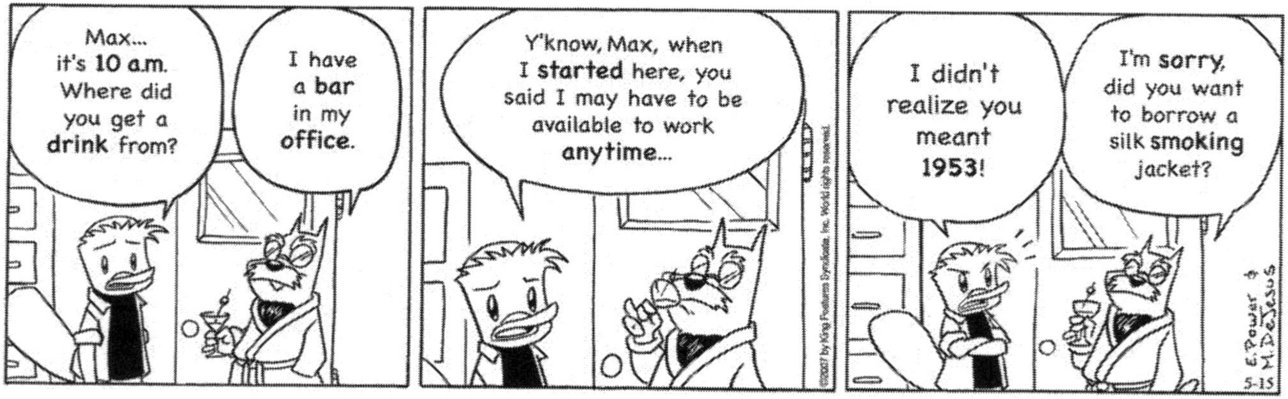
Max... it's 10 a.m. Where did you get a drink from?
I have a bar in my office.
Y'know, Max, when I started here, you said I may have to be available to work anytime...
I didn't realize you meant 1953!
I'm sorry, did you want to borrow a silk smoking jacket?
E. Power & M. DeJesus
5-15

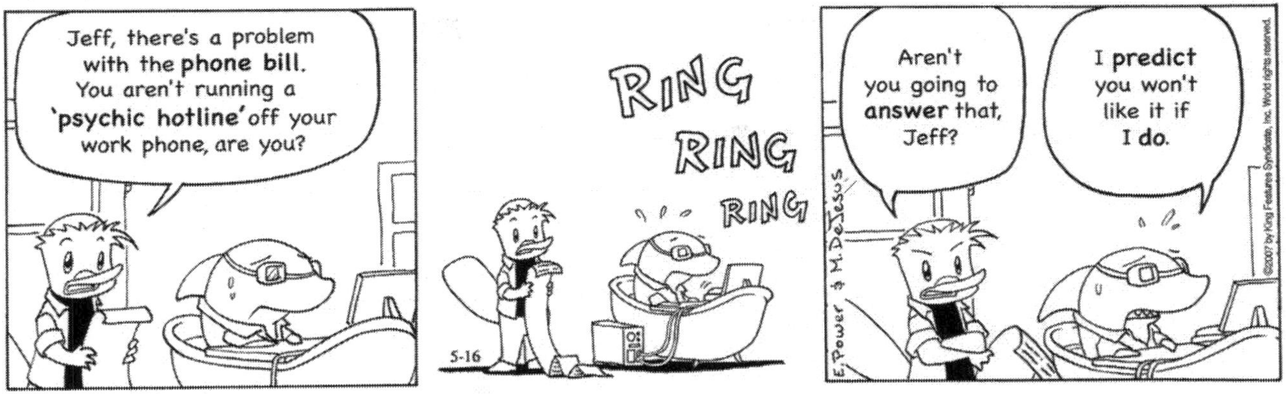
Jeff, there's a problem with the **phone bill**. You aren't running a **'psychic hotline'** off your work phone, are you?
RING RING RING
5-16
Aren't you going to **answer** that, Jeff?
I **predict** you won't like it if **I do**.
E. Power & M. DeJesus
©2007 by King Features Syndicate, Inc. World rights reserved.

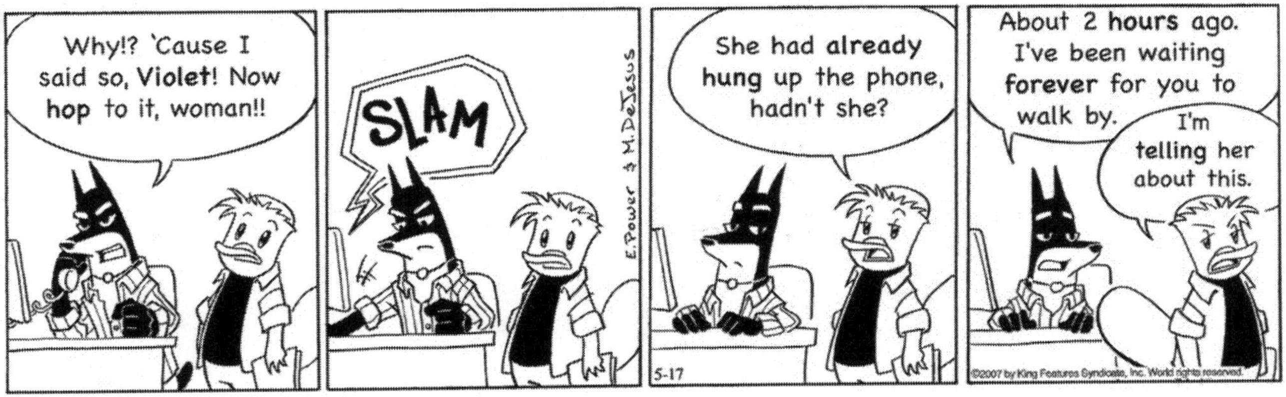
Why!? 'Cause I said so, **Violet**! Now **hop** to it, woman!!
SLAM
E. Power & M. DeJesus
She had **already hung** up the phone, hadn't she?
5-17
About 2 **hours** ago. I've been waiting **forever** for you to walk by.
I'm **telling** her about this.
©2007 by King Features Syndicate, Inc. World rights reserved.

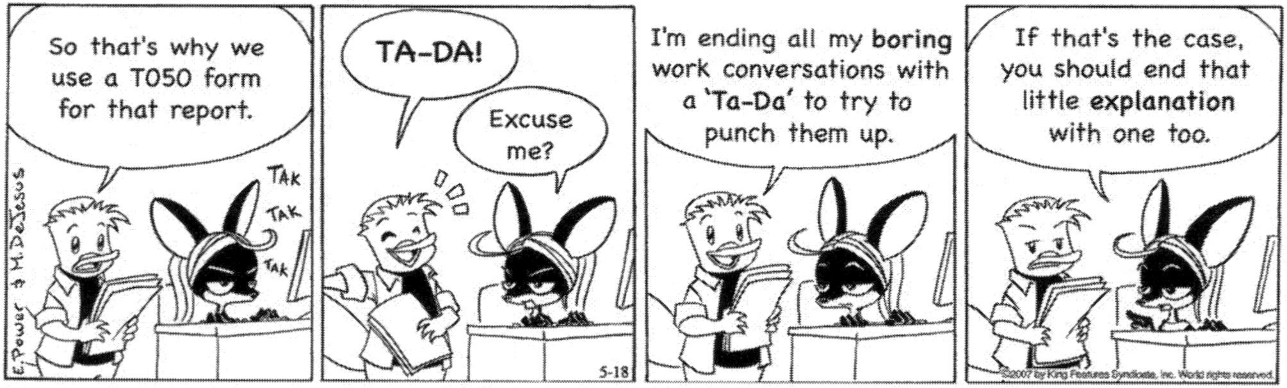
E. Power & M. DeJesus
So that's why we use a T050 form for that report.
TAK
TAK
TAK
TA-DA!
Excuse me?
5-18
I'm ending all my **boring** work conversations with a **'Ta-Da'** to try to punch them up.
If that's the case, you should end that little **explanation** with one too.
©2007 by King Features Syndicate, Inc. World rights reserved.

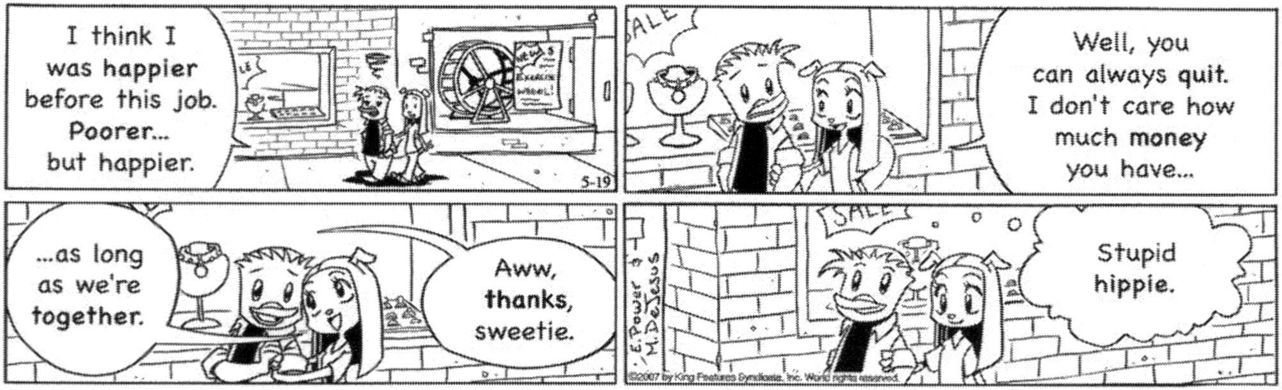
I think I was **happier** before this job. **Poorer...** but happier.
EXERCISE WHEEL!
5-19
SALE
Well, you can always **quit.** I don't care how much **money** you have...
...as long as we're **together.**
Aww, **thanks,** sweetie.
E. Power & M. DeJesus
SALE
Stupid **hippie.**
©2007 by King Features Syndicate, Inc. World rights reserved.

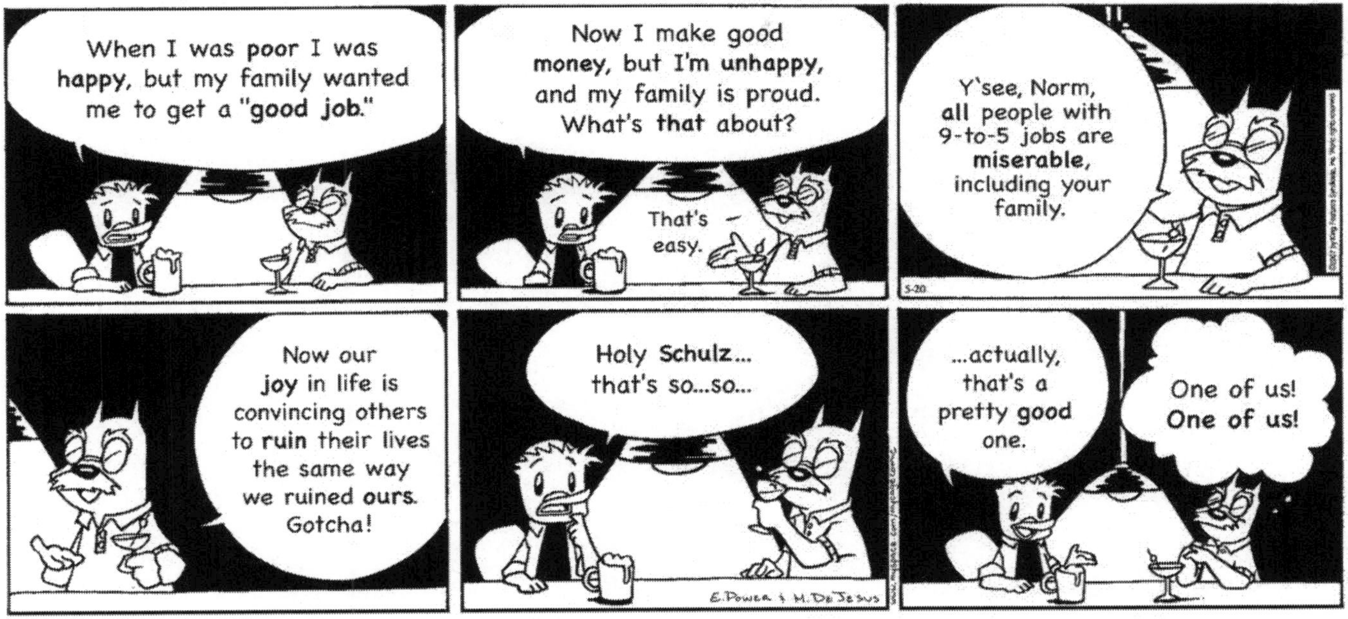
When I was poor I was happy, but my family wanted me to get a "good job."
Now I make good money, but I'm unhappy, and my family is proud. What's that about?
That's easy.
Y'see, Norm, all people with 9-to-5 jobs are miserable, including your family.
Now our joy in life is convincing others to ruin their lives the same way we ruined ours. Gotcha!
Holy Schulz... that's so...so...
E.POWER & M.DeJESUS
...actually, that's a pretty good one.
One of us! One of us!

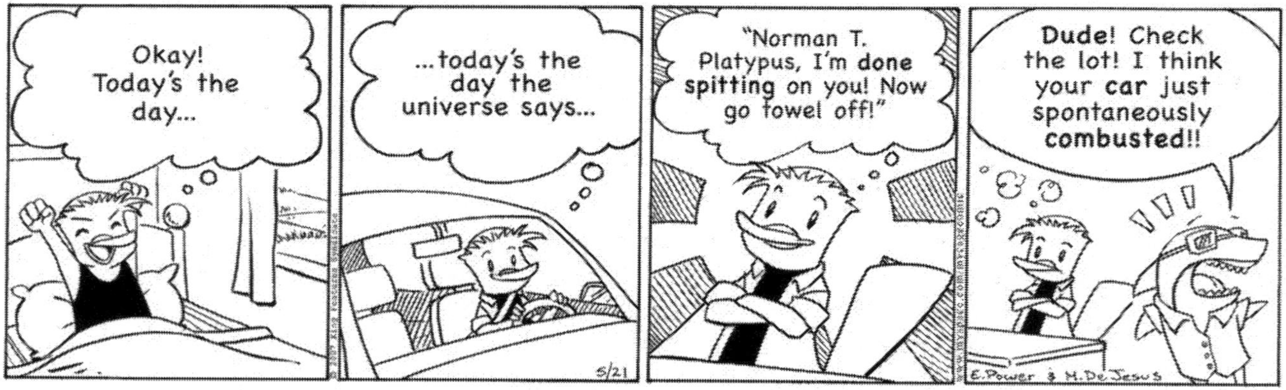
Okay! Today's the day...
...today's the day the universe says...
"Norman T. Platypus, I'm **done spitting** on you! Now go towel off!"
Dude! Check the lot! I think your **car** just spontaneously **combusted**!!
5/21
E. Power & M. De Jesus

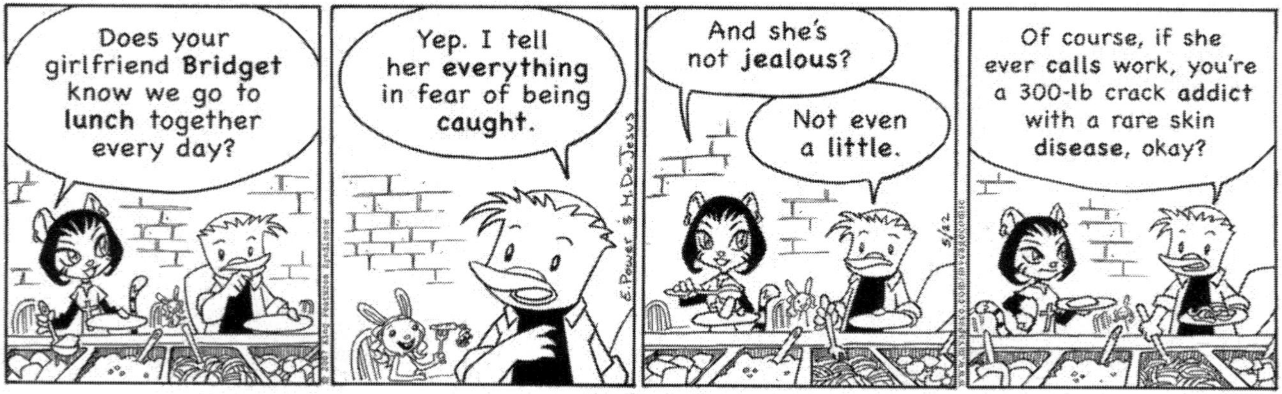
Does your girlfriend **Bridget** know we go to **lunch** together every day?
Yep. I tell her **everything** in fear of being **caught**.
E. Power & M. De Jesus
And she's not **jealous**?
Not even a **little**.
5/22
Of course, if she ever **calls** work, you're a 300-lb crack **addict** with a rare skin **disease**, okay?

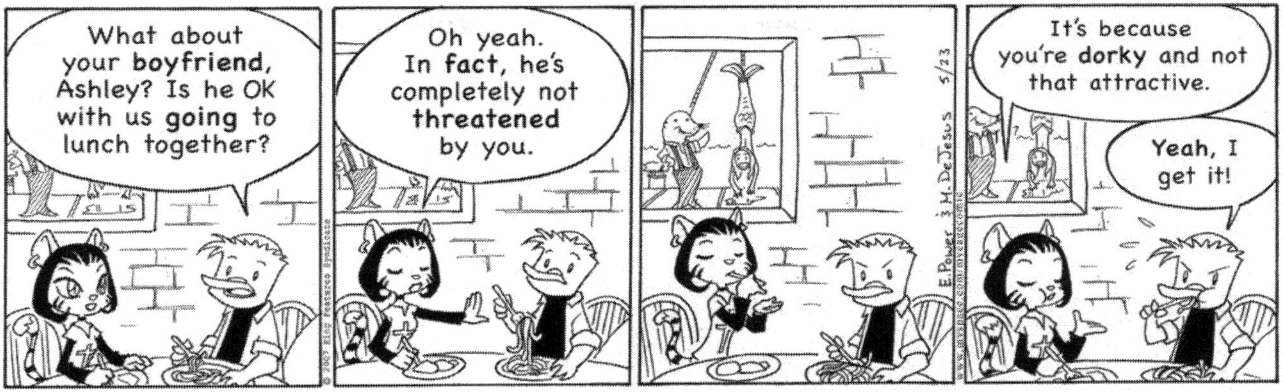
What about your **boyfriend**, Ashley? Is he OK with us **going** to lunch together?
Oh yeah. In **fact**, he's completely not **threatened** by you.
E.Power & H.DeJesus 5/23
It's because you're **dorky** and not that attractive.
Yeah, I get it!

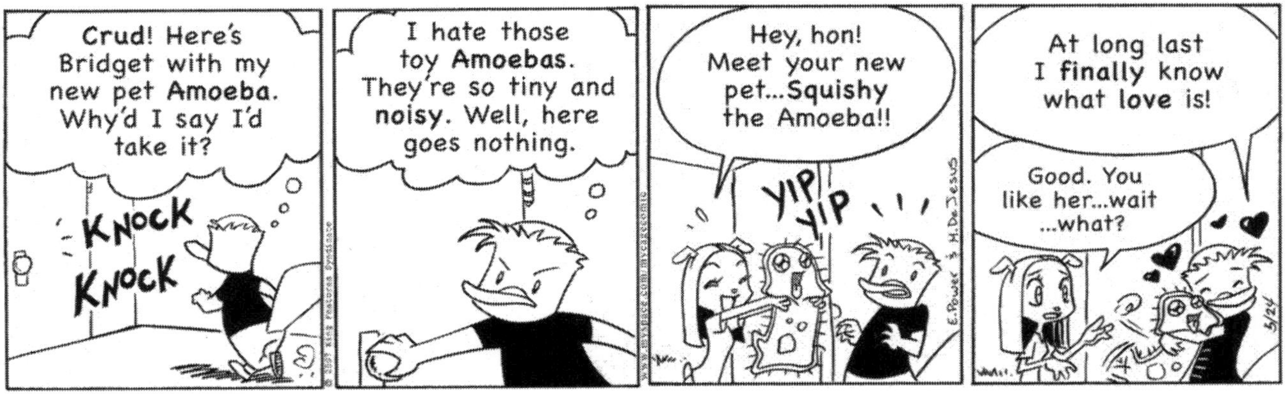
Crud! Here's Bridget with my new pet **Amoeba**. Why'd I say I'd take it?
KNOCK
KNOCK
I hate those toy **Amoebas**. They're so tiny and **noisy**. Well, here goes nothing.
Hey, hon! Meet your new pet...**Squishy** the Amoeba!!
YIP
YIP
E.Power & H.DeJesus
At long last I **finally** know what **love** is!
Good. You like her...wait ...what?
5/24

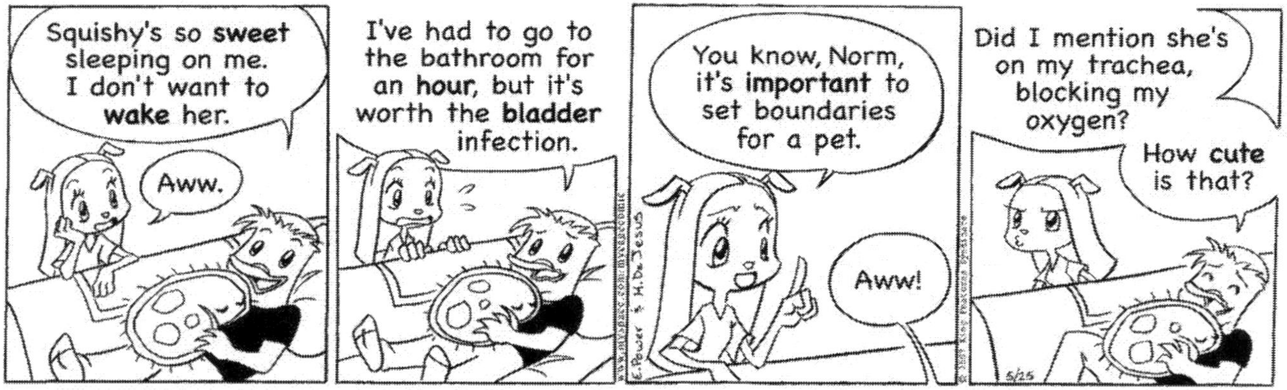
Squishy's so **sweet** sleeping on me. I don't want to **wake** her.
Aww.
I've had to go to the bathroom for an **hour**, but it's worth the **bladder** infection.
You know, Norm, it's **important** to set boundaries for a pet.
Aww!
Did I mention she's on my trachea, blocking my oxygen?
How **cute** is that?
5/25

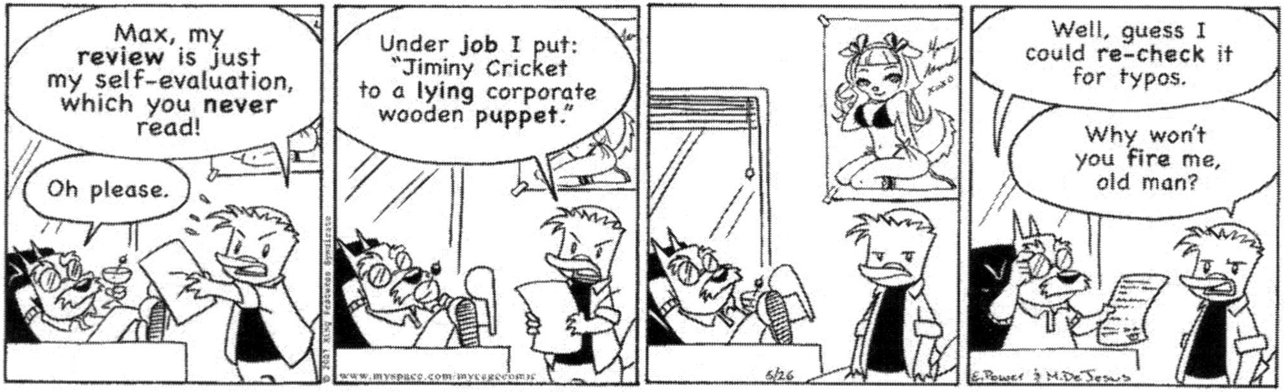
Max, my **review** is just my self-evaluation, which you **never** read!
Oh please.
Under **job** I put: "Jiminy Cricket to a **lying** corporate wooden **puppet**."
Well, guess I could **re-check** it for typos.
Why won't you **fire** me, old man?
5/26
E. Power & M. DeJesus

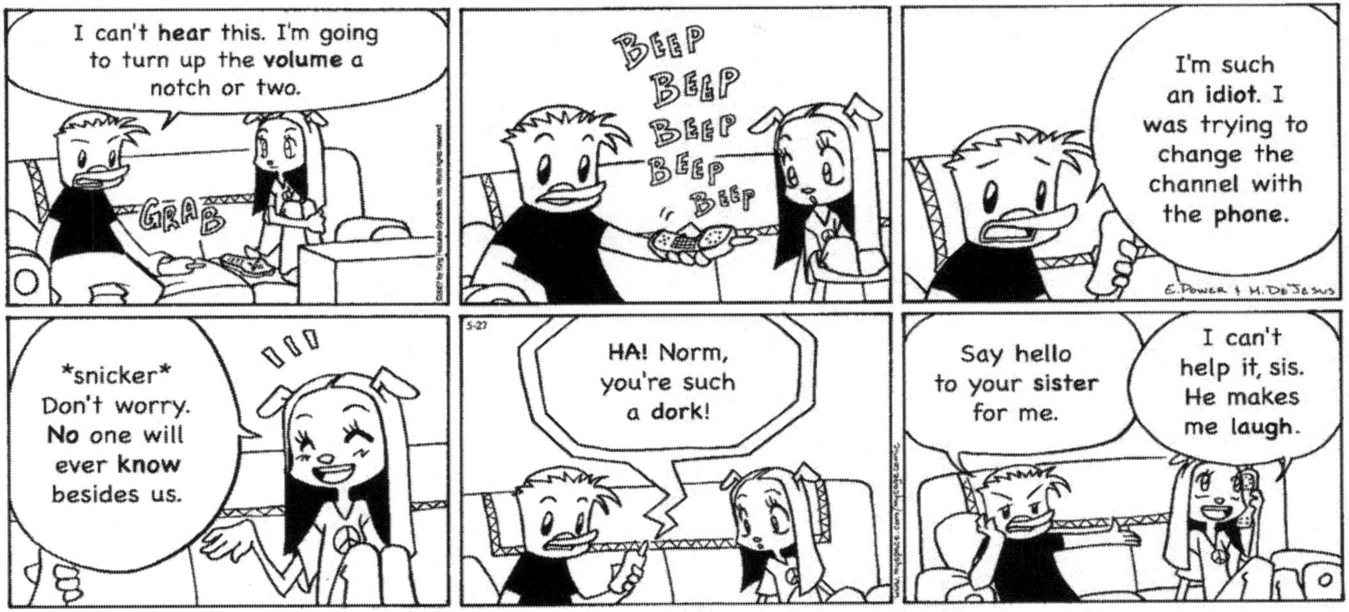
I can't **hear** this. I'm going to turn up the **volume** a notch or two.
GRAB
BEEP BEEP BEEP BEEP BEEP
I'm such an **idiot**. I was trying to change the channel with the **phone**.
E. POWER & H. DEJESUS
snicker Don't worry. **No** one will ever **know** besides us.
5-27
HA! Norm, you're such a **dork**!
Say hello to your **sister** for me.
I can't help it, sis. He makes me **laugh**.

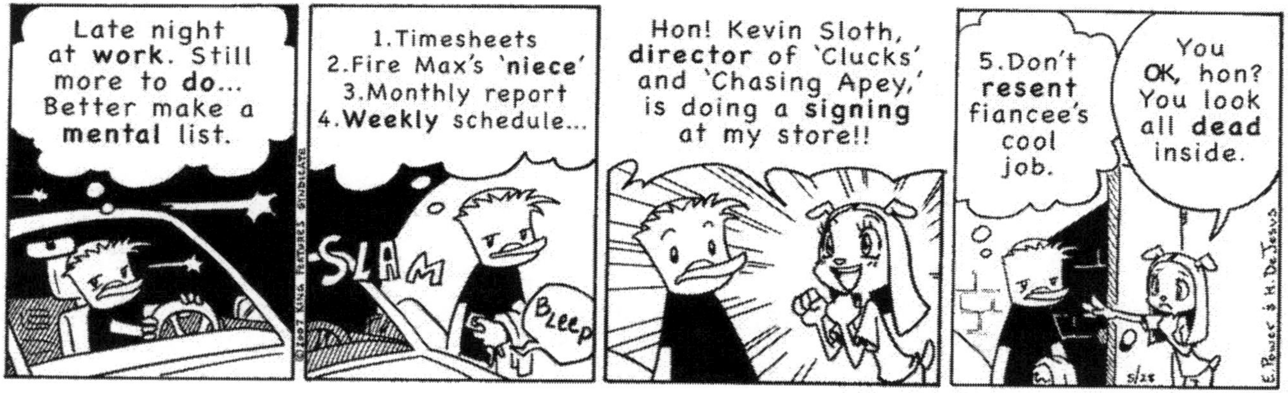

Late night at **work**. Still more to **do**... Better make a **mental** list.
1.Timesheets
2.Fire Max's 'niece'
3.Monthly report
4.Weekly schedule...
SLAM
BLEEP
Hon! Kevin Sloth, director of 'Clucks' and 'Chasing Apey,' is doing a signing at my store!!
5.Don't resent fiancee's cool job.
You OK, hon? You look all dead inside.

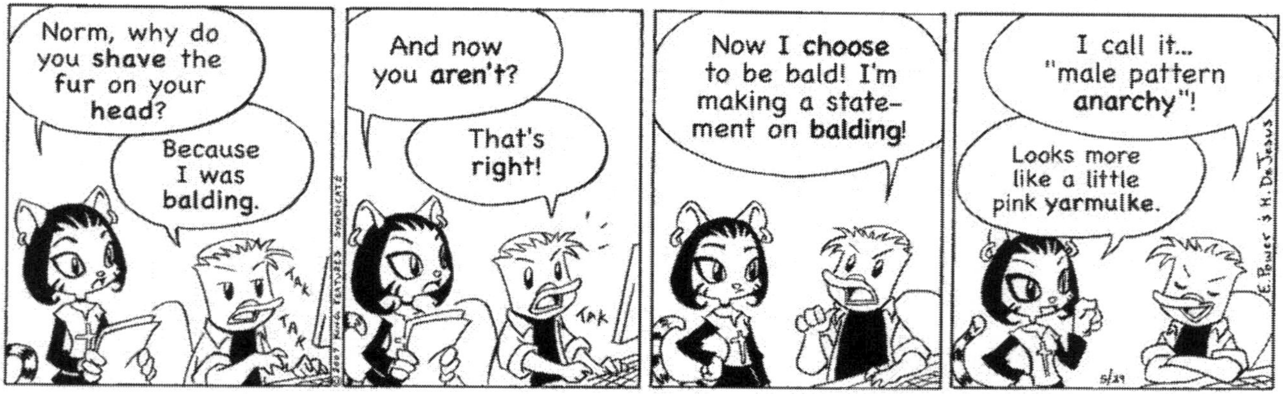

Norm, why do you shave the fur on your head?
Because I was balding.
TAK
TAK
And now you aren't?
That's right!
TAK
Now I choose to be bald! I'm making a statement on balding!
I call it... "male pattern anarchy"!
Looks more like a little pink yarmulke.

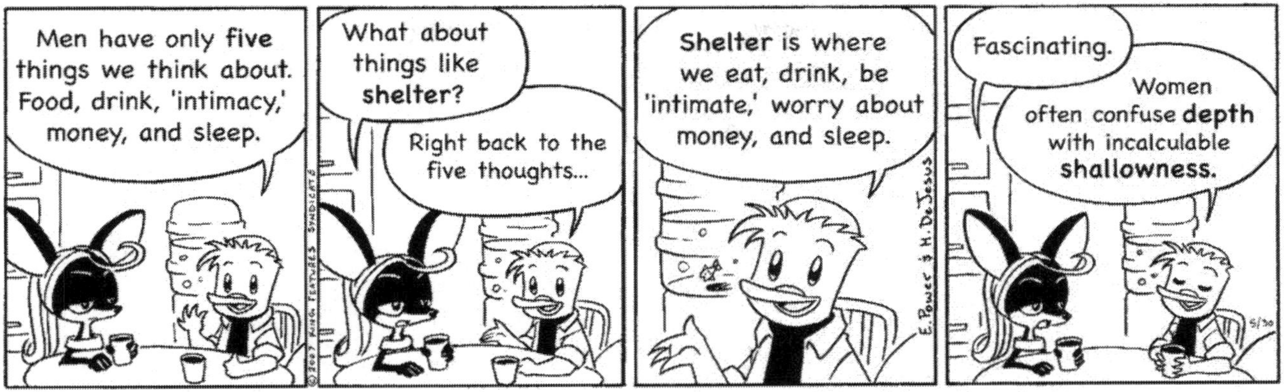
Men have only **five** things we think about. Food, drink, 'intimacy,' money, and sleep.
What about things like **shelter?**
Right back to the five thoughts...
© 2007 King Features Syndicate
Shelter is where we eat, drink, be 'intimate,' worry about money, and sleep.
E. Power & H. DeJesus
Fascinating.
Women often confuse **depth** with incalculable **shallowness.**
5/30

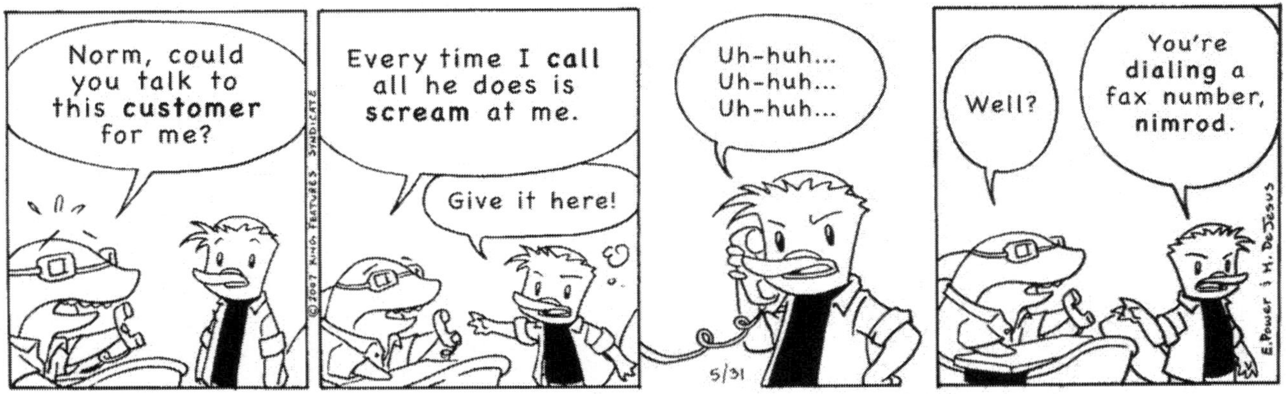
Norm, could you talk to this **customer** for me?
© 2007 King Features Syndicate
Every time I **call** all he does is **scream** at me.
Give it here!
Uh-huh...
Uh-huh...
Uh-huh...
5/31
Well?
You're **dialing** a fax number, **nimrod**.
E. Power & H. DeJesus

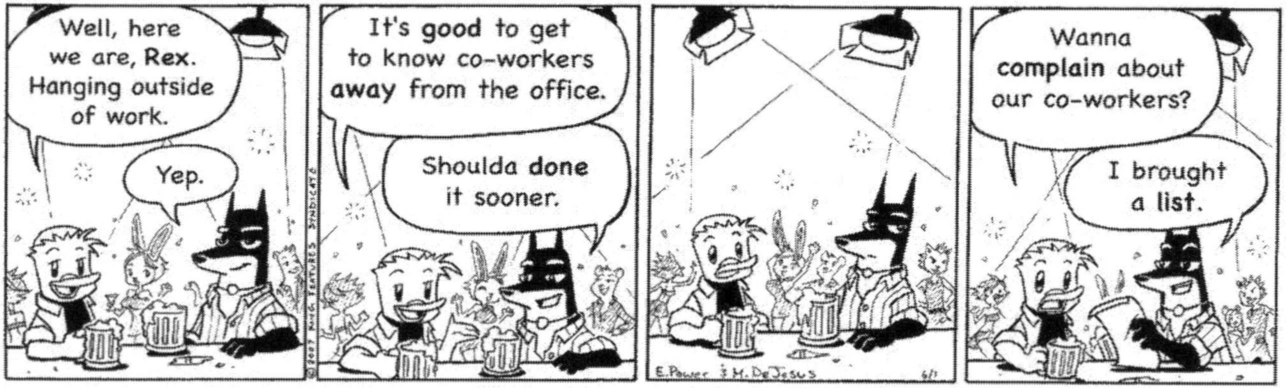
Well, here we are, **Rex**. Hanging outside of work.
Yep.
It's **good** to get to know co-workers **away** from the office.
Shoulda **done** it sooner.
Wanna **complain** about our co-workers?
I brought a **list**.

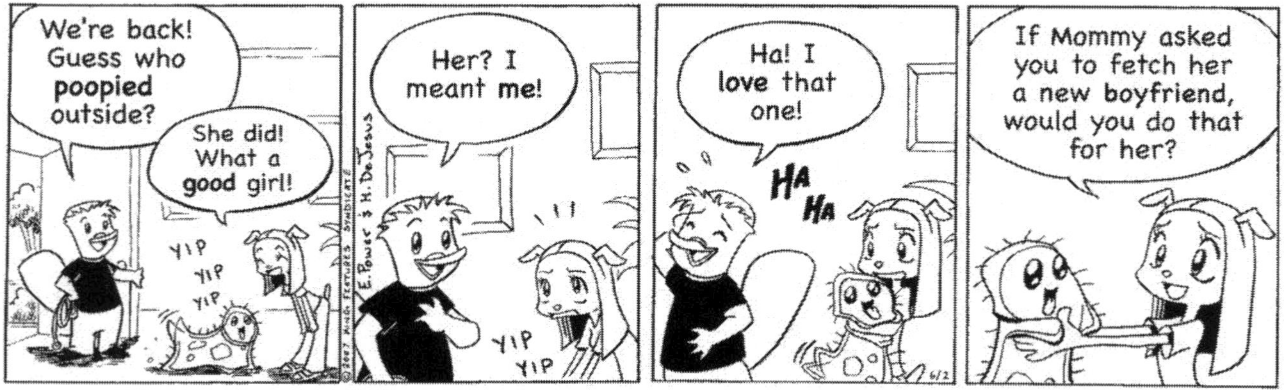
We're back! Guess who **poopied** outside?
She did! What a **good** girl!
YIP
YIP
YIP
Her? I meant **me**!
YIP
YIP
Ha! I **love** that one!
HA
HA
If Mommy asked you to fetch her a new **boyfriend**, would you do that for her?

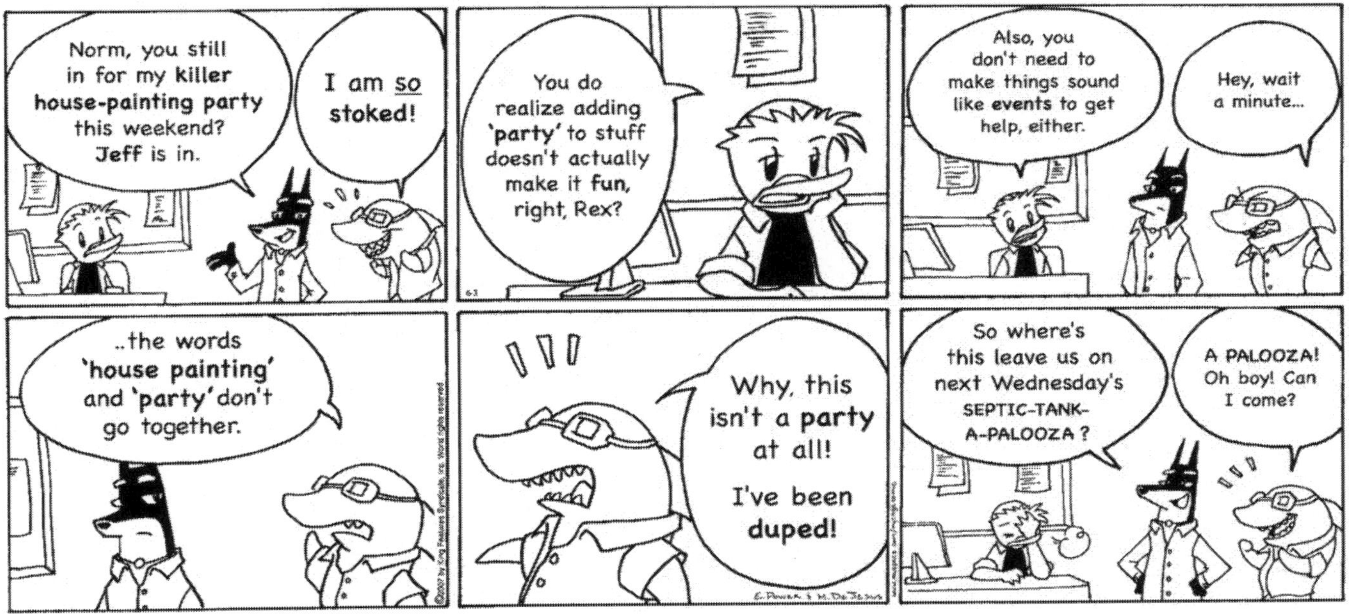
Norm, you still in for my killer house-painting party this weekend? Jeff is in.
I am so stoked!
You do realize adding 'party' to stuff doesn't actually make it fun, right, Rex?
Also, you don't need to make things sound like events to get help, either.
Hey, wait a minute...
..the words 'house painting' and 'party' don't go together.
Why, this isn't a party at all!
I've been duped!
So where's this leave us on next Wednesday's SEPTIC-TANK-A-PALOOZA?
A PALOOZA! Oh boy! Can I come?

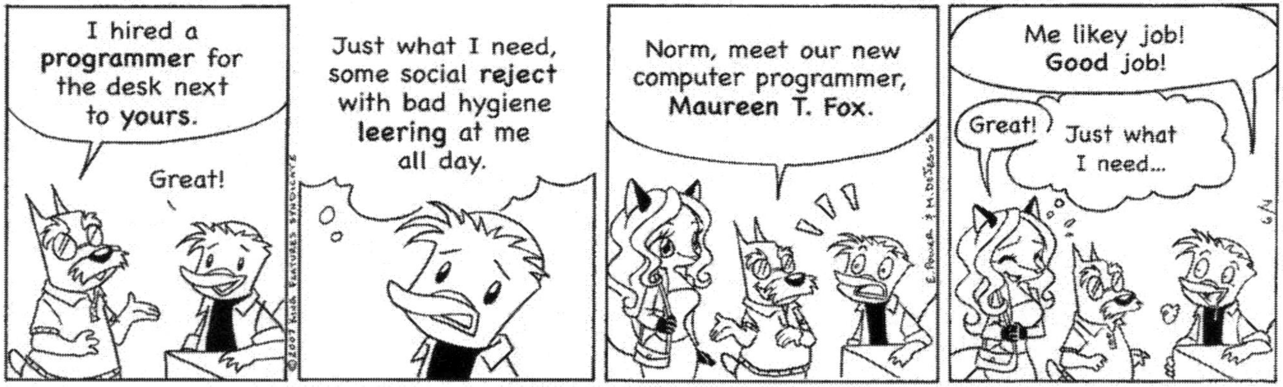
I hired a programmer for the desk next to yours.
Great!
Just what I need, some social reject with bad hygiene leering at me all day.
Norm, meet our new computer programmer, Maureen T. Fox.
!!!
Me likey job! Good job!
Great!
Just what I need...

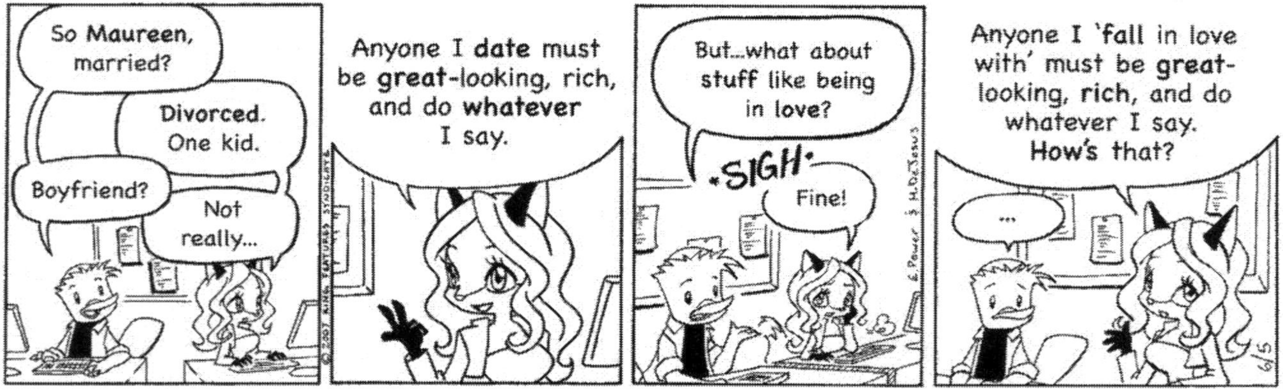
So Maureen, married?
Divorced. One kid.
Boyfriend?
Not really...
Anyone I date must be great-looking, rich, and do whatever I say.
But...what about stuff like being in love?
SIGH
Fine!
Anyone I 'fall in love with' must be great-looking, rich, and do whatever I say. How's that?
...

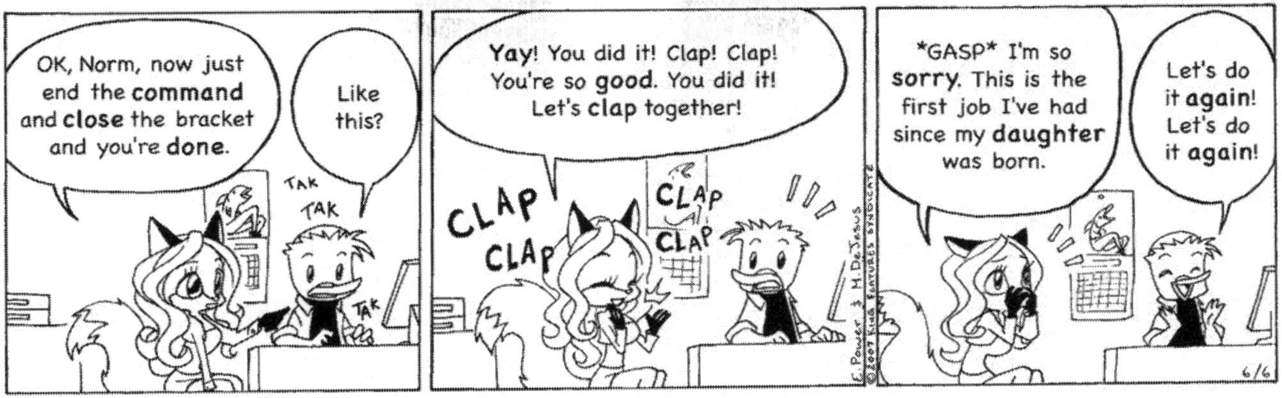
OK, Norm, now just end the command and close the bracket and you're done.
Like this?
TAK TAK TAK
Yay! You did it! Clap! Clap! You're so good. You did it! Let's clap together!
CLAP CLAP
CLAP CLAP
E. Power & M. DeJesus ©2007 King Features Syndicate
GASP I'm so sorry. This is the first job I've had since my daughter was born.
Let's do it again! Let's do it again!
6/6

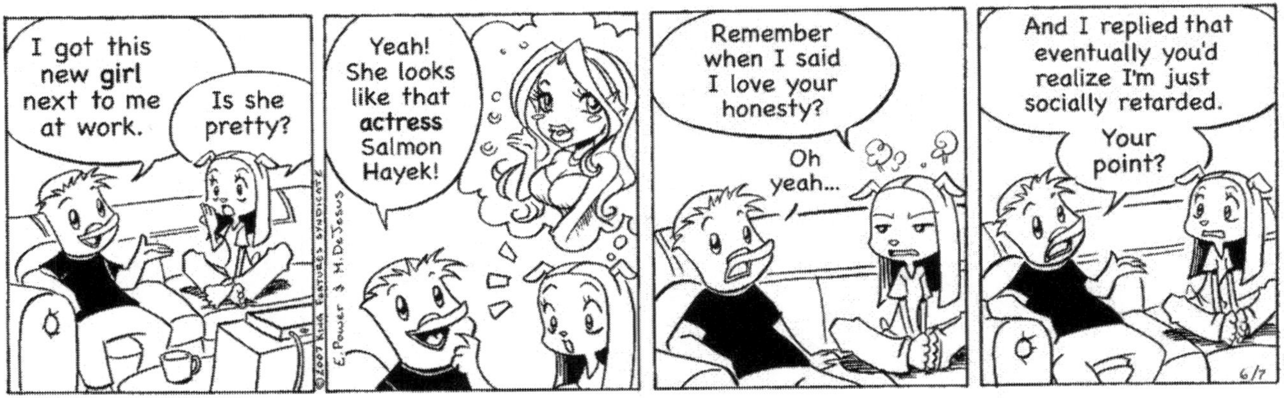
I got this new girl next to me at work.
Is she pretty?
©2007 King Features Syndicate E. Power & M. DeJesus
Yeah! She looks like that actress Salmon Hayek!
Remember when I said I love your honesty?
Oh yeah...
And I replied that eventually you'd realize I'm just socially retarded.
Your point?
6/7

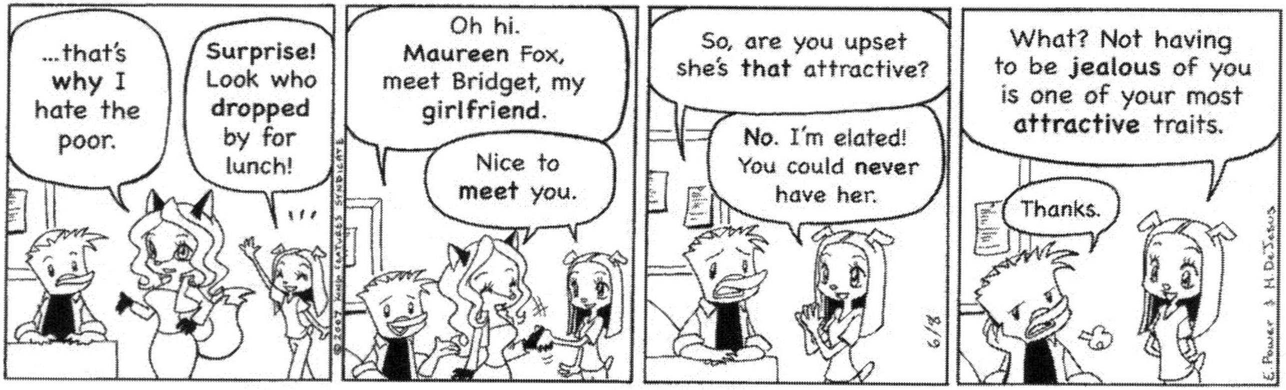
...that's **why** I hate the poor.
Surprise! Look who **dropped** by for lunch!
©2007 King Features Syndicate
Oh hi. **Maureen** Fox, meet Bridget, my **girlfriend**.
Nice to **meet** you.
So, are you upset she's **that** attractive?
No. I'm elated! You could **never** have her.
6/18
What? Not having to be **jealous** of you is one of your most **attractive** traits.
Thanks.
E. Power & H. DeJesus

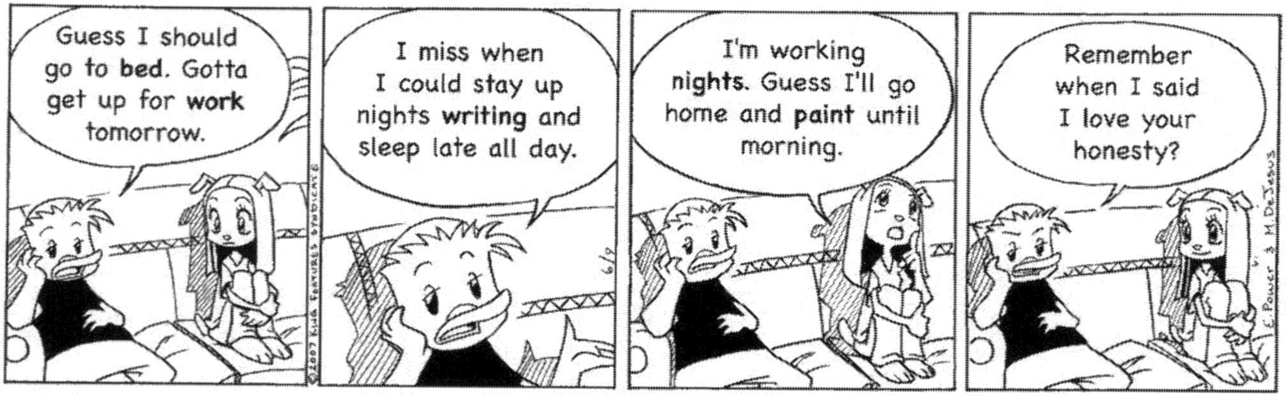
Guess I should go to **bed**. Gotta get up for **work** tomorrow.
©2007 King Features Syndicate
I miss when I could stay up nights **writing** and sleep late all day.
6/19
I'm working **nights**. Guess I'll go home and **paint** until morning.
Remember when I said I love your honesty?
E. Power & H. DeJesus

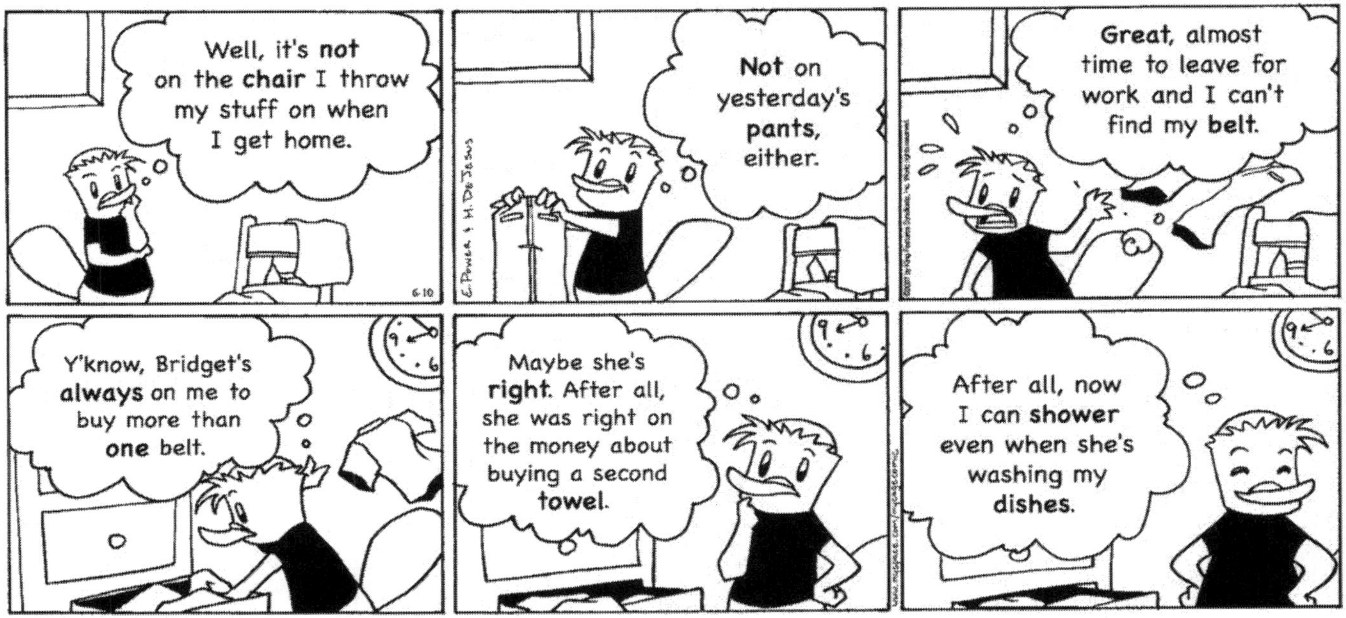
Well, it's **not** on the **chair** I throw my stuff on when I get home.
6-10
E. Power & H. DeJesus
Not on yesterday's **pants,** either.
Great, almost time to leave for work and I can't find my **belt**.
Y'know, Bridget's **always** on me to buy more than **one** belt.
Maybe she's **right**. After all, she was right on the money about buying a second **towel**.
After all, now I can **shower** even when she's washing my **dishes**.

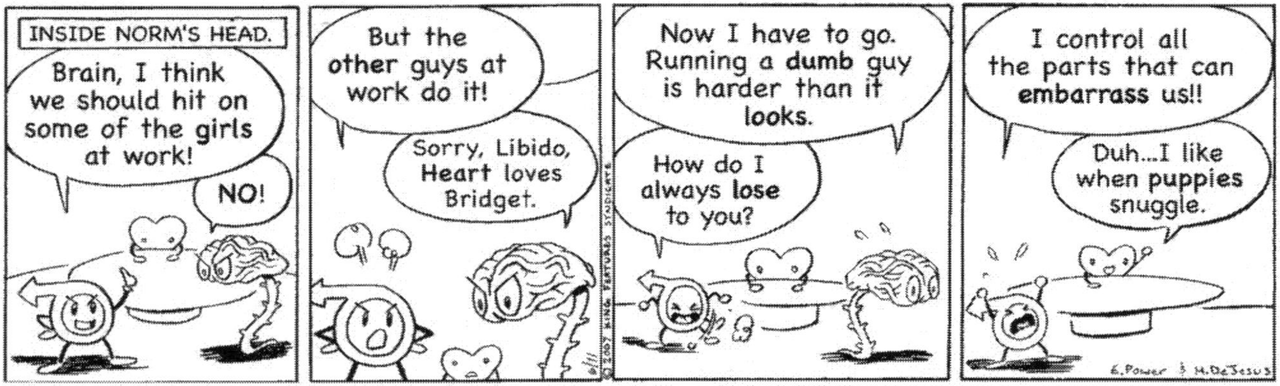
INSIDE NORM'S HEAD.
Brain, I think we should hit on some of the girls at work!
NO!
But the other guys at work do it!
Sorry, Libido, Heart loves Bridget.
Now I have to go. Running a dumb guy is harder than it looks.
How do I always lose to you?
I control all the parts that can embarrass us!!
Duh...I like when puppies snuggle.
E. Power & H. DeJesus

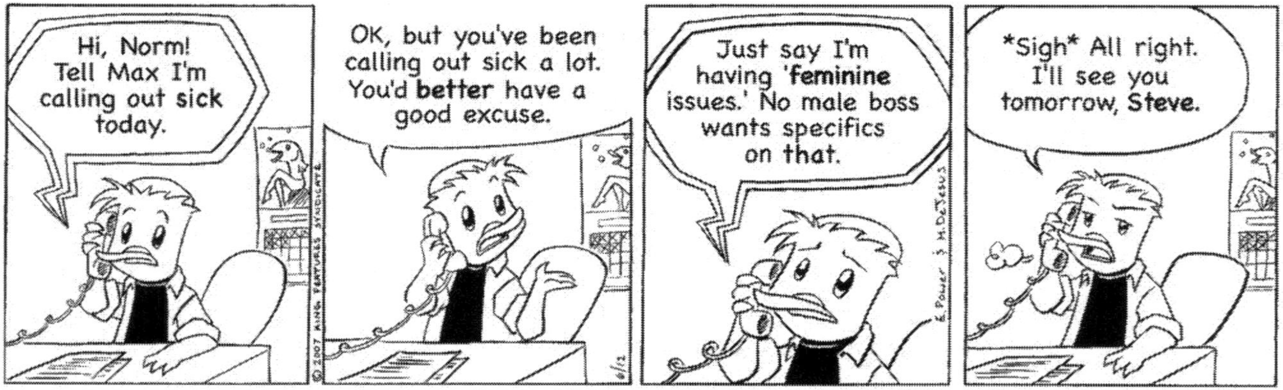
Hi, Norm! Tell Max I'm calling out sick today.
OK, but you've been calling out sick a lot. You'd better have a good excuse.
Just say I'm having 'feminine issues.' No male boss wants specifics on that.
Sigh All right. I'll see you tomorrow, Steve.

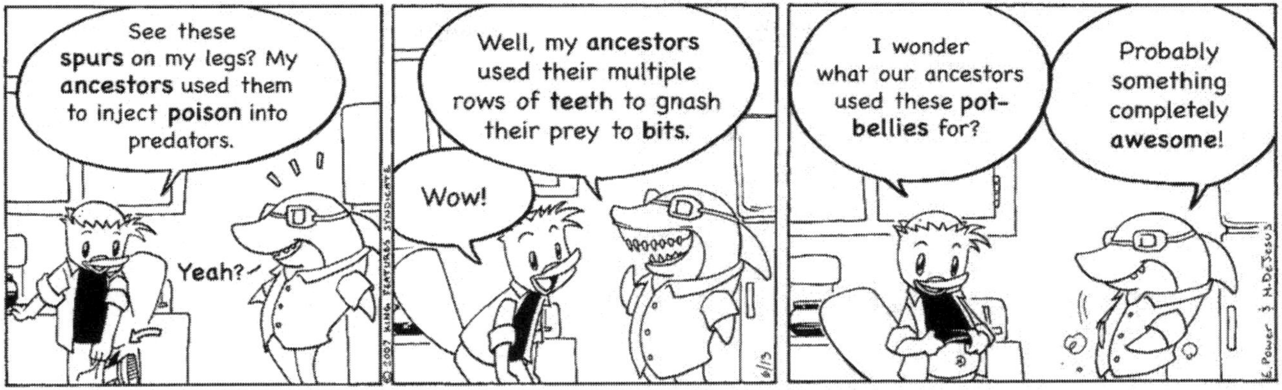
See these spurs on my legs? My ancestors used them to inject poison into predators.
Yeah?
Well, my ancestors used their multiple rows of teeth to gnash their prey to bits.
Wow!
I wonder what our ancestors used these pot-bellies for?
Probably something completely awesome!

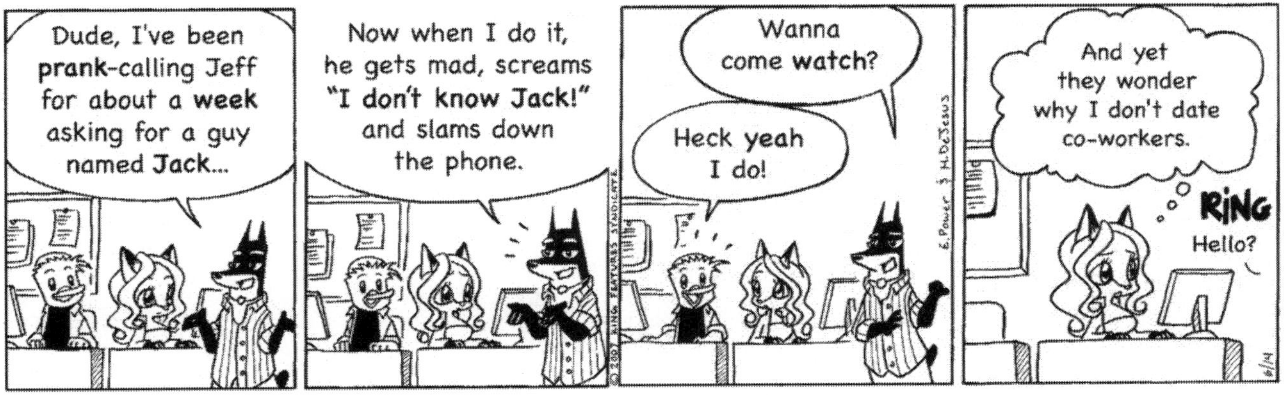
Dude, I've been prank-calling Jeff for about a week asking for a guy named Jack...
Now when I do it, he gets mad, screams "I don't know Jack!" and slams down the phone.
Wanna come watch?
Heck yeah I do!
And yet they wonder why I don't date co-workers.
RING
Hello?

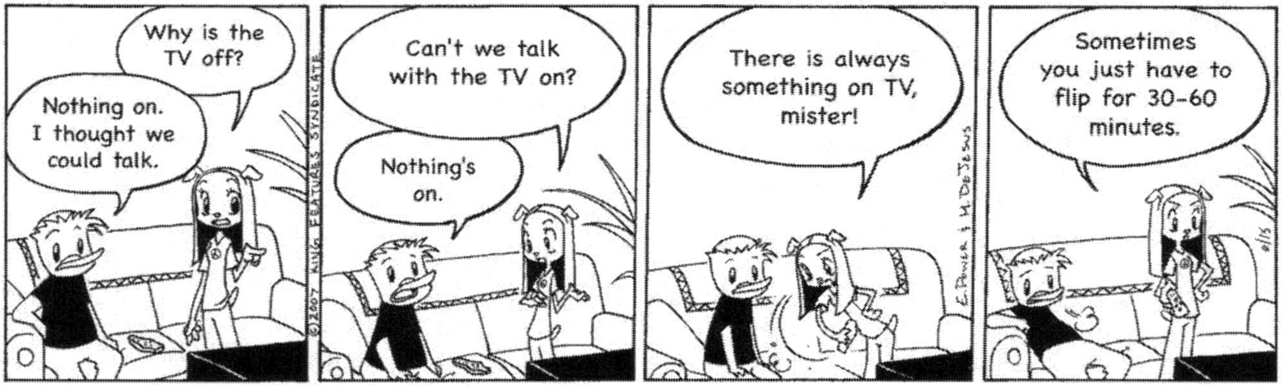
Why is the TV off?
Nothing on. I thought we could talk.
© 2007 King Features Syndicate
Can't we talk with the TV on?
Nothing's on.
There is always something on TV, mister!
E. Power & M. DeJesus
Sometimes you just have to flip for 30-60 minutes.
6/15

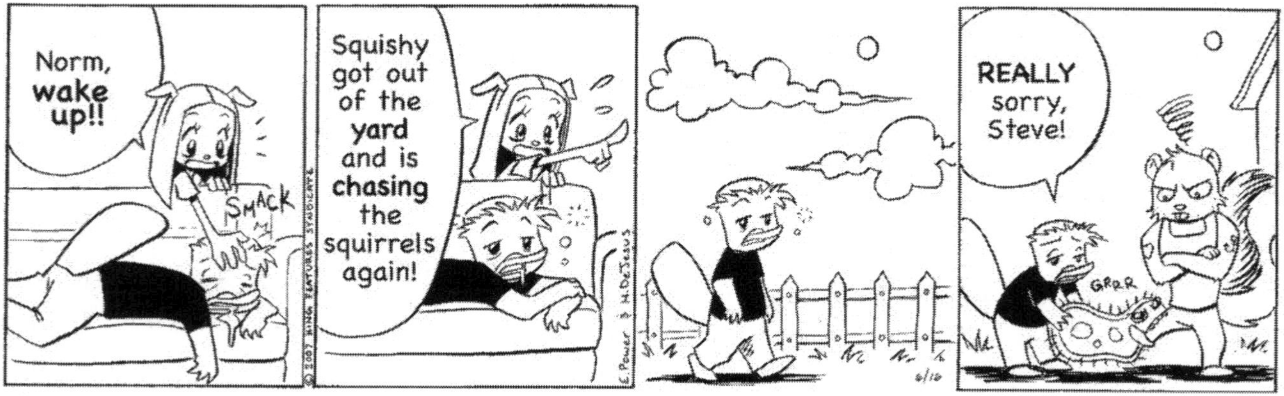
Norm, **wake up!!**
SMACK
© 2007 King Features Syndicate
Squishy got out of the **yard** and is **chasing** the squirrels again!
E. Power & M. DeJesus
6/16
REALLY sorry, Steve!
GRRR

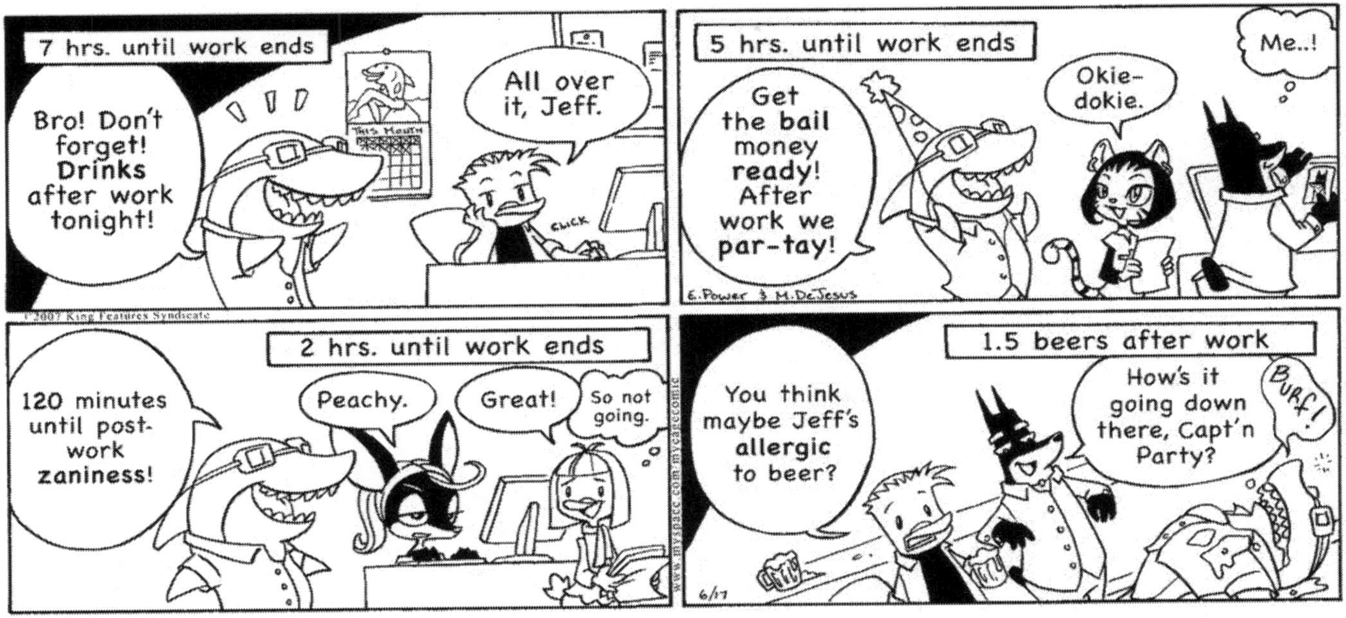
7 hrs. until work ends
Bro! Don't forget! **Drinks** after work tonight!
All over it, Jeff.
This Month
CLICK
5 hrs. until work ends
Get the **bail** money **ready**! After work we **par-tay**!
Okie-dokie.
Me..!
E. Power & M. DeJesus
© 2007 King Features Syndicate
2 hrs. until work ends
120 minutes until post-work **zaniness**!
Peachy.
Great!
So not going.
www.myspace.com/mycagecomic
1.5 beers after work
You think maybe Jeff's **allergic** to beer?
How's it going down there, Capt'n Party?
BURF!
6/17

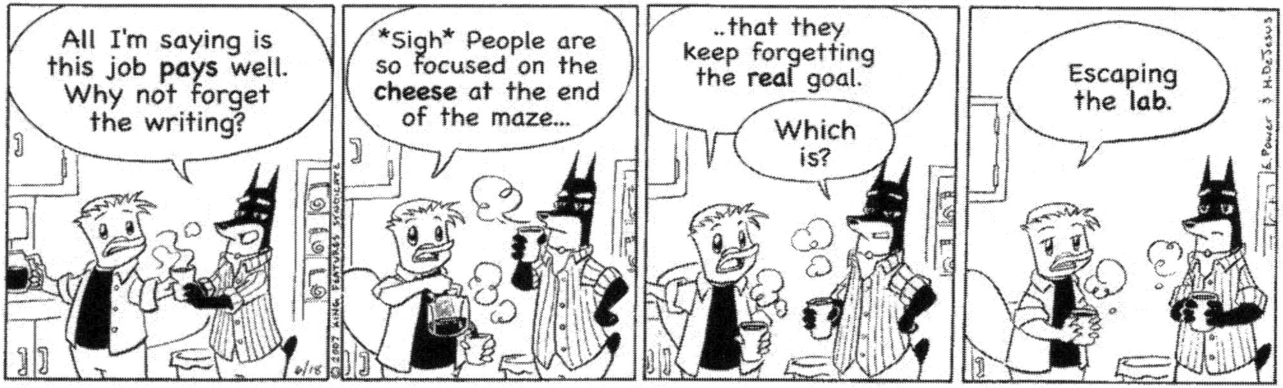
All I'm saying is this job **pays** well. Why not forget the writing?
Sigh People are so focused on the **cheese** at the end of the maze...
..that they keep forgetting the **real** goal.
Which is?
Escaping the **lab**.

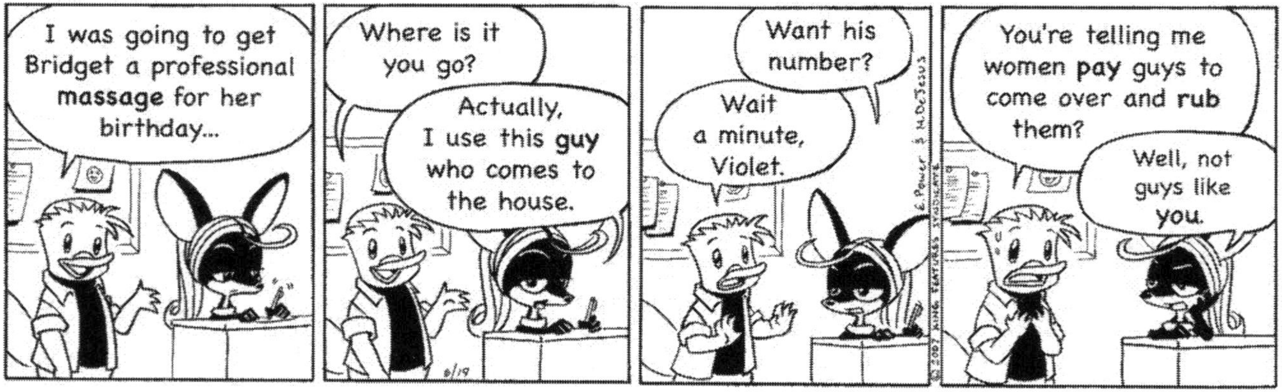
I was going to get Bridget a professional **massage** for her birthday...
Where is it you go?
Actually, I use this **guy** who comes to the house.
Want his number?
Wait a minute, Violet.
You're telling me women **pay** guys to come over and **rub** them?
Well, not guys like **you**.

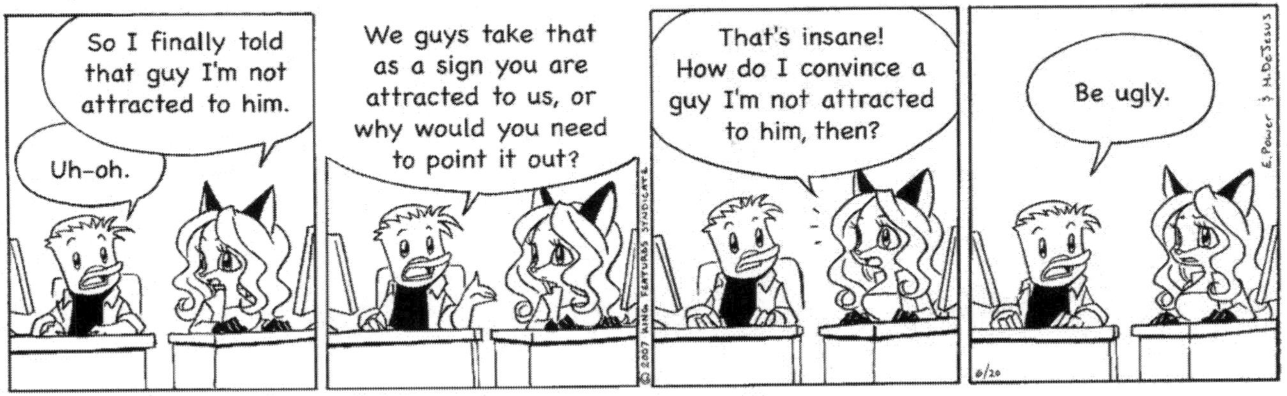
Uh-oh.
So I finally told that guy I'm not attracted to him.
We guys take that as a sign you are attracted to us, or why would you need to point it out?
© 2007 KING FEATURES SYNDICATE
That's insane! How do I convince a guy I'm not attracted to him, then?
Be ugly.
6/20
E. Power & H. DeJesus

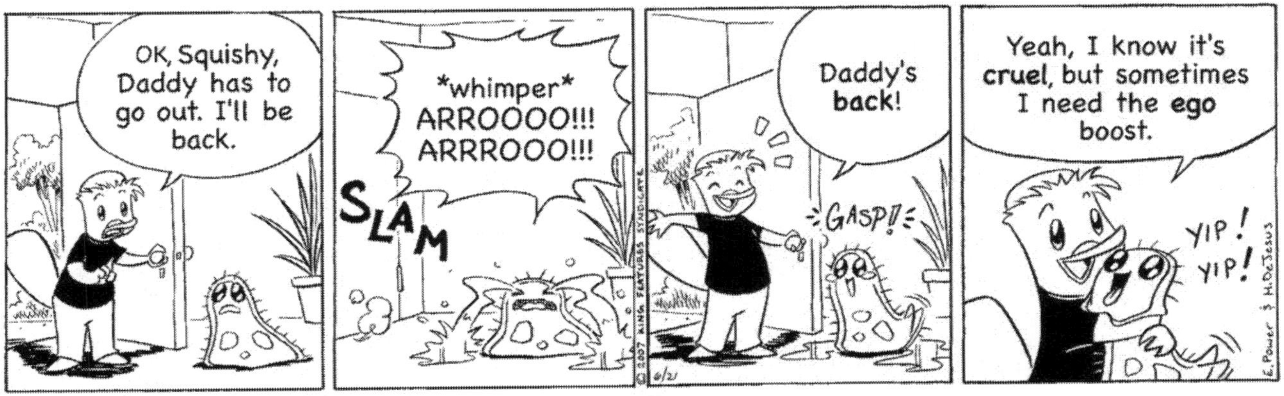
OK, Squishy, Daddy has to go out. I'll be back.
whimper ARROOOO!!! ARRROOO!!!
SLAM
© 2007 KING FEATURES SYNDICATE
6/21
Daddy's **back**!
GASP!!
Yeah, I know it's **cruel**, but sometimes I need the **ego** boost.
YIP! YIP!
E. Power & H. DeJesus

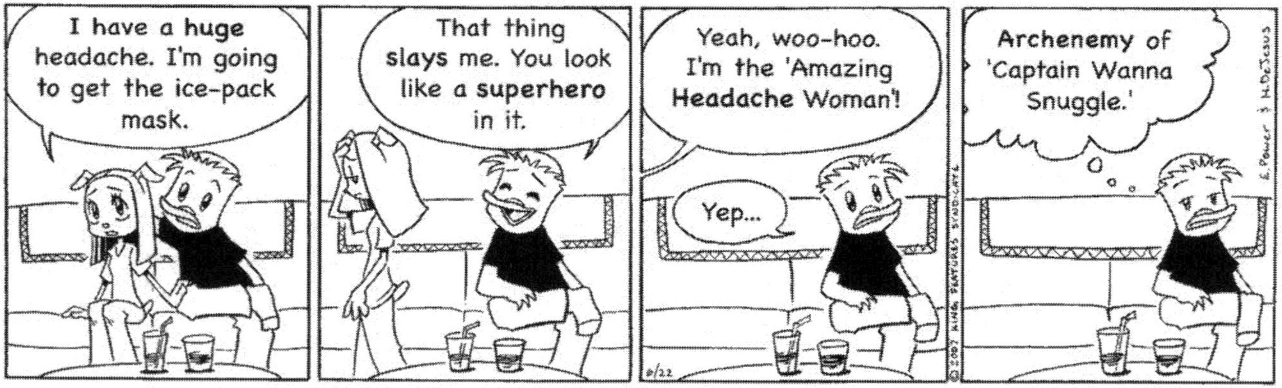
I have a **huge** headache. I'm going to get the ice-pack mask.
That thing **slays** me. You look like a **superhero** in it.
Yeah, woo-hoo. I'm the 'Amazing **Headache** Woman'!
Yep...
Archenemy of 'Captain Wanna Snuggle.'
6/22
© 2007 King Features Syndicate
E. Power & H. DeJesus

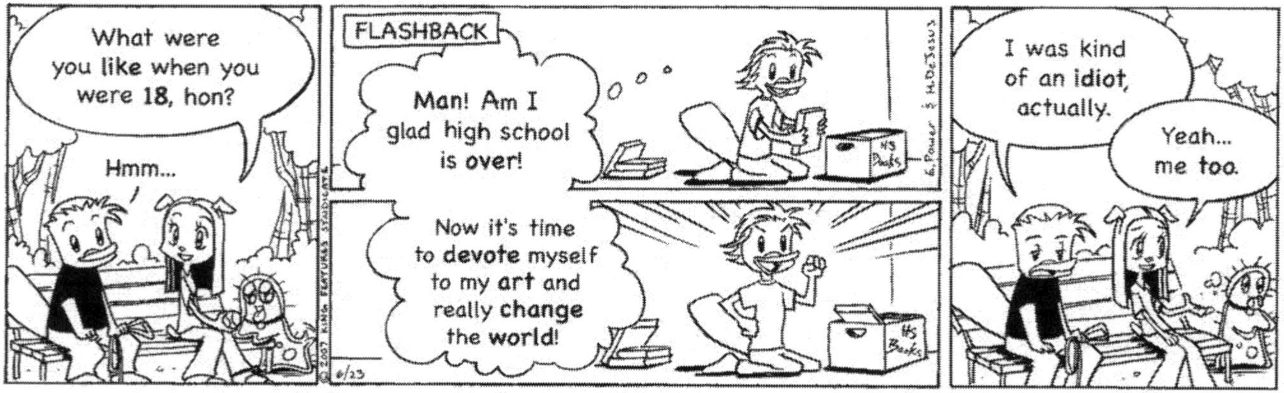
What were you **like** when you were **18**, hon?
Hmm...
FLASHBACK
Man! Am I glad high school is **over**!
HS Books
Now it's time to **devote** myself to my **art** and really **change** the **world**!
I was kind of an **idiot**, actually.
Yeah... me **too**.
6/23
© 2007 King Features Syndicate
E. Power & H. DeJesus

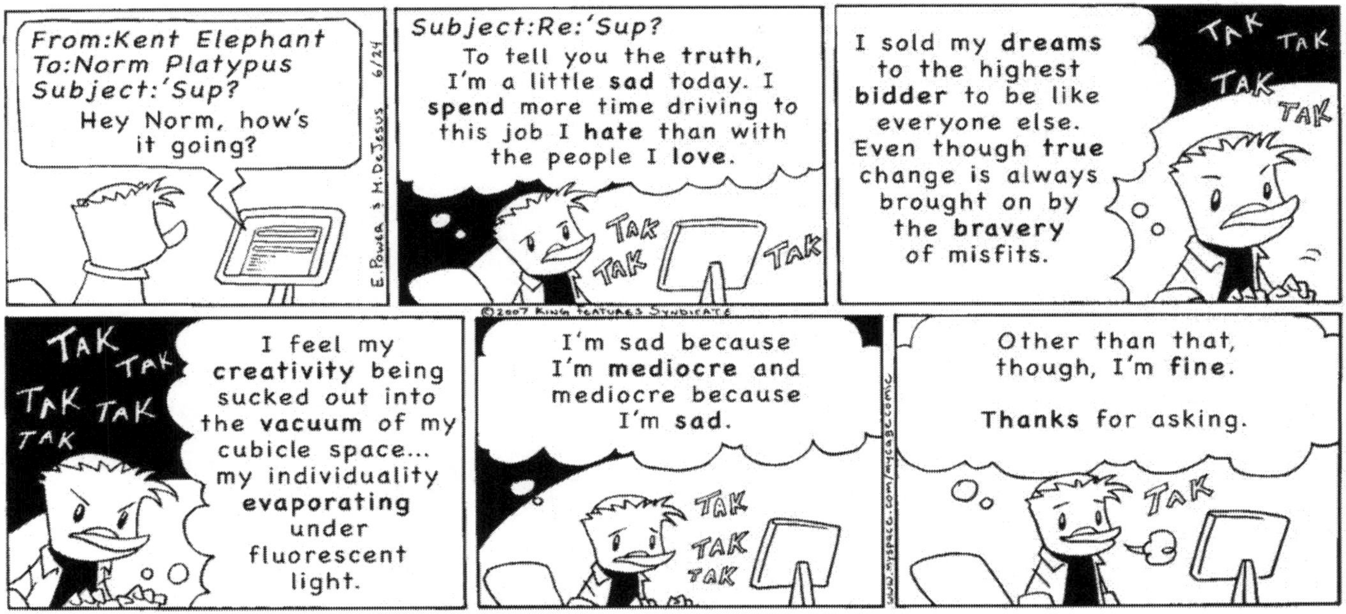
From:Kent Elephant
To:Norm Platypus
Subject:'Sup?
Hey Norm, how's it going?
6/24
E. Power & M. DeJesus
Subject:Re:'Sup?
To tell you the truth, I'm a little sad today. I spend more time driving to this job I hate than with the people I love.
TAK TAK TAK
©2007 King Features Syndicate
I sold my dreams to the highest bidder to be like everyone else. Even though true change is always brought on by the bravery of misfits.
TAK TAK TAK TAK
TAK TAK TAK TAK TAK
I feel my creativity being sucked out into the vacuum of my cubicle space... my individuality evaporating under fluorescent light.
I'm sad because I'm mediocre and mediocre because I'm sad.
TAK TAK TAK
www.myspace.com/mycagecomic
Other than that, though, I'm fine.
Thanks for asking.
TAK

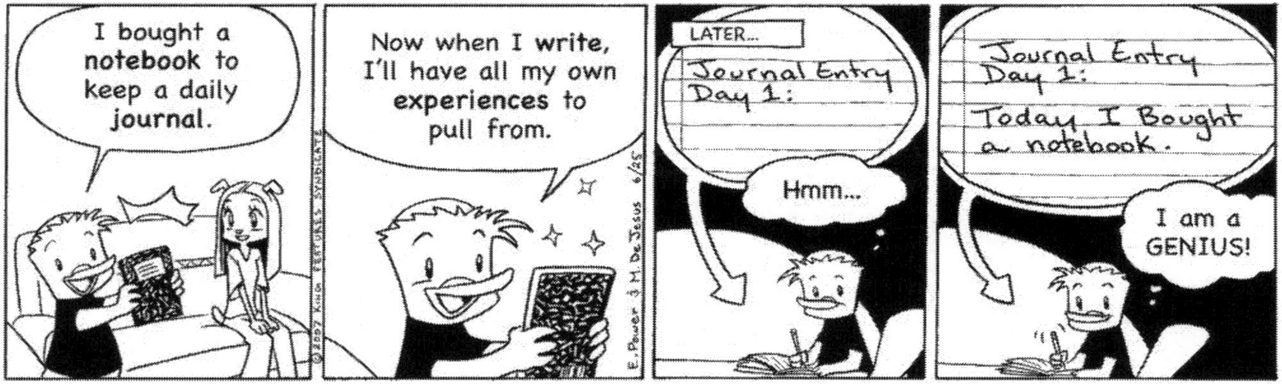
I bought a **notebook** to keep a daily **journal**.
Now when I **write**, I'll have all my own **experiences** to pull from.
LATER...
Journal Entry Day 1:
Hmm...
Journal Entry Day 1:
Today I Bought a notebook.
I am a GENIUS!
© 2007 King Features Syndicate
E. Power & M. De Jesus 6/25

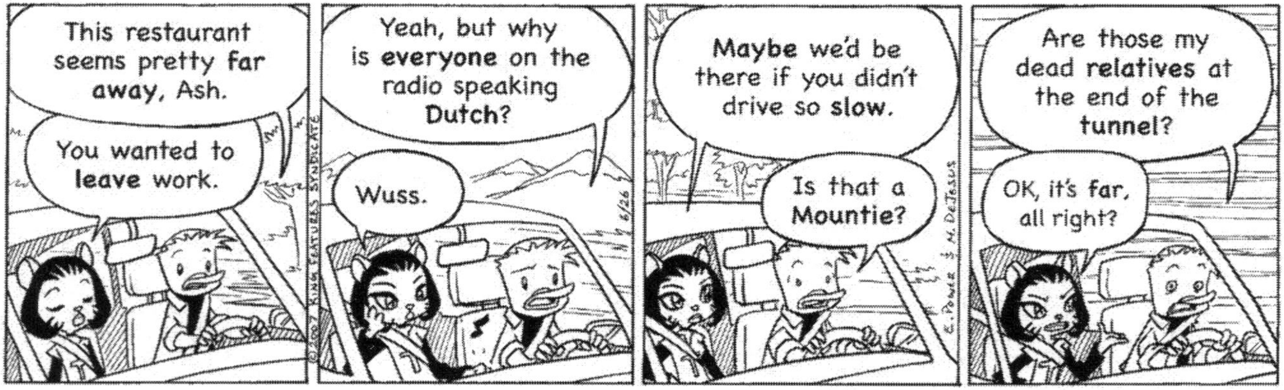
This restaurant seems pretty **far away**, Ash.
You wanted to **leave** work.
Yeah, but why is **everyone** on the radio speaking **Dutch**?
Wuss.
Maybe we'd be there if you didn't drive so **slow**.
Is that a **Mountie**?
Are those my dead **relatives** at the end of the **tunnel**?
OK, it's **far**, all right?
© 2007 King Features Syndicate
6/26
E. Power & M. DeJesus

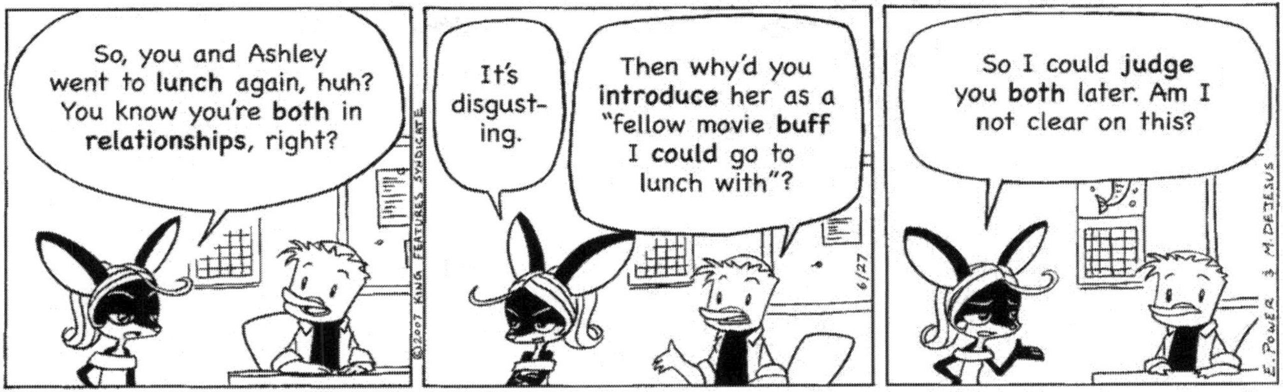
So, you and Ashley went to lunch again, huh? You know you're both in relationships, right?
©2007 King Features Syndicate
It's disgust-ing.
Then why'd you introduce her as a "fellow movie buff I could go to lunch with"?
6/27
So I could judge you both later. Am I not clear on this?
E. Power & M. DeJesus

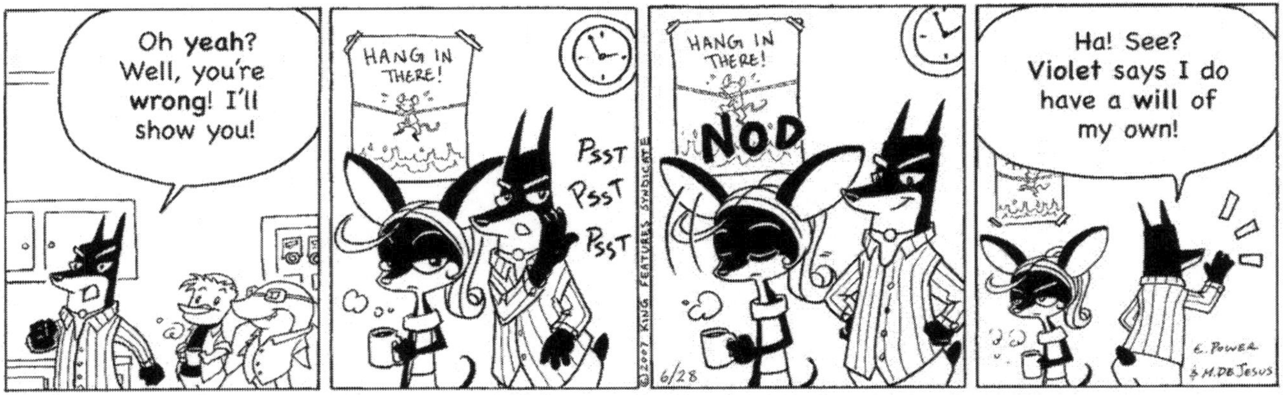
Oh yeah? Well, you're wrong! I'll show you!
HANG IN THERE!
PSST
PSST
PSST
©2007 King Features Syndicate
6/28
HANG IN THERE!
NOD
Ha! See? Violet says I do have a will of my own!
E. Power & M. DeJesus

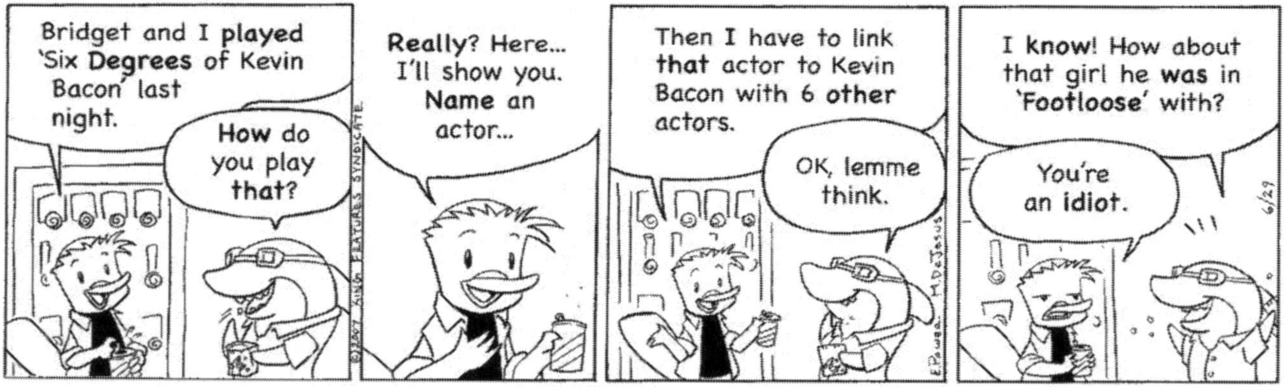

Bridget and I played 'Six Degrees of Kevin Bacon' last night.
How do you play that?
Really? Here... I'll show you. Name an actor...
Then I have to link that actor to Kevin Bacon with 6 other actors.
OK, lemme think.
I know! How about that girl he was in 'Footloose' with?
You're an idiot.
©2007 King Features Syndicate
E.Power M.DeJesus
6/29

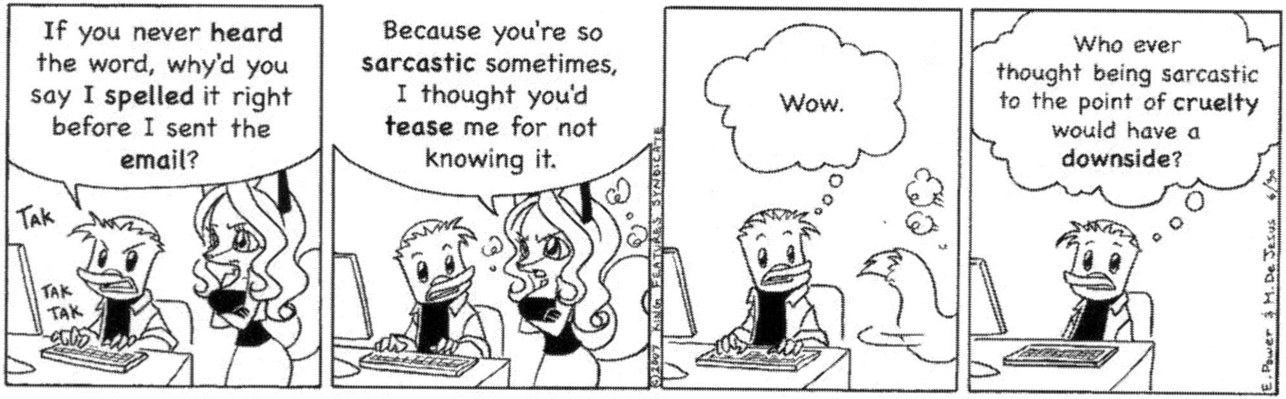

If you never heard the word, why'd you say I spelled it right before I sent the email?
TAK
TAK TAK
Because you're so sarcastic sometimes, I thought you'd tease me for not knowing it.
Wow.
Who ever thought being sarcastic to the point of cruelty would have a downside?
©2007 King Features Syndicate
E.Power & M.DeJesus 6/30

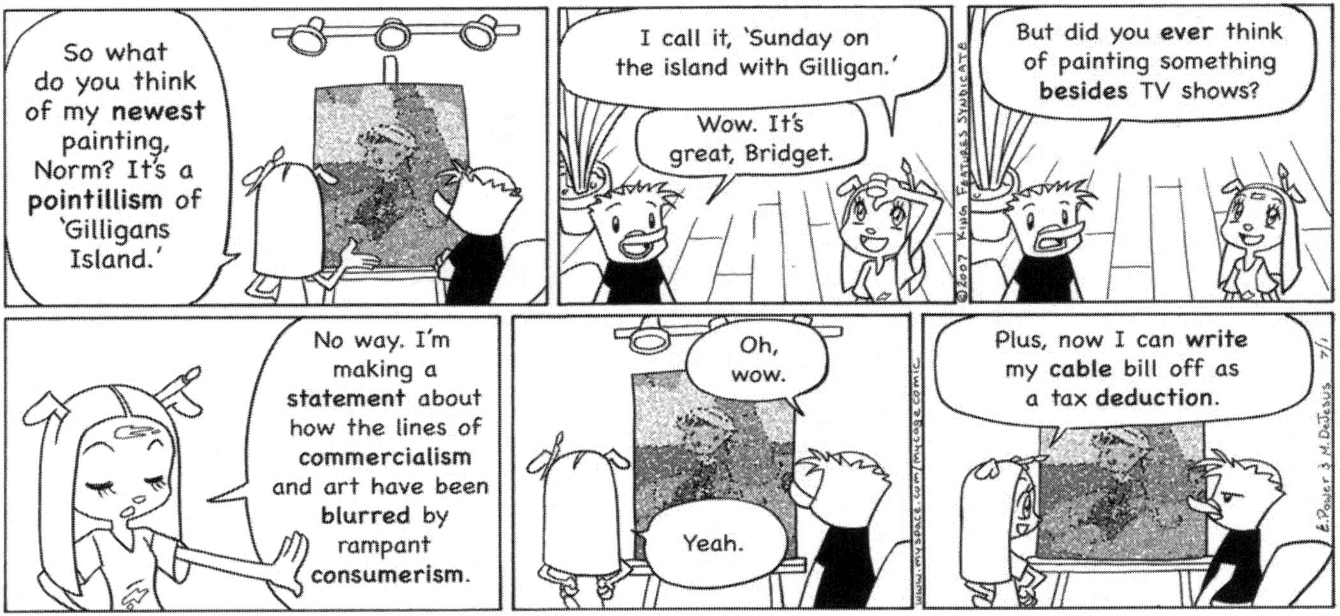
So what do you think of my **newest** painting, Norm? It's a **pointillism** of 'Gilligans Island.'
I call it, 'Sunday on the island with Gilligan.'
Wow. It's great, Bridget.
©2007 King Features Syndicate
But did you **ever** think of painting something **besides** TV shows?
No way. I'm making a **statement** about how the lines of **commercialism** and art have been **blurred** by rampant **consumerism**.
Oh, wow.
Yeah.
www.myspace.com/mycage comic
Plus, now I can **write** my **cable** bill off as a tax **deduction**.
E. Power & M. DeJesus 7/1

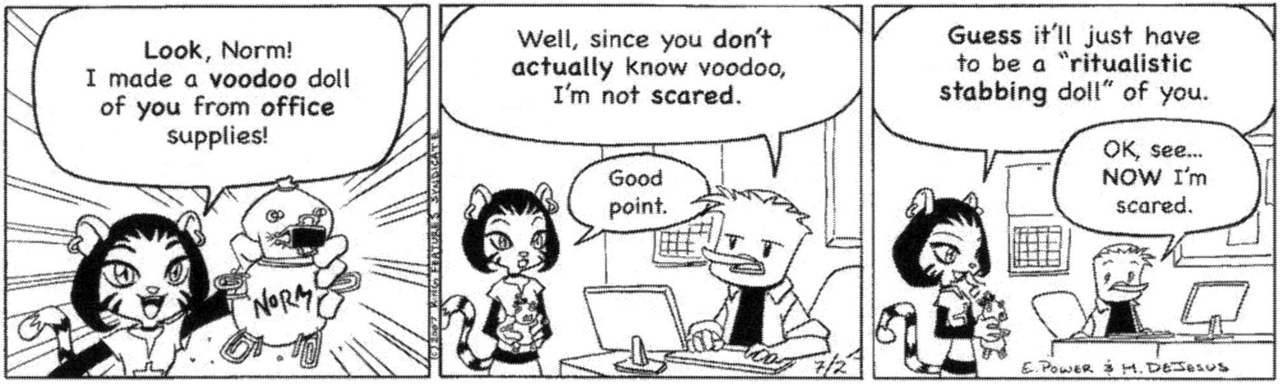
Look, Norm!
I made a voodoo doll of you from office supplies!
NORM
Well, since you don't actually know voodoo, I'm not scared.
Good point.
7/2
Guess it'll just have to be a "ritualistic stabbing doll" of you.
OK, see... NOW I'm scared.
E. POWER & M. DEJESUS

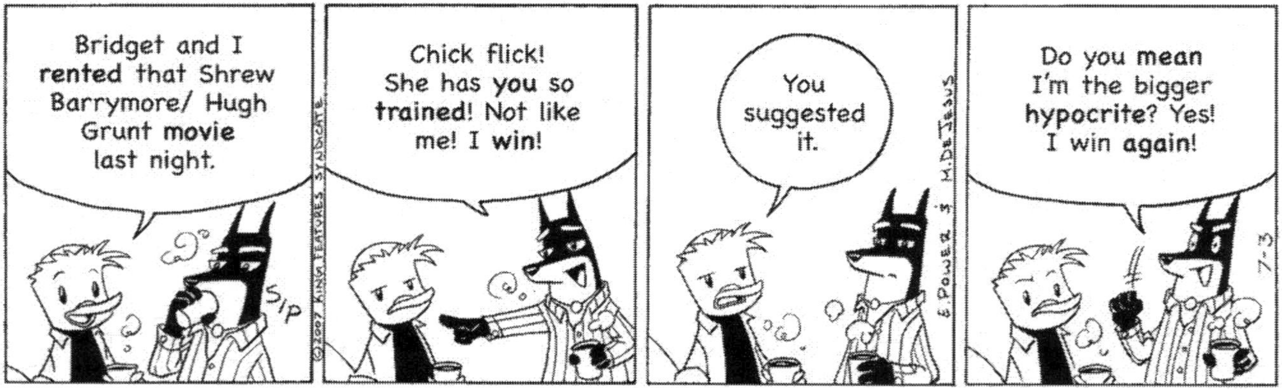
Bridget and I rented that Shrew Barrymore/ Hugh Grunt movie last night.
SIP
©2007 KING FEATURES SYNDICATE
Chick flick! She has you so trained! Not like me! I win!
You suggested it.
E. POWER & M. DEJESUS
Do you mean I'm the bigger hypocrite? Yes! I win again!
7-3

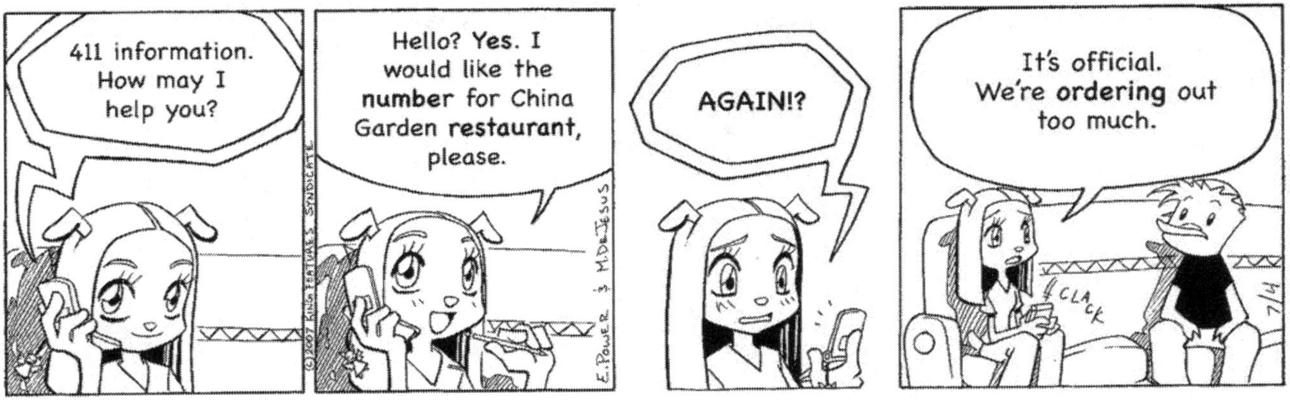
411 information. How may I help you?
Hello? Yes. I would like the number for China Garden restaurant, please.
©2007 KING FEATURES SYNDICATE
E. POWER & M. DEJESUS
AGAIN!?
It's official. We're ordering out too much.
CLACK
7/4

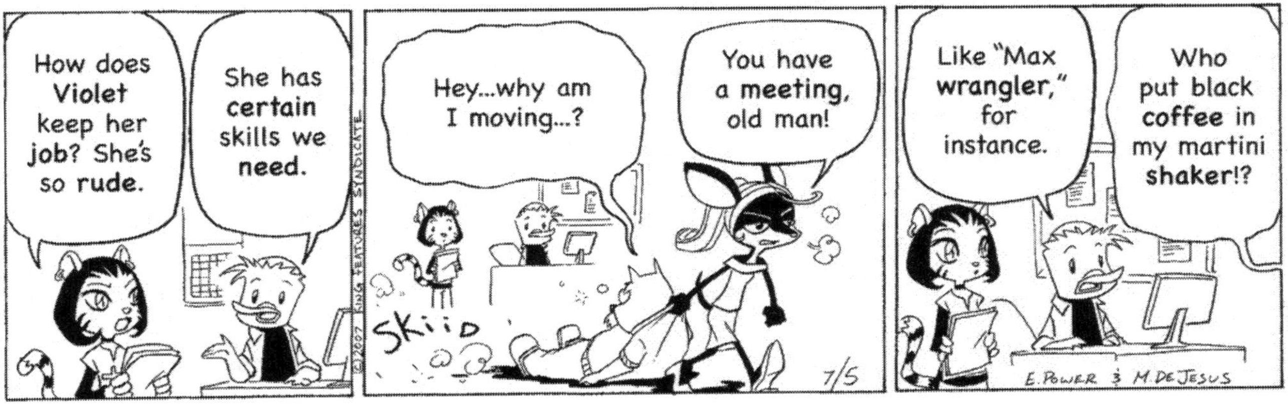
How does Violet keep her job? She's so rude.
She has certain skills we need.
©2007 KING FEATURES SYNDICATE
Hey...why am I moving...?
You have a meeting, old man!
SKiiD
7/5
Like "Max wrangler," for instance.
Who put black coffee in my martini shaker!?
E. POWER & M. DEJESUS

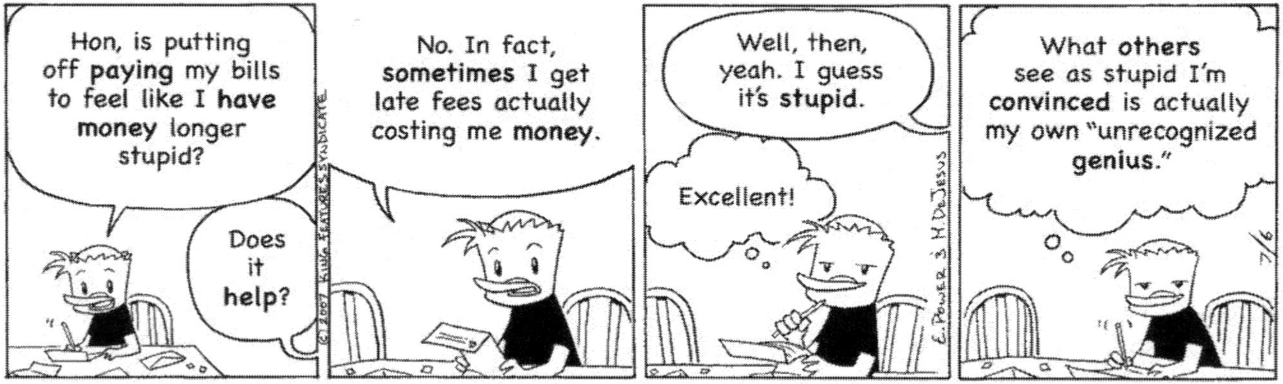
Hon, is putting off **paying** my bills to feel like I **have money** longer stupid?
Does it **help?**
No. In fact, **sometimes** I get late fees actually costing me **money**.
Well, then, yeah. I guess it's **stupid**.
Excellent!
What **others** see as stupid I'm **convinced** is actually my own "unrecognized **genius**."
7/6

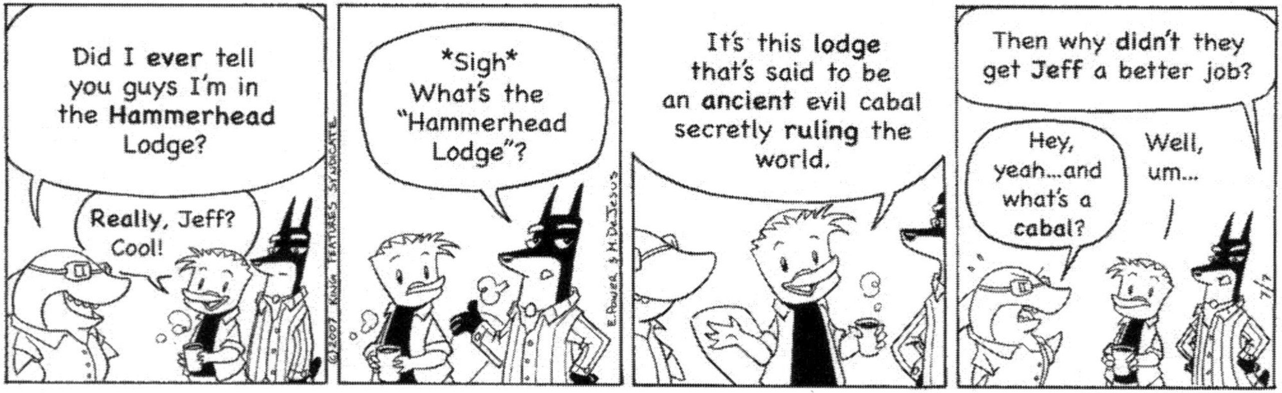
Did I **ever** tell you guys I'm in the **Hammerhead** Lodge?
Really, Jeff? Cool!
Sigh What's the "Hammerhead Lodge"?
It's this **lodge** that's said to be an **ancient** evil cabal secretly **ruling** the world.
Then why **didn't** they get **Jeff** a better job?
Hey, yeah...and what's a **cabal?**
Well, um...
7/7

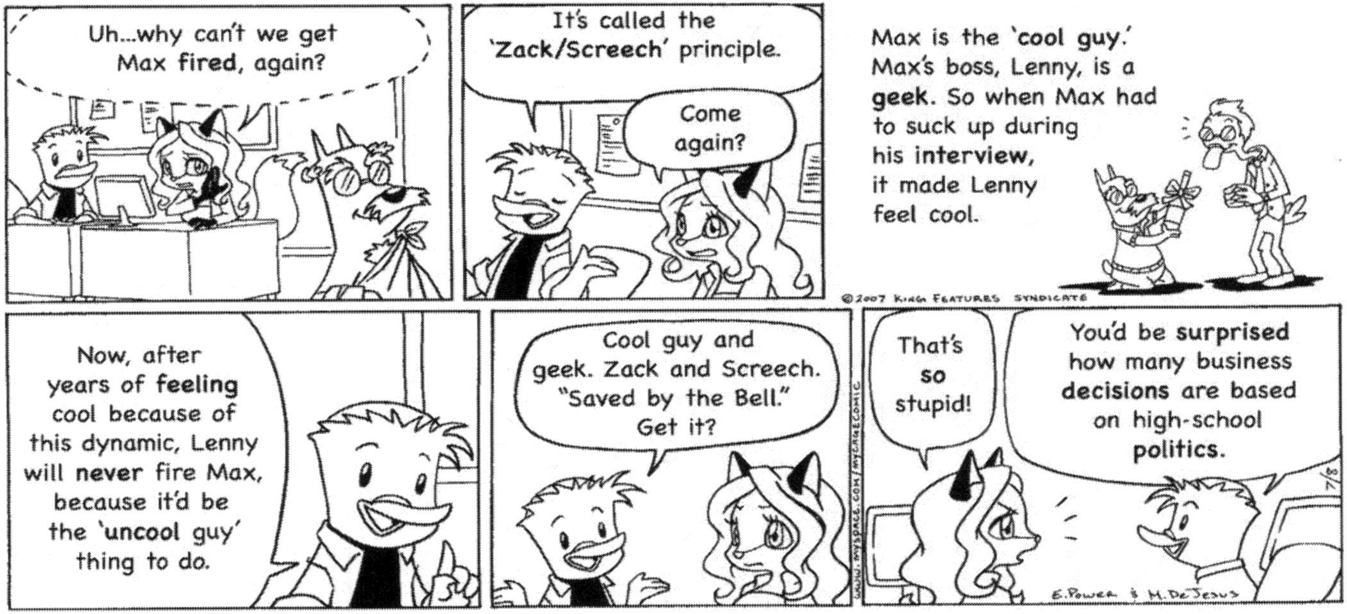
Uh...why can't we get Max **fired**, again?
It's called the '**Zack/Screech**' principle.
Come again?
Max is the '**cool guy**.' Max's boss, Lenny, is a **geek**. So when Max had to suck up during his **interview**, it made Lenny feel cool.
©2007 King Features Syndicate
Now, after years of **feeling** cool because of this dynamic, Lenny will **never** fire Max, because it'd be the '**uncool** guy' thing to do.
Cool guy and geek. Zack and Screech. "Saved by the Bell." Get it?
That's **so** stupid!
You'd be **surprised** how many business **decisions** are based on high-school **politics**.
7/8
E.Power & M.DeJesus

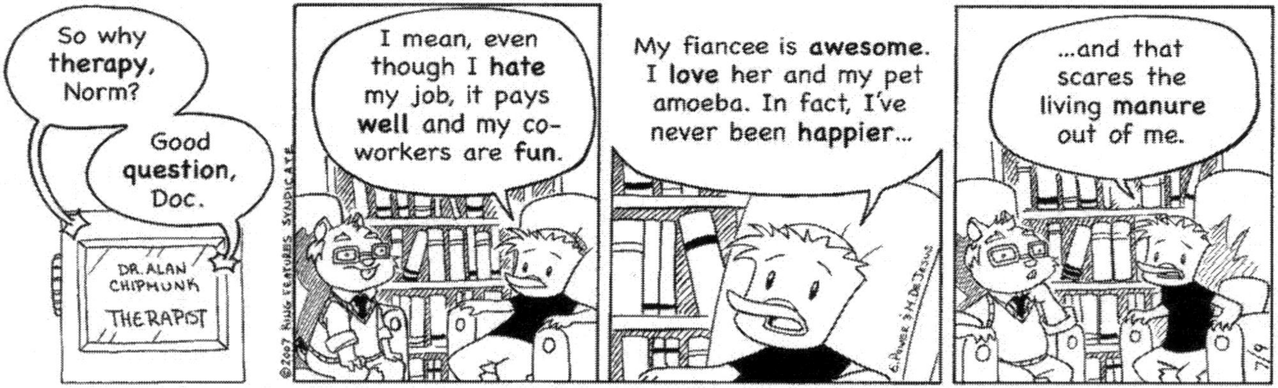
So why **therapy**, Norm?
Good **question**, Doc.
DR. ALAN CHIPMUNK THERAPIST
©2007 King Features Syndicate
I mean, even though I **hate** my job, it pays **well** and my co-workers are **fun**.
My fiancee is **awesome**. I **love** her and my pet amoeba. In fact, I've never been **happier**...
E. Power & M. De Jesus
...and that scares the living **manure** out of me.
7/9

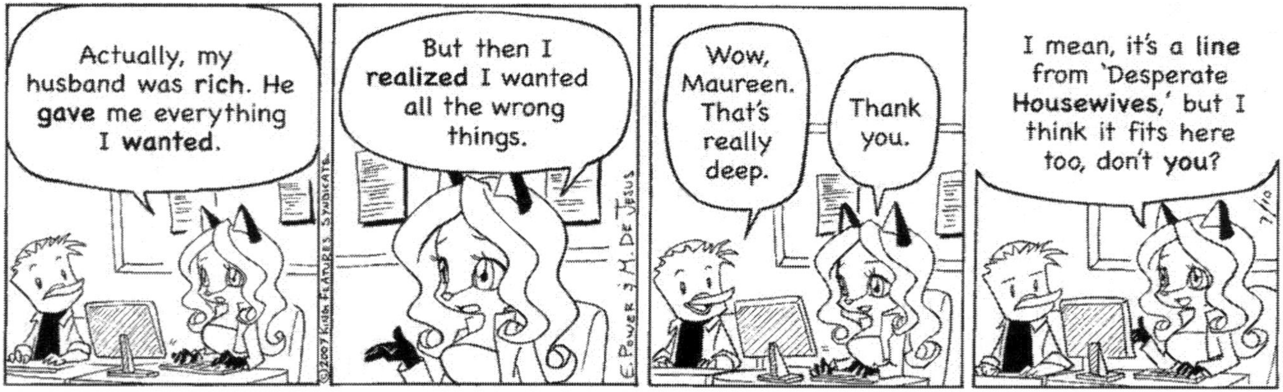
Actually, my husband was **rich**. He **gave** me everything I **wanted**.
©2007 King Features Syndicate
But then I **realized** I wanted all the wrong things.
E. Power & M. De Jesus
Wow, Maureen. That's really deep.
Thank you.
I mean, it's a **line** from 'Desperate **Housewives**,' but I think it fits here too, don't **you**?
7/10

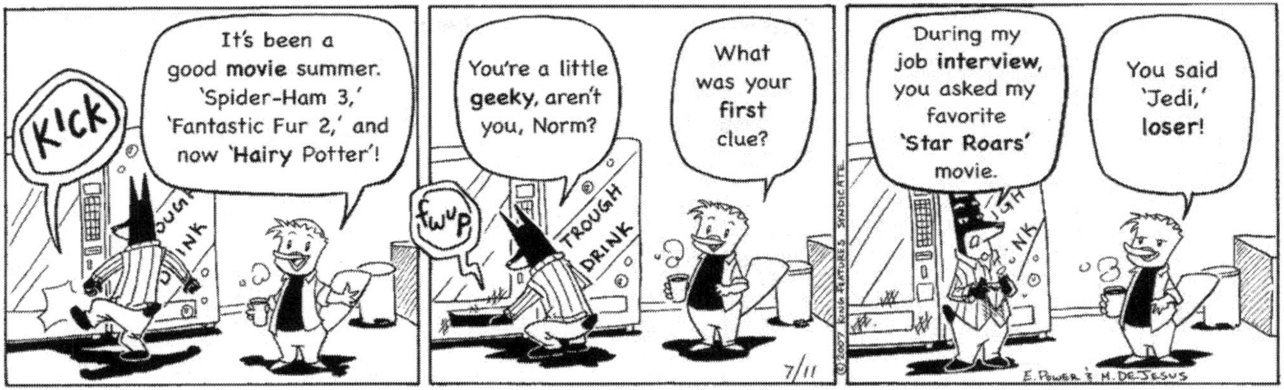
KICK
It's been a good movie summer. 'Spider-Ham 3,' 'Fantastic Fur 2,' and now 'Hairy Potter'!
TROUGH DRINK
FWUP
You're a little geeky, aren't you, Norm?
What was your first clue?
7/11
During my job interview, you asked my favorite 'Star Roars' movie.
You said 'Jedi,' loser!
©2007 KING FEATURES SYNDICATE
E. POWER & M. DEJESUS

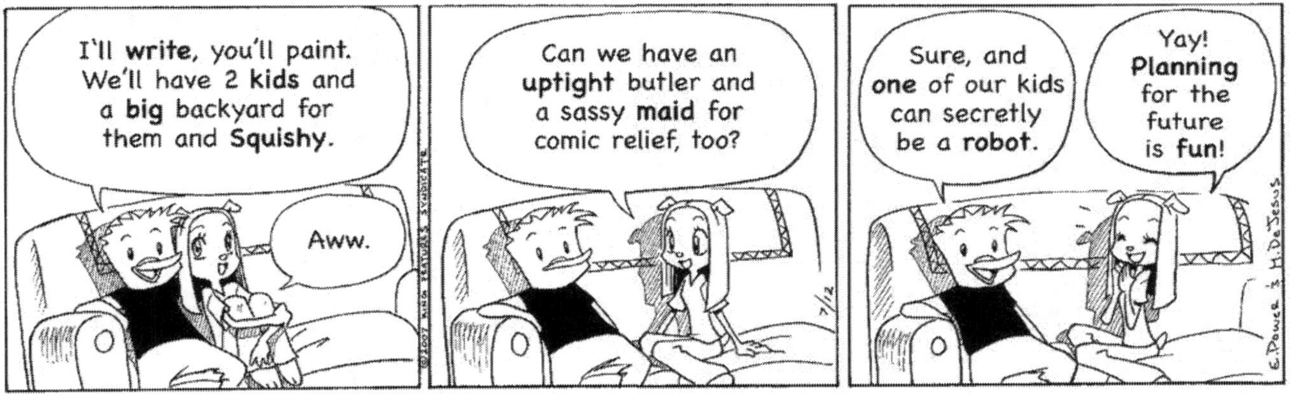
I'll write, you'll paint. We'll have 2 kids and a big backyard for them and Squishy.
Aww.
©2007 KING FEATURES SYNDICATE
Can we have an uptight butler and a sassy maid for comic relief, too?
7/12
Sure, and one of our kids can secretly be a robot.
Yay! Planning for the future is fun!
E. POWER & M. DEJESUS

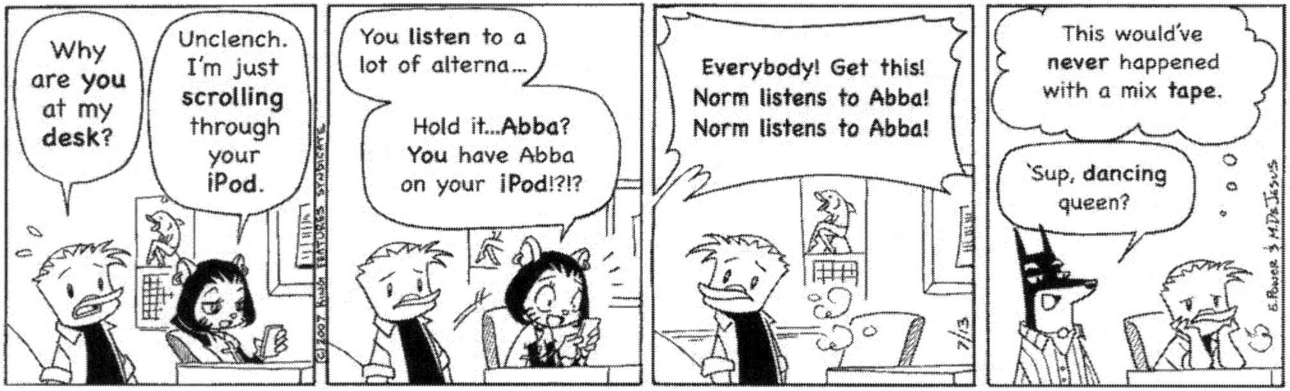
Why are you at my desk?
Unclench. I'm just scrolling through your iPod.
©2007 King Features Syndicate
You listen to a lot of alterna...
Hold it...Abba? You have Abba on your iPod!?!?
Everybody! Get this! Norm listens to Abba! Norm listens to Abba!
7/13
This would've never happened with a mix tape.
'Sup, dancing queen?
E.Power & M.DeJesus

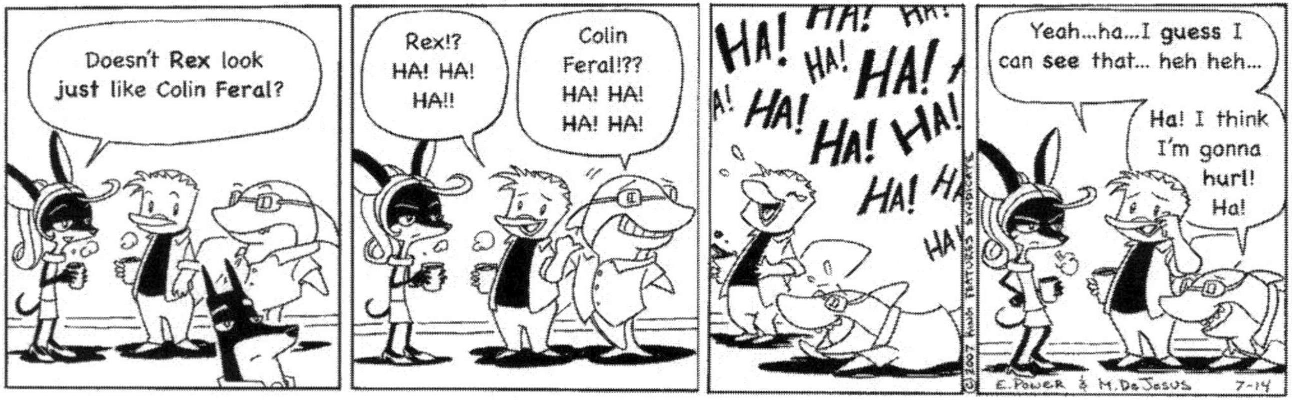
Doesn't Rex look just like Colin Feral?
Rex!? HA! HA! HA!!
Colin Feral!?? HA! HA! HA! HA!
HA! HA! HA! HA! HA! HA! HA! HA! HA! HA! HA!
©2007 King Features Syndicate
Yeah...ha...I guess I can see that... heh heh...
Ha! I think I'm gonna hurl! Ha!
E.Power & M.DeJesus
7-14

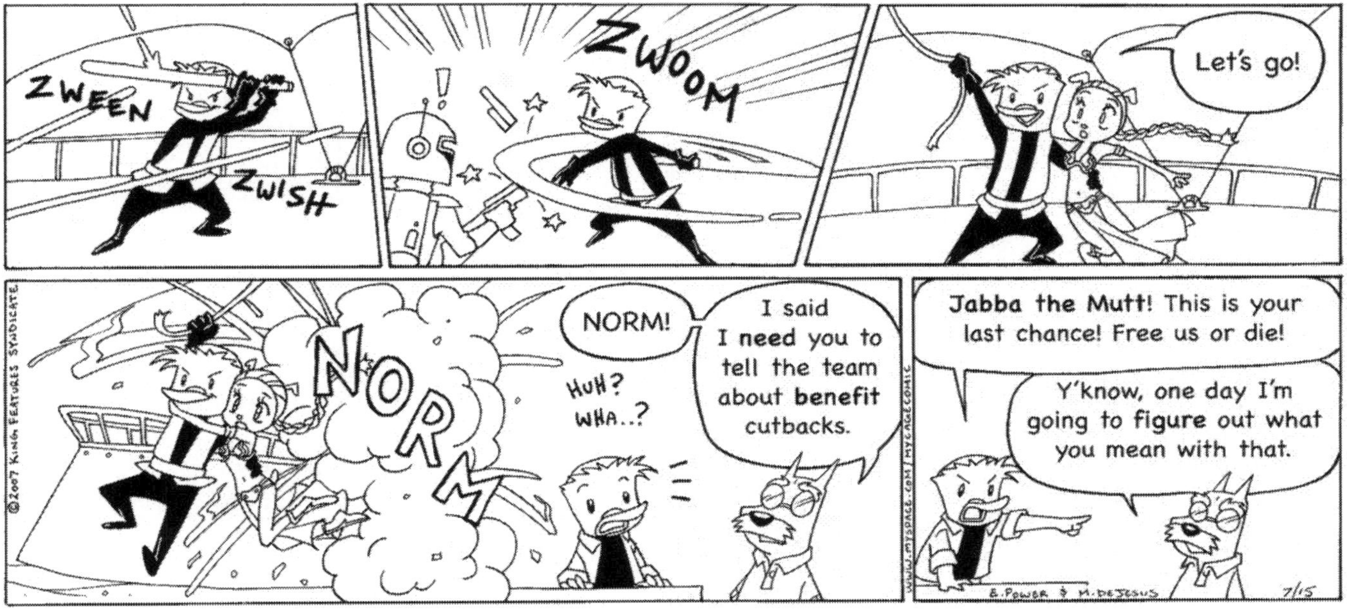
ZWEEN
ZWISH
!
ZWOOM
Let's go!
©2007 King Features Syndicate
NORM
NORM!
HUH?
WHA..?
I said
I **need** you to
tell the team
about **benefit**
cutbacks.
WWW.MYSPACE.COM/MYCAGECOMIC
Jabba the Mutt! This is your last chance! Free us or die!
Y'know, one day I'm going to **figure** out what you mean with that.
B. Power & M. DeJesus
7/15

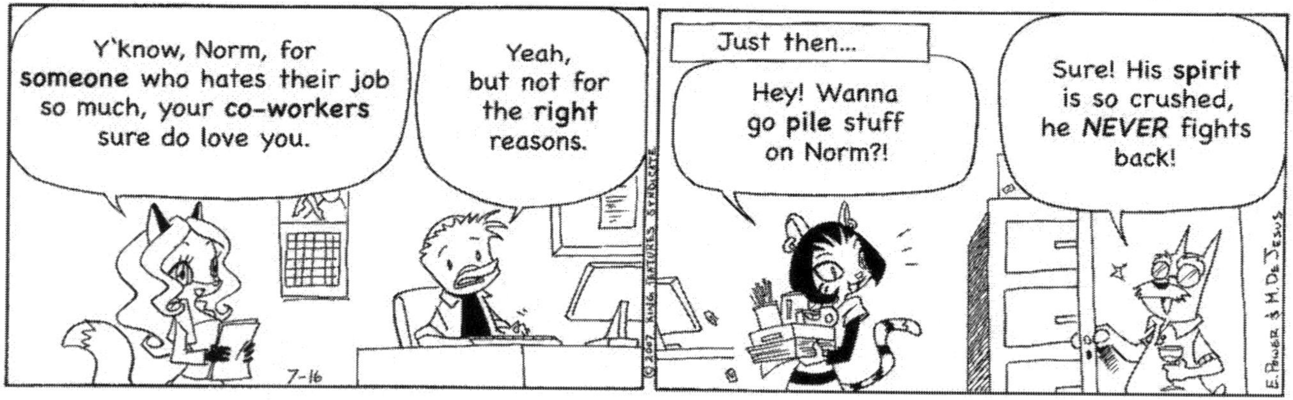
Y'know, Norm, for **someone** who hates their job so much, your **co-workers** sure do love you.
Yeah, but not for the **right** reasons.
Just then...
Hey! Wanna go **pile** stuff on Norm?!
Sure! His **spirit** is so crushed, he ***NEVER*** fights back!

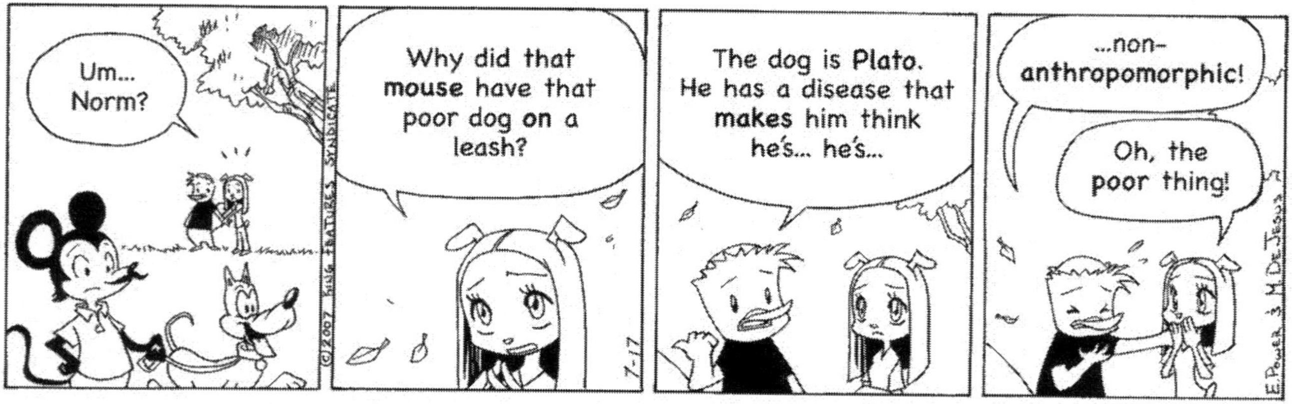
Um... Norm?
Why did that **mouse** have that poor dog **on** a leash?
The dog is **Plato**. He has a disease that **makes** him think he's... he's...
...non-**anthropomorphic**!
Oh, the **poor** thing!

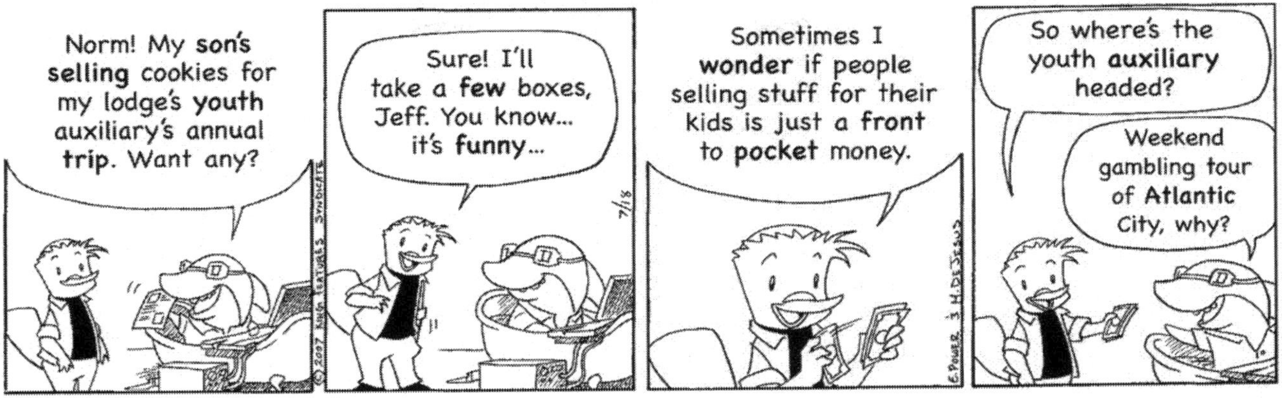
Norm! My **son's selling** cookies for my lodge's **youth** auxiliary's annual **trip**. Want any?
Sure! I'll take a **few** boxes, Jeff. You know... it's **funny**...
7/18
Sometimes I **wonder** if people selling stuff for their kids is just a **front** to **pocket** money.
So where's the youth **auxiliary** headed?
Weekend gambling tour of **Atlantic** City, why?

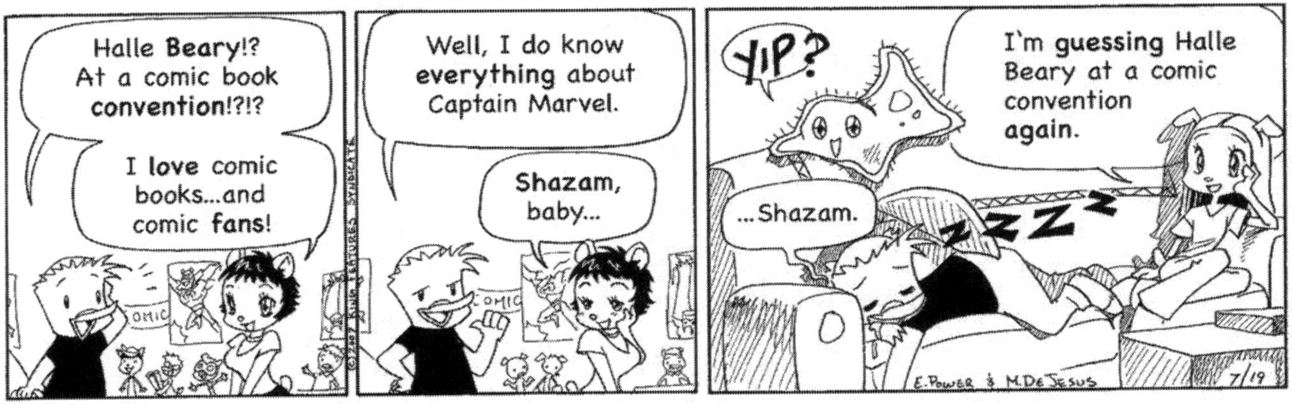
Halle **Beary**!? At a comic book **convention**!?!?
I **love** comic books...and comic **fans**!
Well, I do know **everything** about Captain Marvel.
Shazam, baby...
YIP?
I'm **guessing** Halle Beary at a comic convention **again**.
...Shazam.
ZZZZZ
E. POWER & M. DEJESUS
7/19

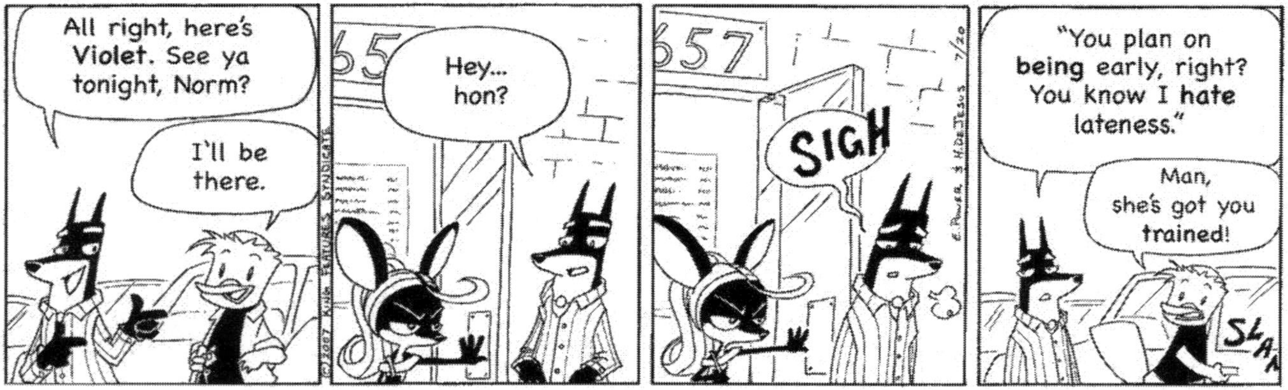
All right, here's Violet. See ya tonight, Norm?
I'll be there.
Hey... hon?
SIGH
"You plan on being early, right? You know I hate lateness."
Man, she's got you trained!

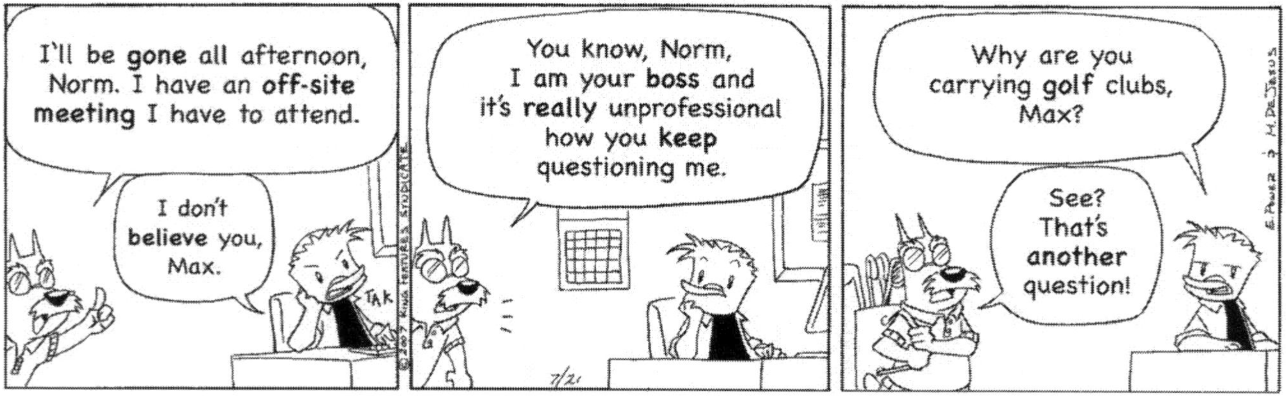
I'll be gone all afternoon, Norm. I have an off-site meeting I have to attend.
I don't believe you, Max.
TAK
You know, Norm, I am your boss and it's really unprofessional how you keep questioning me.
Why are you carrying golf clubs, Max?
See? That's another question!

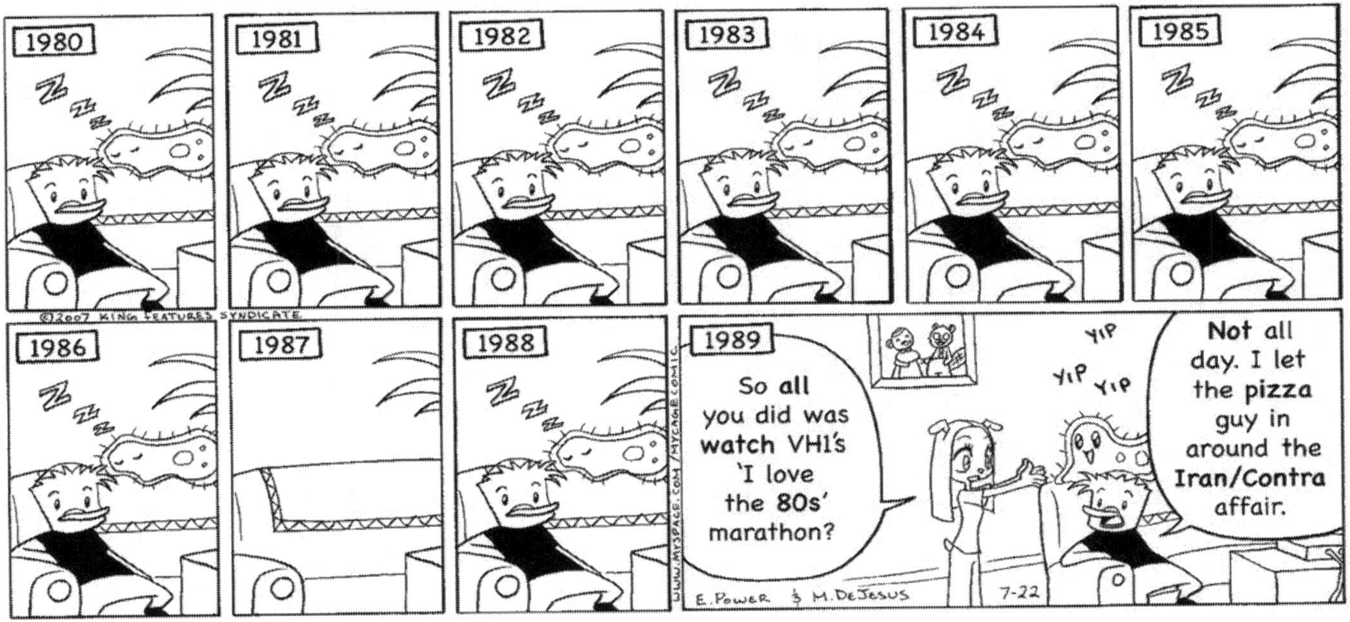
1980
1981
1982
1983
1984
1985
©2007 KING FEATURES SYNDICATE
1986
1987
1988
WWW.MYSPACE.COM/MYCAGECOMIC
1989
So **all** you did was **watch** VH1's 'I love the **80s**' marathon?
YIP YIP YIP
Not all day. I let the **pizza** guy in around the **Iran/Contra** affair.
E. POWER & M. DEJESUS
7-22

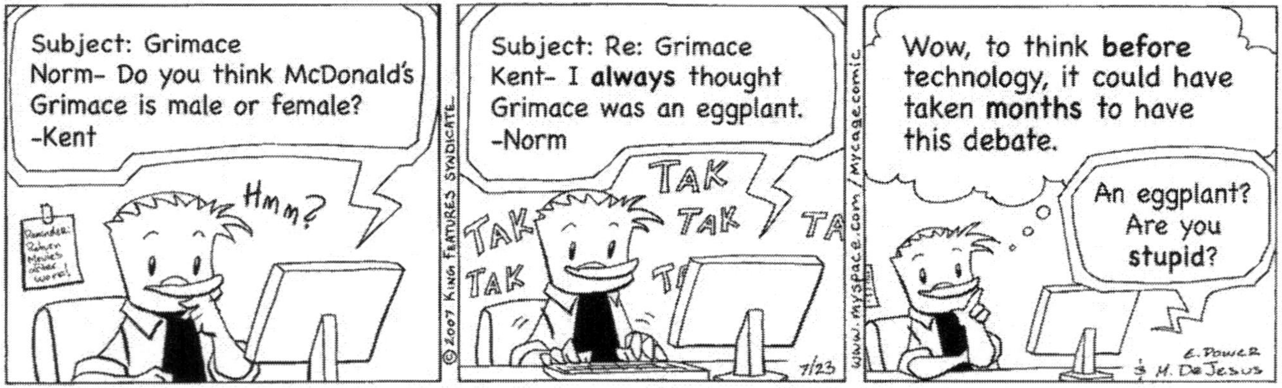
Subject: Grimace
Norm- Do you think McDonald's Grimace is male or female? -Kent
Hmm?
© 2007 King Features Syndicate
Subject: Re: Grimace
Kent- I **always** thought Grimace was an eggplant. -Norm
TAK TAK TAK TAK TA
7/23
www.myspace.com/mycage.comic
Wow, to think **before** technology, it could have taken **months** to have this debate.
An eggplant? Are you **stupid?**
E. Power & M. DeJesus

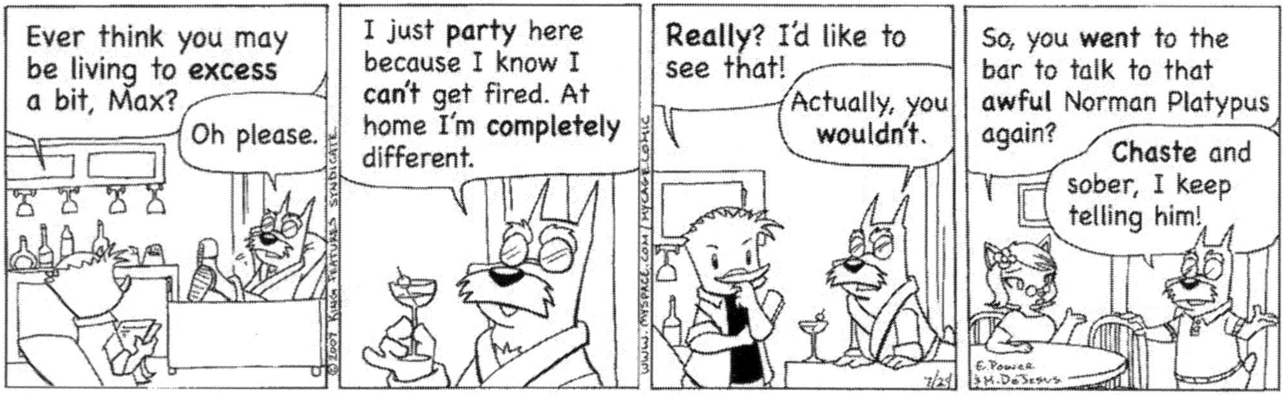
Ever think you may be living to **excess** a bit, Max?
Oh please.
© 2007 King Features Syndicate
I just **party** here because I know I **can't** get fired. At home I'm **completely** different.
www.myspace.com/mycage.comic
Really? I'd like to see that!
Actually, you **wouldn't**.
So, you **went** to the bar to talk to that **awful** Norman Platypus again?
Chaste and sober, I keep telling him!
E. Power & M. DeJesus

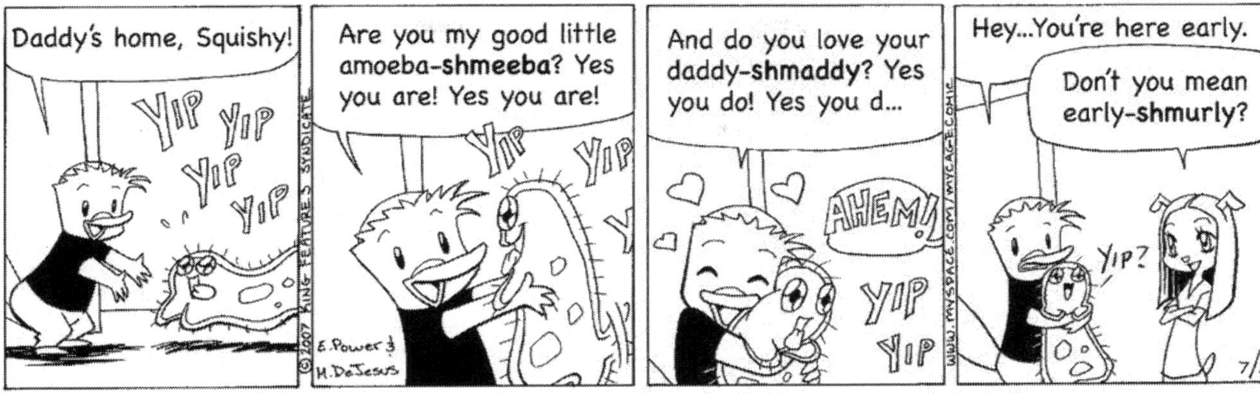

Daddy's home, Squishy!
YIP YIP YIP YIP
Are you my good little amoeba-**shmeeba**? Yes you are! Yes you are!
YIP YIP
E. Power & M. DeJesus
And do you love your daddy-**shmaddy**? Yes you do! Yes you d...
AHEM!
YIP YIP
Hey...You're here early.
Don't you mean early-**shmurly**?
YIP?
7/25

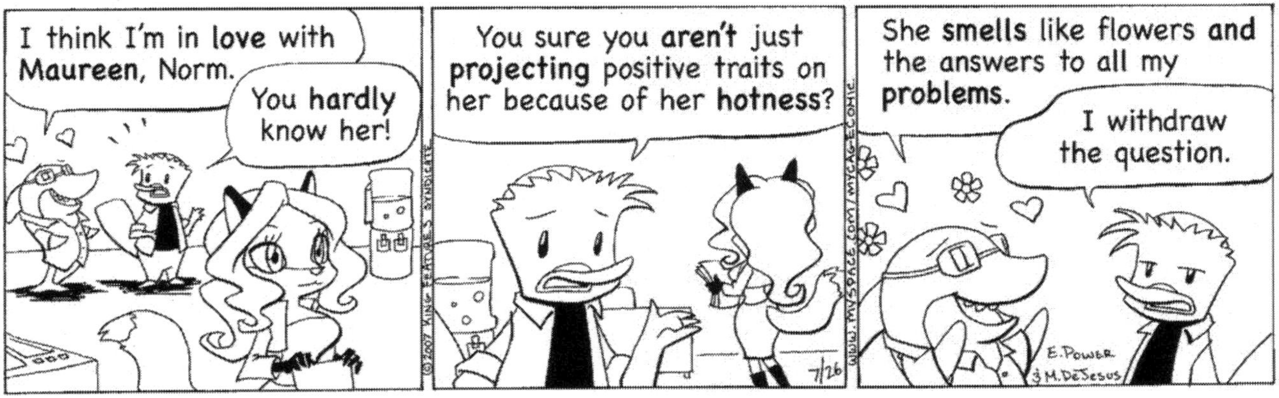

I think I'm in **love** with **Maureen**, Norm.
You **hardly** know her!
You sure you **aren't** just **projecting** positive traits on her because of her **hotness**?
7/26
She **smells** like flowers **and** the answers to all my **problems**.
I withdraw the question.
E. Power & M. DeJesus

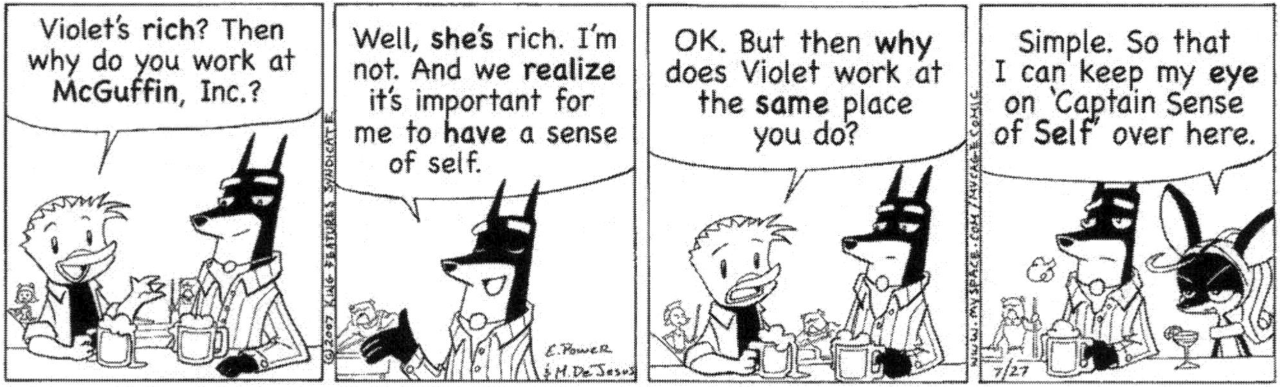
Violet's rich? Then why do you work at McGuffin, Inc.?
Well, she's rich. I'm not. And we realize it's important for me to have a sense of self.
OK. But then why does Violet work at the same place you do?
Simple. So that I can keep my eye on 'Captain Sense of Self' over here.
©2007 KING FEATURES SYNDICATE
E. POWER & M. DeJESUS
WWW.MYSPACE.COM/MYCAGECOMIC
7/27

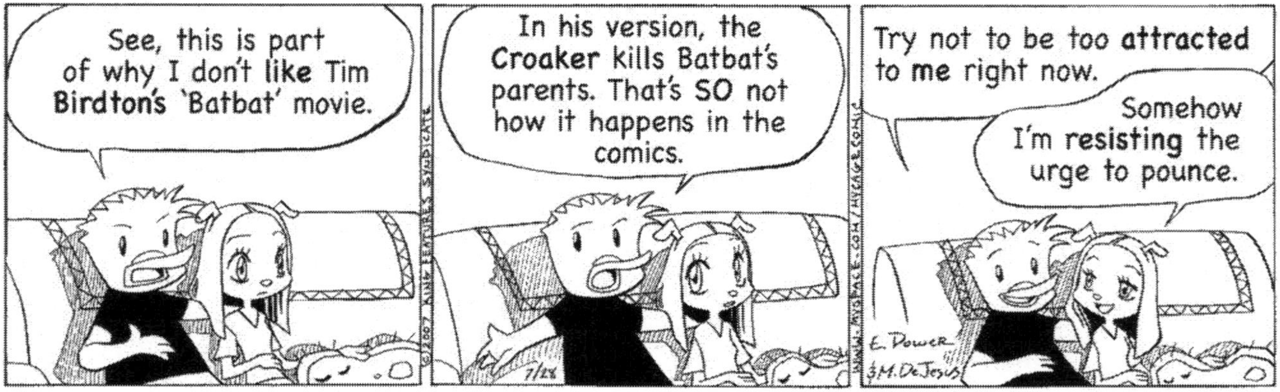
See, this is part of why I don't like Tim Birdton's 'Batbat' movie.
In his version, the Croaker kills Batbat's parents. That's SO not how it happens in the comics.
Try not to be too attracted to me right now.
Somehow I'm resisting the urge to pounce.
©2007 KING FEATURES SYNDICATE
WWW.MYSPACE.COM/MYCAGECOMIC
7/28
E. POWER & M. DeJESUS

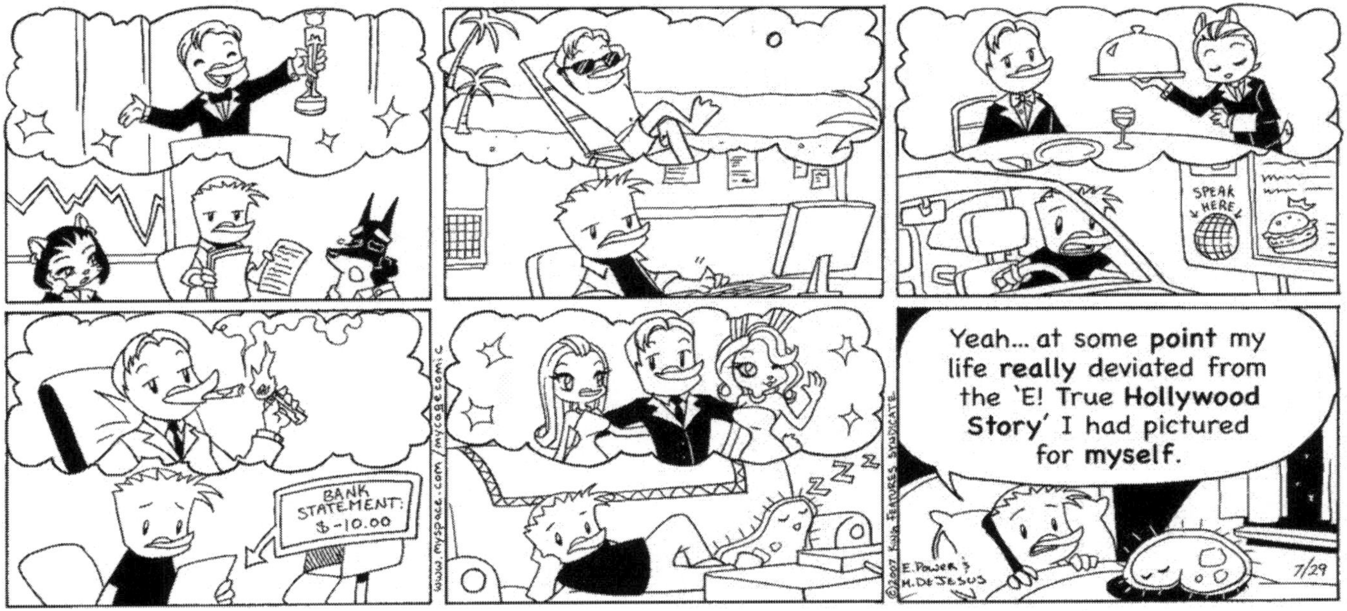
SPEAK HERE
BANK STATEMENT: $-10.00
www.myspace.com/mycagecomic
©2007 KING FEATURES SYNDICATE
Yeah... at some **point** my life **really** deviated from the 'E! True **Hollywood Story**' I had pictured for **myself**.
E. POWER & H. DEJESUS
7/29

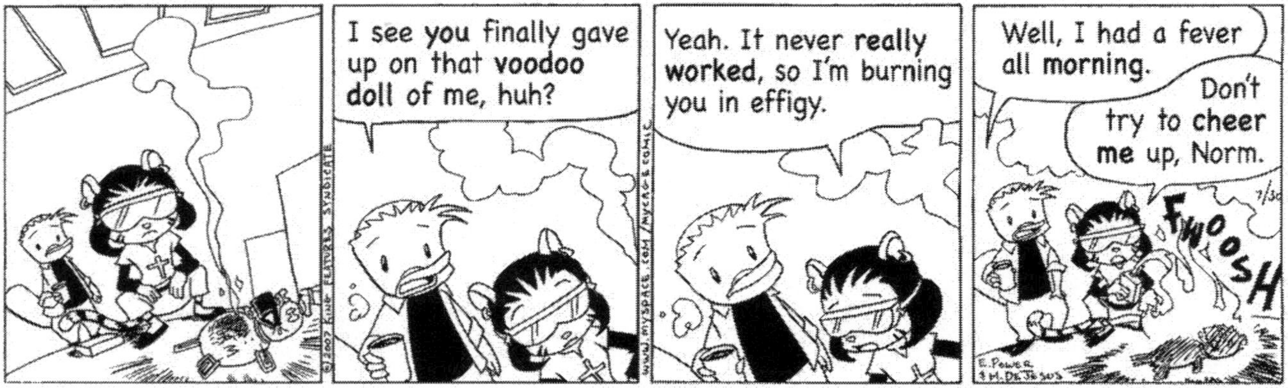
I see you finally gave up on that voodoo doll of me, huh?
Yeah. It never really worked, so I'm burning you in effigy.
Well, I had a fever all morning.
Don't try to cheer me up, Norm.
FWOOSH
E. POWER & M. DEJESUS

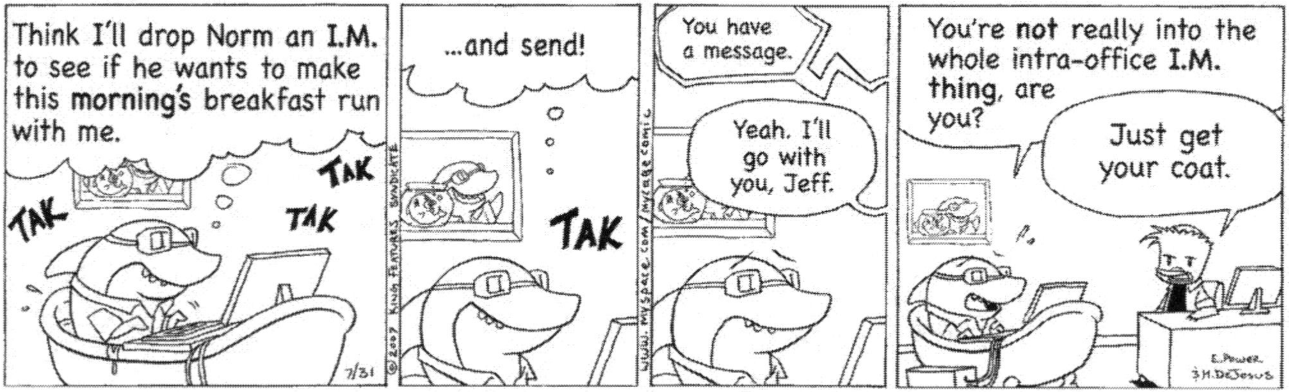
Think I'll drop Norm an I.M. to see if he wants to make this morning's breakfast run with me.
TAK
TAK
TAK
7/31
...and send!
TAK
You have a message.
Yeah. I'll go with you, Jeff.
You're not really into the whole intra-office I.M. thing, are you?
Just get your coat.
E. POWER & M. DEJESUS

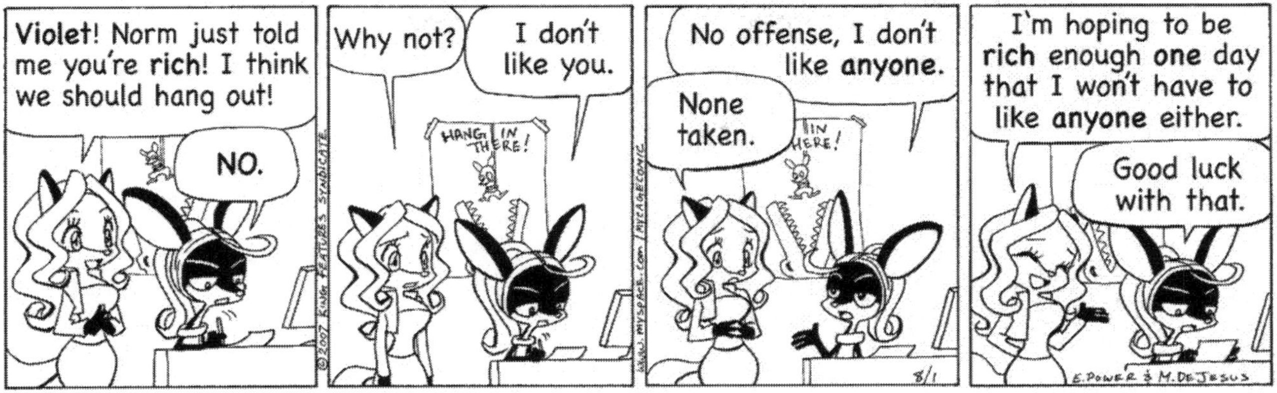
Violet! Norm just told me you're rich! I think we should hang out!
NO.
Why not?
I don't like you.
HANG IN THERE!
No offense, I don't like anyone.
None taken.
I'm hoping to be rich enough one day that I won't have to like anyone either.
Good luck with that.
©2007 King Features Syndicate
www.myspace.com/mycagecomic
8/1
E. Power & M. DeJesus

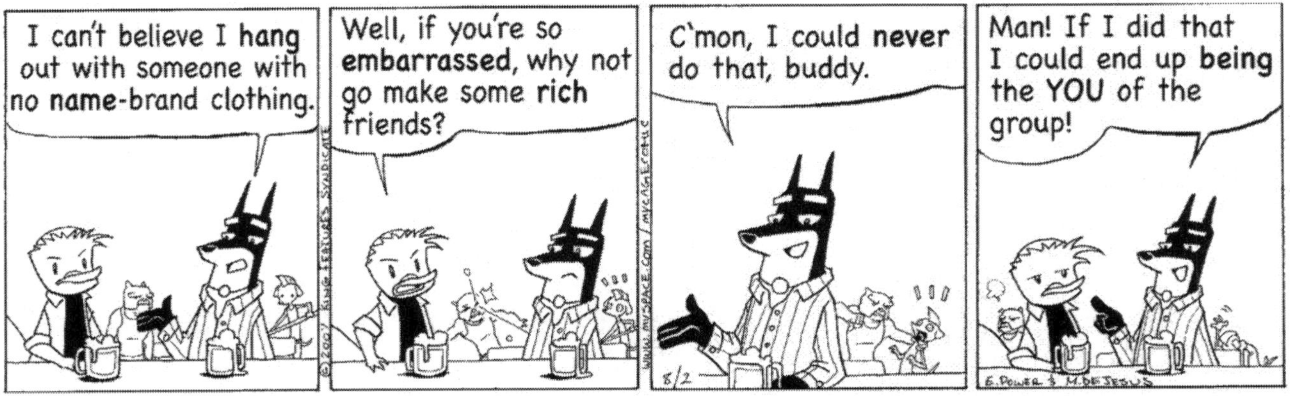
I can't believe I hang out with someone with no name-brand clothing.
Well, if you're so embarrassed, why not go make some rich friends?
C'mon, I could never do that, buddy.
Man! If I did that I could end up being the YOU of the group!
©2007 King Features Syndicate
www.myspace.com/mycagecomic
8/2
E. Power & M. DeJesus

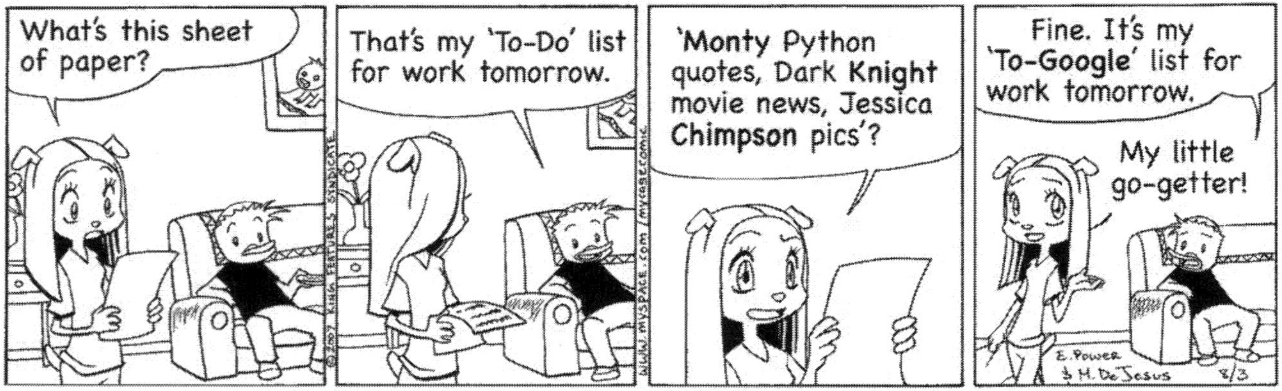
What's this sheet of paper?
That's my 'To-Do' list for work tomorrow.
© 2007 King Features Syndicate
www.myspace.com/mycagecomic
'Monty Python quotes, Dark Knight movie news, Jessica Chimpson pics'?
Fine. It's my 'To-Google' list for work tomorrow.
My little go-getter!
E. Power
& M. DeJesus
8/3

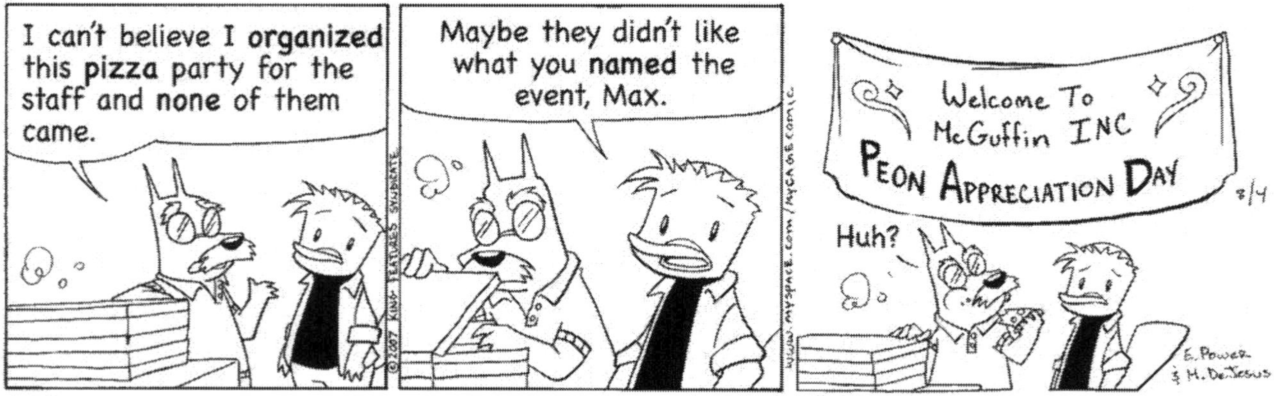
I can't believe I organized this pizza party for the staff and none of them came.
© 2007 King Features Syndicate
Maybe they didn't like what you named the event, Max.
www.myspace.com/mycagecomic
Welcome To McGuffin INC
Peon Appreciation Day
8/4
Huh?
E. Power
& M. DeJesus

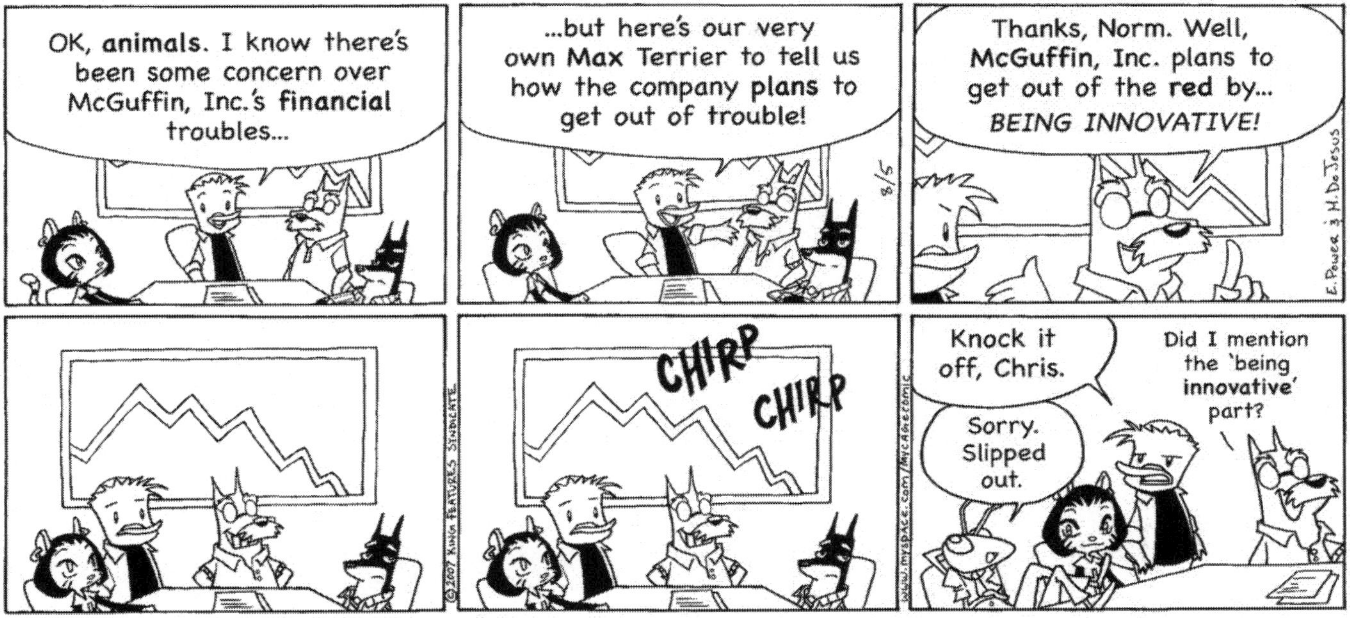

OK, **animals**. I know there's been some concern over McGuffin, Inc.'s **financial** troubles...
...but here's our very own **Max** Terrier to tell us how the company **plans** to get out of trouble!
8/5
Thanks, Norm. Well, **McGuffin**, Inc. plans to get out of the **red** by... *BEING INNOVATIVE!*
E. Power & M. DeJesus
©2007 King Features Syndicate
CHIRP
CHIRP
www.myspace.com/mycagecomic
Knock it off, Chris.
Sorry. Slipped out.
Did I mention the 'being **innovative**' part?

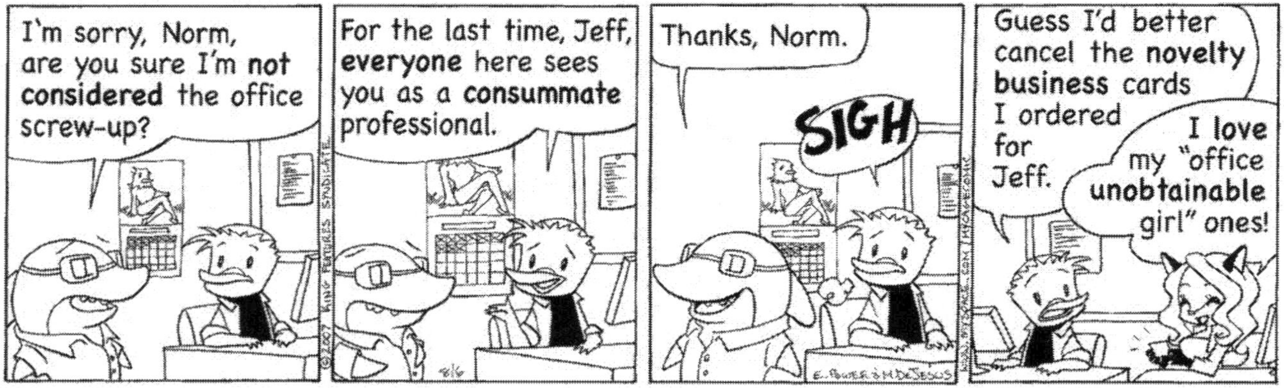
I'm sorry, Norm, are you sure I'm **not considered** the office screw-up?
For the last time, Jeff, **everyone** here sees you as a **consummate** professional.
8/6
Thanks, Norm.
SIGH
Guess I'd better cancel the **novelty business** cards I ordered for Jeff.
I love my "office **unobtainable** girl" ones!

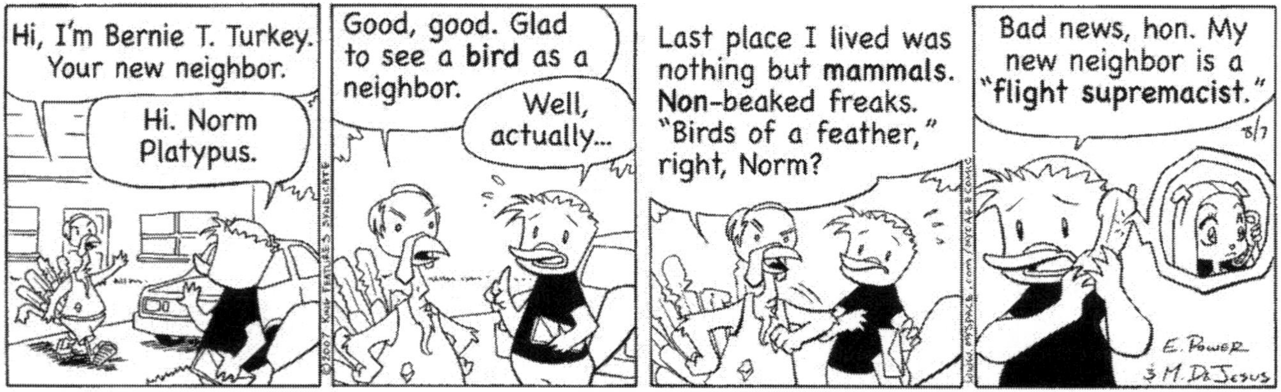
Hi, I'm Bernie T. Turkey. Your new neighbor.
Hi. Norm Platypus.
Good, good. Glad to see a **bird** as a neighbor.
Well, actually...
Last place I lived was nothing but **mammals. Non**-beaked freaks. "Birds of a feather," right, Norm?
Bad news, hon. My new neighbor is a "**flight supremacist.**"
8/7
E. Power
& M. DeJesus

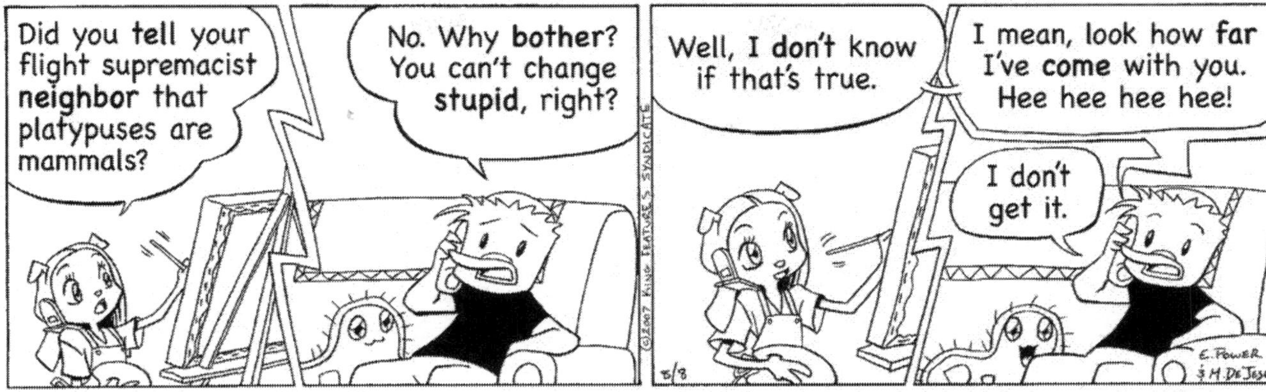
Did you **tell** your flight supremacist **neighbor** that platypuses are mammals?
No. Why **bother**? You can't change **stupid**, right?
Well, I **don't** know if that's true.
I mean, look how **far** I've **come** with you. Hee hee hee hee!
I don't get it.

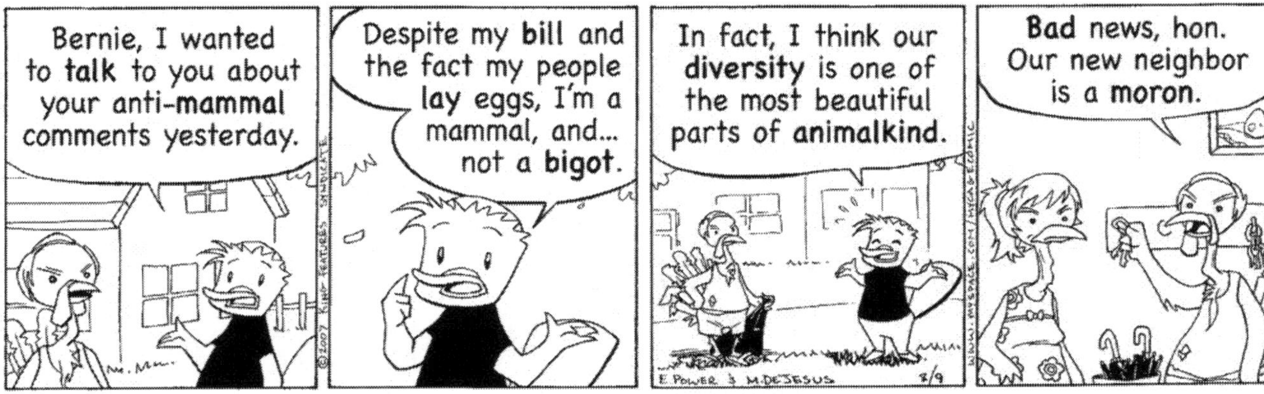
Bernie, I wanted to **talk** to you about your anti-**mammal** comments yesterday.
Despite my **bill** and the fact my people **lay** eggs, I'm a mammal, and... not a **bigot**.
In fact, I think our **diversity** is one of the most beautiful parts of **animalkind**.
Bad news, hon. Our new neighbor is a **moron**.

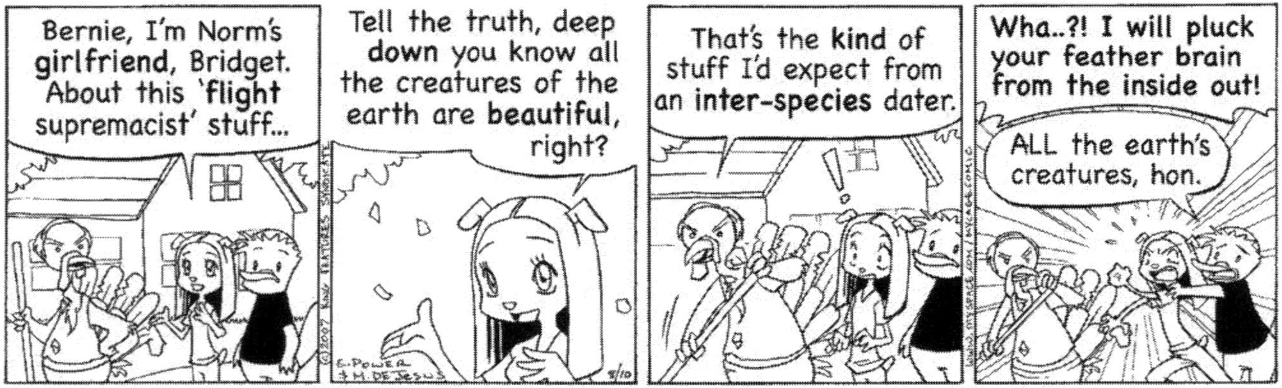
Bernie, I'm Norm's girlfriend, Bridget. About this 'flight supremacist' stuff...
Tell the truth, deep down you know all the creatures of the earth are beautiful, right?
That's the kind of stuff I'd expect from an inter-species dater.
!
Wha..?! I will pluck your feather brain from the inside out!
ALL the earth's creatures, hon.
E. POWER & M. DE JESUS

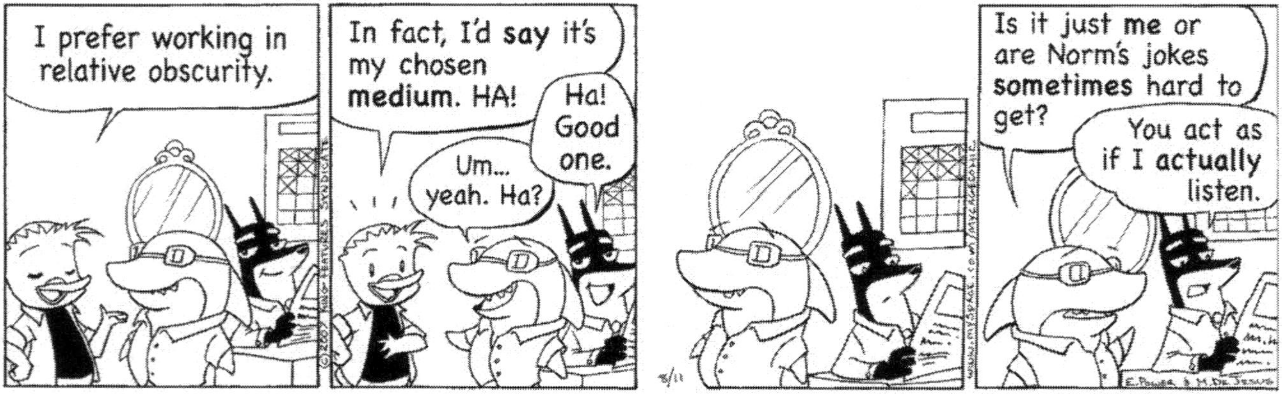
I prefer working in relative obscurity.
In fact, I'd say it's my chosen medium. HA!
Um... yeah. Ha?
Ha! Good one.
Is it just me or are Norm's jokes sometimes hard to get?
You act as if I actually listen.
E. POWER & M. DE JESUS

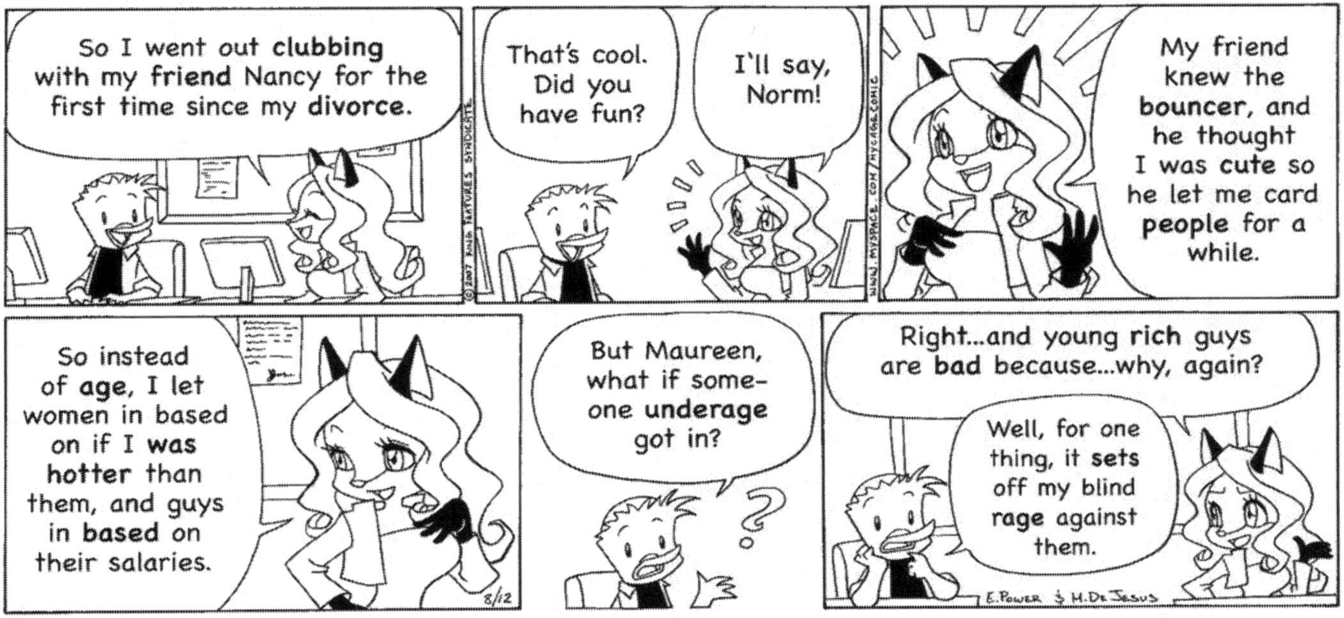
So I went out **clubbing** with my **friend** Nancy for the first time since my **divorce**.
That's cool. Did you have fun?
I'll say, Norm!
My friend knew the **bouncer**, and he thought I was **cute** so he let me card **people** for a while.
So instead of **age**, I let women in based on if I **was hotter** than them, and guys in **based** on their salaries.
8/12
But Maureen, what if some-one **underage** got in?
Right...and young **rich** guys are **bad** because...why, again?
Well, for one thing, it **sets** off my blind **rage** against them.
E.Power & H.De Jesus

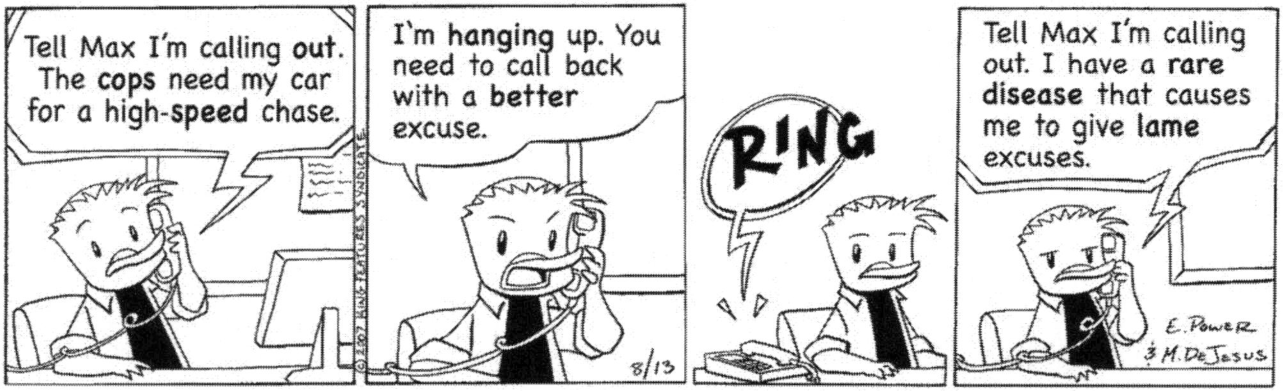
Tell Max I'm calling out. The cops need my car for a high-speed chase.
I'm hanging up. You need to call back with a better excuse.
RING
Tell Max I'm calling out. I have a rare disease that causes me to give lame excuses.
8/13
E. Power & M. DeJesus

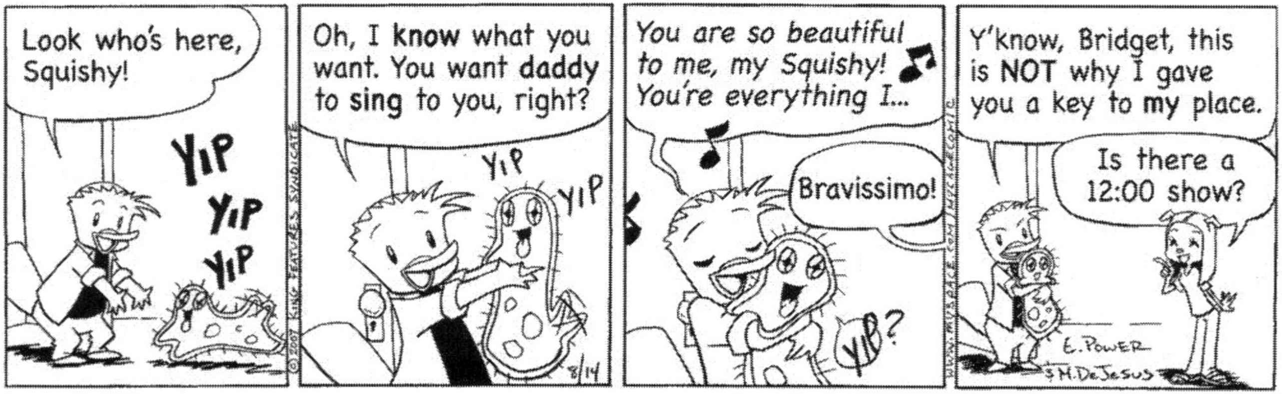
Look who's here, Squishy!
YIP YIP YIP
Oh, I know what you want. You want daddy to sing to you, right?
YIP YIP
You are so beautiful to me, my Squishy! You're everything I...
Bravissimo!
YIP?
Y'know, Bridget, this is NOT why I gave you a key to my place.
Is there a 12:00 show?
8/14
E. Power & M. DeJesus

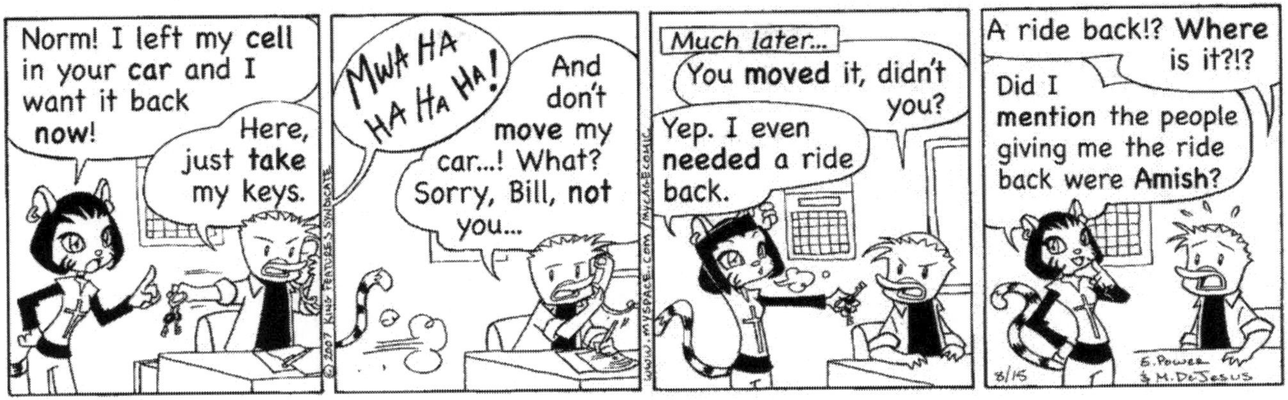
Norm! I left my **cell** in your **car** and I want it back **now**!
Here, just **take** my keys.
© 2007 King Features Syndicate
MWAHA HA HA HA!
And don't **move** my car...! What? Sorry, Bill, **not** you...
www.myspace.com/mycagecomic
Much later...
You **moved** it, didn't you?
Yep. I even **needed** a ride back.
A ride back!? **Where** is it?!?
Did I **mention** the people giving me the ride back were **Amish**?
8/15
E. Power & M. DeJesus

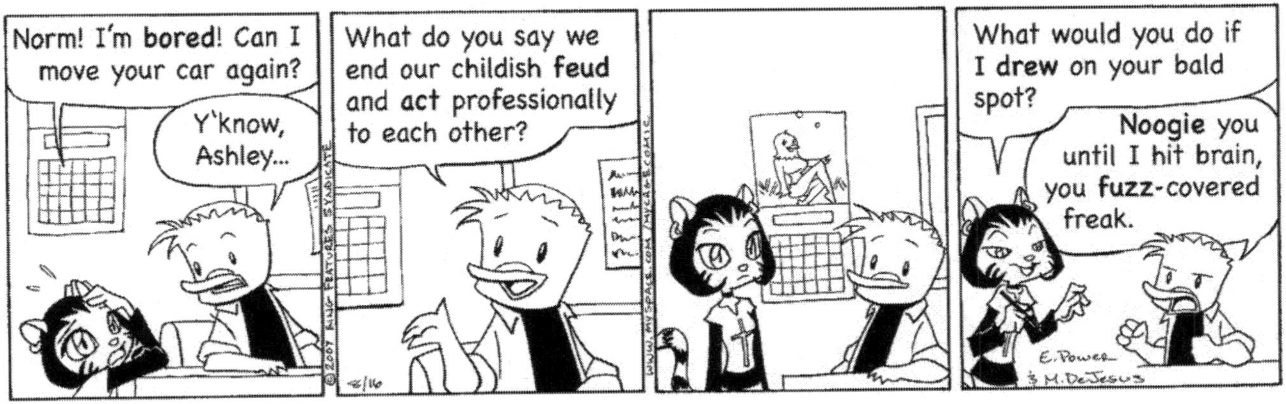
Norm! I'm **bored**! Can I move your car again?
Y'know, Ashley...
© 2007 King Features Syndicate
What do you say we end our childish **feud** and **act** professionally to each other?
8/16
www.myspace.com/mycagecomic
What would you do if **I drew** on your bald spot?
Noogie you until I hit **brain**, you **fuzz**-covered freak.
E. Power & M. DeJesus

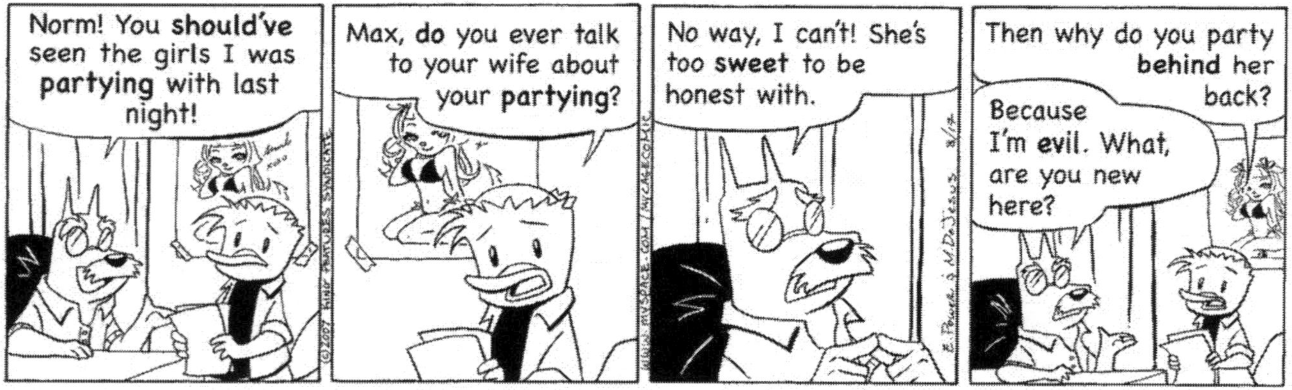
Norm! You **should've** seen the girls I was **partying** with last night!
Max, **do** you ever talk to your wife about your **partying**?
No way, I can't! She's too **sweet** to be honest with.
Then why do you party **behind** her back?
Because I'm **evil**. What, are you new here?
©2007 King Features Syndicate
www.myspace.com/mycagecomic
E. Power & M. DeJesus 8/17

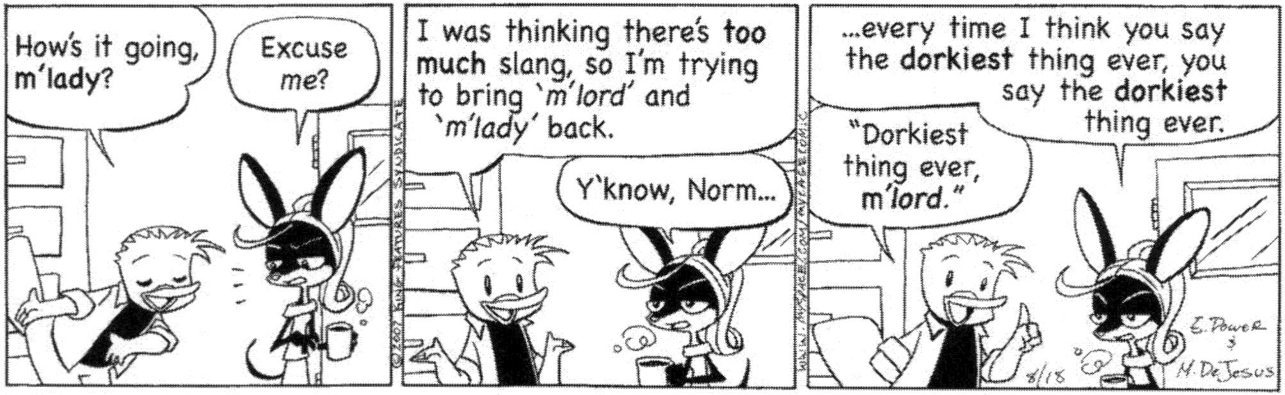
How's it going, **m'lady**?
Excuse *me*?
I was thinking there's **too much** slang, so I'm trying to bring *'m'lord'* and *'m'lady'* back.
Y'know, Norm...
...every time I think you say the **dorkiest** thing ever, you say the **dorkiest** thing ever.
"Dorkiest thing ever, **m'*lord*.**"
©2007 King Features Syndicate
www.myspace.com/mycagecomic
E. Power & M. DeJesus
8/18

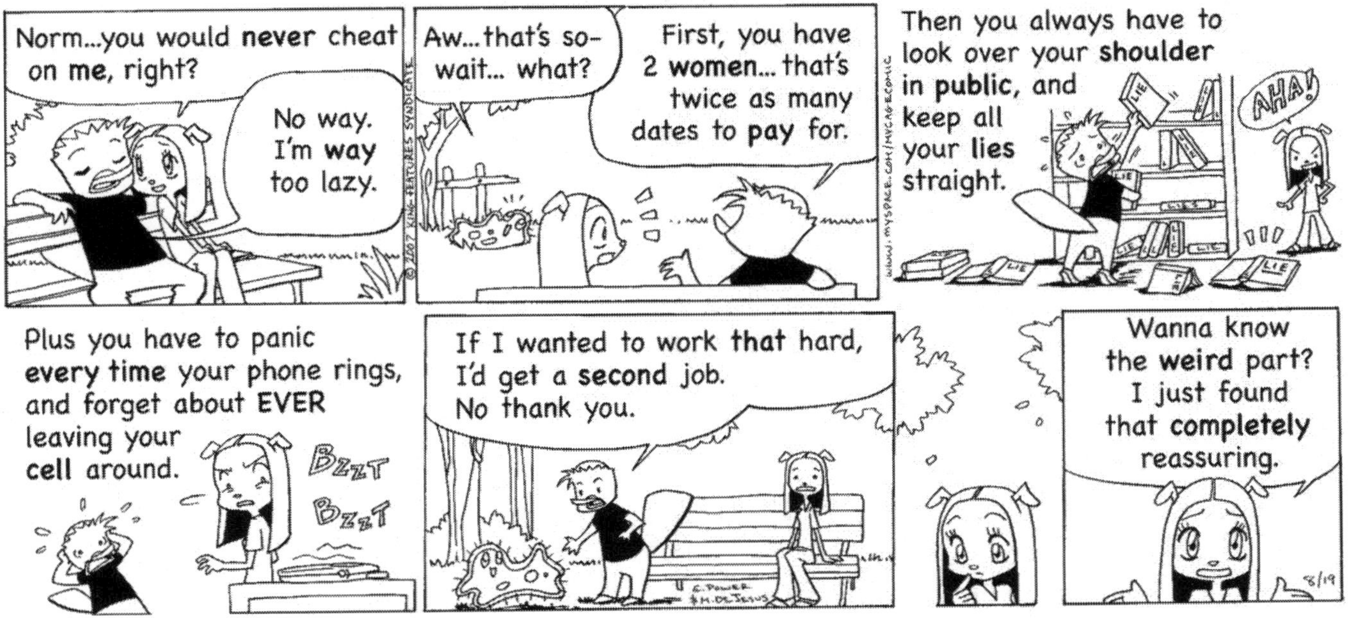
Norm...you would **never** cheat on **me**, right?
No way. I'm **way** too lazy.
© 2007 KING FEATURES SYNDICATE
Aw...that's so- wait... what?
First, you have 2 **women**... that's twice as many dates to **pay** for.
Then you always have to look over your **shoulder** in **public**, and keep all your **lies** straight.
AHA!
LIE
Plus you have to panic **every time** your phone rings, and forget about **EVER** leaving your **cell** around.
BZZT
BZZT
If I wanted to work **that** hard, I'd get a **second** job. No thank you.
Wanna know the **weird** part? I just found that **completely** reassuring.
8/19

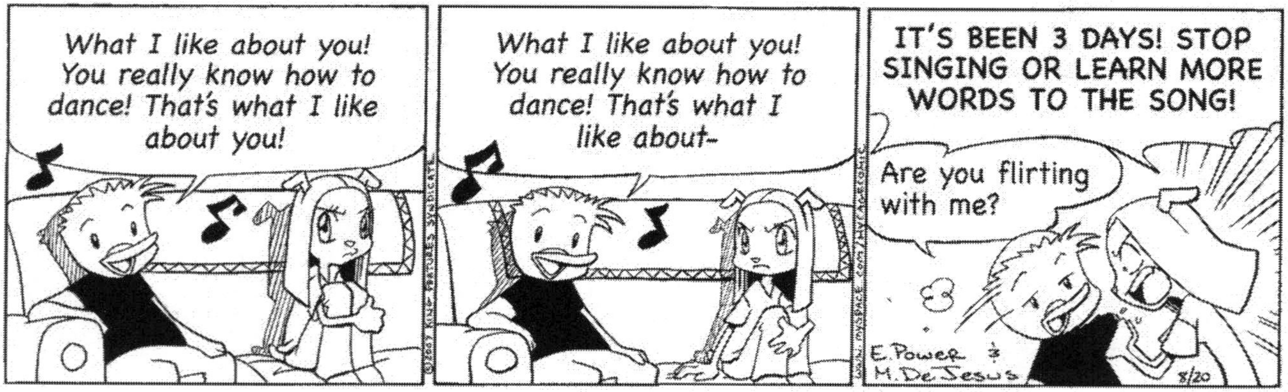
What I like about you! You really know how to dance! That's what I like about you!
What I like about you! You really know how to dance! That's what I like about-
IT'S BEEN 3 DAYS! STOP SINGING OR LEARN MORE WORDS TO THE SONG!
Are you flirting with me?
E. Power & M. DeJesus
8/20

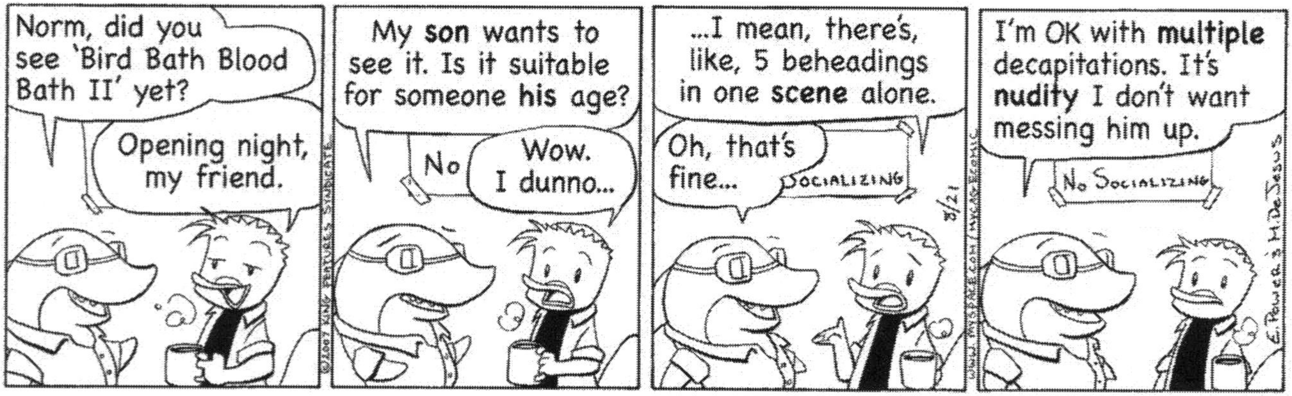
Norm, did you see 'Bird Bath Blood Bath II' yet?
Opening night, my friend.
My **son** wants to see it. Is it suitable for someone **his** age?
Wow. I dunno...
No
...I mean, there's, like, 5 beheadings in one **scene** alone.
Oh, that's fine...
SOCIALIZING
8/21
I'm OK with **multiple** decapitations. It's **nudity** I don't want messing him up.
No Socializing
E. Power & M. DeJesus

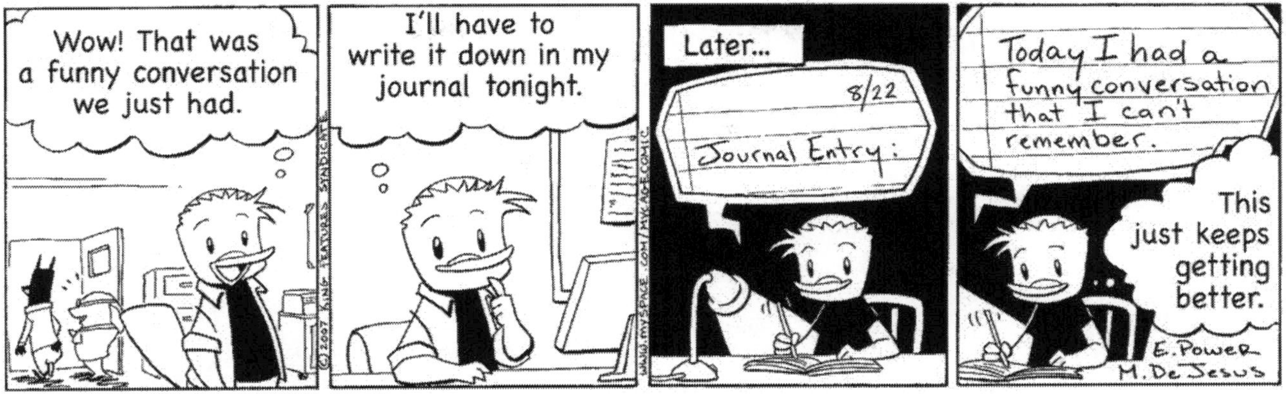

Wow! That was a funny conversation we just had.
I'll have to write it down in my journal tonight.
© 2007 KING FEATURES SYNDICATE
WWW.MYSPACE.COM/MYCAGECOMIC
Later...
8/22
Journal Entry:
Today I had a funny conversation that I can't remember.
This just keeps getting better.
E. POWER
M. DE JESUS

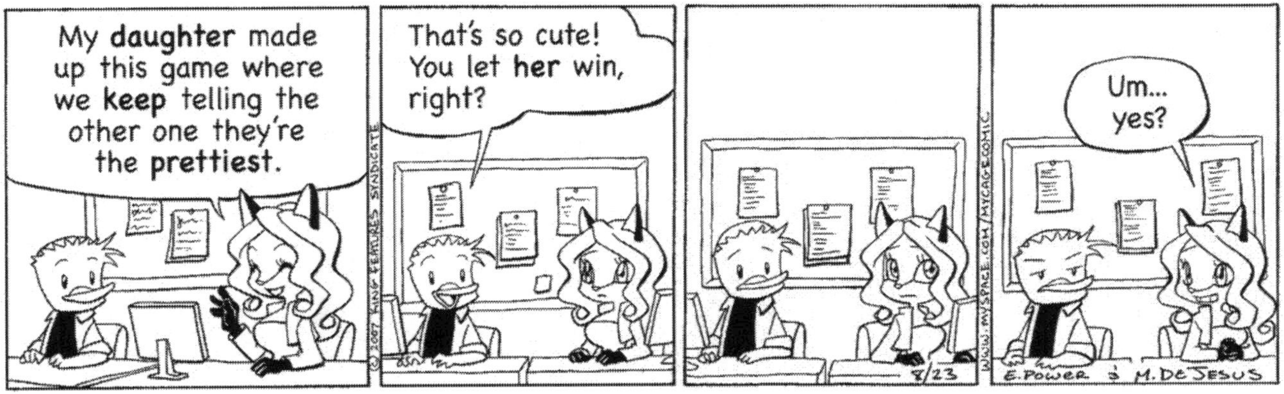

My **daughter** made up this game where we **keep** telling the other one they're the **prettiest**.
© 2007 KING FEATURES SYNDICATE
That's so cute! You let **her** win, right?
8/23
WWW.MYSPACE.COM/MYCAGECOMIC
Um... yes?
E. POWER & M. DE JESUS

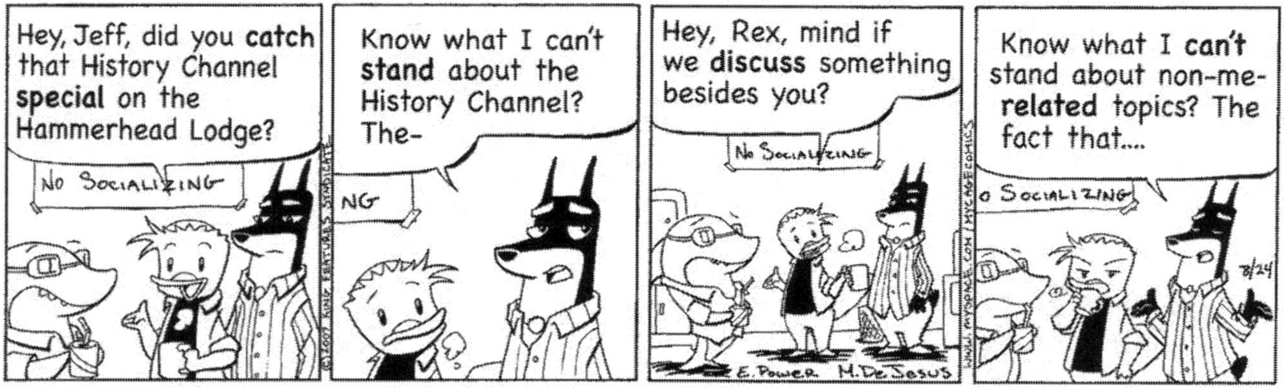
Hey, Jeff, did you **catch** that History Channel **special** on the Hammerhead Lodge?
NO SOCIALIZING
©2007 KING FEATURES SYNDICATE
Know what I can't **stand** about the History Channel? The-
NG
Hey, Rex, mind if we **discuss** something besides you?
No Socializing
E. Power M. DeJesus
WWW.MYSPACE.COM/MYCAGECOMICS
Know what I **can't** stand about non-me-**related** topics? The fact that....
o Socializing
8/24

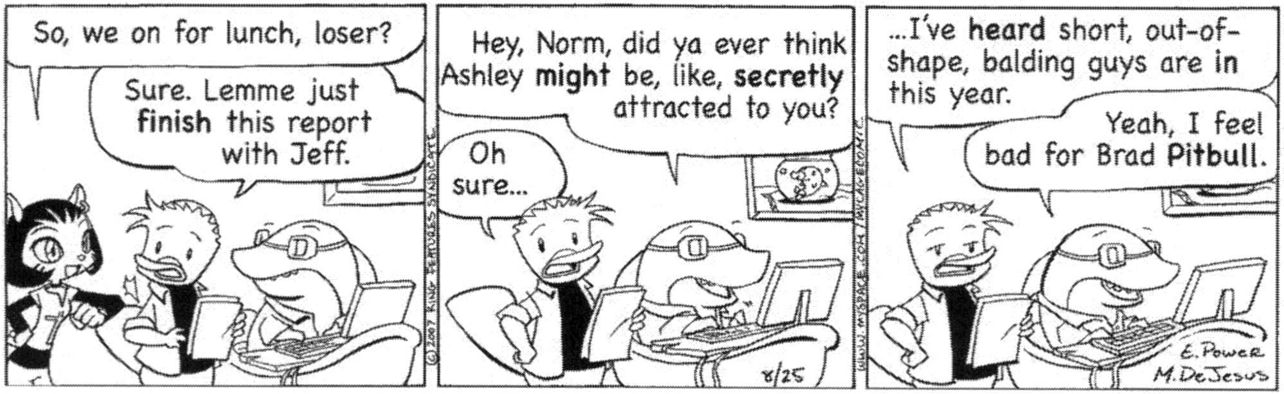
So, we on for lunch, loser?
Sure. Lemme just **finish** this report with Jeff.
©2007 KING FEATURES SYNDICATE
Hey, Norm, did ya ever think Ashley **might** be, like, **secretly** attracted to you?
Oh sure...
8/25
WWW.MYSPACE.COM/MYCAGECOMIC
...I've **heard** short, out-of-shape, balding guys are **in** this year.
Yeah, I feel bad for Brad **Pitbull**.
E. Power
M. DeJesus

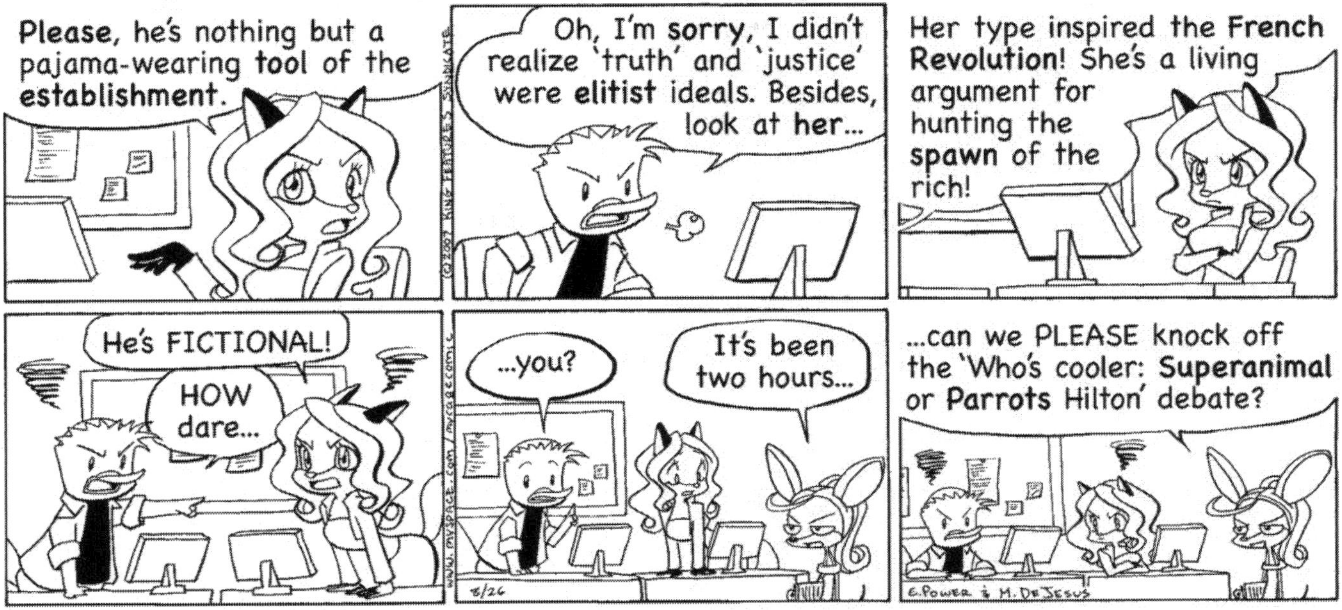
Please, he's nothing but a pajama-wearing tool of the establishment.
Oh, I'm sorry, I didn't realize 'truth' and 'justice' were elitist ideals. Besides, look at her...
Her type inspired the French Revolution! She's a living argument for hunting the spawn of the rich!
He's FICTIONAL!
HOW dare...
...you?
It's been two hours...
...can we PLEASE knock off the 'Who's cooler: Superanimal or Parrots Hilton' debate?
8/26
E. POWER & M. DEJESUS

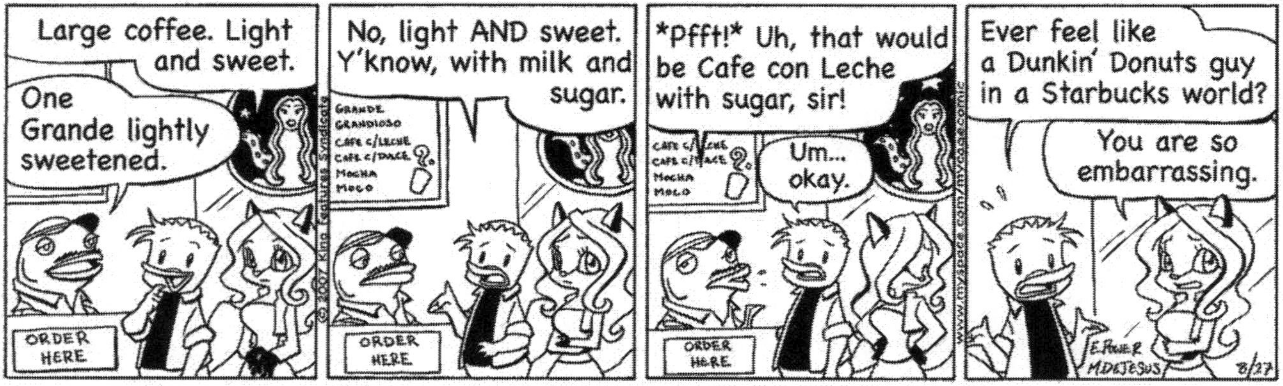
Large coffee. Light and sweet.
One Grande lightly sweetened.
ORDER HERE
© 2007 King Features Syndicate
No, light AND sweet. Y'know, with milk and sugar.
ORDER HERE
Pfft! Uh, that would be Cafe con Leche with sugar, sir!
Um... okay.
ORDER HERE
www.myspace.com/mycagecomic
Ever feel like a Dunkin' Donuts guy in a Starbucks world?
You are so embarrassing.
E. POWER
M. DEJESUS
8/27

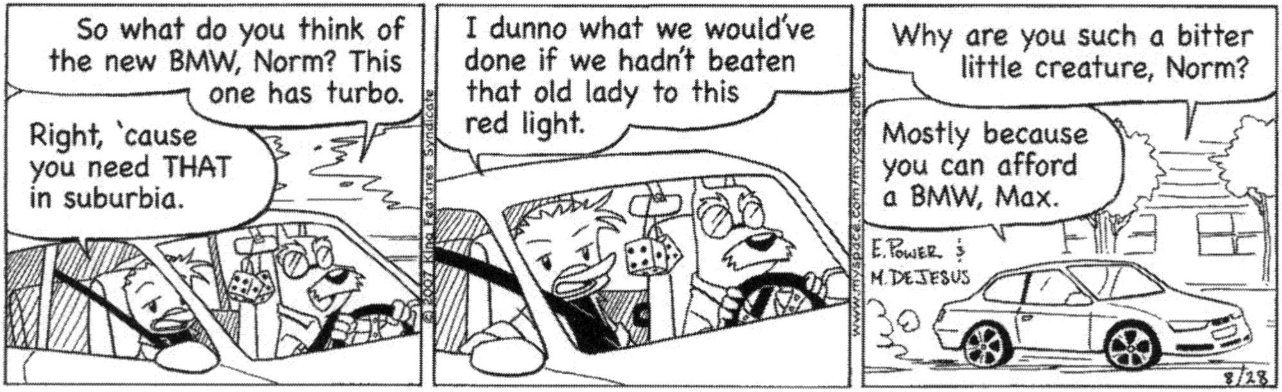
So what do you think of the new BMW, Norm? This one has turbo.
Right, 'cause you need THAT in suburbia.
© 2007 King Features Syndicate
I dunno what we would've done if we hadn't beaten that old lady to this red light.
www.myspace.com/mycagecomic
Why are you such a bitter little creature, Norm?
Mostly because you can afford a BMW, Max.
E. POWER &
M. DEJESUS
8/28

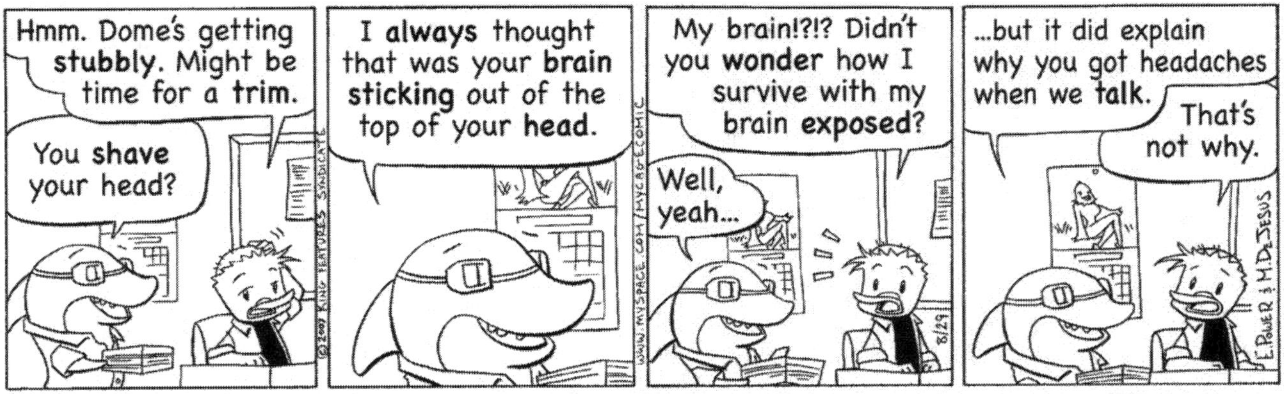
Hmm. Dome's getting **stubbly**. Might be time for a **trim**.
You **shave** your head?
I **always** thought that was your **brain sticking** out of the top of your **head**.
My brain!?!? Didn't you **wonder** how I survive with my brain **exposed**?
Well, yeah...
...but it did explain why you got headaches when we **talk**.
That's not why.
©2009 KING FEATURES SYNDICATE
WWW.MYSPACE.COM/MYCAGECOMIC
8/29
E. POWER & M. DEJESUS

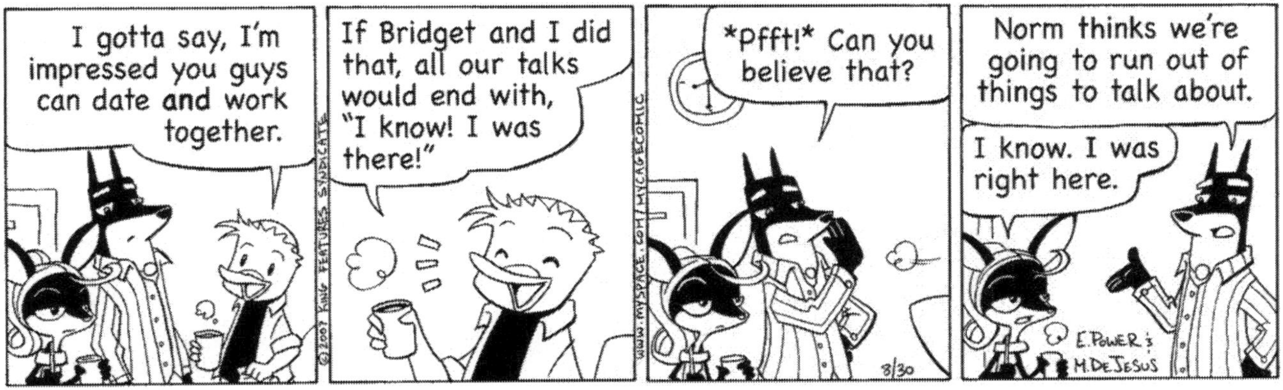
I gotta say, I'm impressed you guys can date **and** work together.
If Bridget and I did that, all our talks would end with, "I know! I was there!"
Pfft! Can you believe that?
Norm thinks we're going to run out of things to talk about.
I know. I was right here.
©2009 KING FEATURES SYNDICATE
WWW.MYSPACE.COM/MYCAGECOMIC
8/30
E. POWER & M. DEJESUS

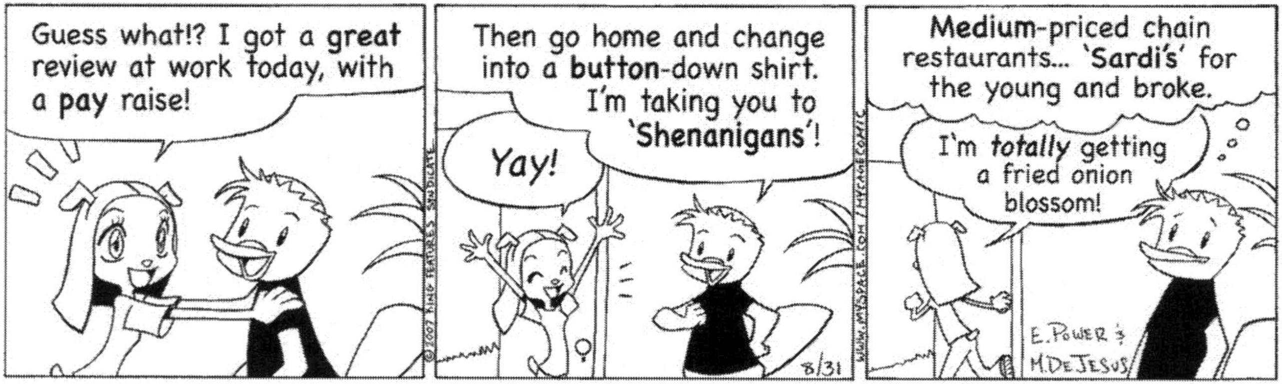

Guess what!? I got a **great** review at work today, with a **pay** raise!
Then go home and change into a **button**-down shirt. I'm taking you to **'Shenanigans'**!
Yay!
© 2007 KING FEATURES SYNDICATE
8/31
WWW.MYSPACE.COM/MYCAGECOMIC
Medium-priced chain restaurants... **'Sardi's'** for the young and broke.
I'm ***totally*** getting a fried onion blossom!
E. POWER & M. DEJESUS

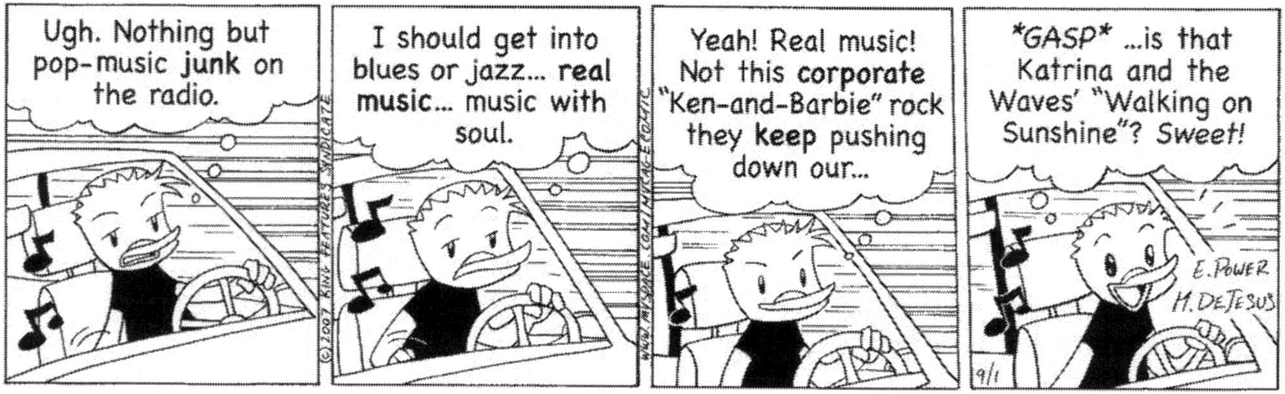

Ugh. Nothing but pop-music **junk** on the radio.
© 2007 KING FEATURES SYNDICATE
I should get into blues or jazz... **real music**... music with soul.
WWW.MYSPACE.COM/MYCAGECOMIC
Yeah! Real music! Not this **corporate** "Ken-and-Barbie" rock they **keep** pushing down our...
**GASP* ...is that Katrina and the Waves' "Walking on Sunshine"? *Sweet!*
E. POWER
M. DEJESUS
9/1

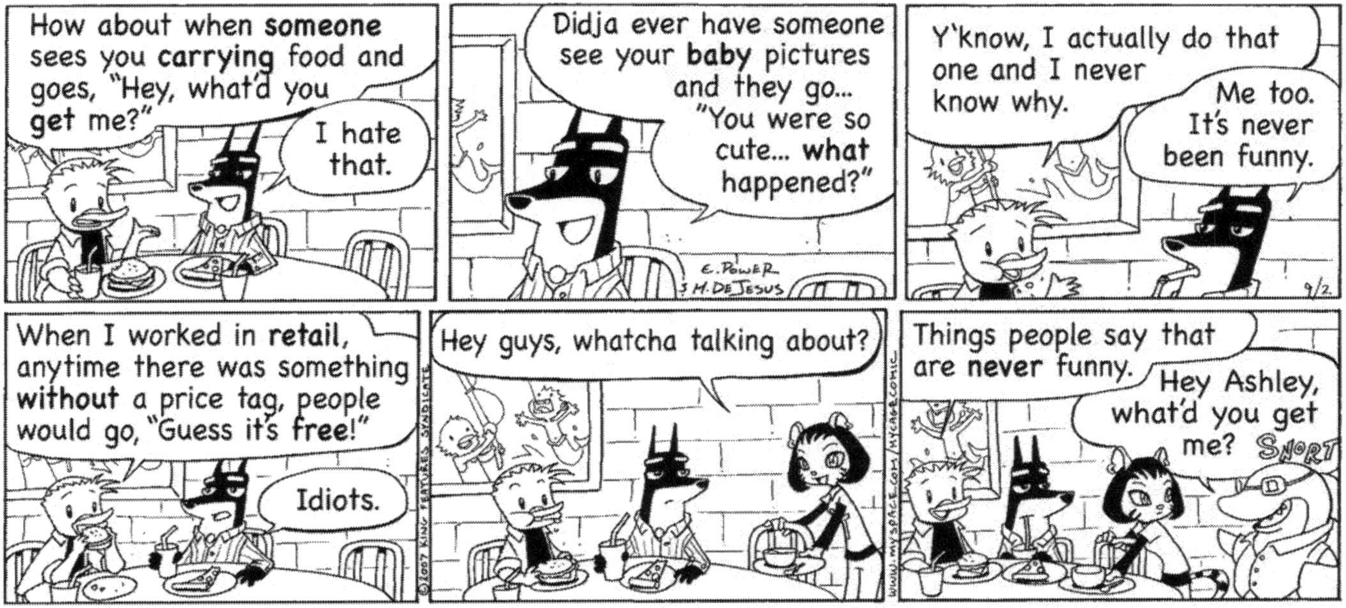
How about when **someone** sees you **carrying** food and goes, "Hey, what'd you **get** me?"
I hate that.
Didja ever have someone see your **baby** pictures and they go... "You were so cute... **what** happened?"
E. POWER
& M. DEJESUS
Y'know, I actually do that one and I never know why.
Me too. It's never been funny.
When I worked in **retail**, anytime there was something **without** a price tag, people would go, "Guess it's **free**!"
Idiots.
©2007 KING FEATURES SYNDICATE
Hey guys, whatcha talking about?
Things people say that are **never** funny.
Hey Ashley, what'd you get me?
SNORT

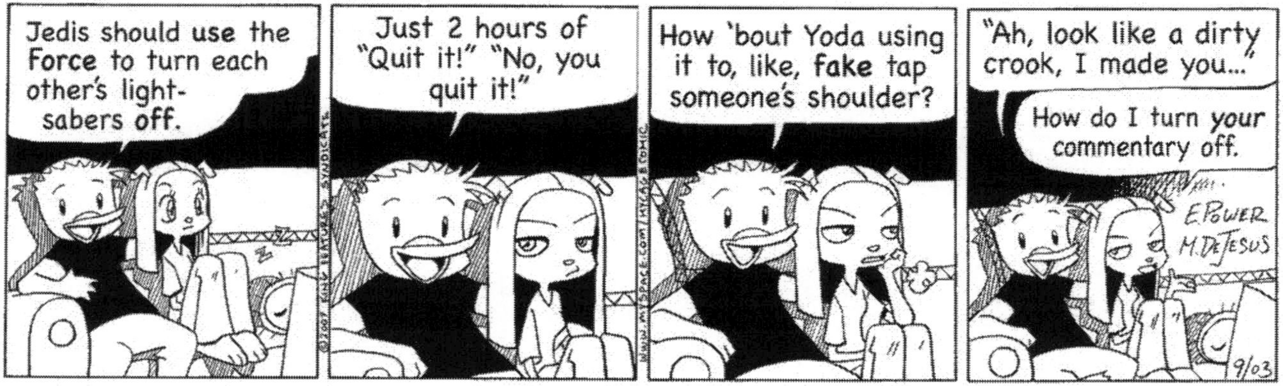
Jedis should use the Force to turn each other's light-sabers off.
Just 2 hours of "Quit it!" "No, you quit it!"
How 'bout Yoda using it to, like, fake tap someone's shoulder?
"Ah, look like a dirty crook, I made you..."
How do I turn your commentary off.
E. POWER
M. DEJESUS
9/03

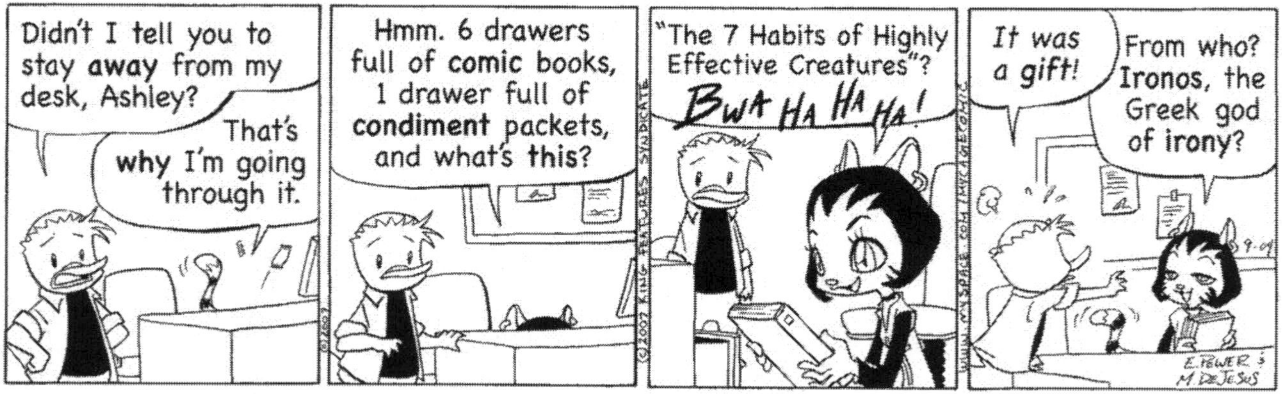
Didn't I tell you to stay away from my desk, Ashley?
That's why I'm going through it.
Hmm. 6 drawers full of comic books, 1 drawer full of condiment packets, and what's this?
"The 7 Habits of Highly Effective Creatures"?
BWA HA HA HA!
It was a gift!
From who? Ironos, the Greek god of irony?
9-04
E. POWER &
M. DEJESUS

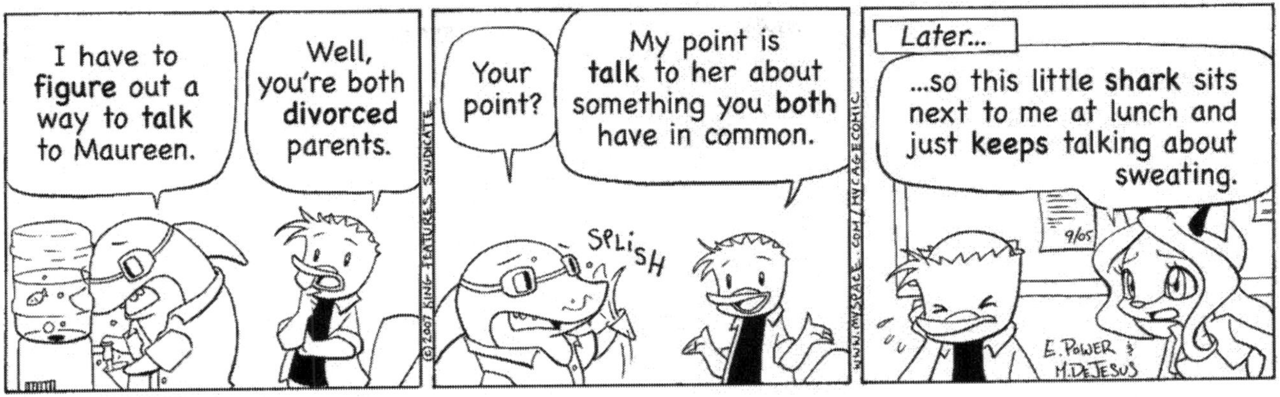
I have to figure out a way to talk to Maureen.
Well, you're both divorced parents.
©2007 KING FEATURES SYNDICATE
Your point?
My point is talk to her about something you both have in common.
SPLISH
WWW.MYSPACE.COM/MYCAGECOMIC
Later...
...so this little shark sits next to me at lunch and just keeps talking about sweating.
9/05
E. POWER & M. DEJESUS

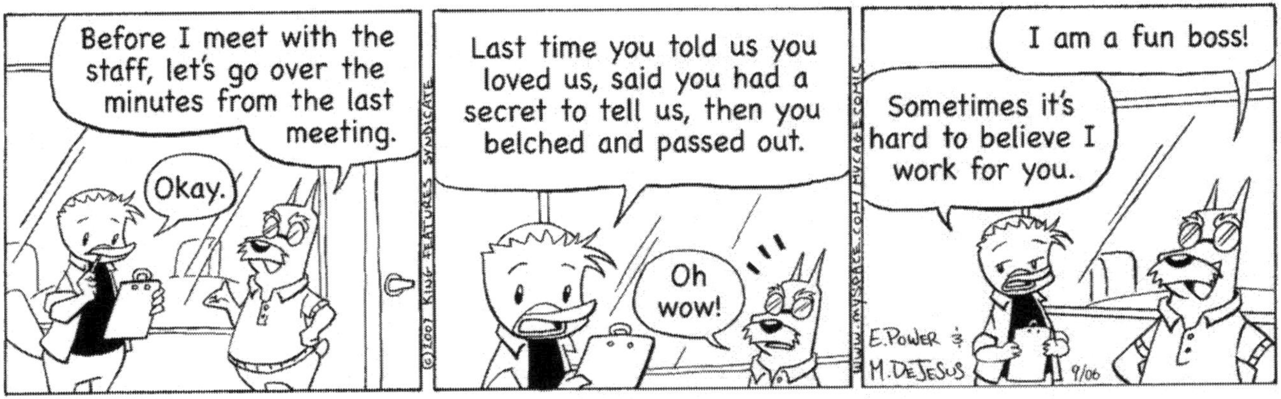
Before I meet with the staff, let's go over the minutes from the last meeting.
Okay.
©2007 KING FEATURES SYNDICATE
Last time you told us you loved us, said you had a secret to tell us, then you belched and passed out.
Oh wow!
WWW.MYSPACE.COM/MYCAGECOMIC
I am a fun boss!
Sometimes it's hard to believe I work for you.
E. POWER & M. DEJESUS
9/06

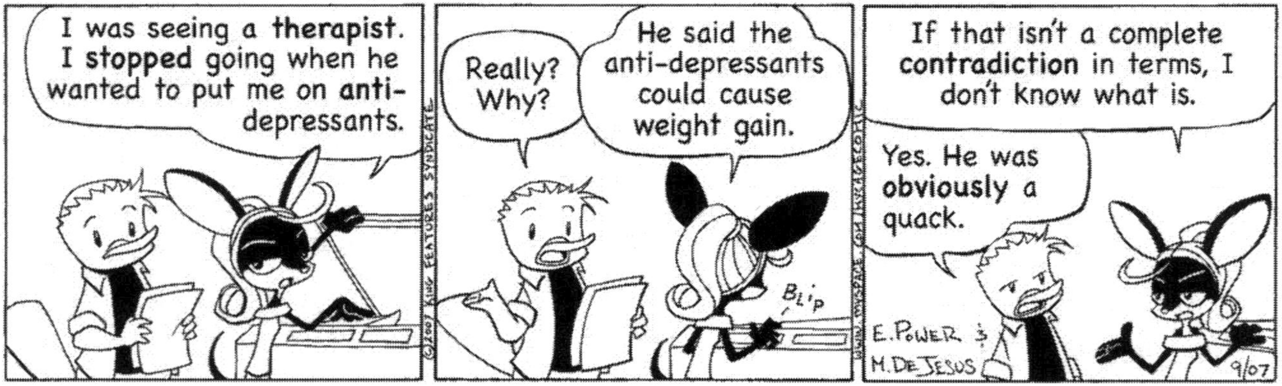
I was seeing a therapist. I stopped going when he wanted to put me on anti-depressants.
©2007 King Features Syndicate
Really? Why?
He said the anti-depressants could cause weight gain.
Blip
www.myspace.com/mycagecomic
If that isn't a complete contradiction in terms, I don't know what is.
Yes. He was obviously a quack.
E. Power & M. DeJesus
9/07

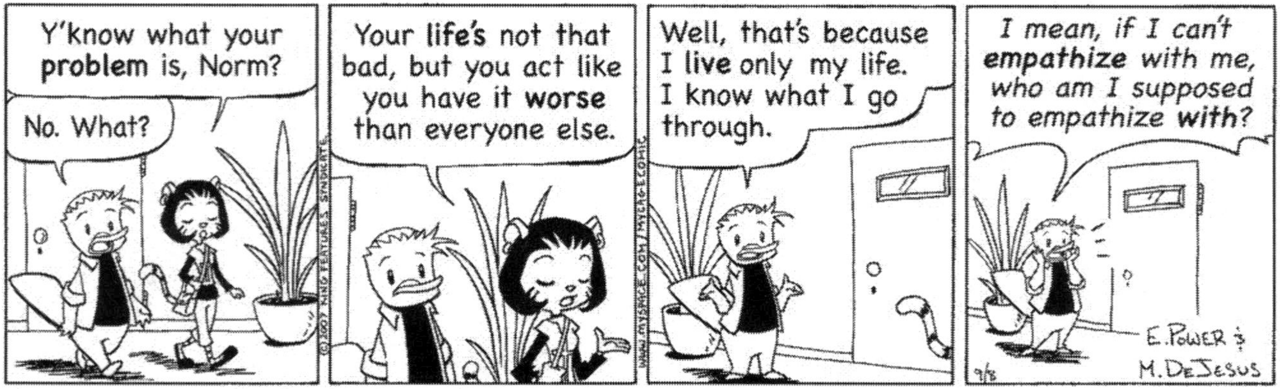
Y'know what your problem is, Norm?
No. What?
©2007 King Features Syndicate
Your life's not that bad, but you act like you have it worse than everyone else.
www.myspace.com/mycagecomic
Well, that's because I live only my life. I know what I go through.
I mean, if I can't empathize with me, who am I supposed to empathize with?
9/8
E. Power & M. DeJesus

Hey, I'm **Norm** Platypus. I'm just going to sit here and **doodle** while pretending to take **notes**.

©2007 King Features Syndicate

Hi, I'm Max Terrier. I got **married** young and didn't **party** enough, so now that **my kids** are grown, I'm **sewing** some wild oats.

I'm Rex Doberman. I'm **obsessed** with status. This is Violet. She's **insecure** and wants a boyfriend who won't leave her. We're **engaged**.

I'm Jeff. I'm **recently** divorced because my ex-wife said I'm an **idiot**. I'm confused by that because I'm no **smarter** than I was on our wedding day.

I'm Maureen. I **was** the pretty girl in high school and **married** money. Well, "money" **cheated** on me — and now I'm a single parent forced to **mix** with you people.

www.myspace.com/mycage.comic

Well, **apparently**, having you all stand and introduce **yourselves** to the rest of the class was a **HUGE** mistake!

Todays Class
Better Communication at Work!

9/9

E. Power & M. DeJesus

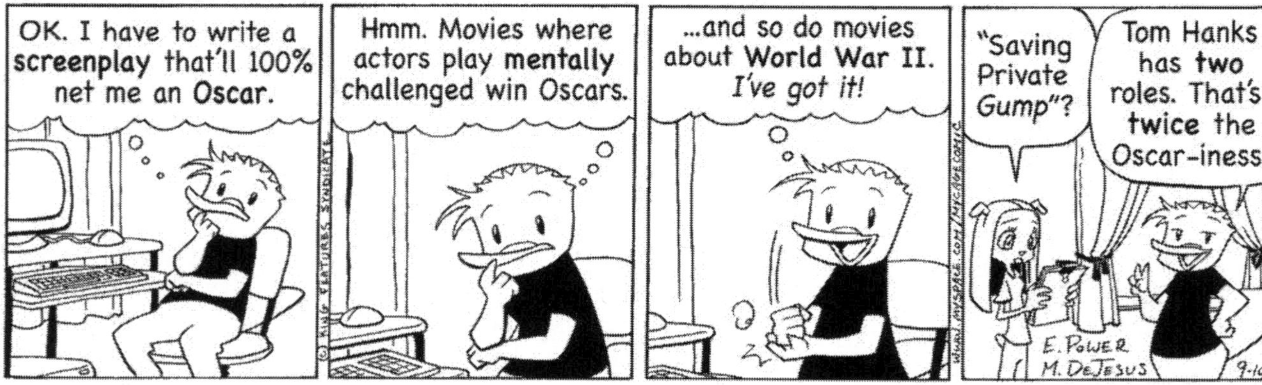
OK. I have to write a **screenplay** that'll 100% net me an **Oscar**.
© KING FEATURES SYNDICATE
Hmm. Movies where actors play **mentally** challenged win Oscars.
...and so do movies about **World War II**. *I've got it!*
WWW.MYSPACE.COM/MYCADECOMIC
"Saving Private *Gump*"?
Tom Hanks has **two** roles. That's **twice** the Oscar-iness.
E. POWER
M. DEJESUS
9-10

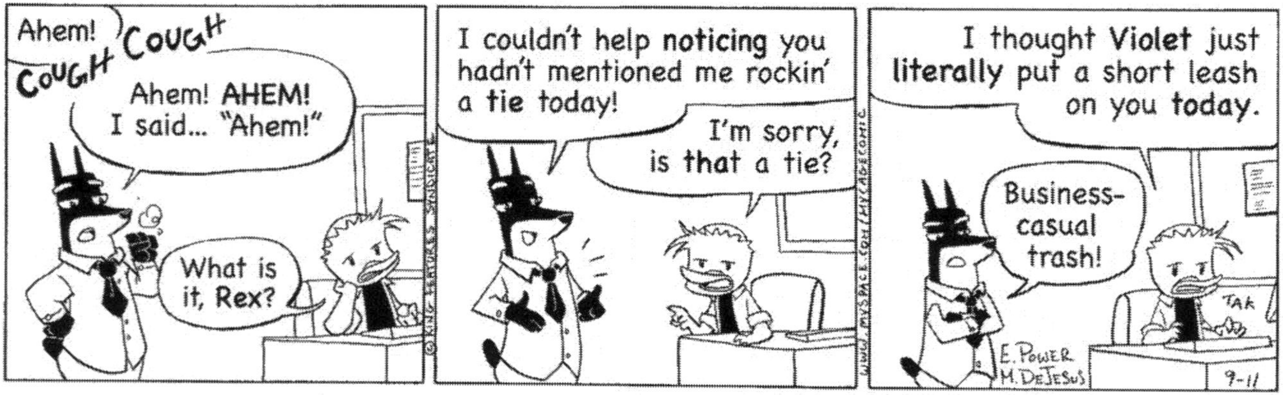
Ahem!
COUGH COUGH
Ahem! **AHEM!** I said... "Ahem!"
What is it, Rex?
© KING FEATURES SYNDICATE
I couldn't help **noticing** you hadn't mentioned me rockin' a **tie** today!
I'm sorry, is **that** a tie?
WWW.MYSPACE.COM/MYCADECOMIC
I thought **Violet** just **literally** put a short leash on you **today**.
Business-casual trash!
TAK
E. POWER
M. DEJESUS
9-11

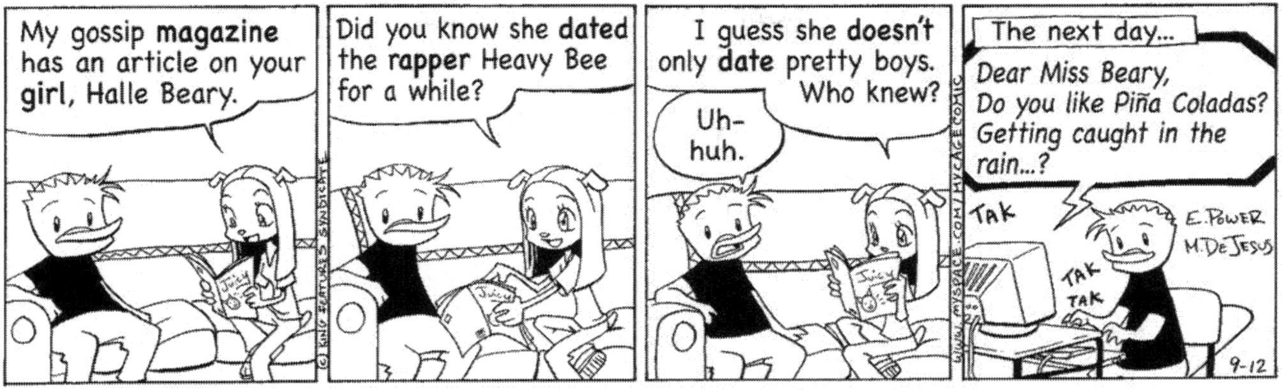
My gossip magazine has an article on your girl, Halle Beary.
Did you know she dated the rapper Heavy Bee for a while?
I guess she doesn't only date pretty boys. Who knew?
Uh-huh.
The next day...
Dear Miss Beary, Do you like Piña Coladas? Getting caught in the rain...?
TAK
TAK
TAK
E. POWER
M. DE JESUS
9-12
© KING FEATURES SYNDICATE
WWW.MYSPACE.COM/MYCAGECOMIC

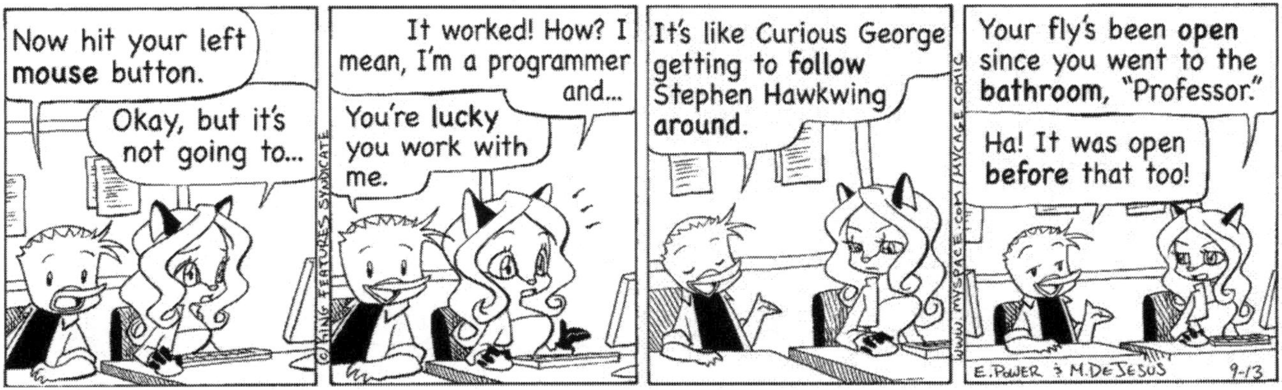
Now hit your left mouse button.
Okay, but it's not going to...
It worked! How? I mean, I'm a programmer and...
You're lucky you work with me.
It's like Curious George getting to follow Stephen Hawkwing around.
Your fly's been open since you went to the bathroom, "Professor."
Ha! It was open before that too!
E. POWER & M. DE JESUS
9-13
© KING FEATURES SYNDICATE
WWW.MYSPACE.COM/MYCAGECOMIC

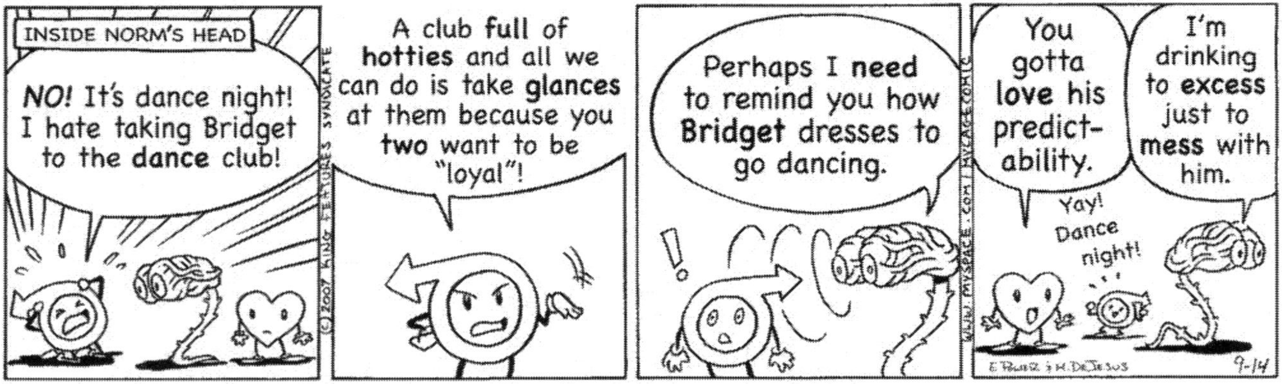
INSIDE NORM'S HEAD
NO! It's dance night! I hate taking Bridget to the dance club!
A club full of hotties and all we can do is take glances at them because you two want to be "loyal"!
© 2007 KING FEATURES SYNDICATE
Perhaps I need to remind you how Bridget dresses to go dancing.
WWW.MYSPACE.COM/MYCAGECOMIC
You gotta love his predict-ability.
I'm drinking to excess just to mess with him.
Yay! Dance night!
E. POWER & M. DEJESUS
9-14

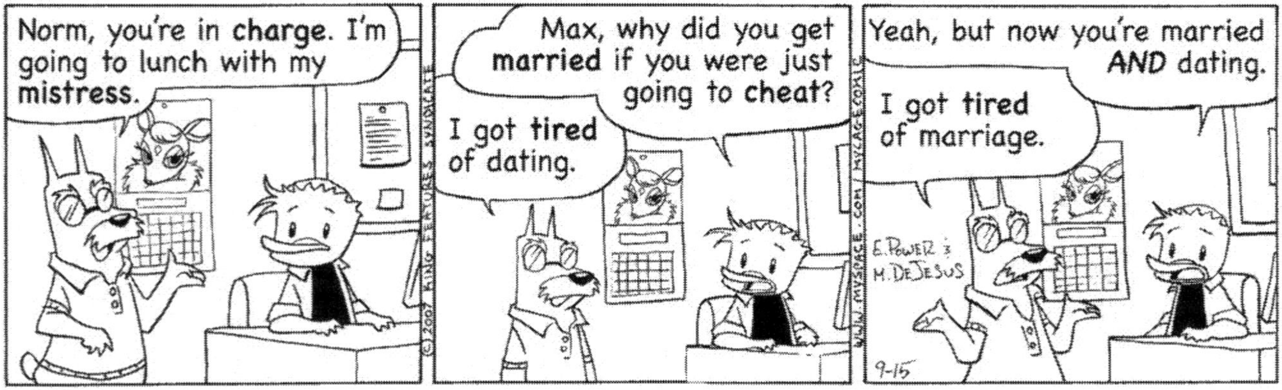
Norm, you're in charge. I'm going to lunch with my mistress.
© 2007 KING FEATURES SYNDICATE
Max, why did you get married if you were just going to cheat?
I got tired of dating.
WWW.MYSPACE.COM/MYCAGECOMIC
Yeah, but now you're married AND dating.
I got tired of marriage.
E. POWER & M. DEJESUS
9-15

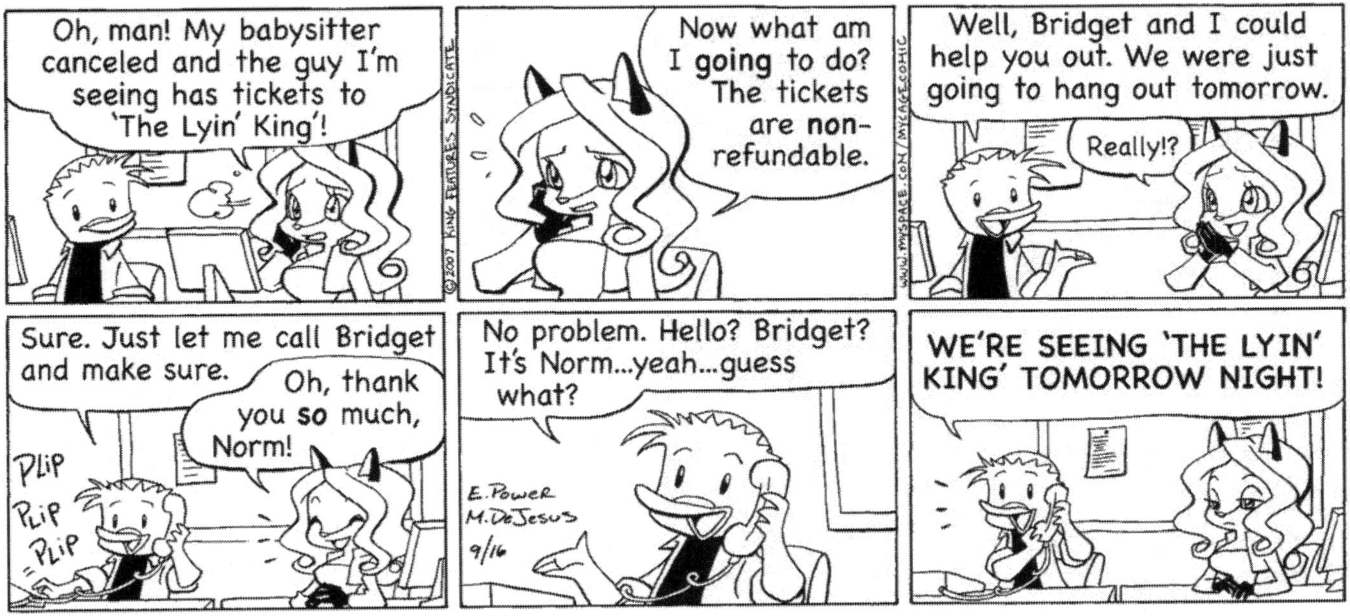
Oh, man! My babysitter canceled and the guy I'm seeing has tickets to 'The Lyin' King'!
©2007 KING FEATURES SYNDICATE
Now what am I **going** to do? The tickets are **non**-refundable.
WWW.MYSPACE.COM/MYCAGECOMIC
Well, Bridget and I could help you out. We were just going to hang out tomorrow.
Really!?
Sure. Just let me call Bridget and make sure.
Oh, thank you **so** much, Norm!
PLIP
PLIP
PLIP
No problem. Hello? Bridget? It's Norm...yeah...guess what?
E. POWER
M. DEJESUS
9/16
WE'RE SEEING 'THE LYIN' KING' TOMORROW NIGHT!

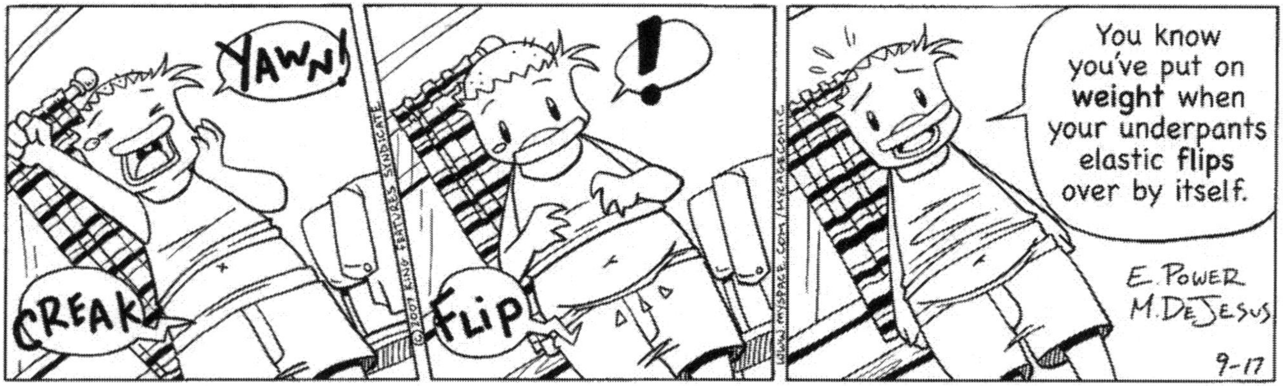
YAWN!
CREAK
© 2007 KING FEATURES SYNDICATE
!
FLIP
WWW.MYSPACE.COM/MYCAGECOMIC
You know you've put on **weight** when your underpants elastic **flips** over by itself.
E. POWER
M. DeJESUS
9-17

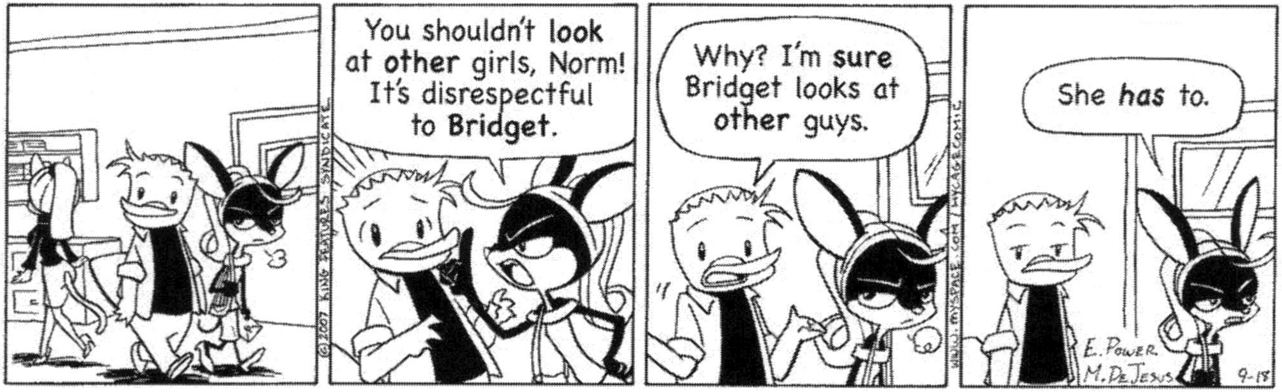
© 2007 KING FEATURES SYNDICATE
You shouldn't **look** at **other** girls, Norm! It's disrespectful to **Bridget**.
WWW.MYSPACE.COM/MYCAGECOMIC
Why? I'm **sure** Bridget looks at **other** guys.
She ***has*** to.
E. POWER
M. DeJESUS
9-18

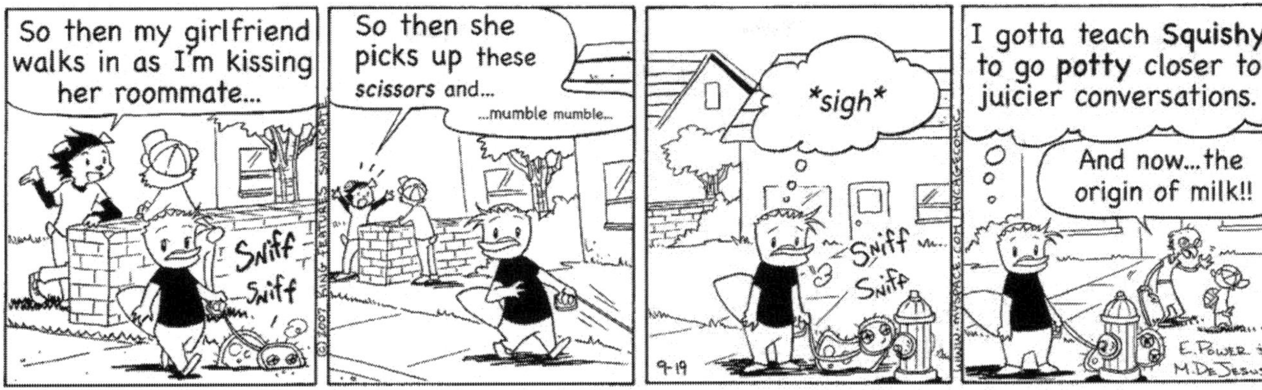
So then my girlfriend walks in as I'm kissing her roommate...
SNIFF
SNIFF
© 2007 KING FEATURES SYNDICATE
So then she picks up these *scissors* and...
...mumble mumble...
sigh
SNIFF
SNIFF
9-19
WWW.MYSPACE.COM/MYCAGECOMIC
I gotta teach **Squishy** to go **potty** closer to juicier conversations.
And now...the origin of milk!!
E. POWER & M. DEJESUS

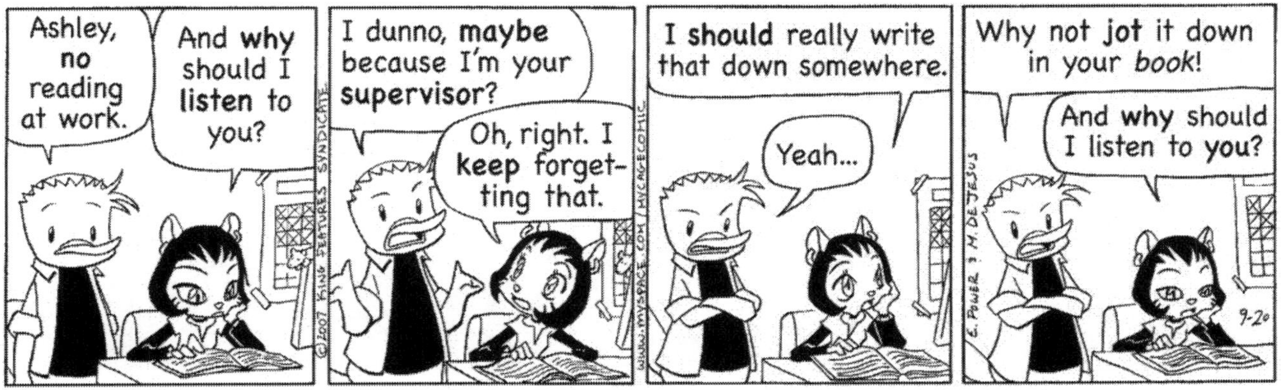
Ashley, **no** reading at work.
And **why** should I **listen** to you?
© 2007 KING FEATURES SYNDICATE
I dunno, **maybe** because I'm your **supervisor**?
Oh, right. I **keep** forgetting that.
WWW.MYSPACE.COM/MYCAGECOMIC
I should really write that down somewhere.
Yeah...
Why not **jot** it down in your *book*!
And **why** should I listen to **you**?
E. POWER & M. DEJESUS
9-20

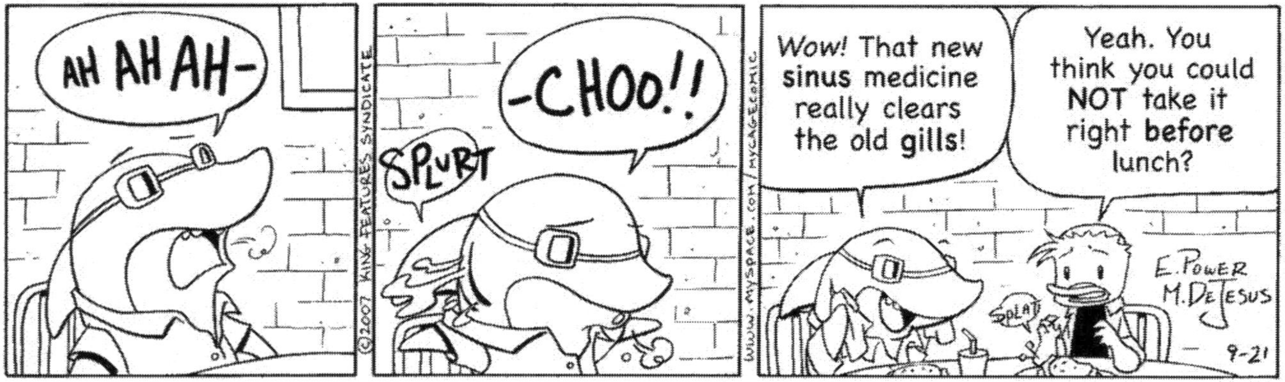
AH AH AH-
SPLURT
-CHOO!!
©2007 KING FEATURES SYNDICATE
WWW.MYSPACE.COM/MYCAGECOMIC
Wow! That new sinus medicine really clears the old gills!
Yeah. You think you could NOT take it right before lunch?
SPLAT
E. POWER
M. DEJESUS
9-21

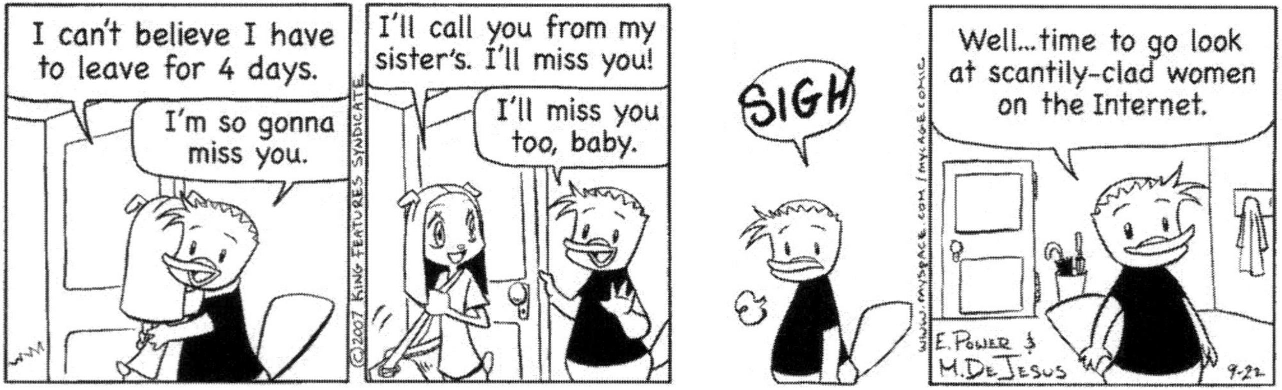
I can't believe I have to leave for 4 days.
I'm so gonna miss you.
©2007 KING FEATURES SYNDICATE
I'll call you from my sister's. I'll miss you!
I'll miss you too, baby.
SIGH
WWW.MYSPACE.COM/MYCAGECOMIC
Well...time to go look at scantily-clad women on the Internet.
E. POWER &
M. DEJESUS
9-22

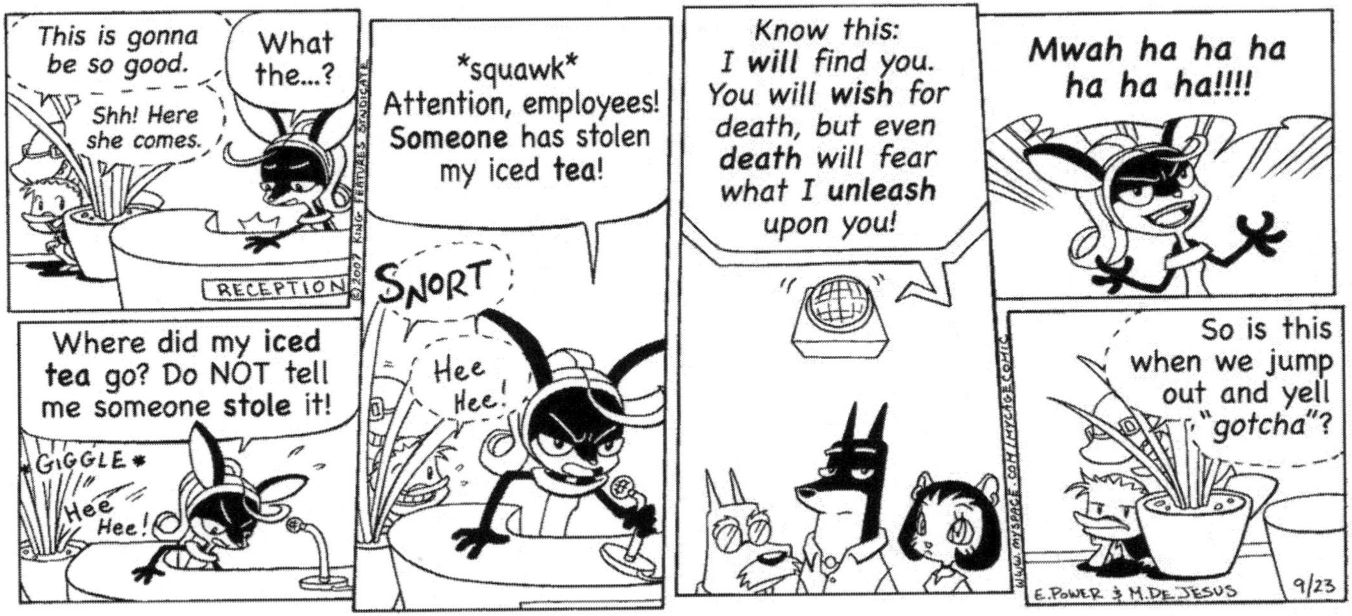
This is gonna be so good.
Shh! Here she comes.
What the...?
RECEPTION
© 2007 KING FEATURES SYNDICATE
Where did my iced tea go? Do NOT tell me someone stole it!
GIGGLE
Hee Hee!
squawk Attention, employees! Someone has stolen my iced tea!
SNORT
Hee Hee!
Know this: I will find you. You will wish for death, but even death will fear what I unleash upon you!
WWW.MYSPACE.COM/MYCAGECOMIC
Mwah ha ha ha ha ha ha!!!!
So is this when we jump out and yell "gotcha"?
E. POWER & M. DE JESUS
9/23

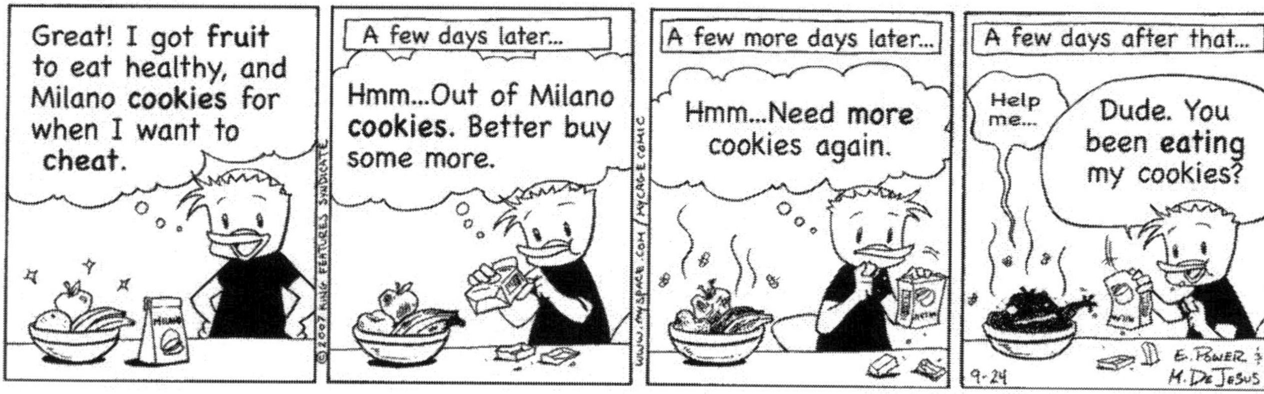
Great! I got fruit to eat healthy, and Milano cookies for when I want to cheat.
© 2007 KING FEATURES SYNDICATE
A few days later...
Hmm...Out of Milano cookies. Better buy some more.
WWW.MYSPACE.COM / MYCAGE COMIC
A few more days later...
Hmm...Need more cookies again.
A few days after that...
Help me...
Dude. You been eating my cookies?
9-24
E. POWER & M. DEJESUS

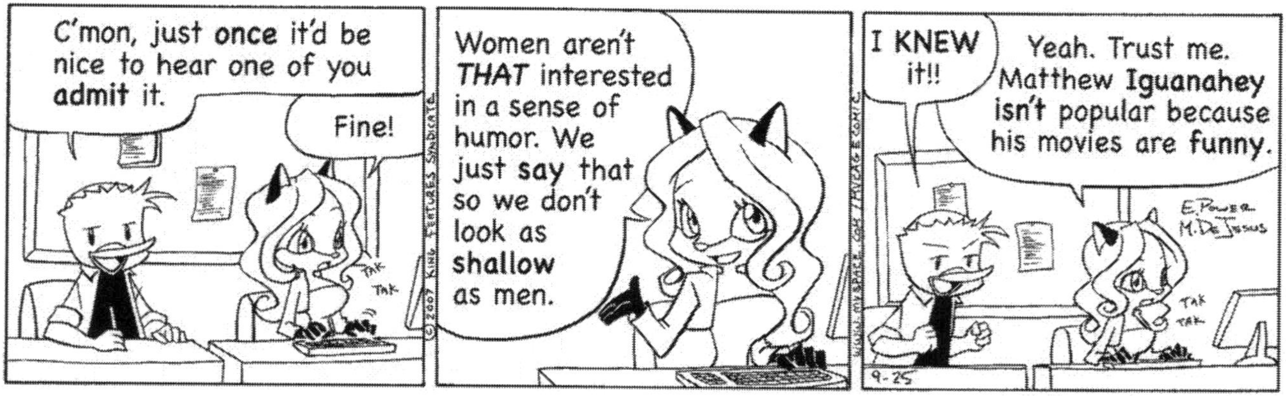
C'mon, just once it'd be nice to hear one of you admit it.
Fine!
TAK
TAK
© 2007 KING FEATURES SYNDICATE
Women aren't THAT interested in a sense of humor. We just say that so we don't look as shallow as men.
WWW.MYSPACE.COM / MYCAGE COMIC
I KNEW it!!
Yeah. Trust me. Matthew Iguanahey isn't popular because his movies are funny.
E. POWER
M. DEJESUS
TAK
TAK
9-25

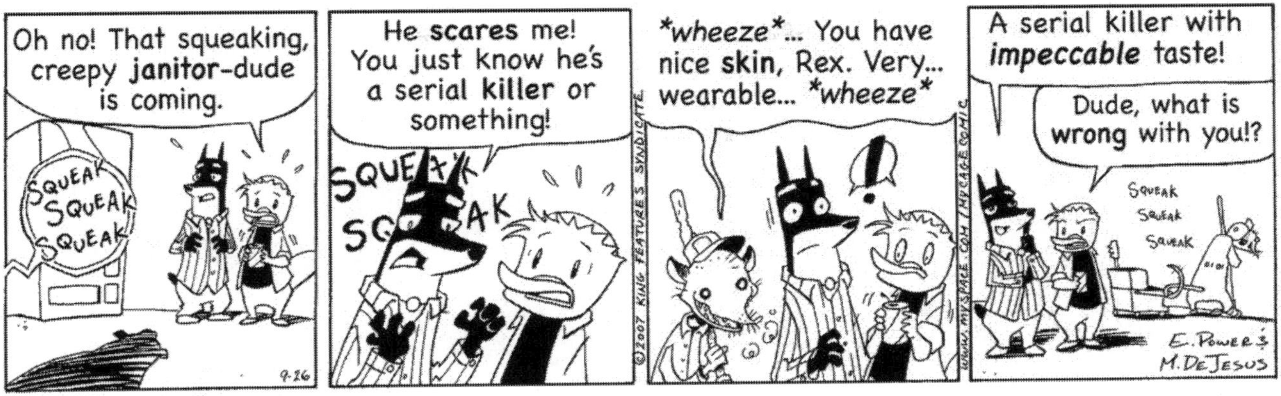
Oh no! That squeaking, creepy janitor-dude is coming.
SQUEAK SQUEAK SQUEAK
9-26
He scares me! You just know he's a serial killer or something!
SQUEAK SQUEAK
©2007 KING FEATURES SYNDICATE
wheeze... You have nice skin, Rex. Very... wearable... *wheeze*
WWW.MYSPACE.COM/MYCAGECOMIC
A serial killer with impeccable taste!
Dude, what is wrong with you!?
SQUEAK SQUEAK SQUEAK
E. POWER & M. DEJESUS

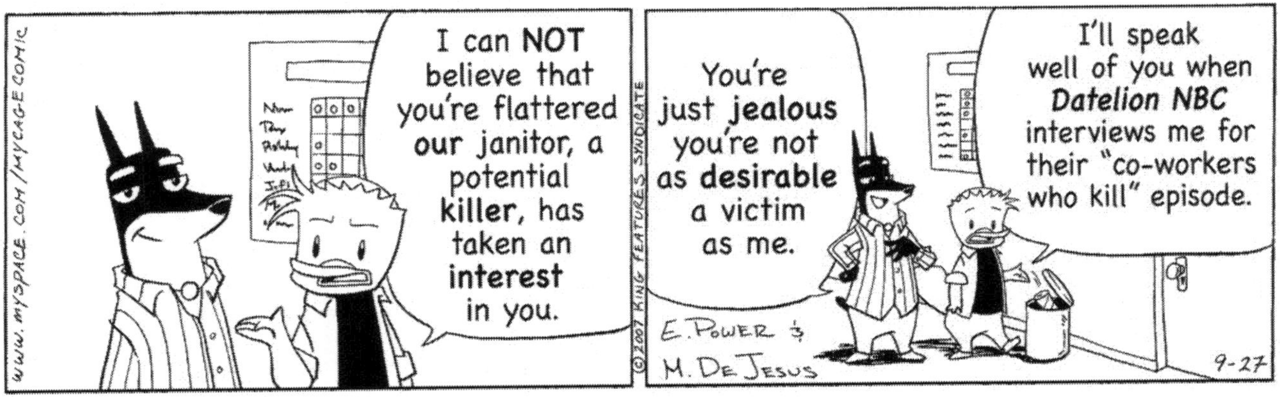
WWW.MYSPACE.COM/MYCAGECOMIC
I can NOT believe that you're flattered our janitor, a potential killer, has taken an interest in you.
©2007 KING FEATURES SYNDICATE
You're just jealous you're not as desirable a victim as me.
I'll speak well of you when Datelion NBC interviews me for their "co-workers who kill" episode.
E. POWER & M. DEJESUS
9-27

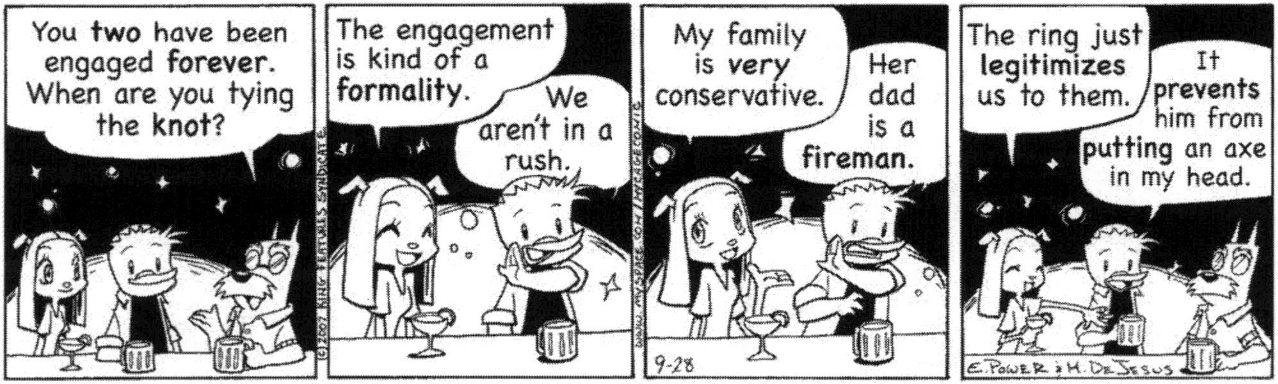
You **two** have been engaged **forever**. When are you tying the **knot**?
The engagement is kind of a **formality**.
We aren't in a rush.
My family is **very** conservative.
Her dad is a **fireman**.
The ring just **legitimizes** us to them.
It **prevents** him from **putting** an axe in my head.
9-28
E. POWER & M. DEJESUS

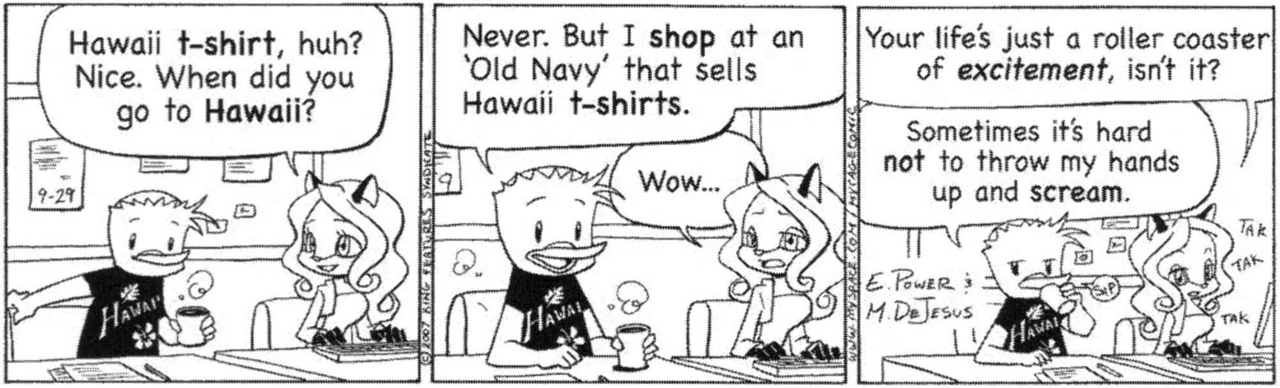
9-29
Hawaii **t-shirt**, huh? Nice. When did you go to **Hawaii**?
Never. But I **shop** at an 'Old Navy' that sells Hawaii **t-shirts**.
Wow...
Your life's just a roller coaster of ***excitement***, isn't it?
Sometimes it's hard **not** to throw my hands up and **scream**.
E. POWER & M. DEJESUS
SIP
TAK
TAK
TAK

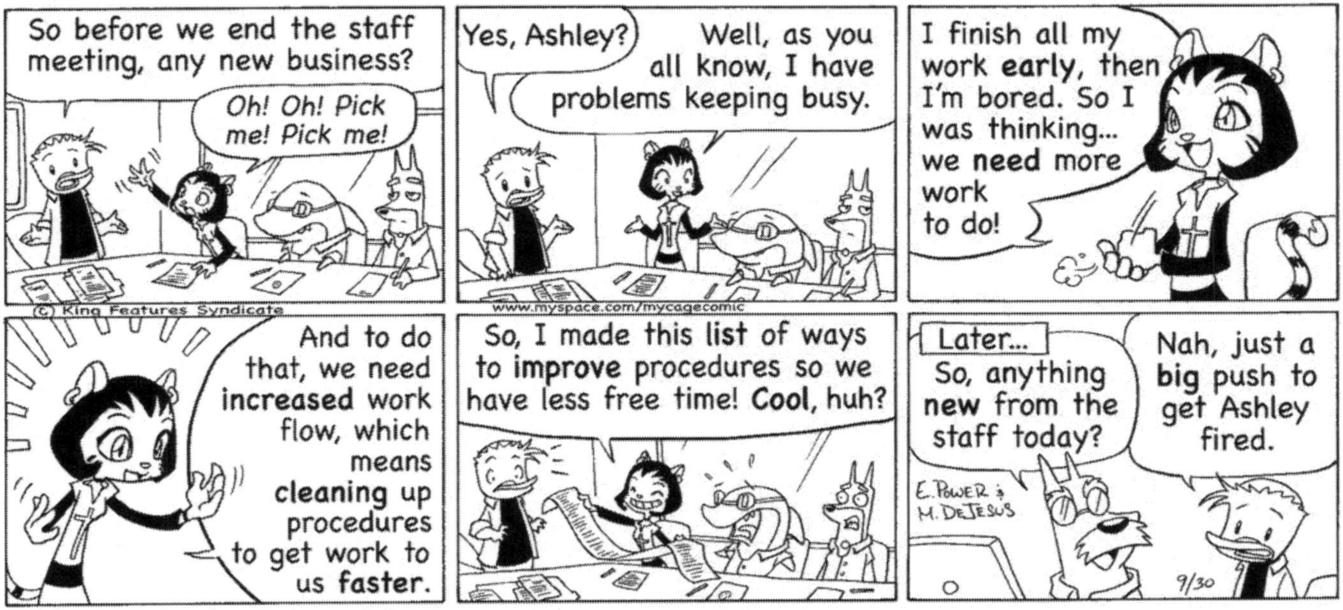
So before we end the staff meeting, any new business?
Oh! Oh! Pick me! Pick me!
© King Features Syndicate
Yes, Ashley?
Well, as you all know, I have problems keeping busy.
www.myspace.com/mycagecomic
I finish all my work early, then I'm bored. So I was thinking... we need more work to do!
And to do that, we need increased work flow, which means cleaning up procedures to get work to us faster.
So, I made this list of ways to improve procedures so we have less free time! Cool, huh?
Later...
So, anything new from the staff today?
Nah, just a big push to get Ashley fired.
E. POWER & M. DEJESUS
9/30

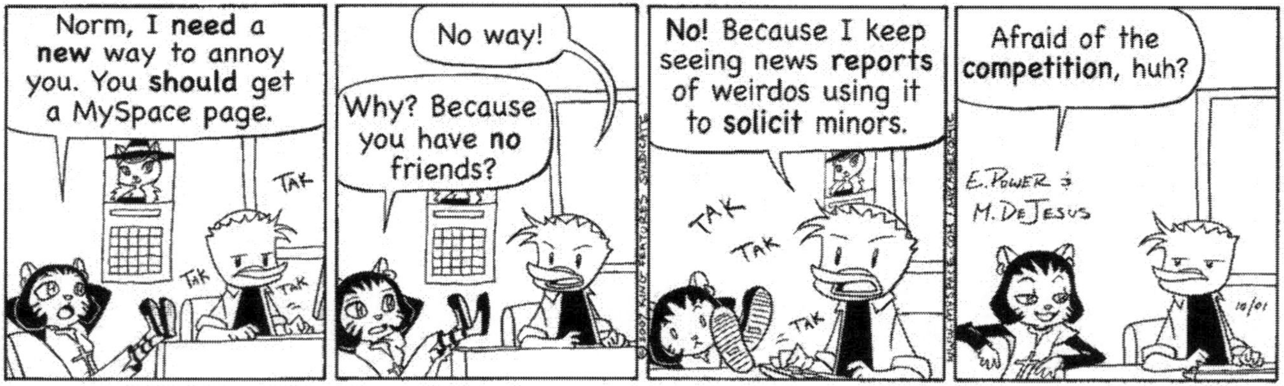
Norm, I **need** a **new** way to annoy you. You **should** get a MySpace page.
TAK
TAK
TAK
No way!
Why? Because you have **no** friends?
No! Because I keep seeing news **reports** of weirdos using it to **solicit** minors.
TAK
TAK
TAK
Afraid of the **competition**, huh?
E. POWER & M. DEJESUS
10/01

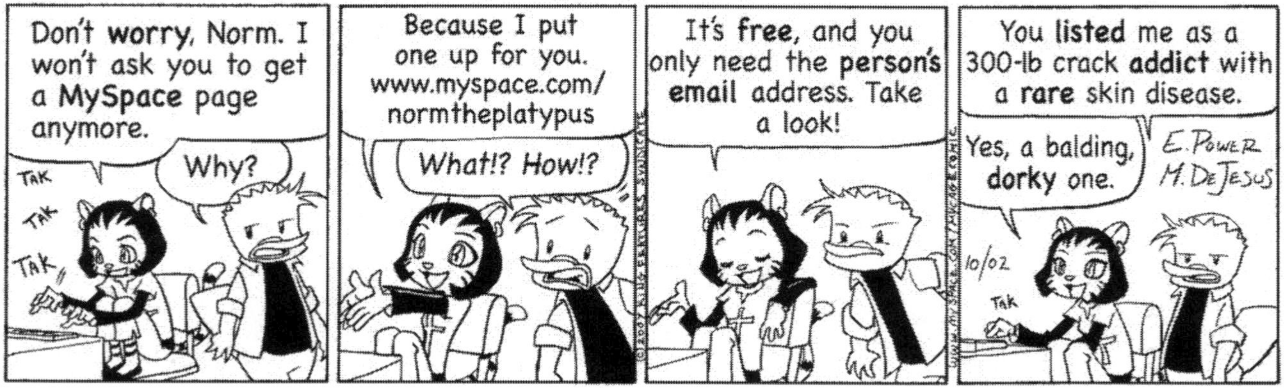
Don't **worry**, Norm. I won't ask you to get a **MySpace** page anymore.
Why?
TAK
TAK
TAK
Because I put one up for you. www.myspace.com/normtheplatypus
What!? How!?
It's **free**, and you only need the **person's email** address. Take a look!
You **listed** me as a 300-lb crack **addict** with a **rare** skin disease.
Yes, a balding, **dorky** one.
E. POWER M. DEJESUS
10/02
TAK

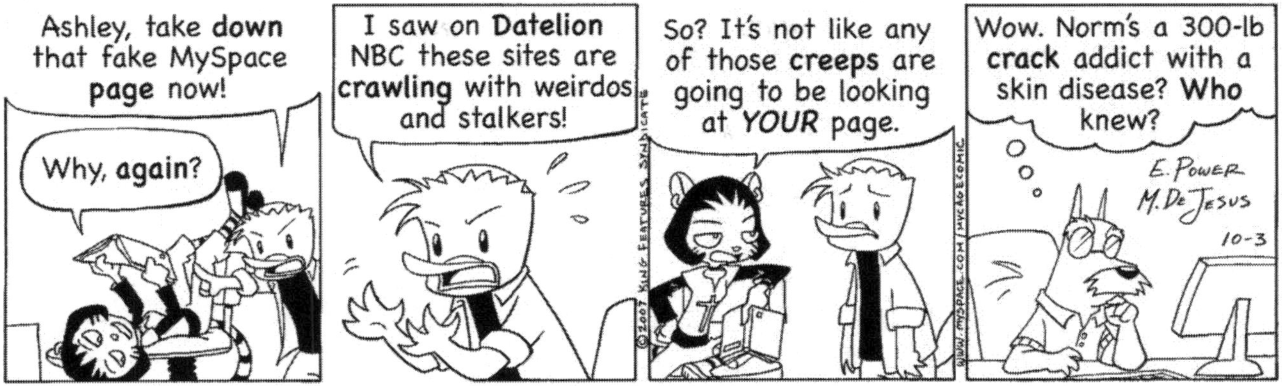
Ashley, take **down** that fake MySpace **page** now!
Why, **again**?
I saw on **Datelion** NBC these sites are **crawling** with weirdos and stalkers!
So? It's not like any of those **creeps** are going to be looking at ***YOUR*** page.
Wow. Norm's a 300-lb **crack** addict with a skin disease? **Who** knew?
E. Power
M. DeJesus
10-3

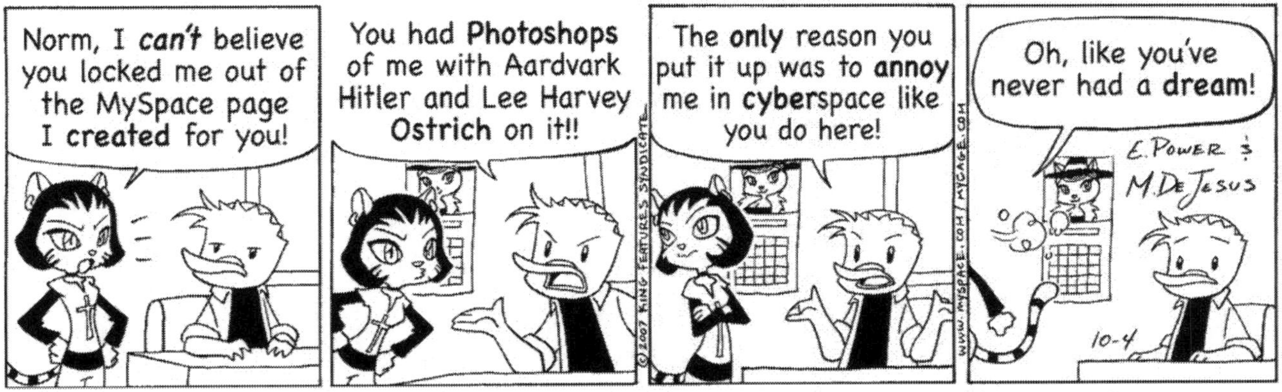
Norm, I ***can't*** believe you locked me out of the MySpace page I **created** for you!
You had **Photoshops** of me with Aardvark Hitler and Lee Harvey **Ostrich** on it!!
The **only** reason you put it up was to **annoy** me in **cyber**space like you do here!
Oh, like you've never had a **dream**!
E. Power &
M. DeJesus
10-4

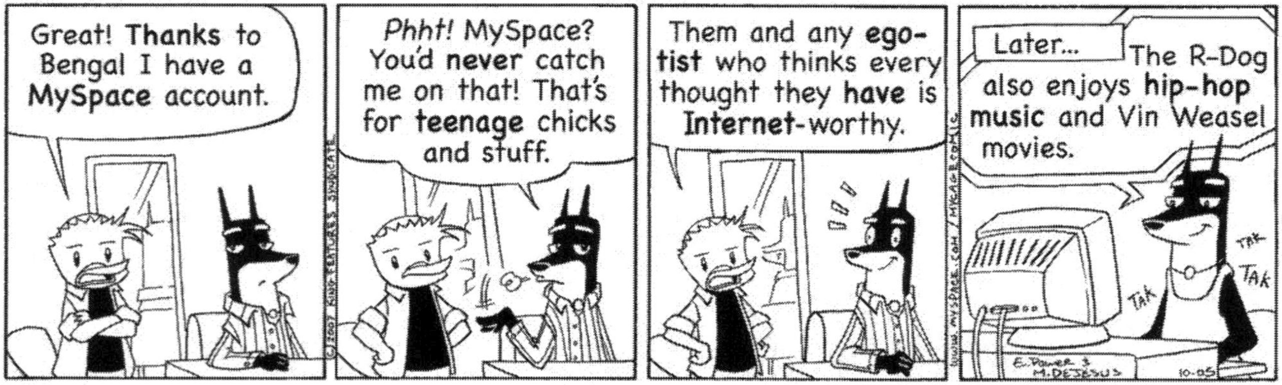
Great! **Thanks** to Bengal I have a **MySpace** account.
Phht! MySpace? You'd **never** catch me on that! That's for **teenage** chicks and stuff.
Them and any **ego-tist** who thinks every thought they **have** is **Internet**-worthy.
Later...
The R-Dog also enjoys **hip-hop music** and Vin Weasel movies.
TAK
TAK
TAK
E. Power & M. DeJesus
10-05

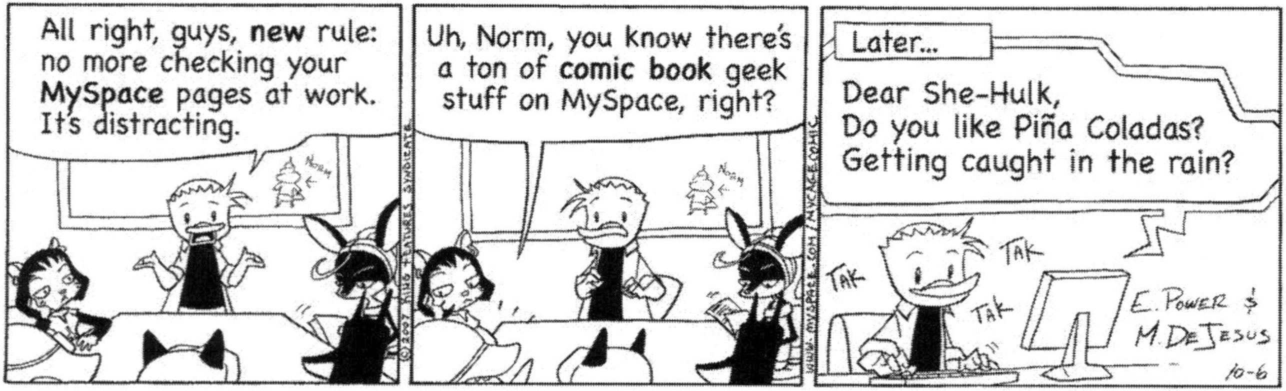
All right, guys, **new** rule: no more checking your **MySpace** pages at work. It's distracting.
Norm
Uh, Norm, you know there's a ton of **comic book** geek stuff on MySpace, right?
Norm
Later...
Dear She-Hulk,
Do you like Piña Coladas?
Getting caught in the rain?
TAK
TAK
TAK
E. Power & M. DeJesus
10-6

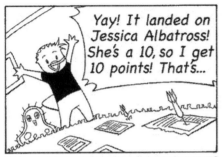

Yay! It landed on Jessica Albatross! She's a 10, so I get 10 points! That's...
Actually, it's **kinda** sad. Y'know, Squishy, there **was** a time when I used to go out on **Friday** nights.
YIP?
©2007 KING FEATURES SYNDICATE
Now I just sit **around making** up games like *Celebrity Carpet Darts* until **Bridget** gets off work.
WWW.MYSPACE.COM/MYCAGECOMIC
Y'know what? I **should** go to the movies! That's it! First I'll find **someone** to go with!
E. POWER & M. DEJESUS
Then I'll **shower**, get dressed, go to the ATM, drive to the **theater**... wait in line for the **ticket**... then wait in **another** line for candy...
So the point of the game is to see if you can eat all your pet food out of my mouth before I gag on it.
YIP! YIP!
10-7

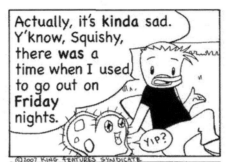

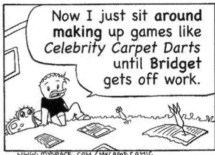

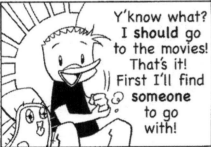

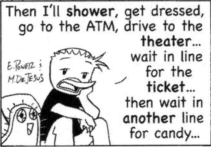

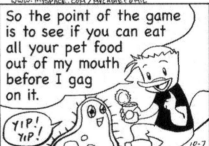

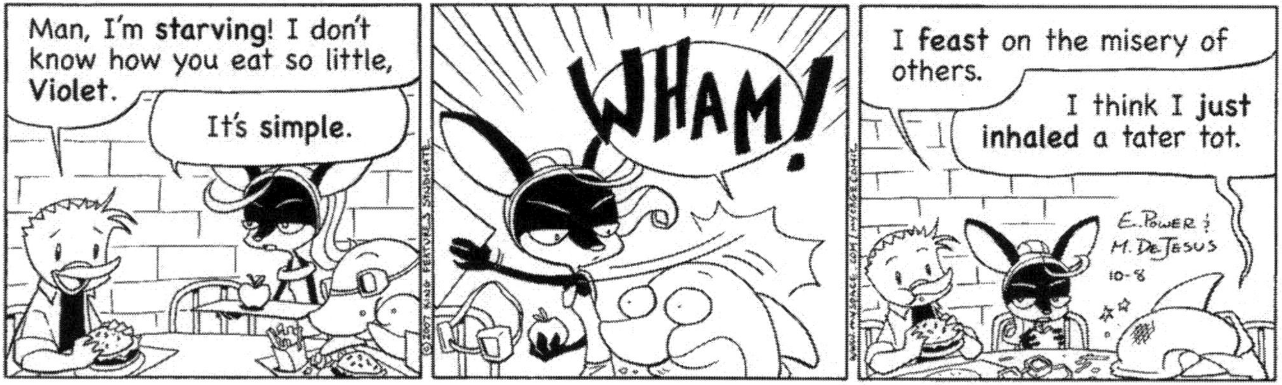
Man, I'm **starving**! I don't know how you eat so little, **Violet**.
It's **simple**.
WHAM!
I **feast** on the misery of others.
I think I **just inhaled** a tater tot.
E. Power & M. DeJesus 10-8

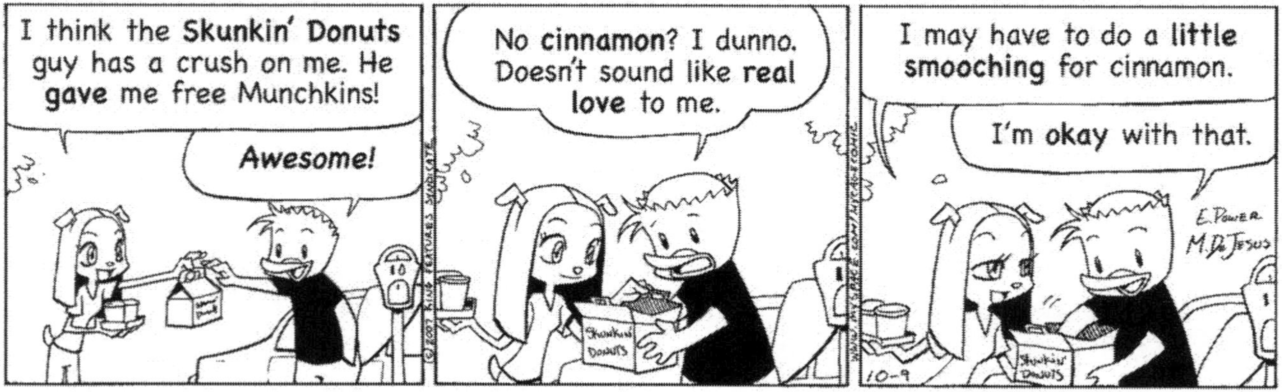
I think the **Skunkin' Donuts** guy has a crush on me. He **gave** me free Munchkins!
Awesome!
No **cinnamon**? I dunno. Doesn't sound like **real love** to me.
Skunkin' Donuts
I may have to do a **little smooching** for cinnamon.
I'm **okay** with that.
E. Power M. DeJesus
10-9

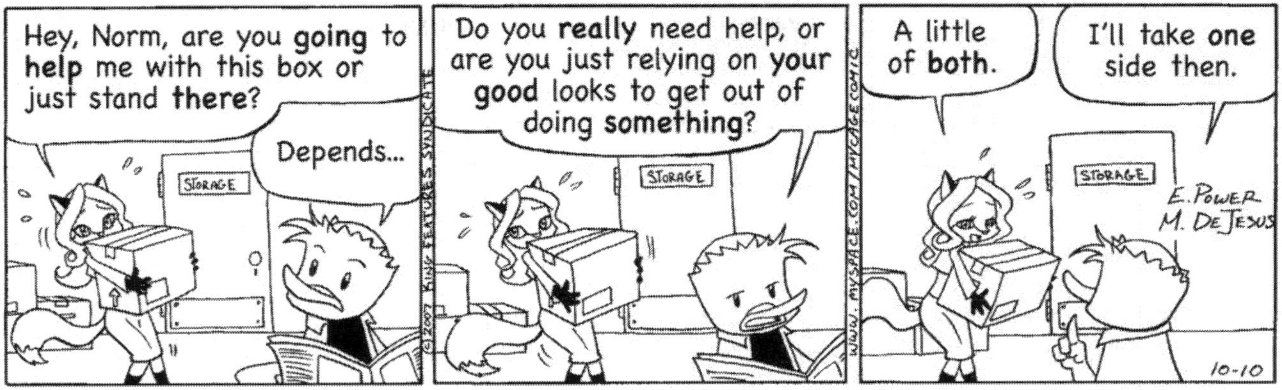
Hey, Norm, are you **going** to **help** me with this box or just stand **there**?
Depends...
STORAGE
© 2007 KING FEATURES SYNDICATE
Do you **really** need help, or are you just relying on **your good** looks to get out of doing **something**?
STORAGE
WWW.MYSPACE.COM/MYCAGECOMIC
A little of **both**.
I'll take **one** side then.
STORAGE
E. POWER
M. DEJESUS
10-10

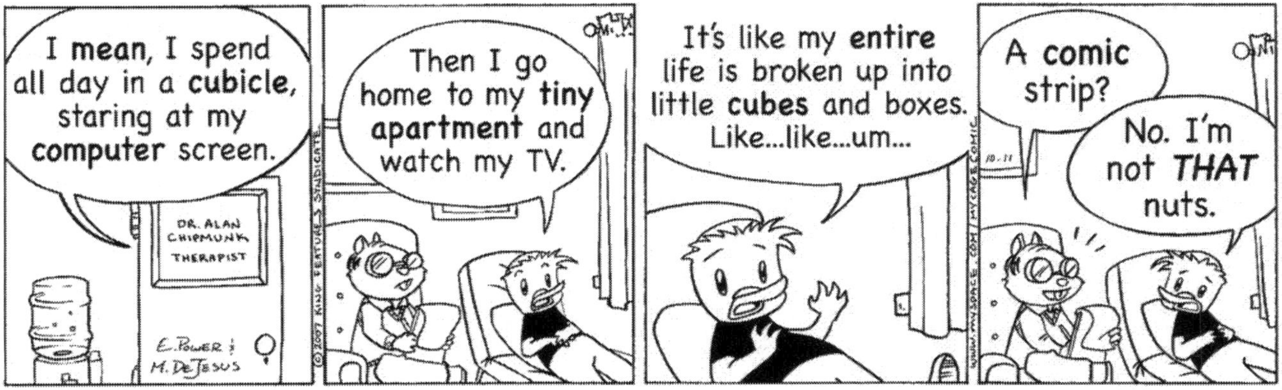
I **mean**, I spend all day in a **cubicle**, staring at my **computer** screen.
DR. ALAN CHIPMUNK
THERAPIST
E. POWER & M. DEJESUS
© 2007 KING FEATURES SYNDICATE
Then I go home to my **tiny apartment** and watch my TV.
It's like my **entire** life is broken up into little **cubes** and boxes. Like...like...um...
WWW.MYSPACE.COM/MYCAGECOMIC
A **comic** strip?
No. I'm not ***THAT*** nuts.

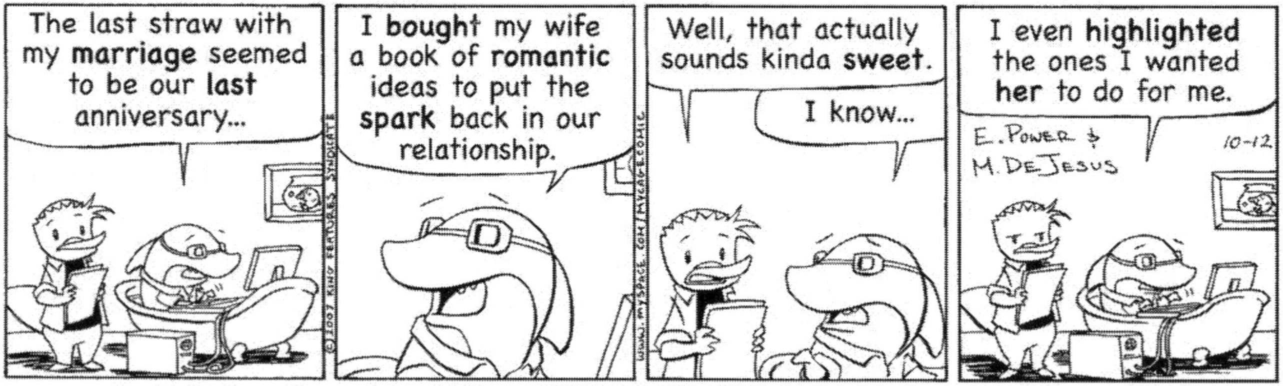
The last straw with my **marriage** seemed to be our **last** anniversary...
I **bought** my wife a book of **romantic** ideas to put the **spark** back in our relationship.
Well, that actually sounds kinda **sweet**.
I know...
I even **highlighted** the ones I wanted **her** to do for me.
E. Power & M. DeJesus
10-12

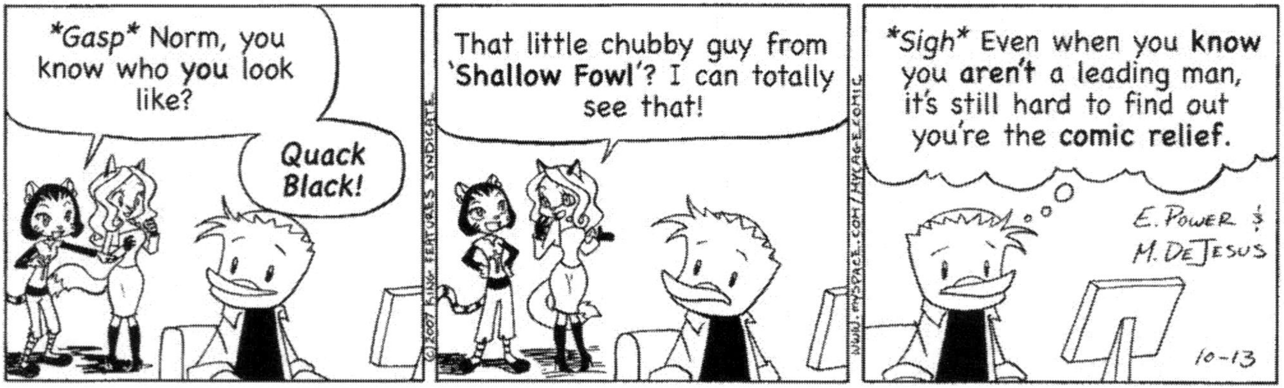
Gasp Norm, you know who **you** look like?
Quack Black!
That little chubby guy from '**Shallow Fowl**'? I can totally see that!
Sigh Even when you **know** you **aren't** a leading man, it's still hard to find out you're the **comic relief**.
E. Power & M. DeJesus
10-13

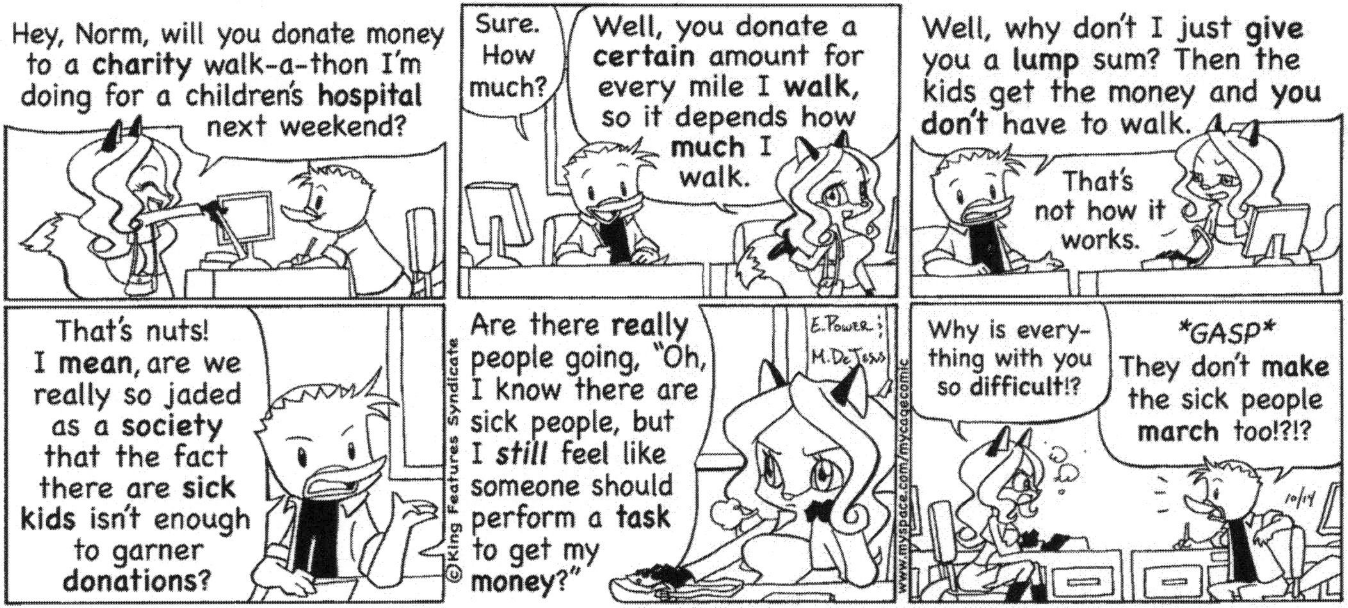
Hey, Norm, will you donate money to a **charity** walk-a-thon I'm doing for a children's **hospital** next weekend?
Sure. How much?
Well, you donate a **certain** amount for every mile I **walk**, so it depends how **much** I walk.
Well, why don't I just **give** you a **lump** sum? Then the kids get the money and **you don't** have to walk.
That's not how it works.
That's nuts! I **mean**, are we really so jaded as a **society** that the fact there are **sick kids** isn't enough to garner **donations**?
©King Features Syndicate
Are there **really** people going, "Oh, I know there are sick people, but I ***still*** feel like someone should perform a **task** to get my **money**?"
E. Power ; M. DeJesus
www.myspace.com/mycagecomic
Why is everything with you so **difficult**!?
GASP They don't **make** the sick people **march** too!?!?
10/14

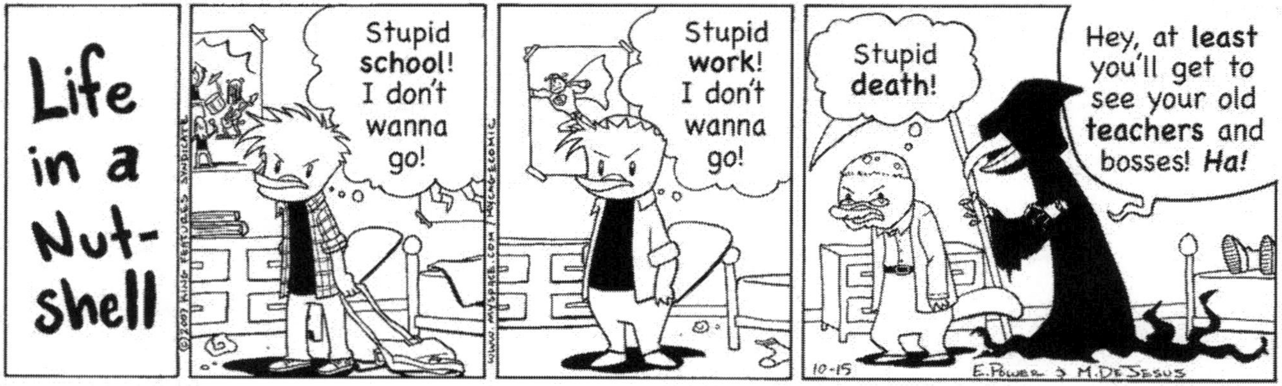
Life in a Nut-shell
Stupid school! I don't wanna go!
Stupid work! I don't wanna go!
Stupid death!
Hey, at least you'll get to see your old teachers and bosses! Ha!
10-15
E. Power & M. DeJesus

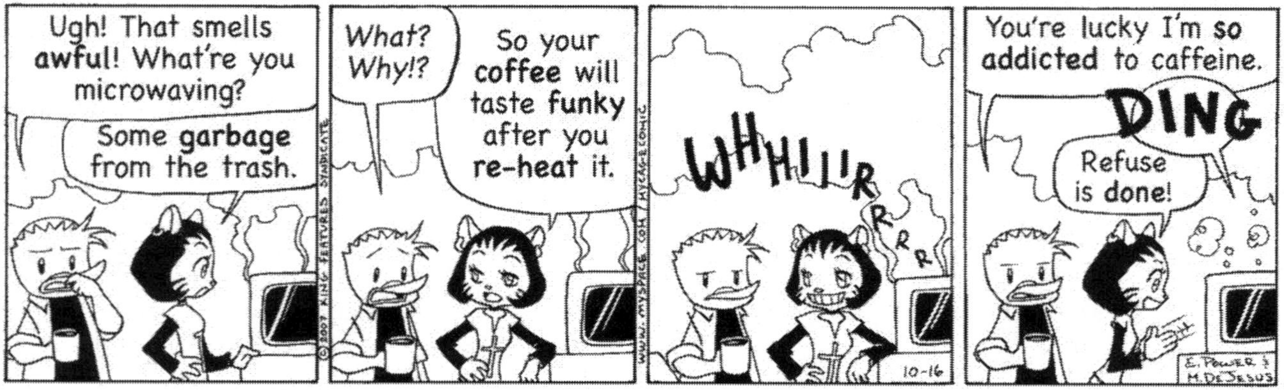
Ugh! That smells awful! What're you microwaving?
Some garbage from the trash.
What? Why!?
So your coffee will taste funky after you re-heat it.
WHHIIIRRRR
You're lucky I'm so addicted to caffeine.
DING
Refuse is done!
10-16
E. Power & M. DeJesus

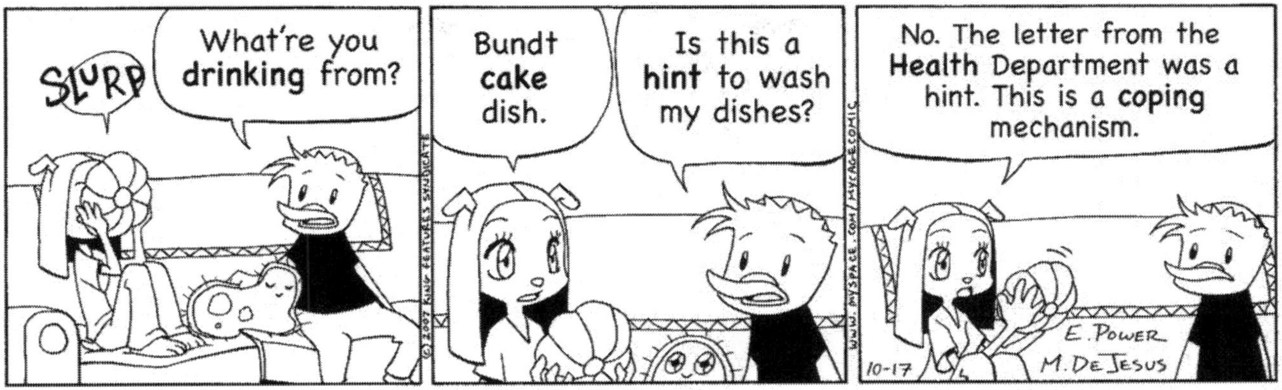
SLURP
What're you drinking from?
Bundt cake dish.
Is this a hint to wash my dishes?
No. The letter from the Health Department was a hint. This is a coping mechanism.
© 2007 King Features Syndicate
www.myspace.com/mycagecomic
10-17
E. Power
M. DeJesus

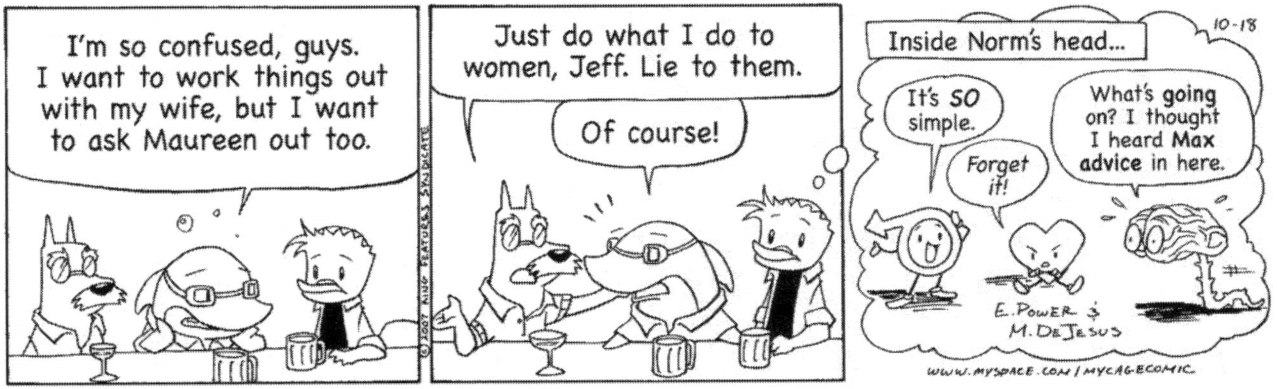
I'm so confused, guys. I want to work things out with my wife, but I want to ask Maureen out too.
Just do what I do to women, Jeff. Lie to them.
Of course!
Inside Norm's head...
It's SO simple.
Forget it!
What's going on? I thought I heard Max advice in here.
10-18
E. Power & M. DeJesus
© 2007 King Features Syndicate
www.myspace.com/mycagecomic

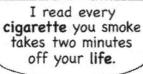

You should **stop smoking**, Rex.
I read every **cigarette** you smoke takes two minutes off your **life**.
See, that's why I have **you** come with me on my **smoke** breaks...
Two minutes with you is like an **eternity**, so it evens out.
You should smoke **more**.
© 2007 King Features Syndicate
www.myspace.com/mycagecomic
E. Power & M. DeJesus
10-19

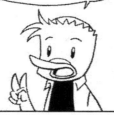

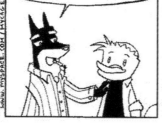

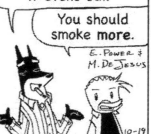

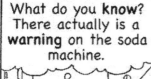

What do you **know**? There actually is a **warning** on the soda machine.
SODA
I **read** there are 35 recorded **deaths** of people being **crushed** by soda vending machines.
My thing is, if you can **shake** a machine to the point it **falls** over on you...
SODA
...the **last** thing you need is more sugar and **caffeine**.
SODA
© 2007 King Features Syndicate
www.myspace.com/mycagecomic
E. Power M. DeJesus
10-20

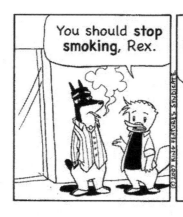

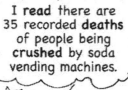

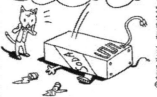

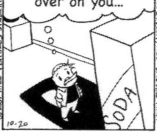

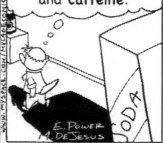

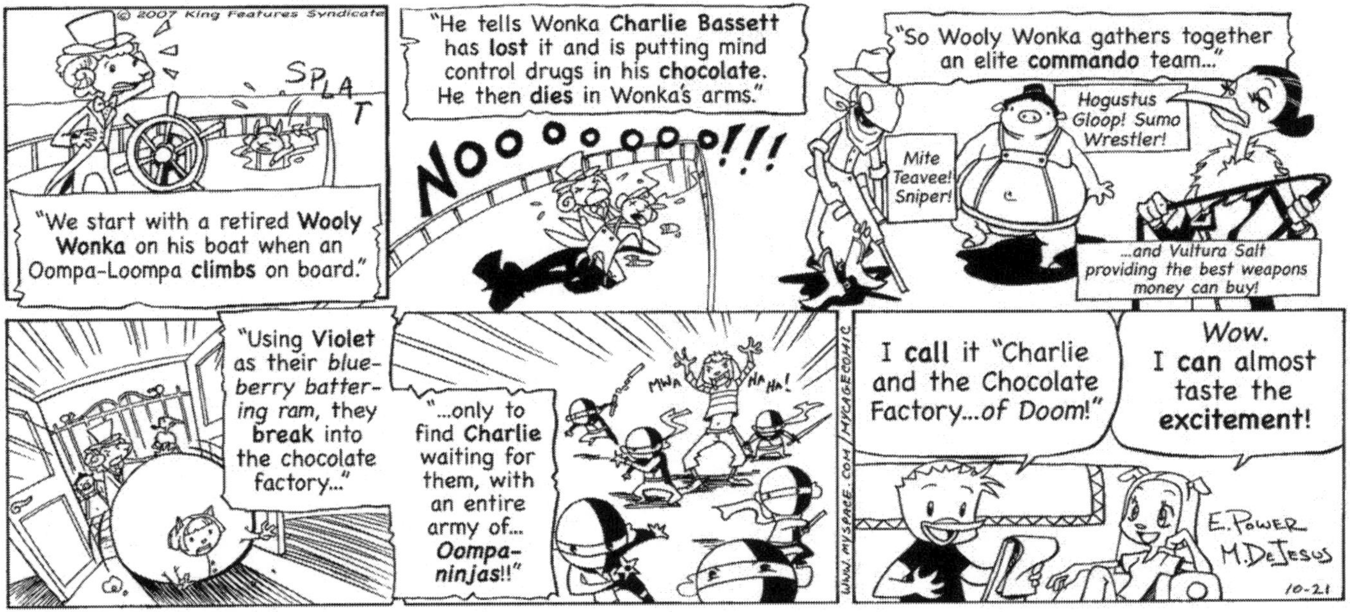
© 2007 King Features Syndicate
SPLAT
"We start with a retired **Wooly Wonka** on his boat when an Oompa-Loompa **climbs** on board."
"He tells Wonka **Charlie Bassett** has **lost** it and is putting mind control drugs in his **chocolate**. He then **dies** in Wonka's arms."
NOOOOOOO!!!
"So Wooly Wonka gathers together an elite **commando** team..."
Mite Teavee! Sniper!
Hogustus Gloop! Sumo Wrestler!
...and Vultura Salt providing the best weapons money can buy!
"Using **Violet** as their *blueberry battering ram*, they **break** into the chocolate factory..."
"...only to find **Charlie** waiting for them, with an entire army of... ***Oompa-ninjas!!***"
MWA HA HA!
WWW.MYSPACE.COM/MYCAGECOMIC
I **call** it "Charlie and the Chocolate Factory...*of Doom!*"
Wow. I **can** almost taste the **excitement!**
E. POWER
M. DEJESUS
10-21

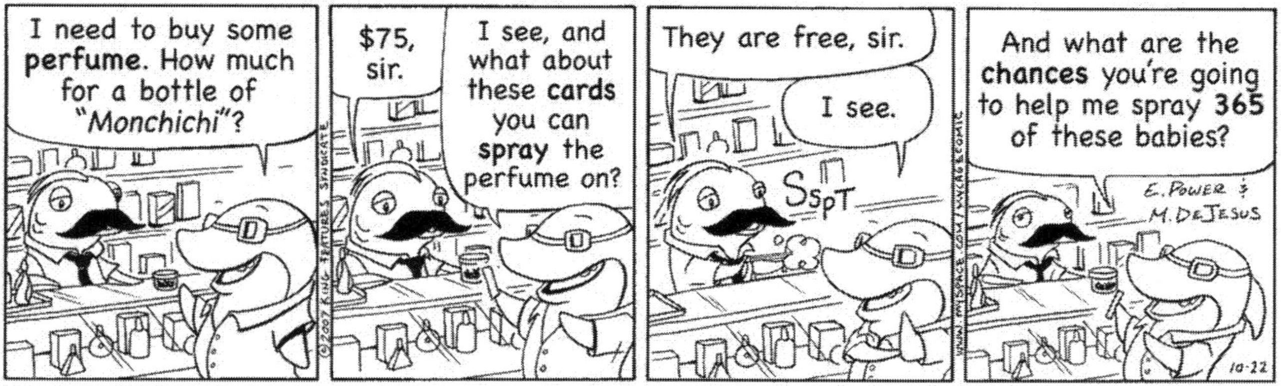
I need to buy some perfume. How much for a bottle of "Monchichi"?
$75, sir.
I see, and what about these cards you can spray the perfume on?
They are free, sir.
I see.
SSPT
And what are the chances you're going to help me spray 365 of these babies?
E. POWER & M. DEJESUS
10-22
©2007 KING FEATURES SYNDICATE
WWW.MYSPACE.COM/MYCAGECOMIC

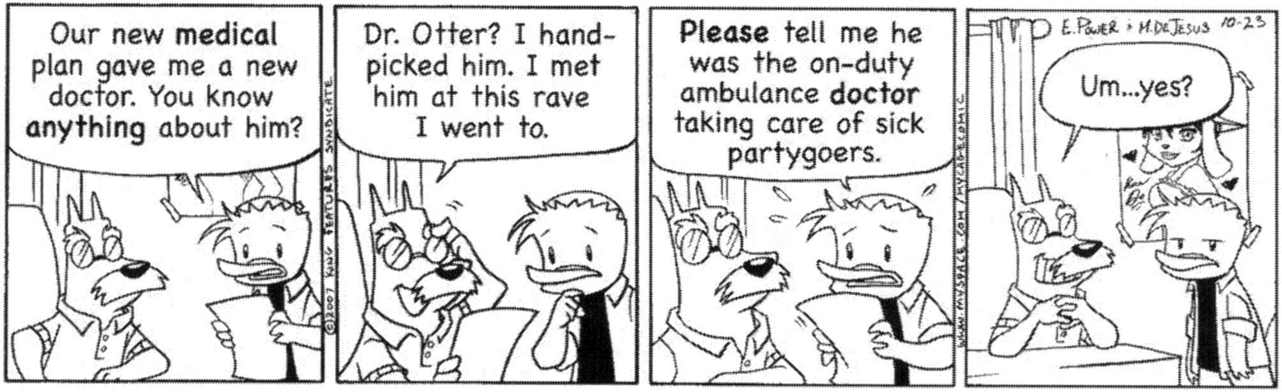
Our new medical plan gave me a new doctor. You know anything about him?
Dr. Otter? I hand-picked him. I met him at this rave I went to.
Please tell me he was the on-duty ambulance doctor taking care of sick partygoers.
Um...yes?
E. POWER & M. DEJESUS 10-23
©2007 KING FEATURES SYNDICATE
WWW.MYSPACE.COM/MYCAGECOMIC

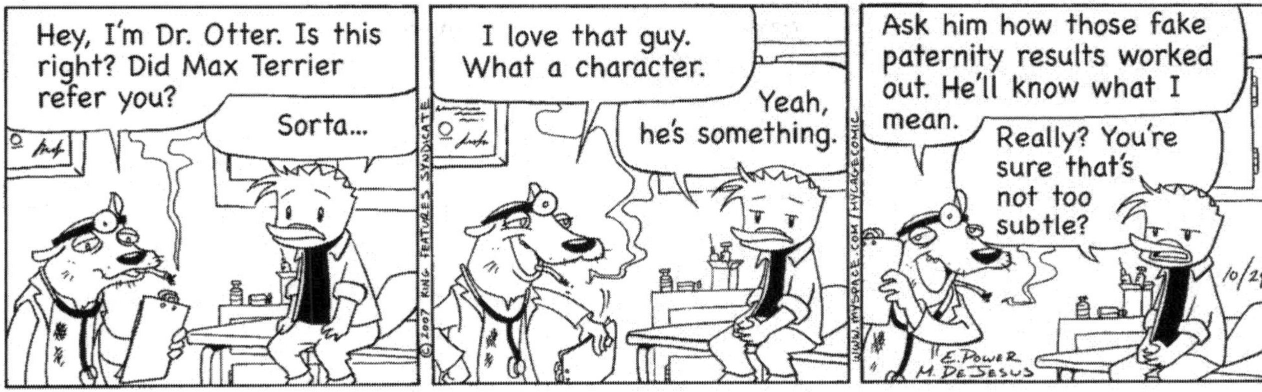
Hey, I'm Dr. Otter. Is this right? Did Max Terrier refer you?
Sorta...
I love that guy. What a character.
Yeah, he's something.
Ask him how those fake paternity results worked out. He'll know what I mean.
Really? You're sure that's not too subtle?
10/24
E. POWER
M. DEJESUS
© 2007 KING FEATURES SYNDICATE
WWW.MYSPACE.COM/MYCAGECOMIC

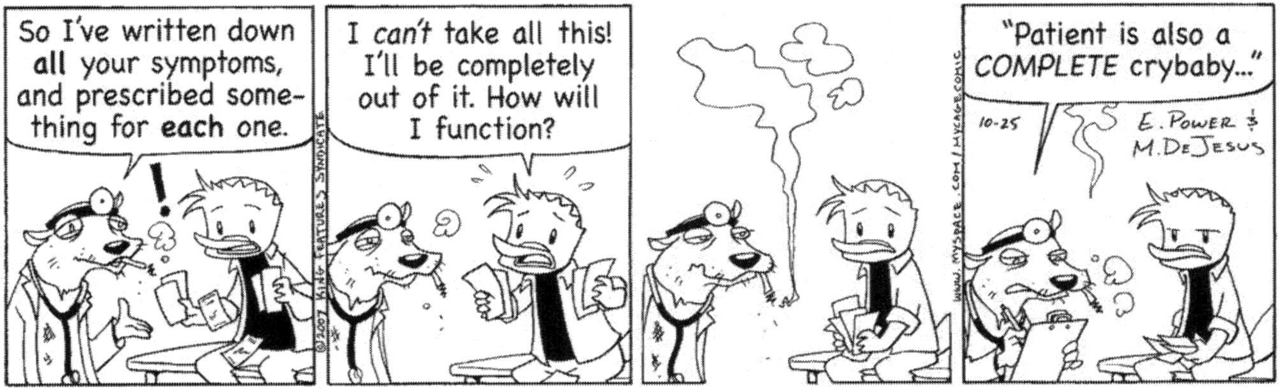
So I've written down **all** your symptoms, and prescribed something for **each** one.
!
I *can't* take all this! I'll be completely out of it. How will I function?
"Patient is also a *COMPLETE* crybaby..."
10-25
E. POWER &
M. DEJESUS
©2007 KING FEATURES SYNDICATE
WWW.MYSPACE.COM/MYCAGECOMIC

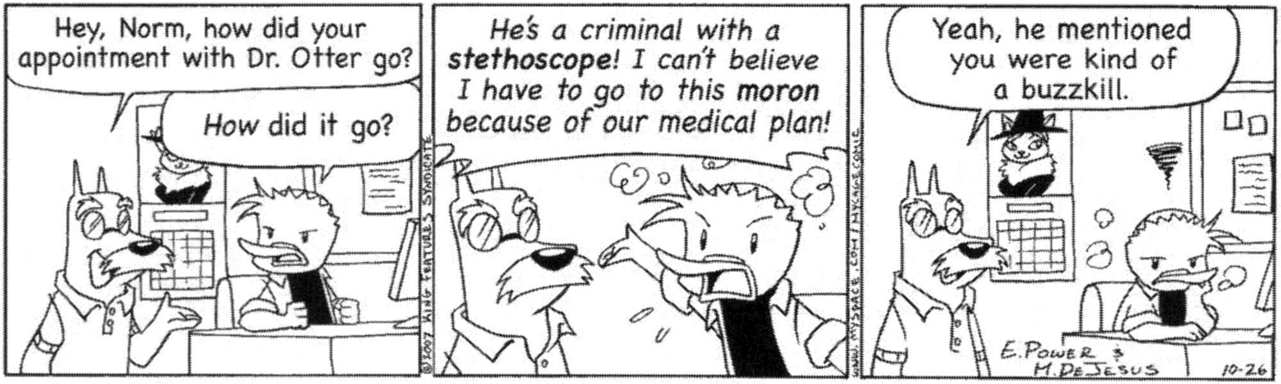
Hey, Norm, how did your appointment with Dr. Otter go?
How did it go?
He's a criminal with a **stethoscope**! I can't believe I have to go to this **moron** because of our medical plan!
Yeah, he mentioned you were kind of a buzzkill.
E. POWER & M. DEJESUS
10-26

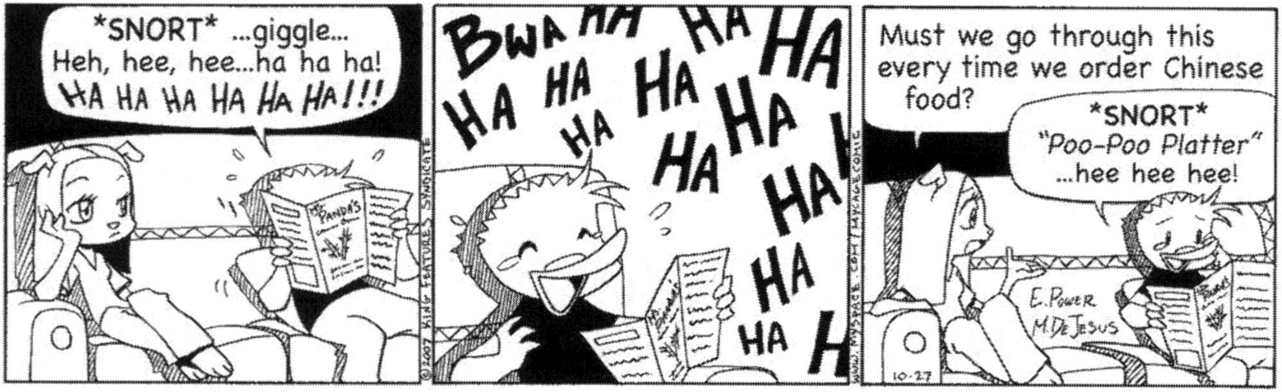
SNORT ...giggle... Heh, hee, hee...ha ha ha! HA HA HA HA HA HA!!!
BWA HA HA HA HA HA HA HA HA HA HA HA HA HA HA H
Must we go through this every time we order Chinese food?
SNORT "Poo-Poo Platter" ...hee hee hee!
E. POWER M. DEJESUS
10-27

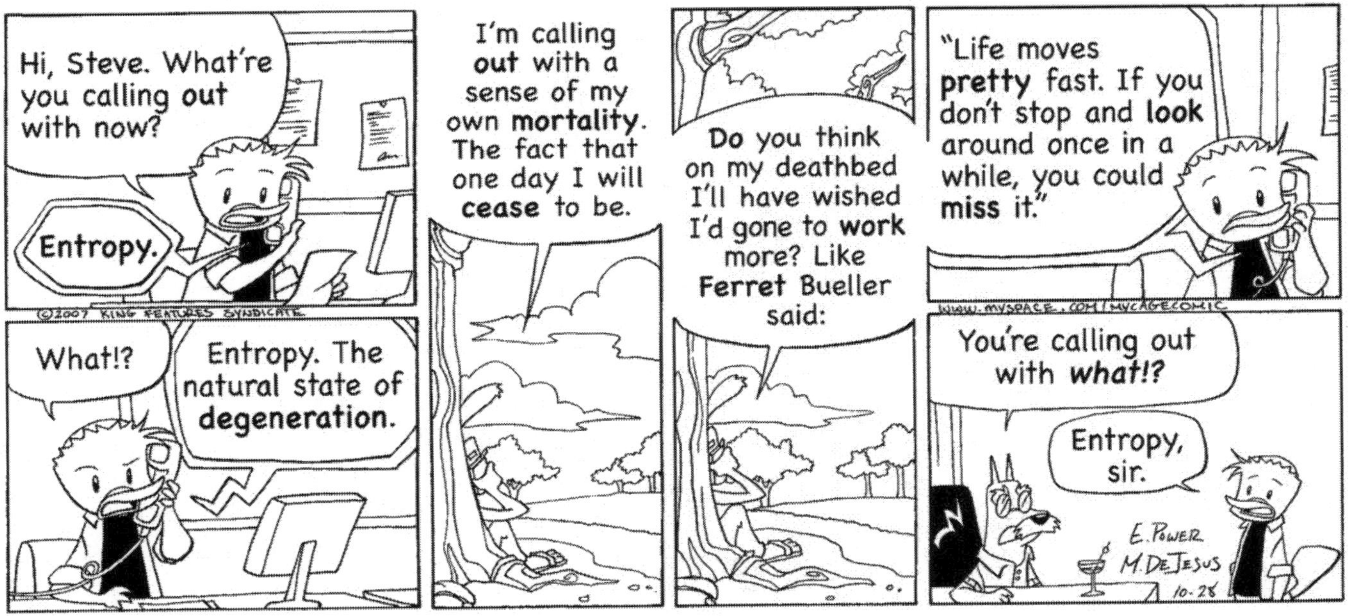
Hi, Steve. What're you calling **out** with now?
Entropy.
©2007 KING FEATURES SYNDICATE
What!?
Entropy. The natural state of **degeneration.**
I'm calling **out** with a sense of my own **mortality**. The fact that one day I will **cease** to be.
Do you think on my deathbed I'll have wished I'd gone to **work** more? Like **Ferret** Bueller said:
"Life moves **pretty** fast. If you don't stop and **look** around once in a while, you could **miss** it."
WWW.MYSPACE.COM/MYCAGECOMIC
You're calling out with ***what!?***
Entropy, sir.
E. POWER
M. DEJESUS
10-28

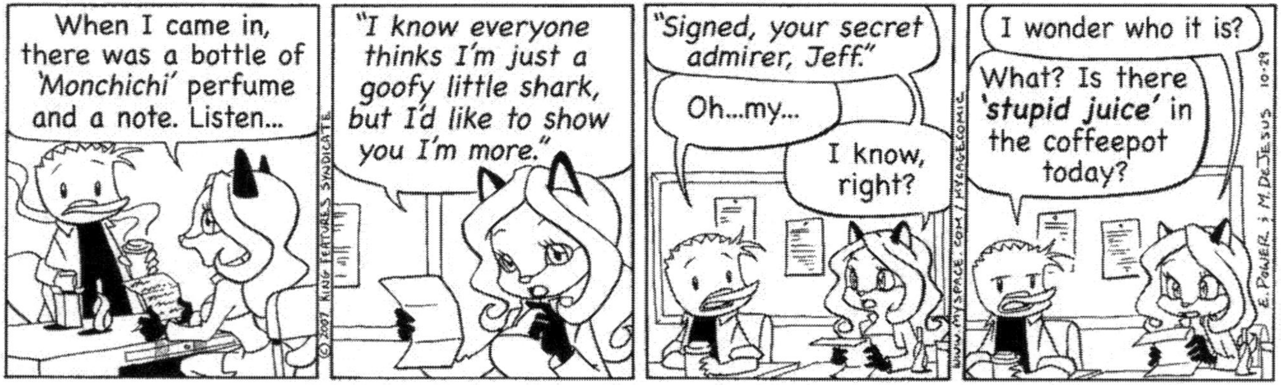
When I came in, there was a bottle of 'Monchichi' perfume and a note. Listen...
© 2007 KING FEATURES SYNDICATE
"I know everyone thinks I'm just a goofy little shark, but I'd like to show you I'm more."
"Signed, your secret admirer, Jeff."
Oh...my...
I know, right?
WWW.MYSPACE.COM/MYCAGECOMIC
I wonder who it is?
What? Is there **'stupid juice'** in the coffeepot today?
E. POWER & M. DEJESUS
10-29

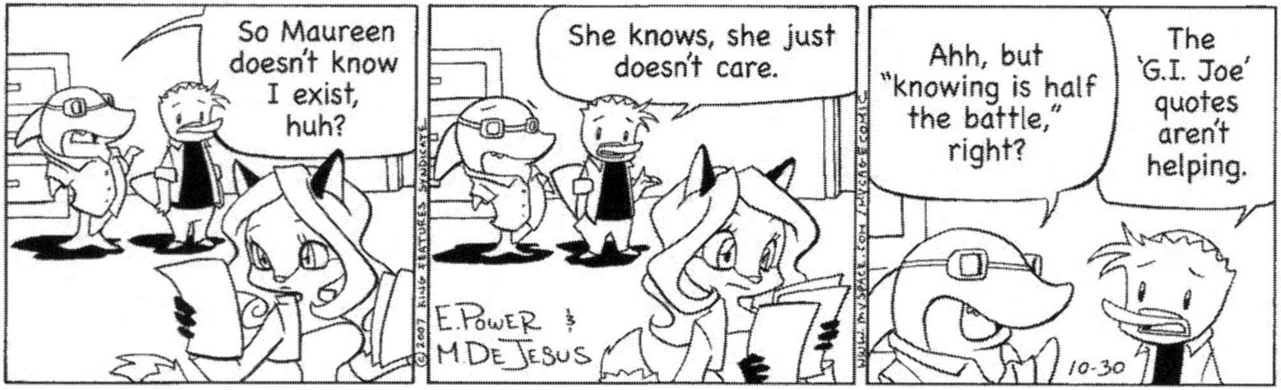
So Maureen doesn't know I exist, huh?
© 2007 KING FEATURES SYNDICATE
E. POWER & M. DEJESUS
She knows, she just doesn't care.
WWW.MYSPACE.COM/MYCAGECOMIC
Ahh, but "knowing is half the battle," right?
The 'G.I. Joe' quotes aren't helping.
10-30

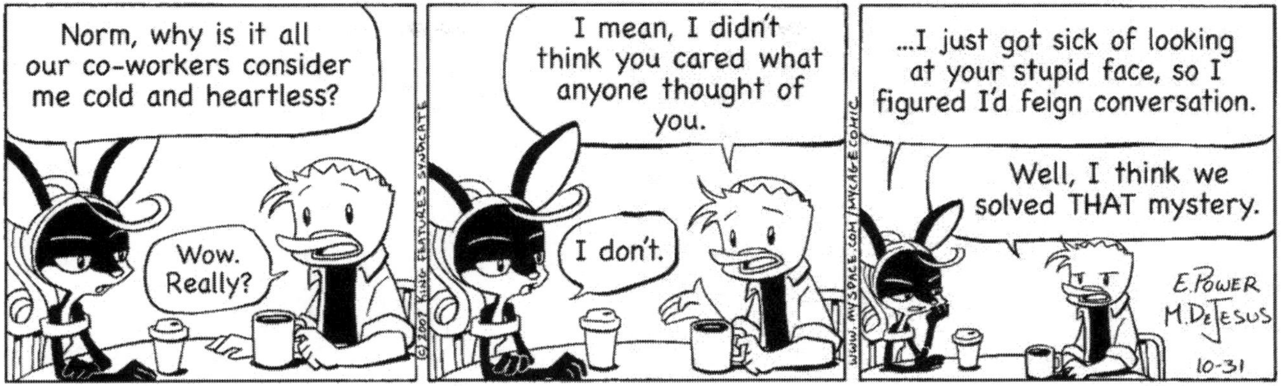
Norm, why is it all our co-workers consider me cold and heartless?
Wow. Really?
© 2007 King Features Syndicate
I mean, I didn't think you cared what anyone thought of you.
I don't.
www.myspace.com/mycagecomic
...I just got sick of looking at your stupid face, so I figured I'd feign conversation.
Well, I think we solved THAT mystery.
E. Power
M. DeJesus
10-31

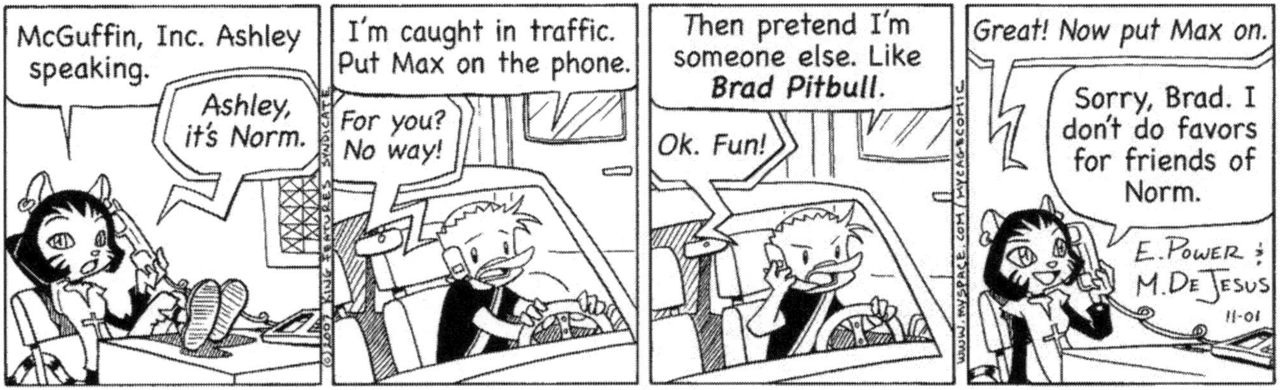
McGuffin, Inc. Ashley speaking.
Ashley, it's Norm.
© 2007 King Features Syndicate
I'm caught in traffic. Put Max on the phone.
For you? No way!
Then pretend I'm someone else. Like **Brad Pitbull**.
Ok. Fun!
www.myspace.com/mycagecomic
Great! Now put Max on.
Sorry, Brad. I don't do favors for friends of Norm.
E. Power & M. DeJesus
11-01

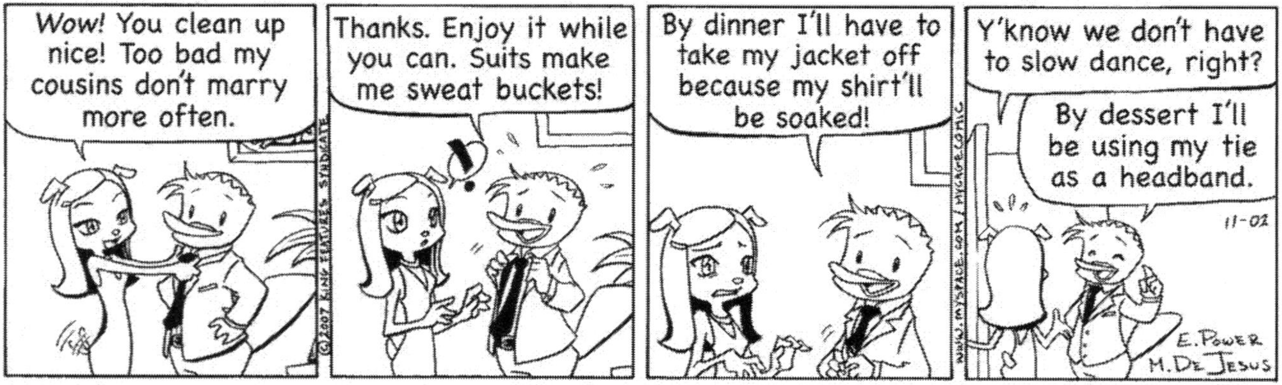
Wow! You clean up nice! Too bad my cousins don't marry more often.
©2007 King Features Syndicate
Thanks. Enjoy it while you can. Suits make me sweat buckets!
By dinner I'll have to take my jacket off because my shirt'll be soaked!
Y'know we don't have to slow dance, right?
By dessert I'll be using my tie as a headband.
11-02
E. Power
M. De Jesus

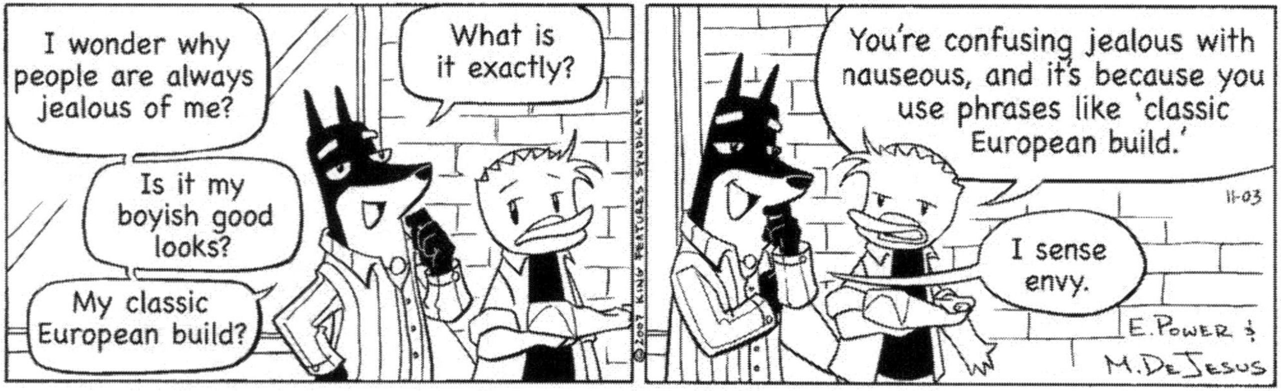
I wonder why people are always jealous of me?
Is it my boyish good looks?
My classic European build?
What is it exactly?
©2007 King Features Syndicate
You're confusing jealous with nauseous, and it's because you use phrases like 'classic European build.'
11-03
I sense envy.
E. Power &
M. De Jesus

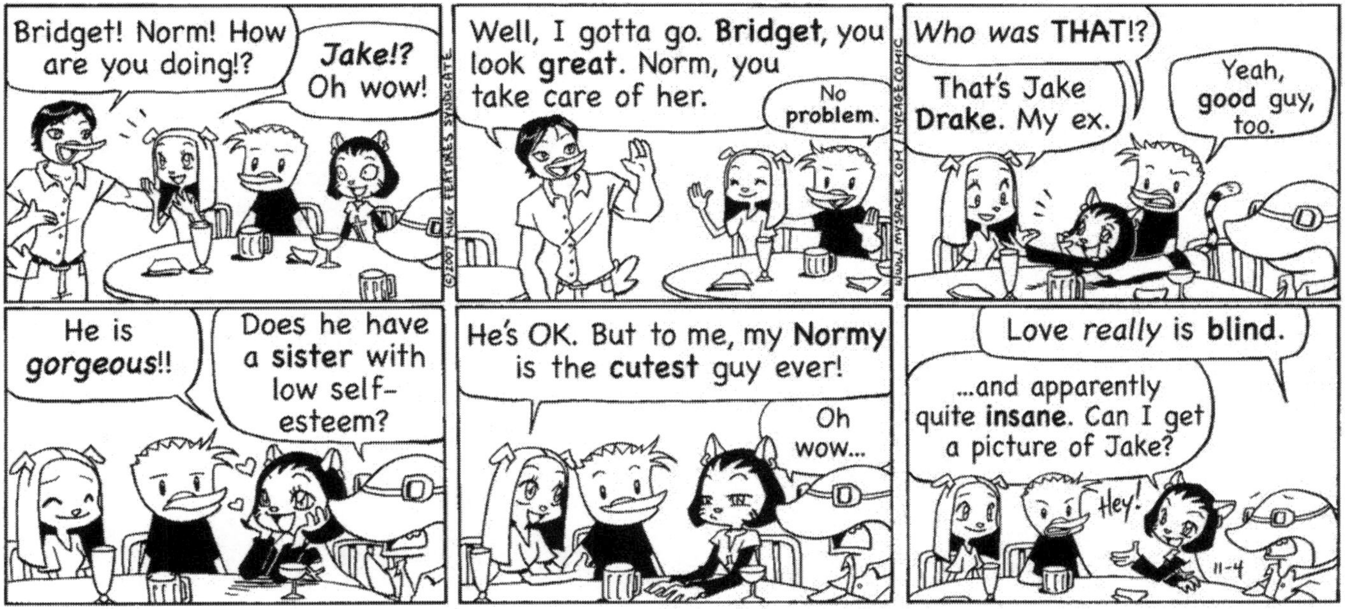
Bridget! Norm! How are you doing!?
Jake!? Oh wow!
©2007 KING FEATURES SYNDICATE
Well, I gotta go. **Bridget**, you look **great**. Norm, you take care of her.
No **problem**.
WWW.MYSPACE.COM/MYCAGECOMIC
Who was **THAT**!?
That's Jake **Drake**. My ex.
Yeah, **good** guy, too.
He is ***gorgeous***!!
Does he have a **sister** with low self-esteem?
He's OK. But to me, my **Normy** is the **cutest** guy ever!
Oh wow...
Love *really* is **blind**.
...and apparently quite **insane**. Can I get a picture of Jake?
Hey!
11-4

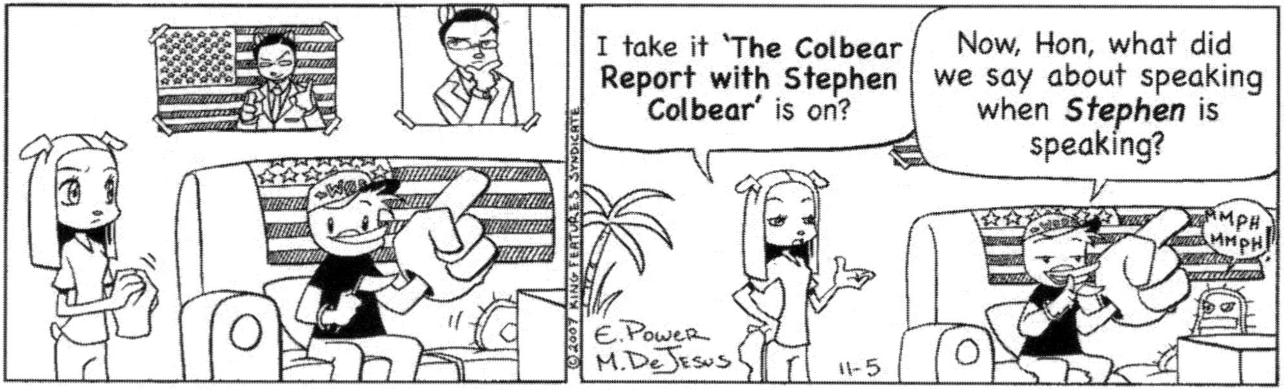

I take it 'The Colbear Report with Stephen Colbear' is on?
Now, Hon, what did we say about speaking when *Stephen* is speaking?
MMPH MMPH!
© 2007 KING FEATURES SYNDICATE
E. POWER M. DeJESUS
11-5

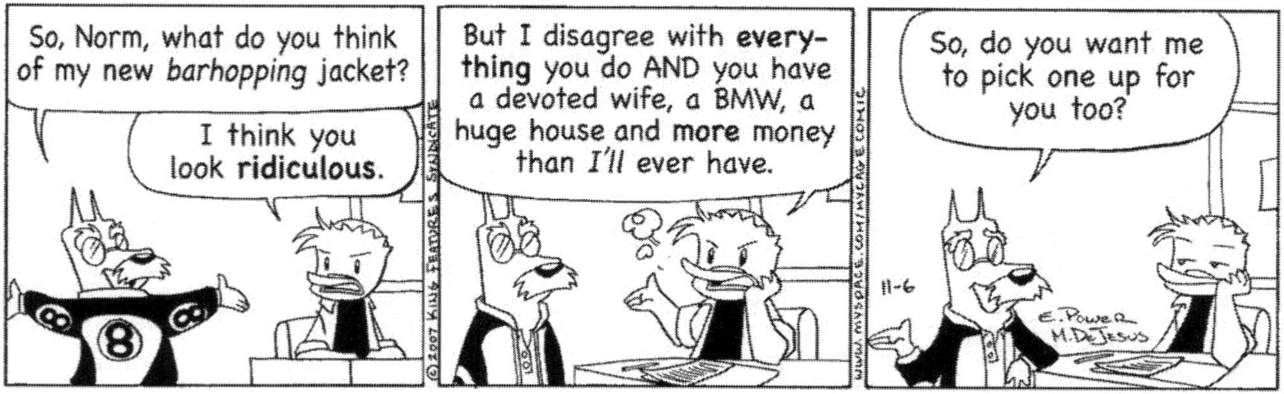

So, Norm, what do you think of my new *barhopping* jacket?
I think you look **ridiculous**.
But I disagree with **everything** you do AND you have a devoted wife, a BMW, a huge house and **more** money than *I'll* ever have.
So, do you want me to pick one up for you too?
© 2007 KING FEATURES SYNDICATE
WWW.MYSPACE.COM/MYCAGECOMIC
11-6
E. POWER M. DeJESUS

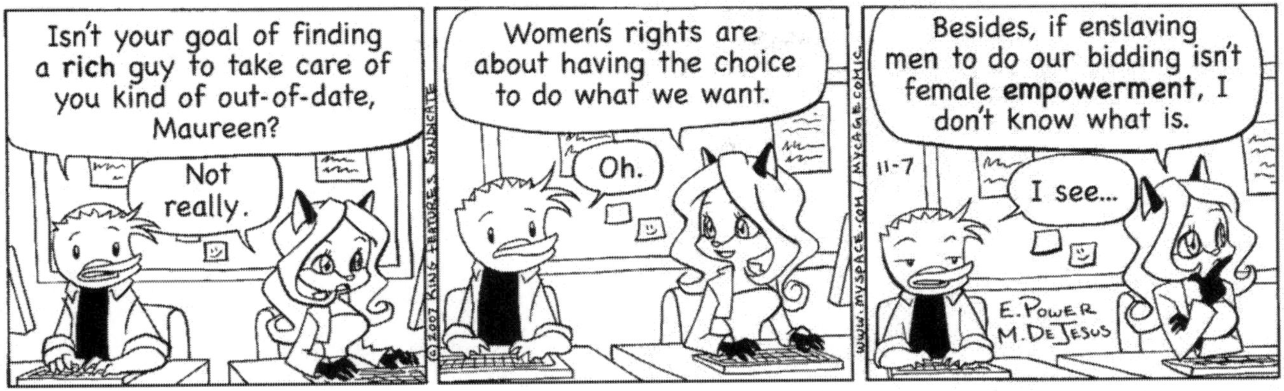

Isn't your goal of finding a **rich** guy to take care of you kind of out-of-date, Maureen?
Not really.
© 2007 King Features Syndicate
Women's rights are about having the choice to do what we want.
Oh.
www.myspace.com/mycagecomic
11-7
Besides, if enslaving men to do our bidding isn't female **empowerment**, I don't know what is.
I see...
E. Power
M. DeJesus

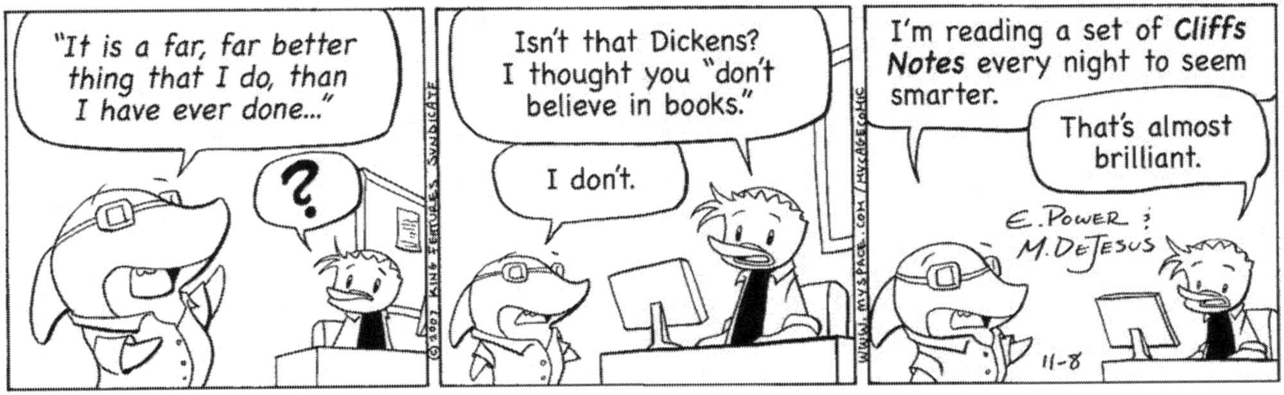

"It is a far, far better thing that I do, than I have ever done..."
?
© 2007 King Features Syndicate
Isn't that Dickens? I thought you "don't believe in books."
I don't.
www.myspace.com/mycagecomic
I'm reading a set of ***Cliffs Notes*** every night to seem smarter.
That's almost brilliant.
E. Power
M. DeJesus
11-8

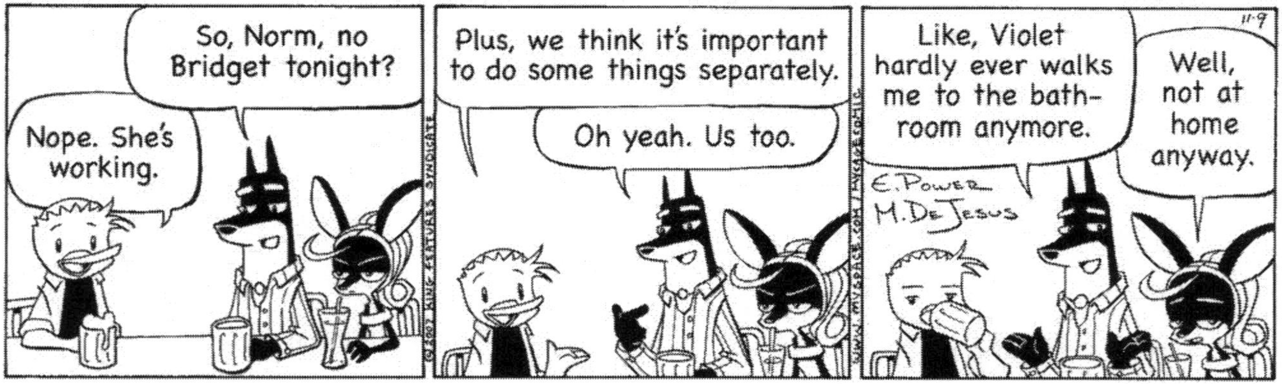
So, Norm, no Bridget tonight?
Nope. She's working.
Plus, we think it's important to do some things separately.
Oh yeah. Us too.
Like, Violet hardly ever walks me to the bathroom anymore.
Well, not at home anyway.
E. POWER
M. DEJESUS
11-9

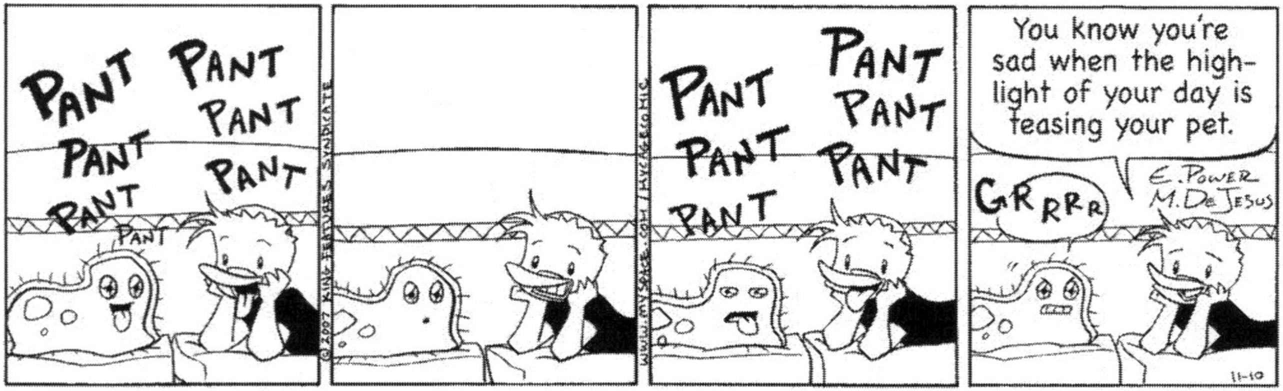
PANT PANT
PANT PANT
PANT PANT
PANT
PANT PANT
PANT PANT
PANT PANT
PANT
You know you're sad when the highlight of your day is teasing your pet.
GRRRR
E. POWER
M. DEJESUS
11-10

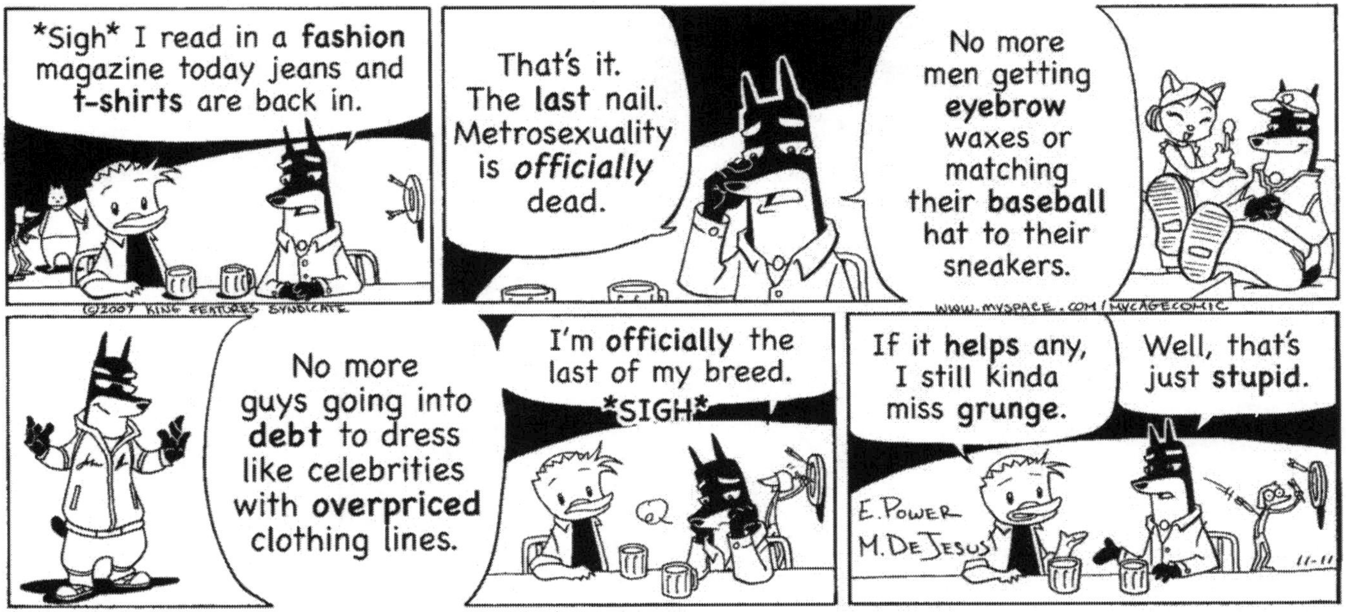
Sigh I read in a **fashion** magazine today jeans and **t-shirts** are back in.
That's it. The **last** nail. Metrosexuality is ***officially*** dead.
No more men getting **eyebrow** waxes or matching their **baseball** hat to their sneakers.
©2007 King Features Syndicate
www.myspace.com/mycagecomic
No more guys going into **debt** to dress like celebrities with **overpriced** clothing lines.
I'm **officially** the last of my breed.
SIGH
If it **helps** any, I still kinda miss **grunge**.
Well, that's just **stupid**.
E. Power
M. DeJesus
11-11

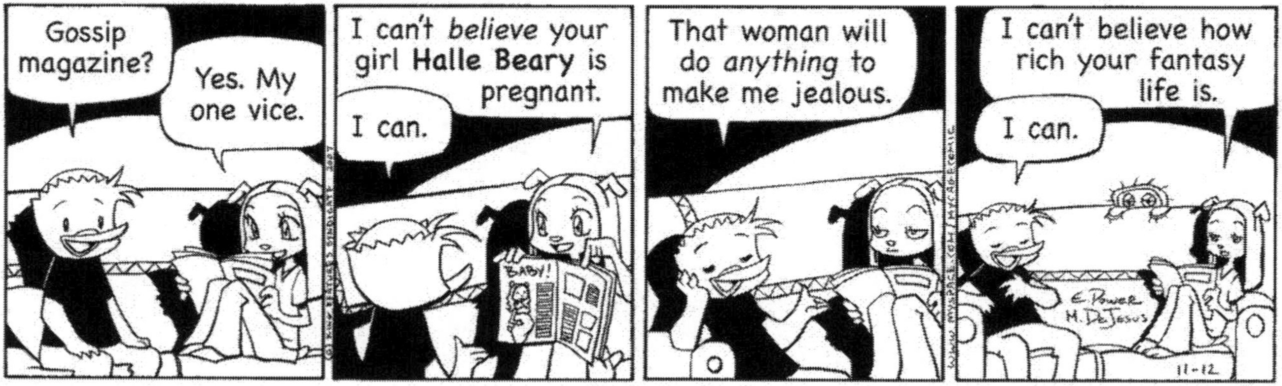
Gossip magazine?
Yes. My one vice.
I can't *believe* your girl **Halle Beary** is pregnant.
I can.
BABY!
That woman will do *anything* to make me jealous.
I can't believe how rich your fantasy life is.
I can.
E. Power
M. DeJesus
11-12

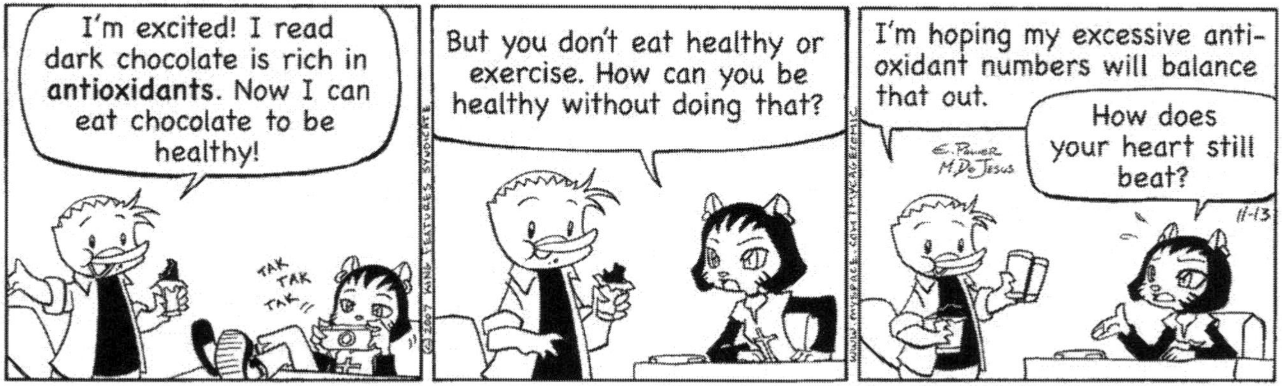
I'm excited! I read dark chocolate is rich in **antioxidants**. Now I can eat chocolate to be healthy!
TAK TAK TAK
But you don't eat healthy or exercise. How can you be healthy without doing that?
I'm hoping my excessive anti-oxidant numbers will balance that out.
How does your heart still beat?
E. Power
M. DeJesus
11-13

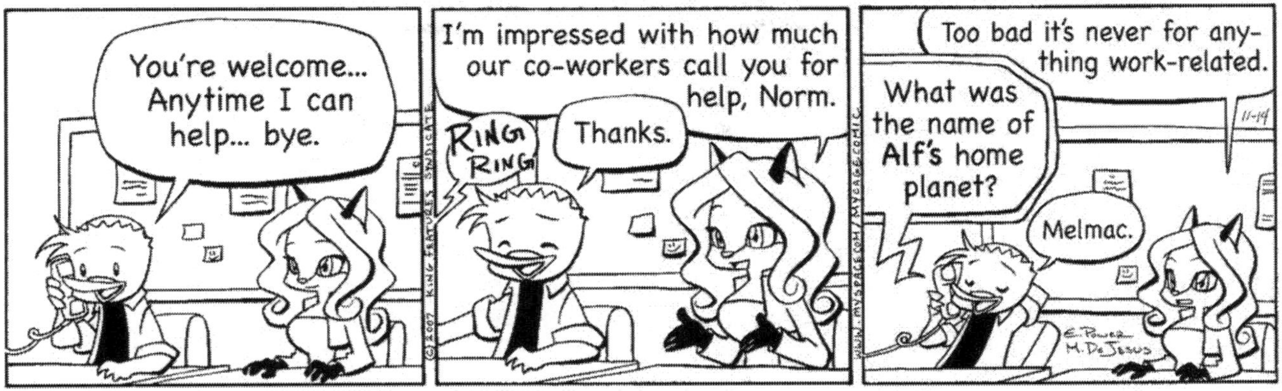
You're welcome... Anytime I can help... bye.
I'm impressed with how much our co-workers call you for help, Norm.
RING RING
Thanks.
Too bad it's never for anything work-related.
What was the name of Alf's home planet?
Melmac.
11-14
E. Power
M. DeJesus

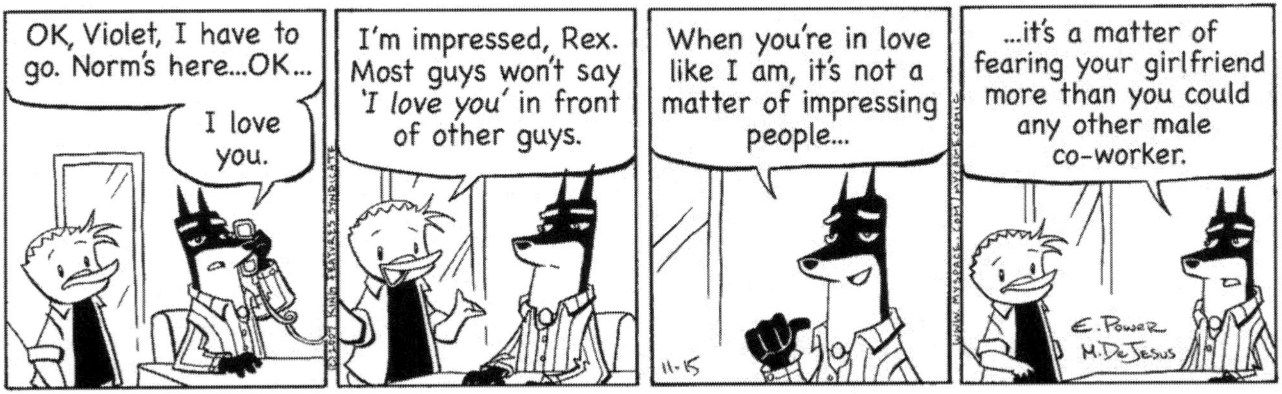
OK, Violet, I have to go. Norm's here...OK...
I love you.
I'm impressed, Rex. Most guys won't say *'I love you'* in front of other guys.
When you're in love like I am, it's not a matter of impressing people...
11-15
...it's a matter of fearing your girlfriend more than you could any other male co-worker.
E. Power
M. DeJesus

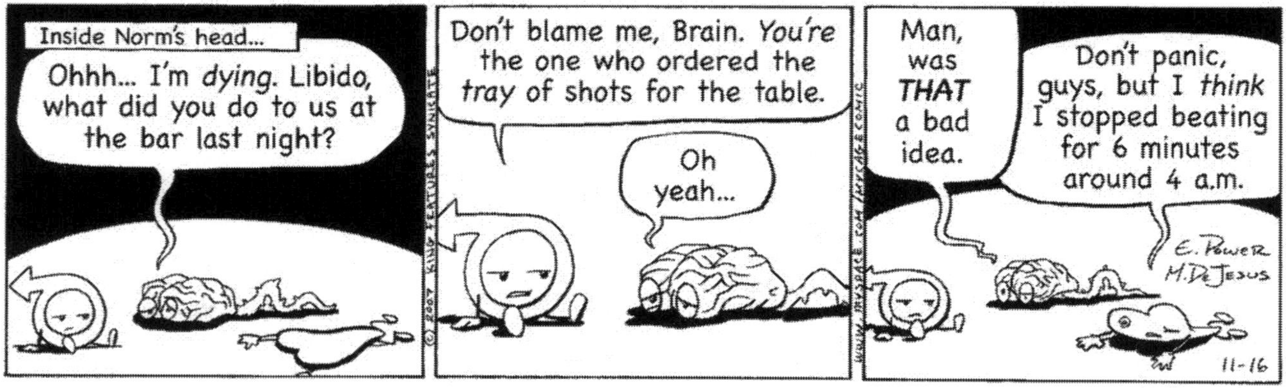
Inside Norm's head...
Ohhh... I'm *dying*. Libido, what did you do to us at the bar last night?
© 2007 KING FEATURES SYNDICATE
Don't blame me, Brain. *You're* the one who ordered the *tray* of shots for the table.
Oh yeah...
Man, was ***THAT*** a bad idea.
Don't panic, guys, but I *think* I stopped beating for 6 minutes around 4 a.m.
E. POWER
M. DEJESUS
11-16

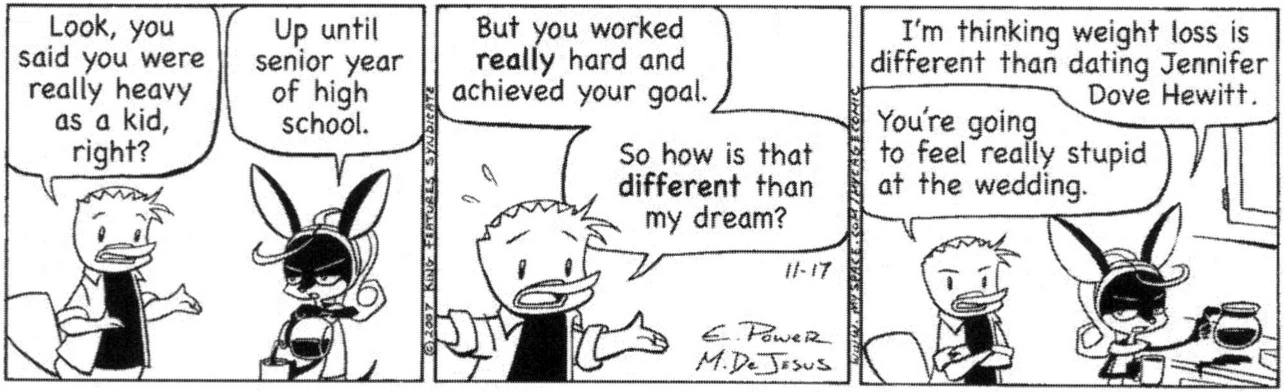
Look, you said you were really heavy as a kid, right?
Up until senior year of high school.
© 2007 KING FEATURES SYNDICATE
But you worked **really** hard and achieved your goal.
So how is that **different** than my dream?
11-17
E. POWER
M. DEJESUS
I'm thinking weight loss is different than dating Jennifer Dove Hewitt.
You're going to feel really stupid at the wedding.

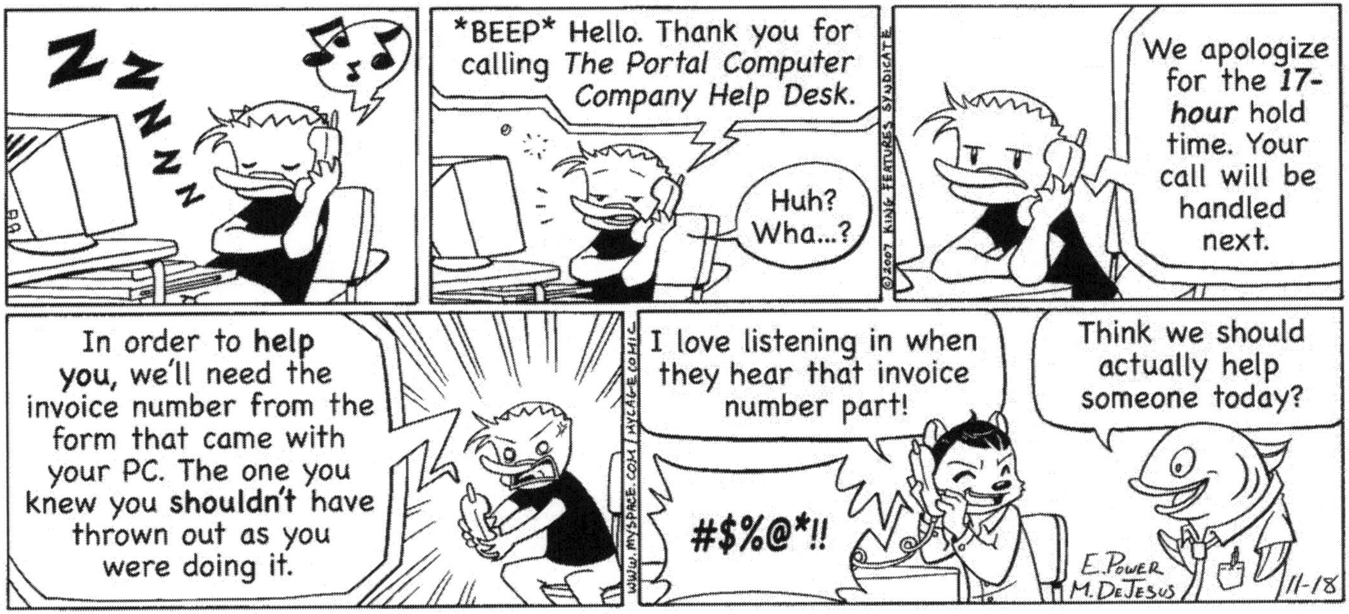
Z Z Z Z Z Z
BEEP Hello. Thank you for calling *The Portal Computer Company Help Desk.*
Huh? Wha...?
©2007 KING FEATURES SYNDICATE
We apologize for the **17-hour** hold time. Your call will be handled next.
In order to **help you,** we'll need the invoice number from the form that came with your PC. The one you knew you **shouldn't** have thrown out as you were doing it.
WWW.MYSPACE.COM/MYCAGECOMIC
I love listening in when they hear that invoice number part!
#$%@*!!
Think we should actually help someone today?
E.POWER
M.DEJESUS
11-18

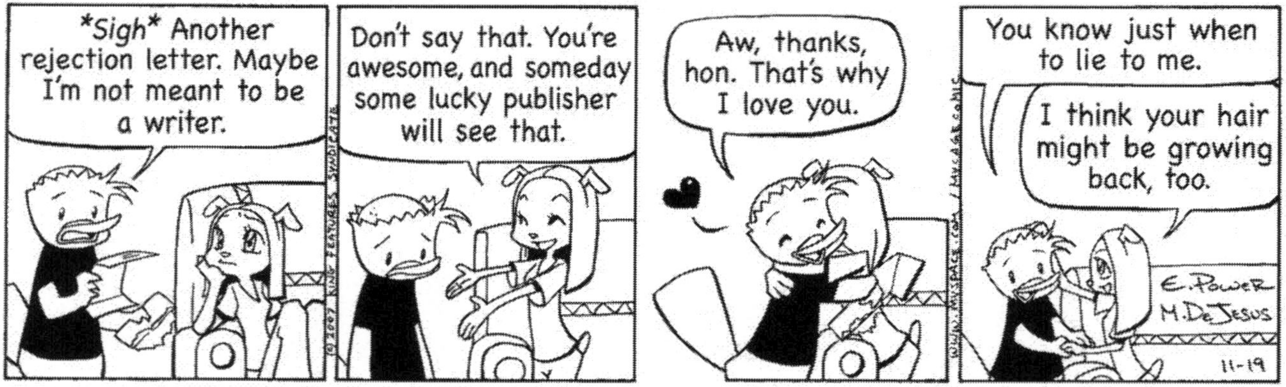
Sigh Another rejection letter. Maybe I'm not meant to be a writer.
Don't say that. You're awesome, and someday some lucky publisher will see that.
Aw, thanks, hon. That's why I love you.
You know just when to lie to me.
I think your hair might be growing back, too.
E. Power
M. DeJesus
11-19

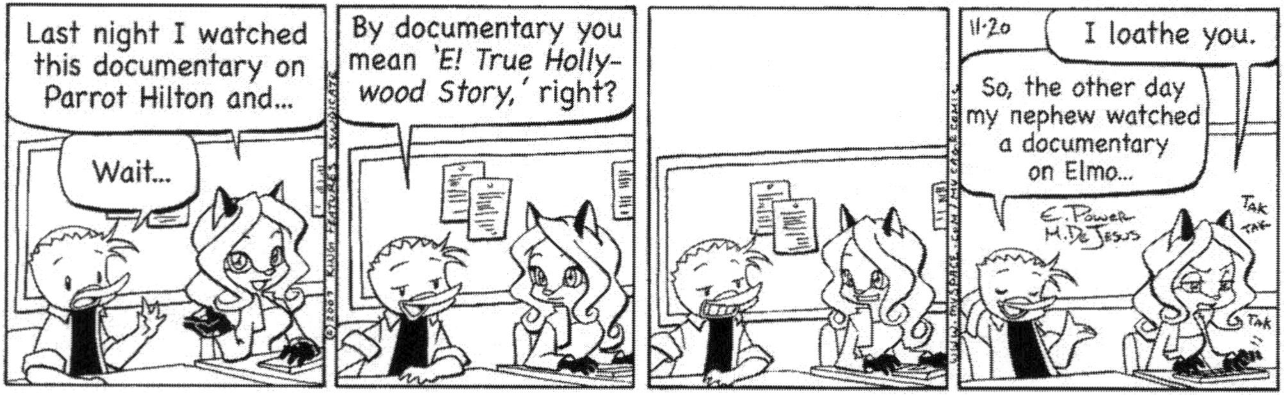
Last night I watched this documentary on Parrot Hilton and...
Wait...
By documentary you mean *'E! True Hollywood Story,'* right?
11·20
I loathe you.
So, the other day my nephew watched a documentary on Elmo...
E. Power
M. DeJesus
TAK
TAK
TAK

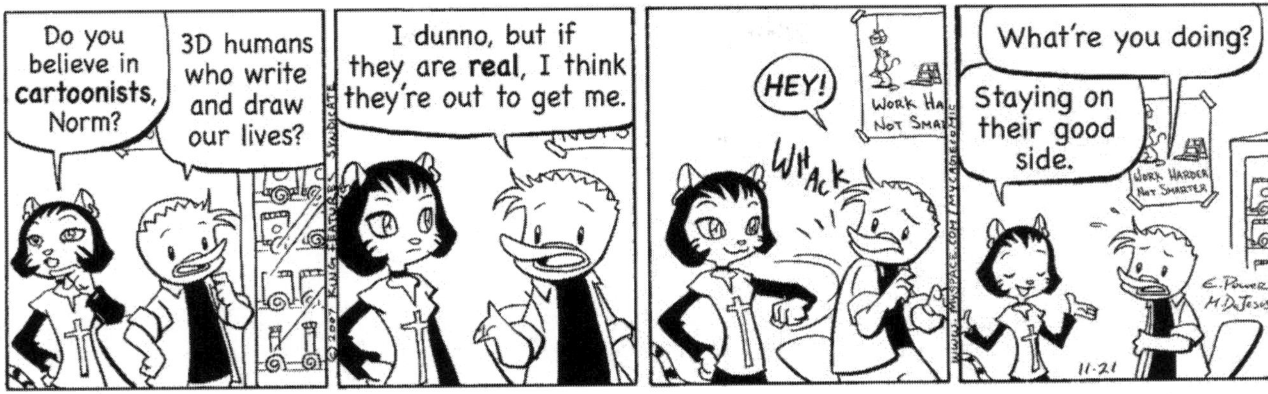
Do you believe in **cartoonists**, Norm?
3D humans who write and draw our lives?
I dunno, but if they are **real**, I think they're out to get me.
HEY!
WHACK
WORK HARDER NOT SMARTER
What're you doing?
Staying on their good side.
E. Power
M. DeJesus
11-21

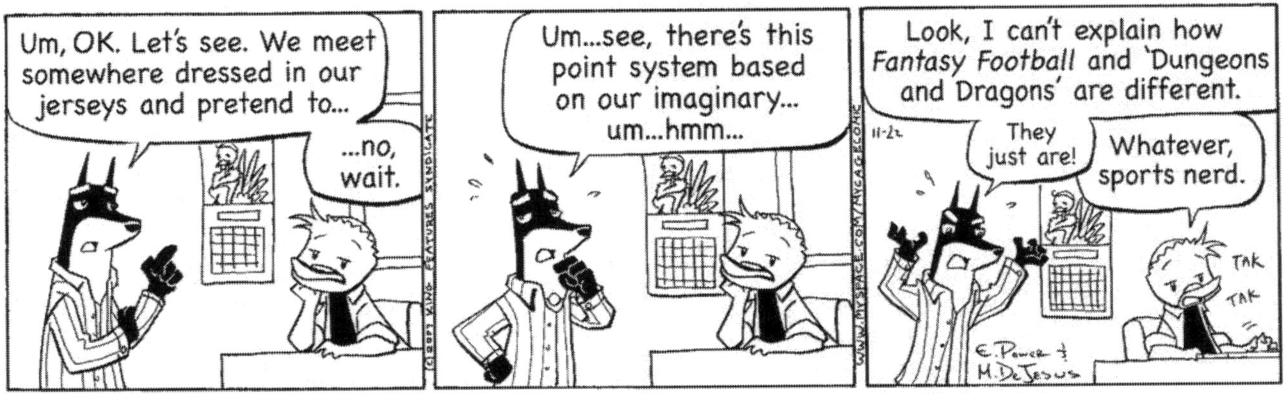
Um, OK. Let's see. We meet somewhere dressed in our jerseys and pretend to...
...no, wait.
Um...see, there's this point system based on our imaginary... um...hmm...
11-22
Look, I can't explain how *Fantasy Football* and 'Dungeons and Dragons' are different.
They just are!
Whatever, sports nerd.
TAK
TAK
E. Power &
M. DeJesus

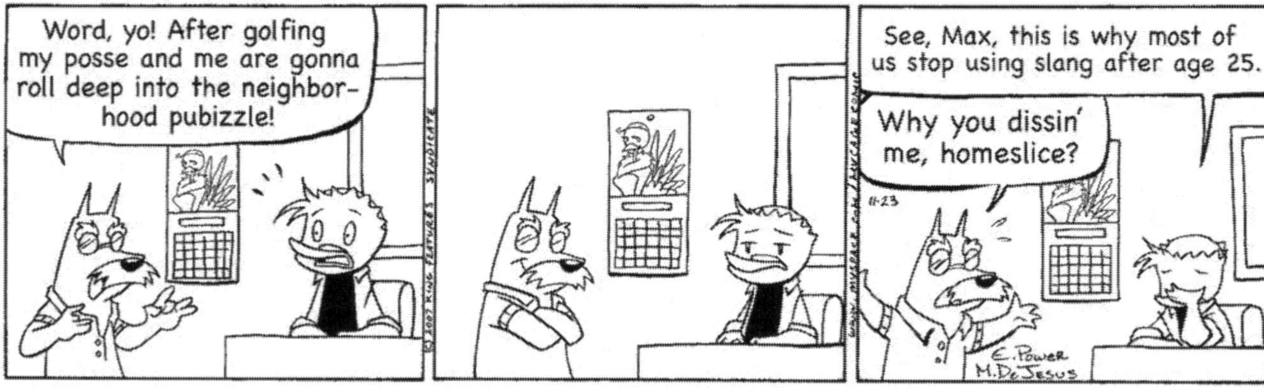
Word, yo! After golfing my posse and me are gonna roll deep into the neighborhood pubizzle!
See, Max, this is why most of us stop using slang after age 25.
Why you dissin' me, homeslice?
E. Power
M. DeJesus

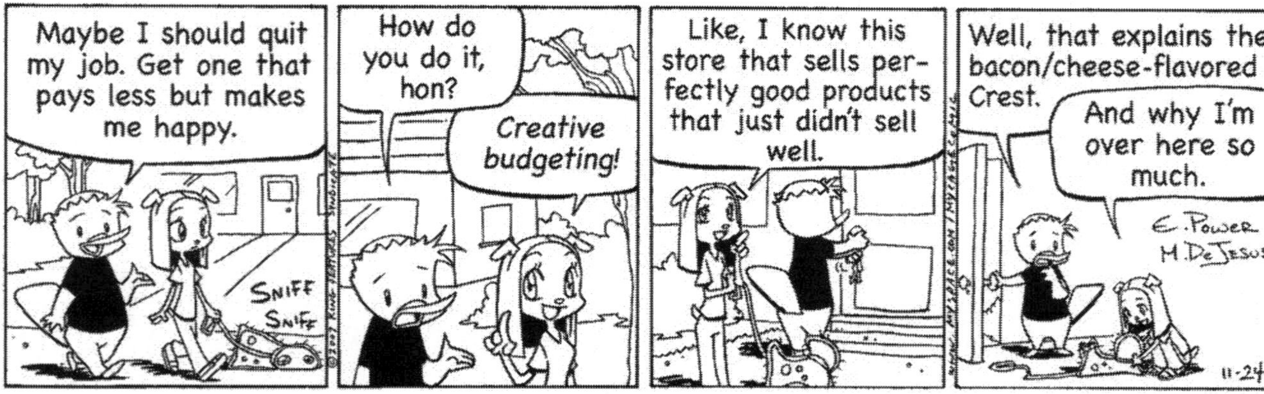
Maybe I should quit my job. Get one that pays less but makes me happy.
SNIFF
SNIFF
How do you do it, hon?
Creative budgeting!
Like, I know this store that sells perfectly good products that just didn't sell well.
Well, that explains the bacon/cheese-flavored Crest.
And why I'm over here so much.
E. Power
M. DeJesus

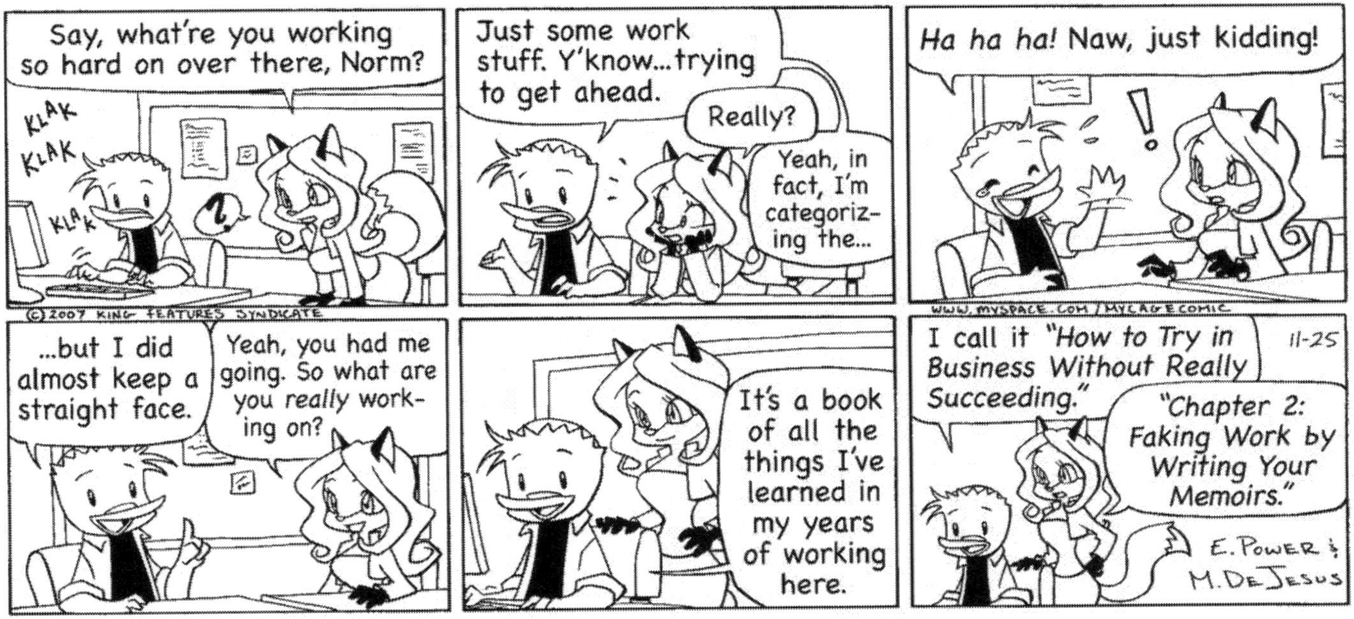

Say, what're you working so hard on over there, Norm?
KLAK KLAK KLAK
Just some work stuff. Y'know...trying to get ahead.
Really?
Yeah, in fact, I'm categoriz-ing the...
Ha ha ha! Naw, just kidding!
©2007 KING FEATURES SYNDICATE
WWW.MYSPACE.COM/MYCAGECOMIC
...but I did almost keep a straight face.
Yeah, you had me going. So what are you really work-ing on?
It's a book of all the things I've learned in my years of working here.
I call it "How to Try in Business Without Really Succeeding."
11-25
"Chapter 2: Faking Work by Writing Your Memoirs."
E. POWER & M. DEJESUS

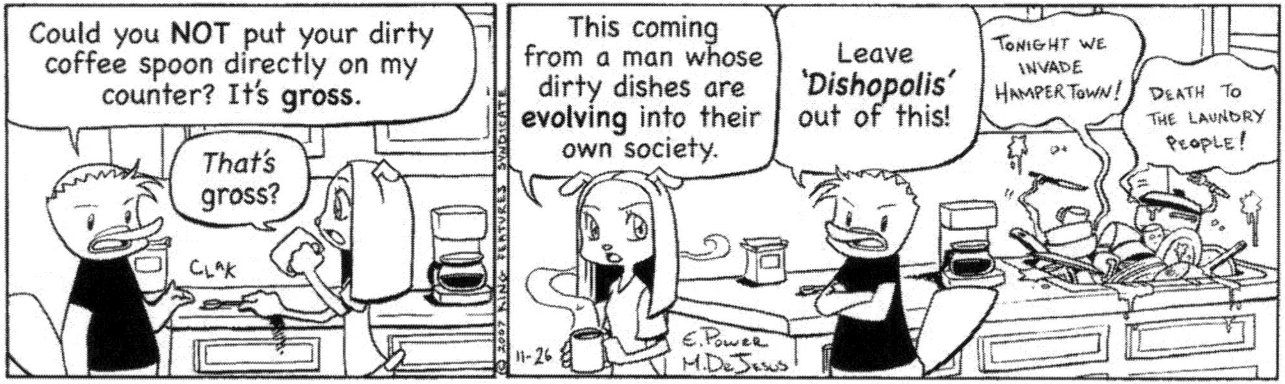
Could you **NOT** put your dirty coffee spoon directly on my counter? It's **gross**.
That's gross?
CLAK
© 2007 KING FEATURES SYNDICATE
11-26
E. Power
M. DeJesus
This coming from a man whose dirty dishes are **evolving** into their own society.
Leave ***'Dishopolis'*** out of this!
TONIGHT WE INVADE HAMPERTOWN!
DEATH TO THE LAUNDRY PEOPLE!

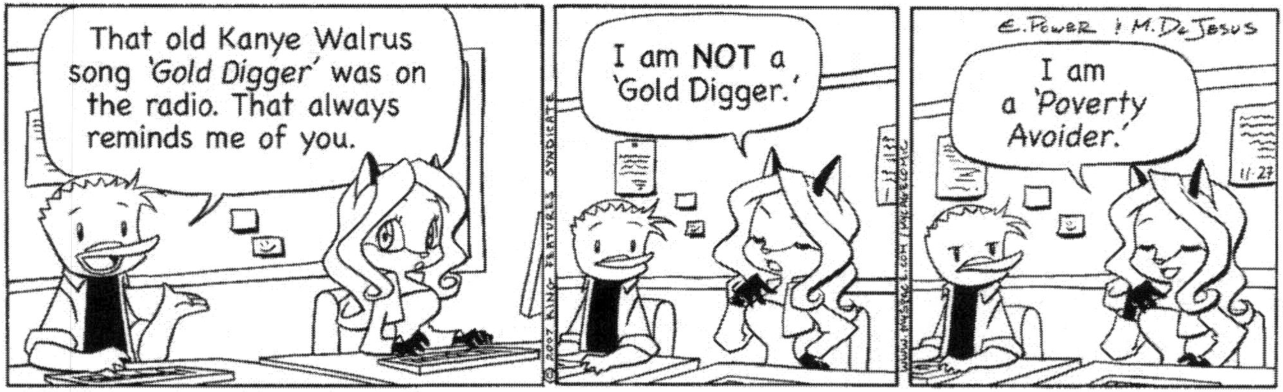
That old Kanye Walrus song *'Gold Digger'* was on the radio. That always reminds me of you.
© 2007 KING FEATURES SYNDICATE
I am **NOT** a 'Gold Digger.'
E. Power & M. DeJesus
I am a *'Poverty Avoider.'*
11-27

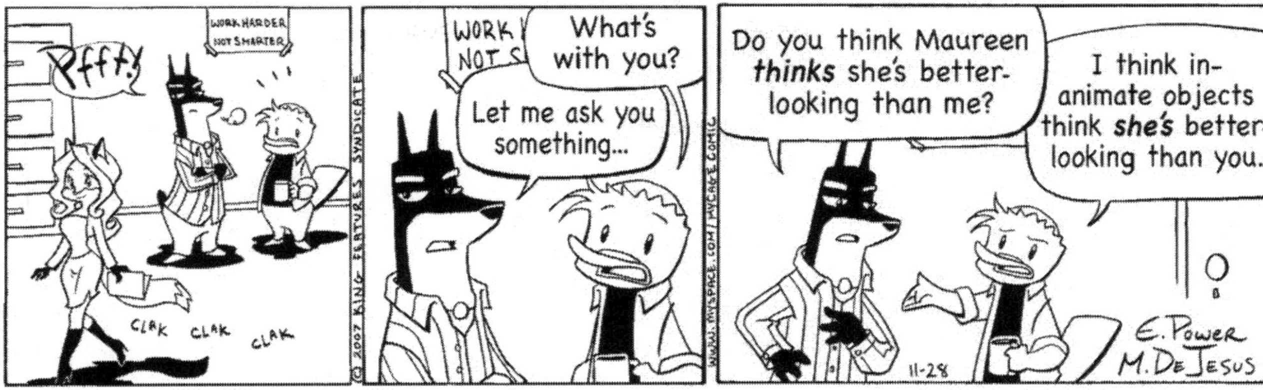
WORK HARDER NOT SMARTER
Pffft!
CLAK CLAK CLAK
© 2007 KING FEATURES SYNDICATE
What's with you?
Let me ask you something...
WWW.MYSPACE.COM/MYCAGECOMIC
Do you think Maureen **thinks** she's better-looking than me?
I think inanimate objects think ***she's*** better-looking than you.
11-28
E. Power
M. DeJesus

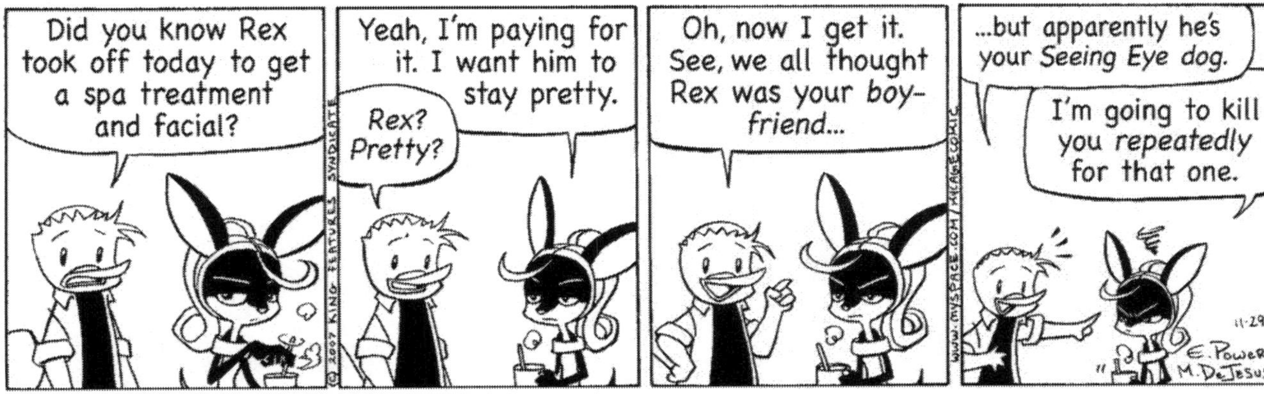
Did you know Rex took off today to get a spa treatment and facial?
© 2007 KING FEATURES SYNDICATE
Yeah, I'm paying for it. I want him to stay pretty.
Rex? Pretty?
WWW.MYSPACE.COM/MYCAGECOMIC
Oh, now I get it. See, we all thought Rex was your *boy-friend*...
...but apparently he's your *Seeing Eye dog.*
I'm going to kill you *repeatedly* for that one.
11-29
E. Power
M. DeJesus

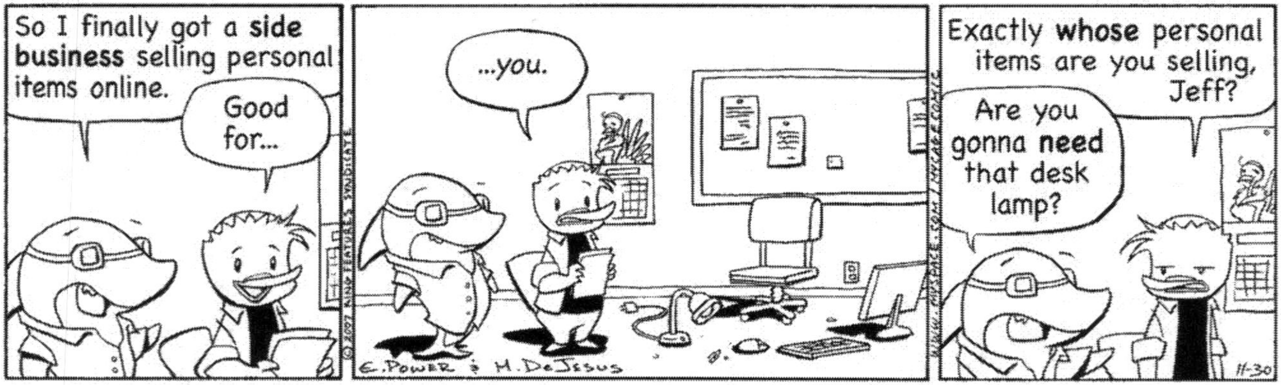
So I finally got a **side business** selling personal items online.
Good for...
...you.
Exactly **whose** personal items are you selling, Jeff?
Are you gonna **need** that desk lamp?
E. Power & M. DeJesus
11-30

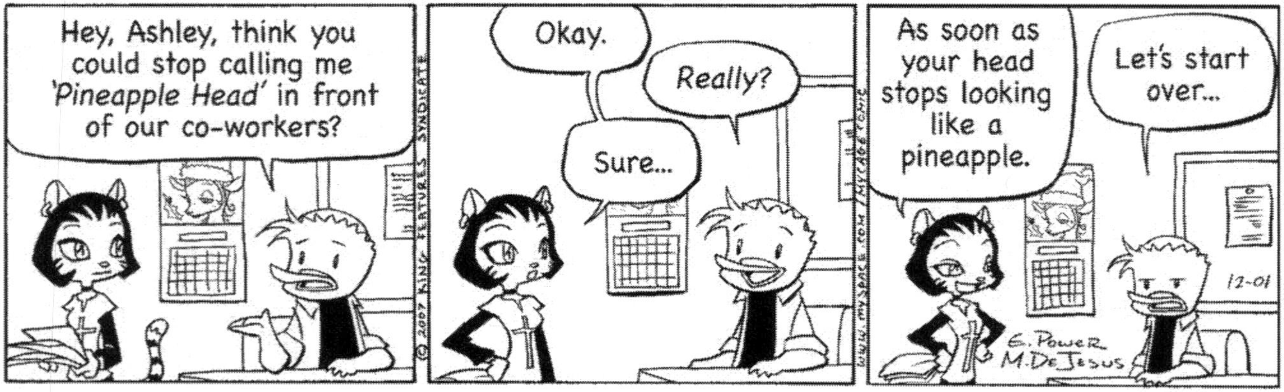
Hey, Ashley, think you could stop calling me *'Pineapple Head'* in front of our co-workers?
Okay.
Really?
Sure...
As soon as your head stops looking like a pineapple.
Let's start over...
E. Power
M. DeJesus
12-01

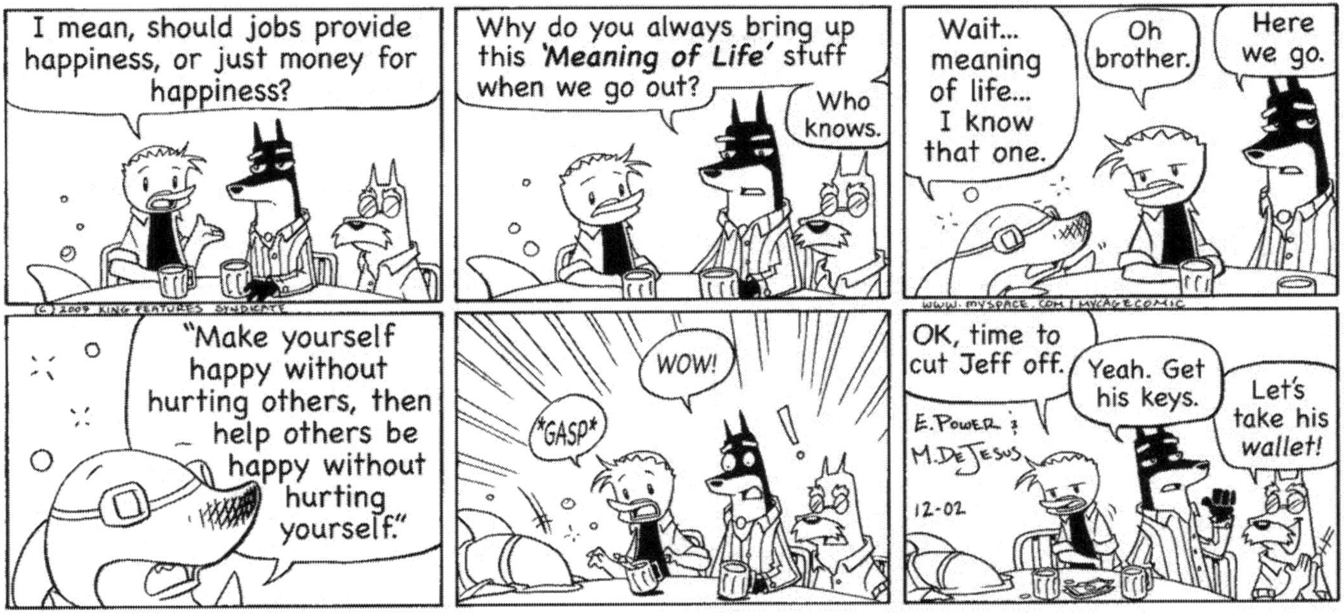
I mean, should jobs provide happiness, or just money for happiness?
(C) 2009 KING FEATURES SYNDICATE
Why do you always bring up this *'Meaning of Life'* stuff when we go out?
Who knows.
Wait... meaning of life... I know that one.
Oh brother.
Here we go.
WWW.MYSPACE.COM/MYCAGECOMIC
"Make yourself happy without hurting others, then help others be happy without hurting yourself."
GASP
WOW!
!
OK, time to cut Jeff off.
Yeah. Get his keys.
Let's take his *wallet!*
E. POWER & M. DEJESUS
12-02

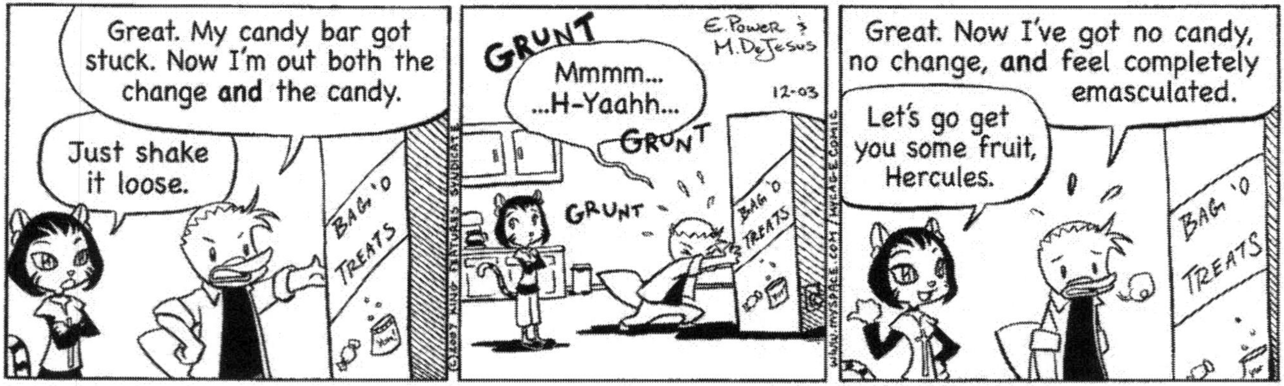
Great. My candy bar got stuck. Now I'm out both the change **and** the candy.
Just shake it loose.
BAG 'O TREATS
E. Power & M. DeJesus
12-03
GRUNT
Mmmm... ...H-Yaahh...
GRUNT
GRUNT
BAG 'O TREATS
©2007 KING FEATURES SYNDICATE
WWW.MYSPACE.COM/MYCAGECOMIC
Great. Now I've got no candy, no change, **and** feel completely emasculated.
Let's go get you some fruit, Hercules.
BAG 'O TREATS

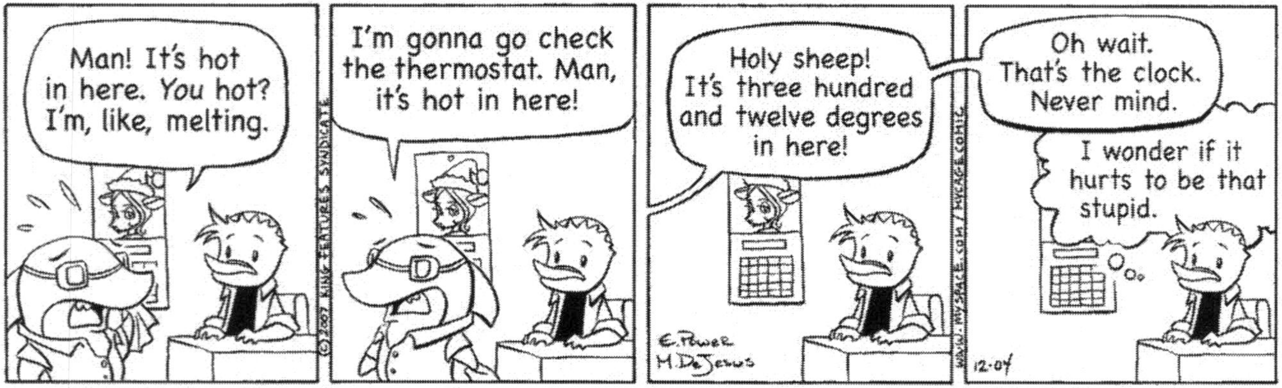
Man! It's hot in here. *You* hot? I'm, like, melting.
©2007 KING FEATURES SYNDICATE
I'm gonna go check the thermostat. Man, it's hot in here!
Holy sheep! It's three hundred and twelve degrees in here!
E. Power
M. DeJesus
WWW.MYSPACE.COM/MYCAGECOMIC
Oh wait. That's the clock. Never mind.
I wonder if it hurts to be that stupid.
12-04

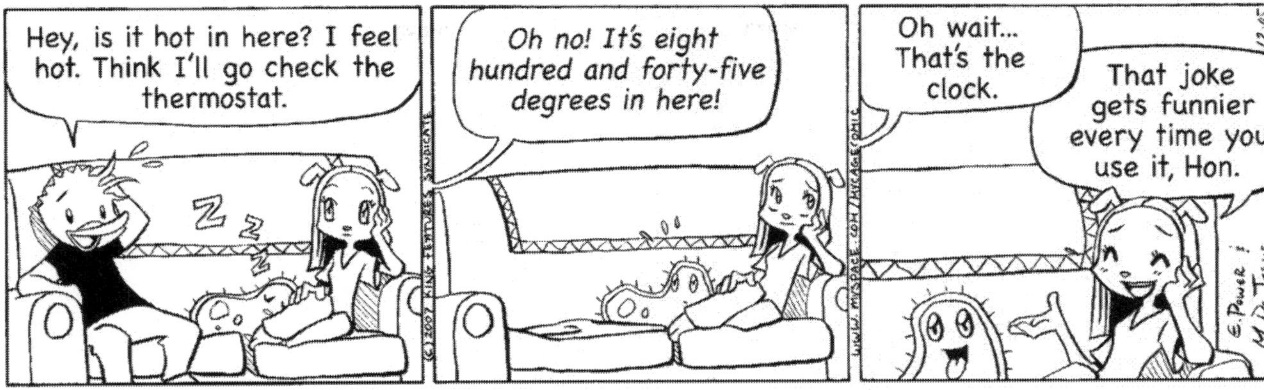
Hey, is it hot in here? I feel hot. Think I'll go check the thermostat.
Z Z Z
Oh no! It's eight hundred and forty-five degrees in here!
Oh wait... That's the clock.
That joke gets funnier every time you use it, Hon.
12-05
E. Power & M. DeJesus
© 2007 KING FEATURES SYNDICATE
WWW.MYSPACE.COM/MYCAGECOMIC

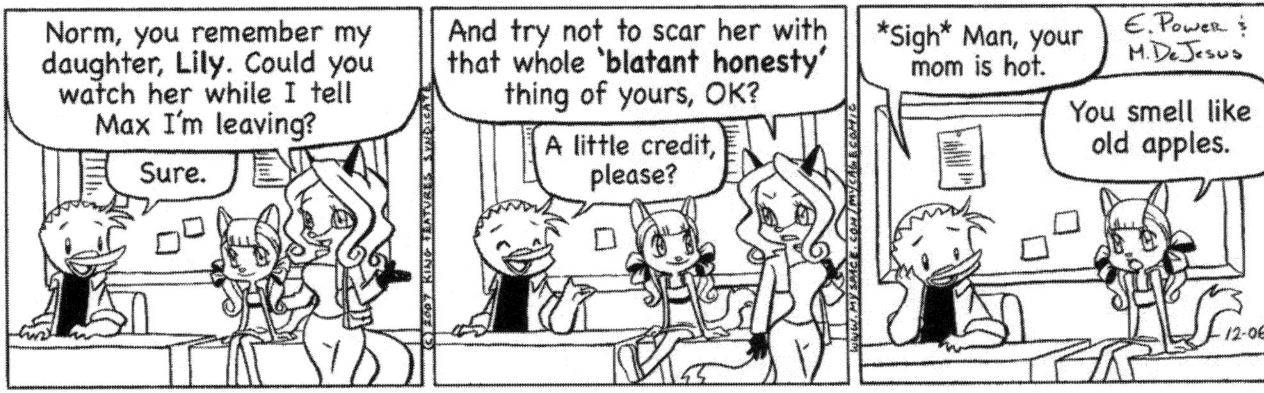
Norm, you remember my daughter, **Lily**. Could you watch her while I tell Max I'm leaving?
Sure.
And try not to scar her with that whole **'blatant honesty'** thing of yours, OK?
A little credit, please?
Sigh Man, your mom is hot.
You smell like old apples.
E. Power & M. DeJesus
12-06
© 2007 KING FEATURES SYNDICATE
WWW.MYSPACE.COM/MYCAGECOMIC

Max, look...The company sprung for a cake for your anniversary here. Congrats!

HAPPY ANNIVERSARY

Any chance a tiny girl is going to jump out of there?

Uh...no.

12-07

I'll be in my office.

HAPPY ANNIVERSARY

E. Power & M. DeJesus

Hey, Violet. You're back. How was yours and Rex's vacation?

How was it, Norm? HOW WAS IT!?

COPY

THE PLANE WAS DELAYED. OUR LUGGAGE WAS LOST. IT RAINED THE ENTIRE TRIP. WE BOTH GOT VERY SICK. REX LOST HIS WALLET W... A... MONEY... ...EN ...D AN A... ...TK! S... ...HAT ...E... EA... ...IT AND WE ...HREW 'T... ...IT IN A VO... ...NO. ZOMBIES AR... ...D.

E. Power
M. DeJesus

But... it was better than being here, right?

Oh yeah. Like, a bijillion times better.

COPY

12-08

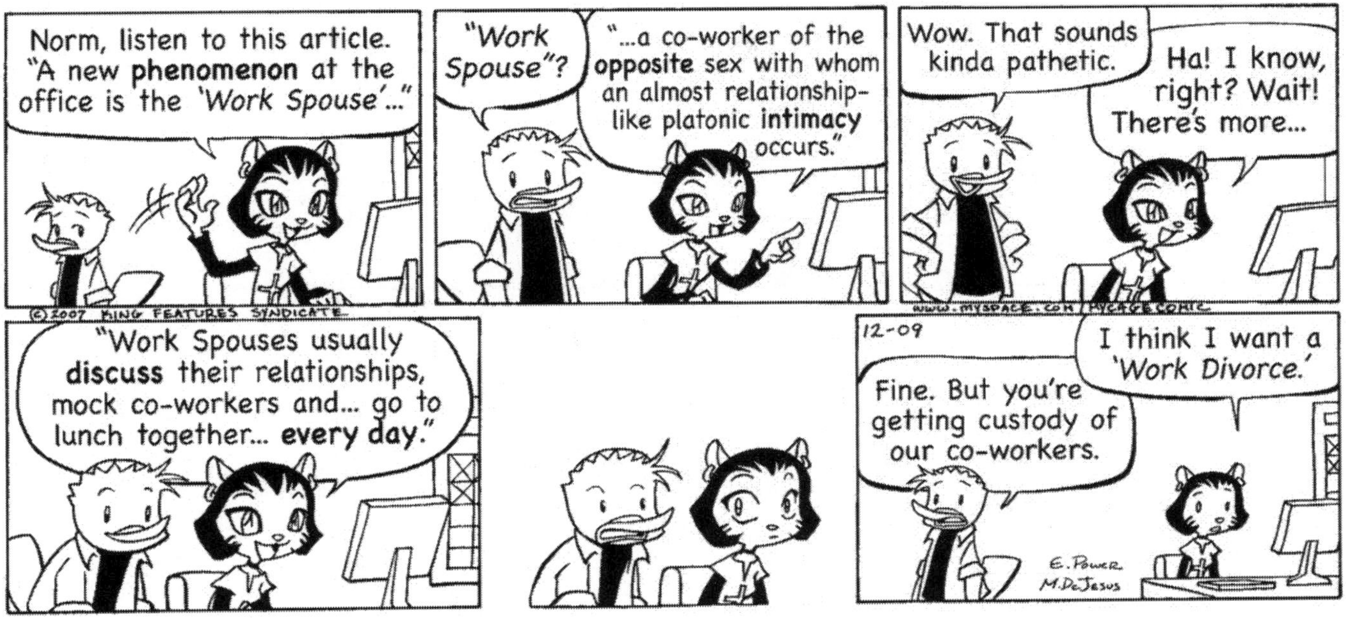
Norm, listen to this article. "A new **phenomenon** at the office is the '*Work Spouse*'..."
"*Work Spouse*"?
"...a co-worker of the **opposite** sex with whom an almost relationship-like platonic **intimacy** occurs."
Wow. That sounds kinda pathetic.
Ha! I know, right? Wait! There's more...
"Work Spouses usually **discuss** their relationships, mock co-workers and... go to lunch together... **every day**."
I think I want a '*Work Divorce*.'
Fine. But you're getting custody of our co-workers.
©2007 KING FEATURES SYNDICATE
WWW.MYSPACE.COM/MYCAGECOMIC
12-09
E. POWER
M. DeJESUS

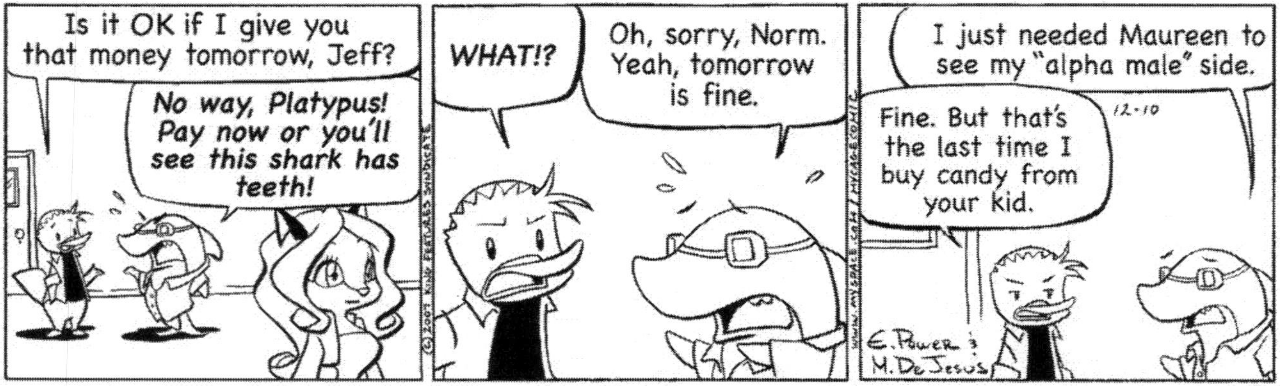
Is it OK if I give you that money tomorrow, Jeff?
No way, Platypus! Pay now or you'll see this shark has teeth!
WHAT!?
Oh, sorry, Norm. Yeah, tomorrow is fine.
I just needed Maureen to see my "alpha male" side.
Fine. But that's the last time I buy candy from your kid.
12-10
E. Power & M. DeJesus

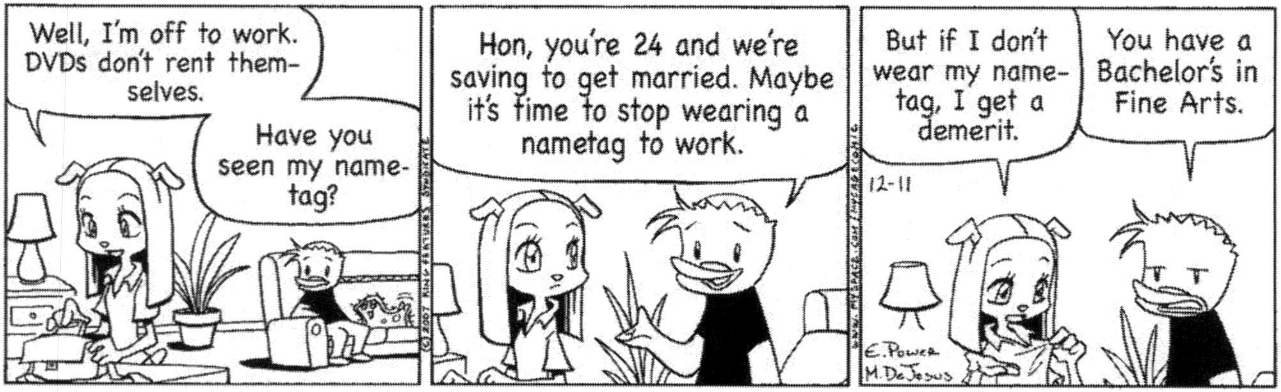
Well, I'm off to work. DVDs don't rent themselves.
Have you seen my nametag?
Hon, you're 24 and we're saving to get married. Maybe it's time to stop wearing a nametag to work.
12-11
But if I don't wear my nametag, I get a demerit.
You have a Bachelor's in Fine Arts.
E. Power
M. DeJesus

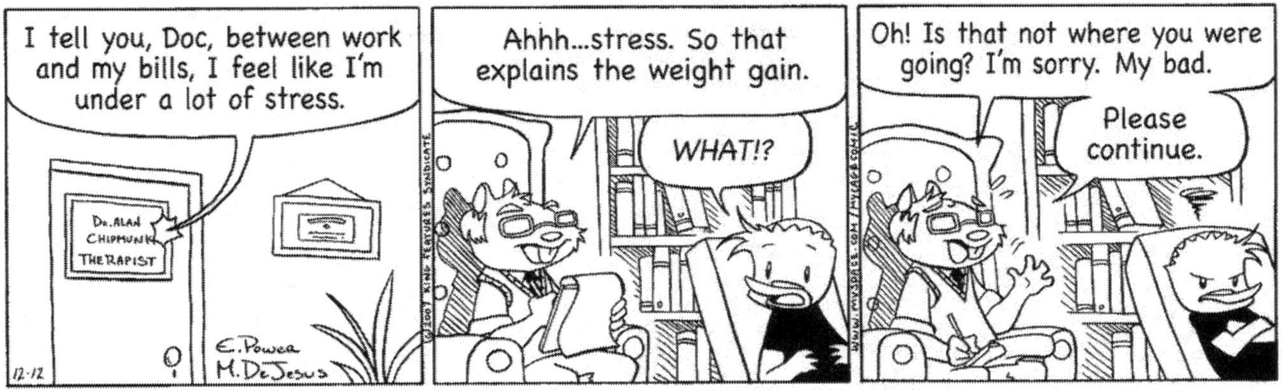
I tell you, Doc, between work and my bills, I feel like I'm under a lot of stress.
Dr. ALAN CHIPMUNK THERAPIST
E. Power
M. DeJesus
12-12
Ahhh...stress. So that explains the weight gain.
WHAT!?
Oh! Is that not where you were going? I'm sorry. My bad.
Please continue.

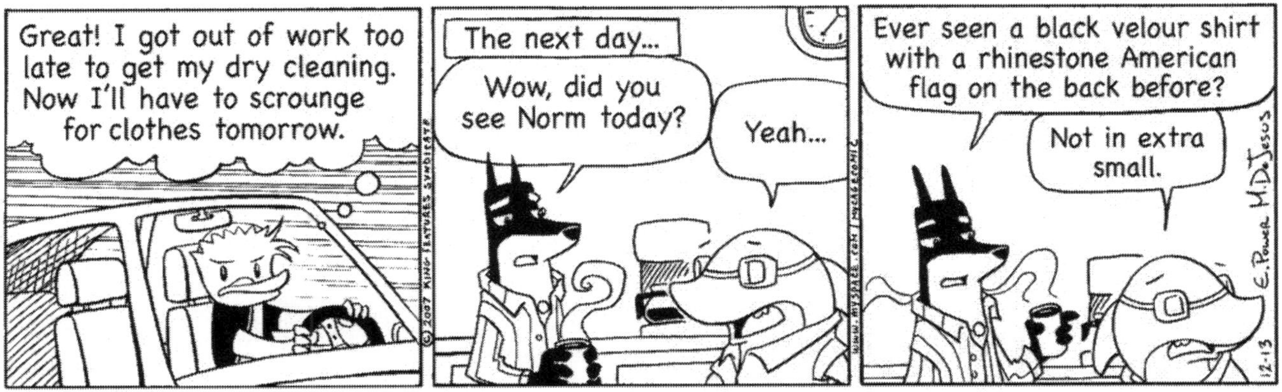
Great! I got out of work too late to get my dry cleaning. Now I'll have to scrounge for clothes tomorrow.
The next day...
Wow, did you see Norm today?
Yeah...
Ever seen a black velour shirt with a rhinestone American flag on the back before?
Not in extra small.
E. Power M. DeJesus
12-13

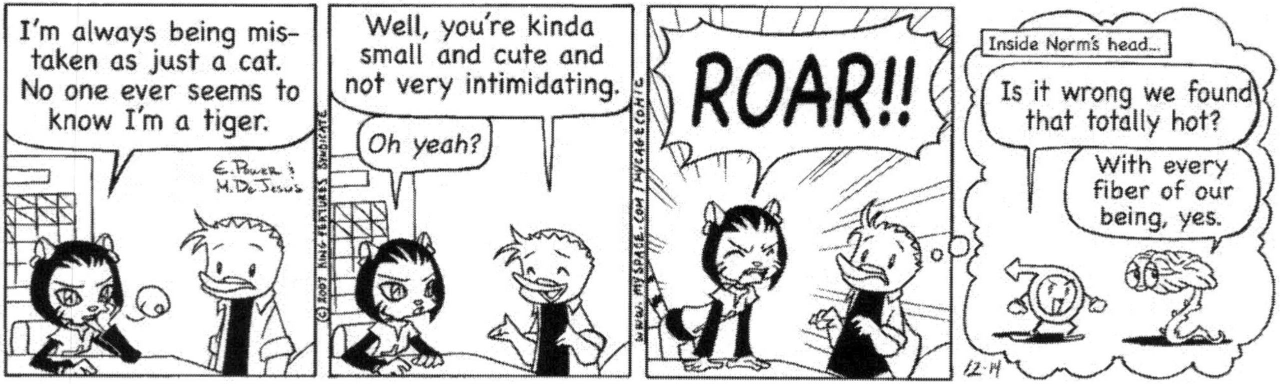
I'm always being mistaken as just a cat. No one ever seems to know I'm a tiger.
E. Power & M. DeJesus
Well, you're kinda small and cute and not very intimidating.
Oh yeah?
© 2007 King Features Syndicate
www.myspace.com/mycagecomic
ROAR!!
Inside Norm's head...
Is it wrong we found that totally hot?
With every fiber of our being, yes.
12-14

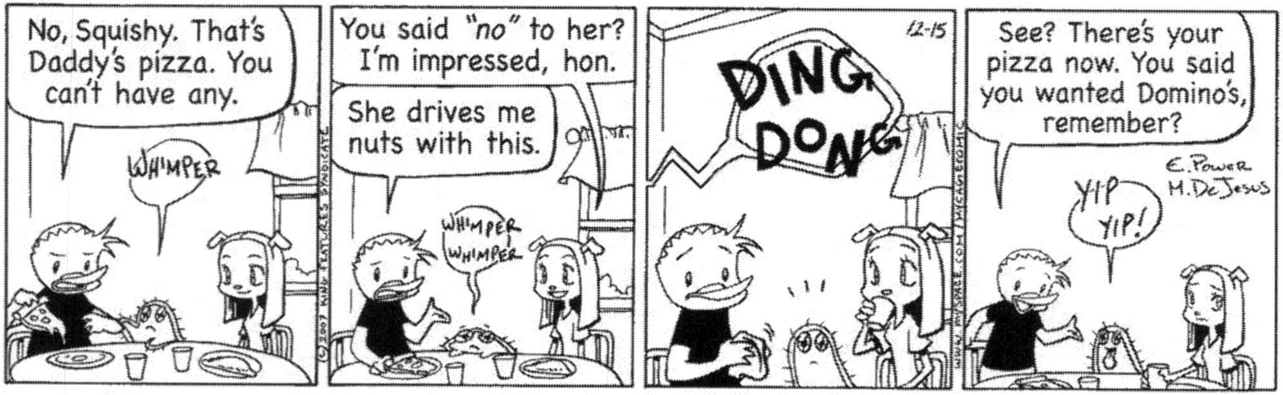
No, Squishy. That's Daddy's pizza. You can't have any.
WHIMPER
You said "no" to her? I'm impressed, hon.
She drives me nuts with this.
WHIMPER WHIMPER
© 2007 King Features Syndicate
12-15
DING DONG
www.myspace.com/mycagecomic
See? There's your pizza now. You said you wanted Domino's, remember?
E. Power M. DeJesus
YIP YIP!

I'm a huge fan of both **Vince Prawn** and **Paul Giamanatee**. I just haven't seen it ye...Let me call you back.
So, still **shamelessly** flirting with Ashley, huh?
Oh please.
CLAK
You think I try to flirt with **every** female friend I have. Why is that?
Name **one** female friend you have who isn't attractive.
Your heart is dark as night and twice as cold, does **that** count?
I mean physically, and quit trying to flatter me.
© 2007 KING FEATURES SYNDICATE
WWW.MYSPACE.COM/MYCAGECOMIC
E. POWER
M. DEJESUS
12-16

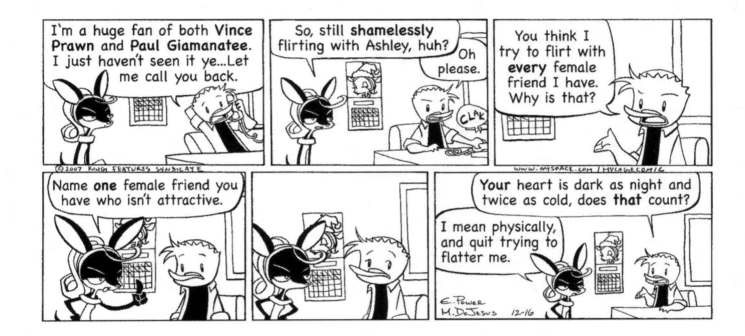

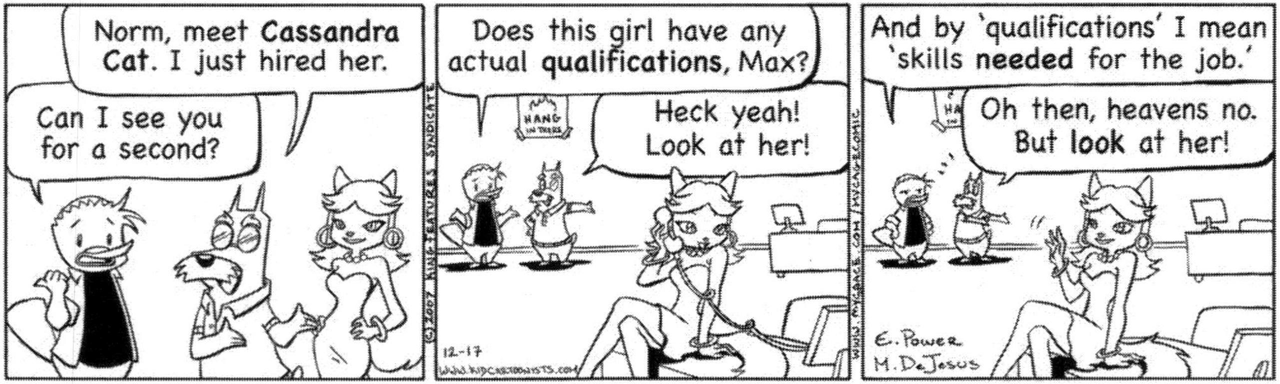
Norm, meet **Cassandra Cat**. I just hired her.
Can I see you for a second?
Does this girl have any actual **qualifications**, Max?
Heck yeah! Look at her!
HANG IN THERE
And by 'qualifications' I mean 'skills **needed** for the job.'
Oh then, heavens no. But **look** at her!
©2007 KING FEATURES SYNDICATE
12-17
WWW.KIDCARTOONISTS.COM
WWW.MYSPACE.COM/MYCAGECOMIC
E. Power
M. DeJesus

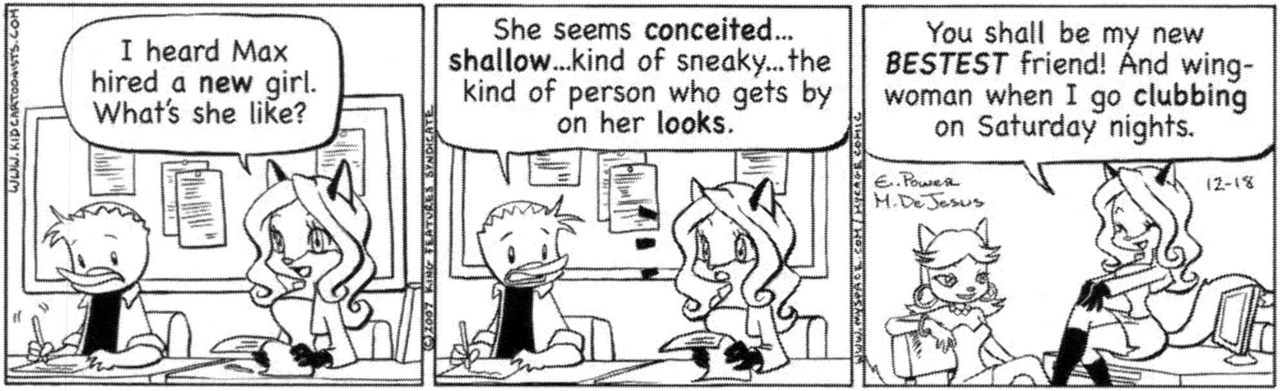
WWW.KIDCARTOONISTS.COM
I heard Max hired a **new** girl. What's she like?
She seems **conceited**... **shallow**...kind of sneaky...the kind of person who gets by on her **looks**.
©2007 KING FEATURES SYNDICATE
You shall be my new ***BESTEST*** friend! And wing-woman when I go **clubbing** on Saturday nights.
E. Power
M. DeJesus
12-18
WWW.MYSPACE.COM/MYCAGECOMIC

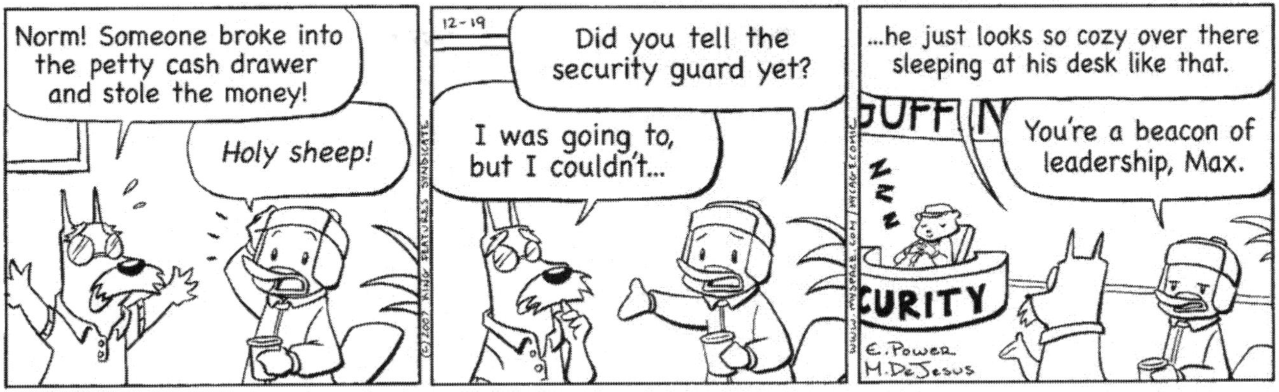
12-19
Norm! Someone broke into the petty cash drawer and stole the money!
Holy sheep!
Did you tell the security guard yet?
I was going to, but I couldn't...
...he just looks so cozy over there sleeping at his desk like that.
You're a beacon of leadership, Max.
(c) 2007 KING FEATURES SYNDICATE
WWW.MYSPACE.COM/MICAGECOMIC
E. POWER
M. DeJESUS

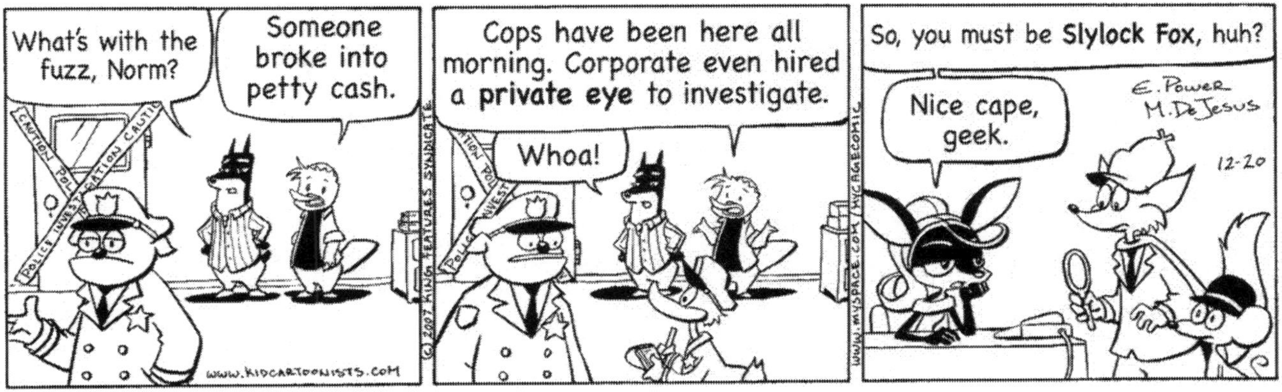
What's with the fuzz, Norm?
Someone broke into petty cash.
WWW.KIDCARTOONISTS.COM
Cops have been here all morning. Corporate even hired a **private eye** to investigate.
Whoa!
(c) 2007 KING FEATURES SYNDICATE
WWW.MYSPACE.COM/MICAGECOMIC
So, you must be **Slylock Fox**, huh?
Nice cape, geek.
E. POWER
M. DeJESUS
12-20

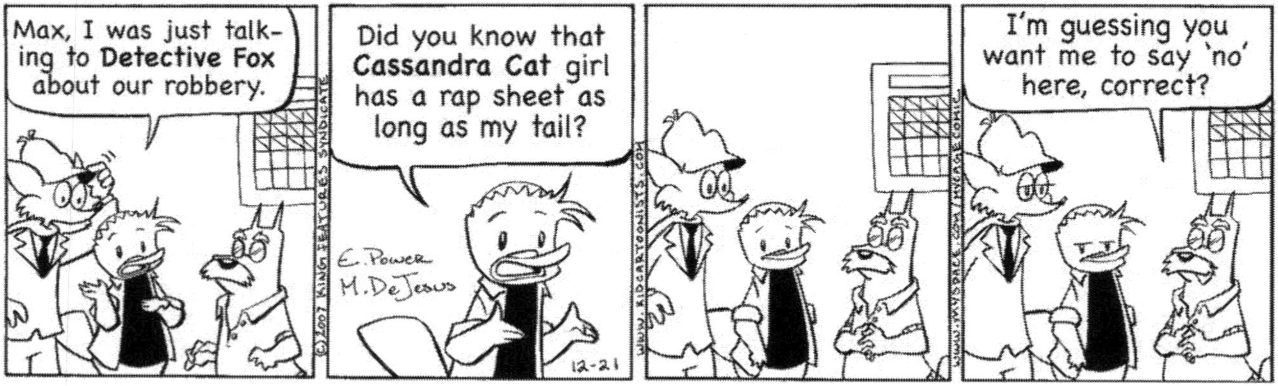

Max, I was just talk-ing to **Detective Fox** about our robbery.
Did you know that **Cassandra Cat** girl has a rap sheet as long as my tail?
I'm guessing you want me to say 'no' here, correct?
E. Power
M. DeJesus
12-21

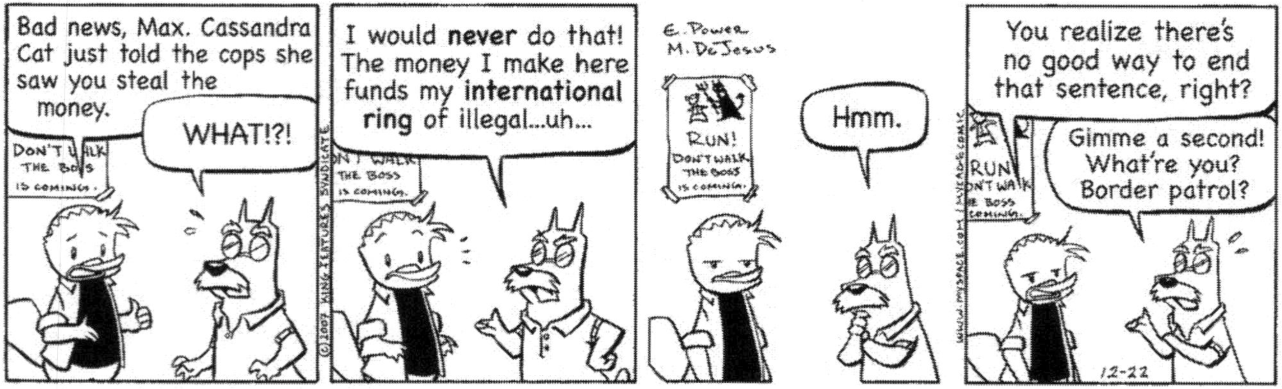

Bad news, Max. Cassandra Cat just told the cops she saw you steal the money.
WHAT!?!
I would **never** do that! The money I make here funds my **international ring** of illegal...uh...
Hmm.
You realize there's no good way to end that sentence, right?
Gimme a second! What're you? Border patrol?
RUN!
DON'T WALK
THE BOSS IS COMING.
E. Power
M. DeJesus
12-22

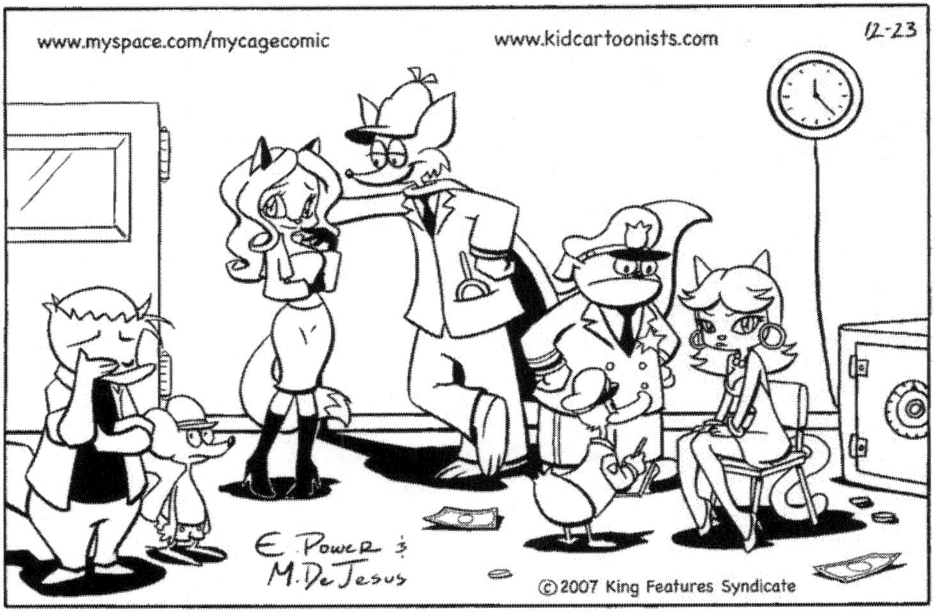

www.myspace.com/mycagecomic
www.kidcartoonists.com
12-23
E. Power & M. DeJesus
©2007 King Features Syndicate

After getting Cassandra Cat to confess to stealing McGuffin Inc.'s money, Slylock Fox sticks around to hit on Maureen. Why is Norm convinced Slylock is doomed to fail?

Solution - The average income of a private eye is $40,000 a year. Maureen requires at least twice that amount for Slylock to even get her secondary email address. (The cape ain't helping either.)

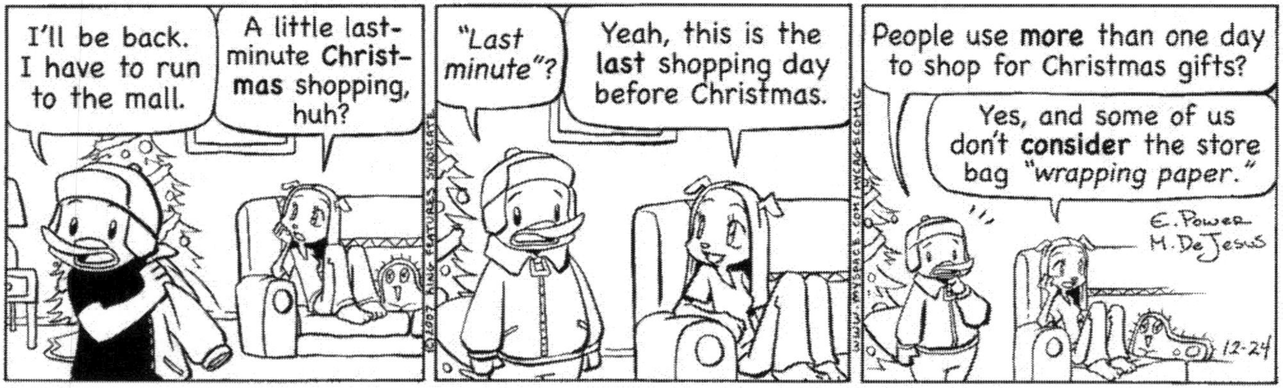
I'll be back. I have to run to the mall.
A little last-minute **Christmas** shopping, huh?
"Last minute"?
Yeah, this is the **last** shopping day before Christmas.
People use **more** than one day to shop for Christmas gifts?
Yes, and some of us don't **consider** the store bag *"wrapping paper."*
E. Power
M. DeJesus
12-24

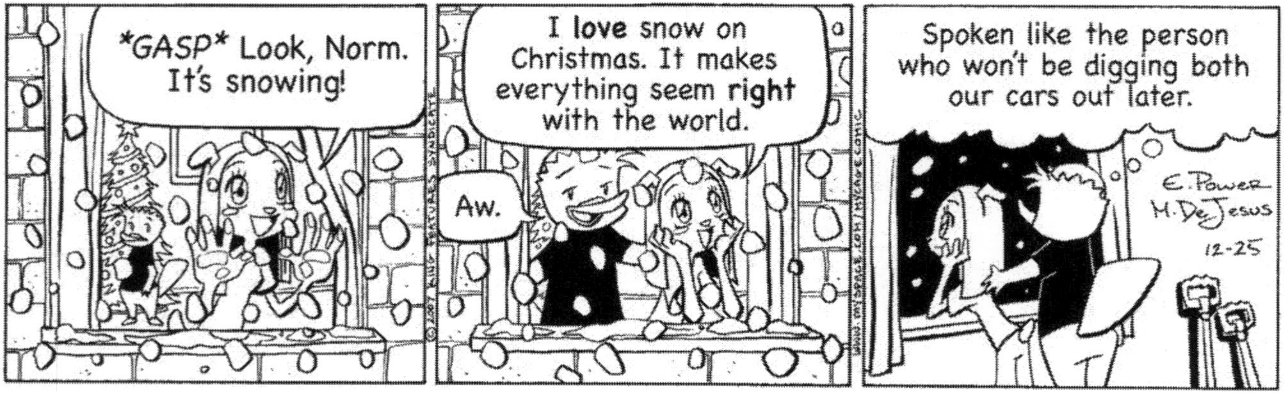
GASP Look, Norm. It's snowing!
I **love** snow on Christmas. It makes everything seem **right** with the world.
Aw.
Spoken like the person who won't be digging both our cars out later.
E. Power
M. DeJesus
12-25

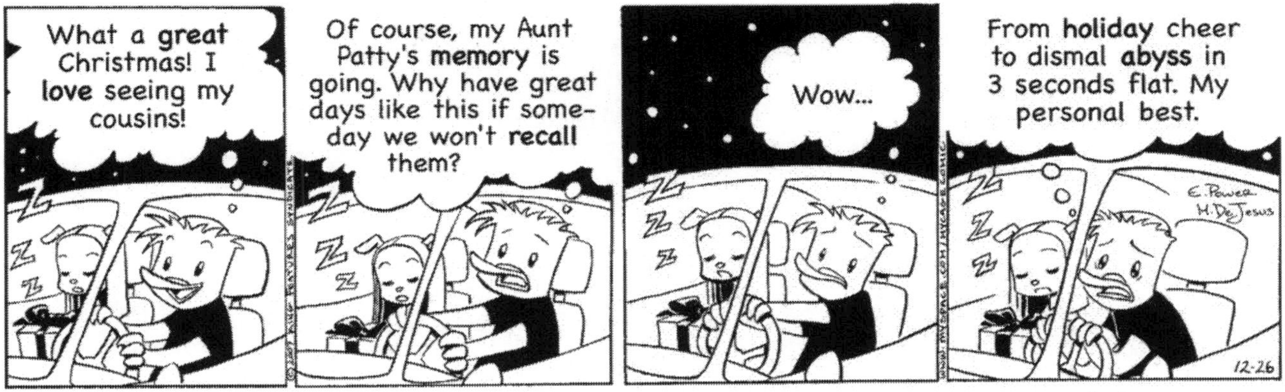
What a **great** Christmas! I **love** seeing my cousins!
Of course, my Aunt Patty's **memory** is going. Why have great days like this if someday we won't **recall** them?
Wow...
From **holiday** cheer to dismal **abyss** in 3 seconds flat. My personal best.
E. Power
M. DeJesus
12-26

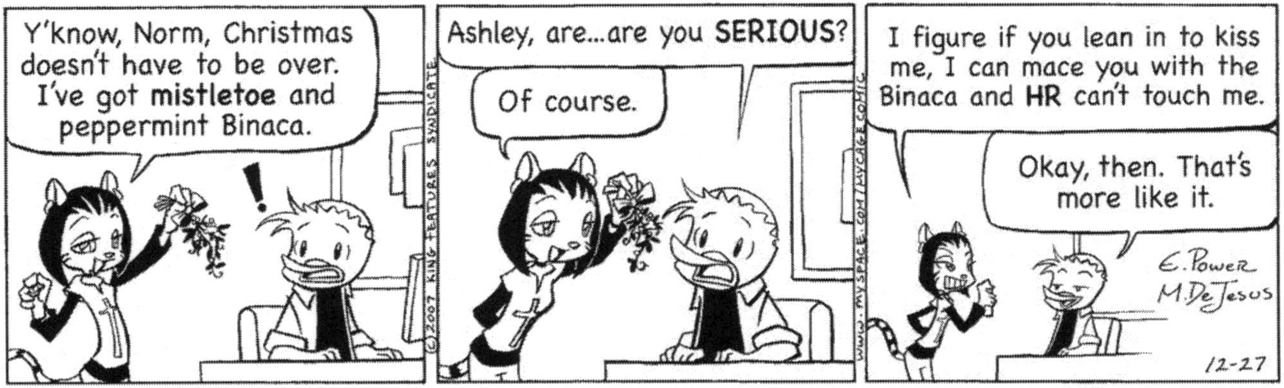
Y'know, Norm, Christmas doesn't have to be over. I've got **mistletoe** and peppermint Binaca.
!
Ashley, are...are you **SERIOUS**?
Of course.
I figure if you lean in to kiss me, I can mace you with the Binaca and **HR** can't touch me.
Okay, then. That's more like it.
E. Power
M. DeJesus
12-27
©2007 KING FEATURES SYNDICATE
WWW.MYSPACE.COM/MYCAGECOMIC

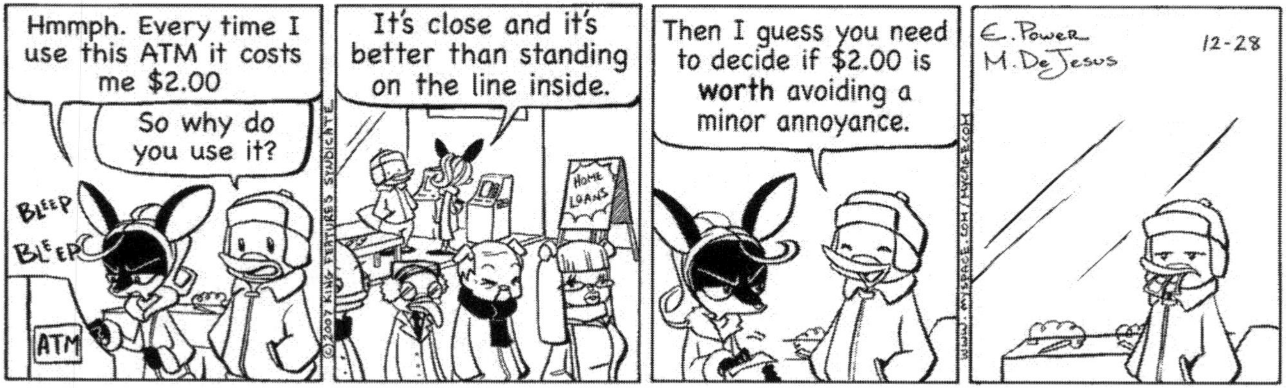
Hmmph. Every time I use this ATM it costs me $2.00
So why do you use it?
BLEEP
BLEEP
ATM
©2007 KING FEATURES SYNDICATE
It's close and it's better than standing on the line inside.
HOME LOANS
Then I guess you need to decide if $2.00 is **worth** avoiding a minor annoyance.
E. Power
M. DeJesus
12-28

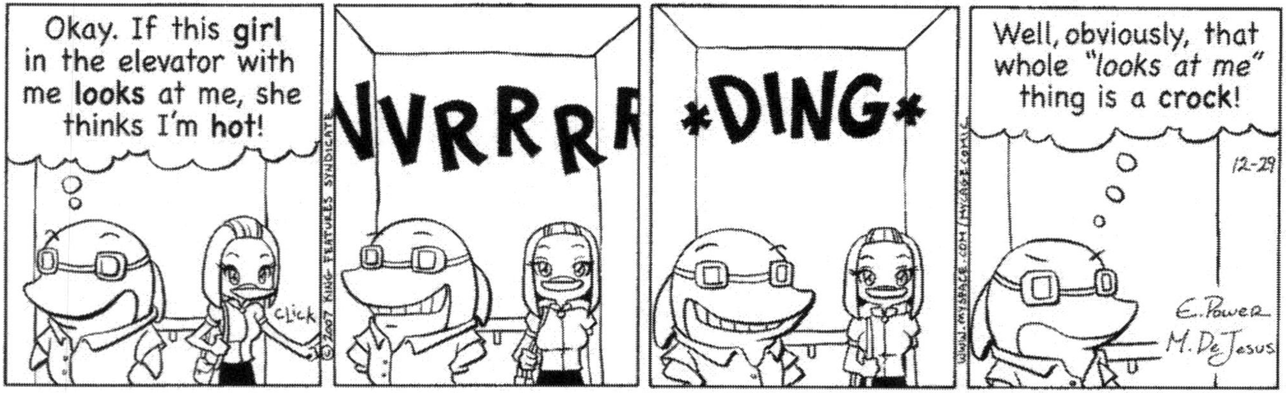
Okay. If this **girl** in the elevator with me **looks** at me, she thinks I'm **hot**!
CLICK
©2007 KING FEATURES SYNDICATE
NVRRRRR
DING
Well, obviously, that whole *"looks at me"* thing is a **crock**!
12-29
E. Power
M. DeJesus

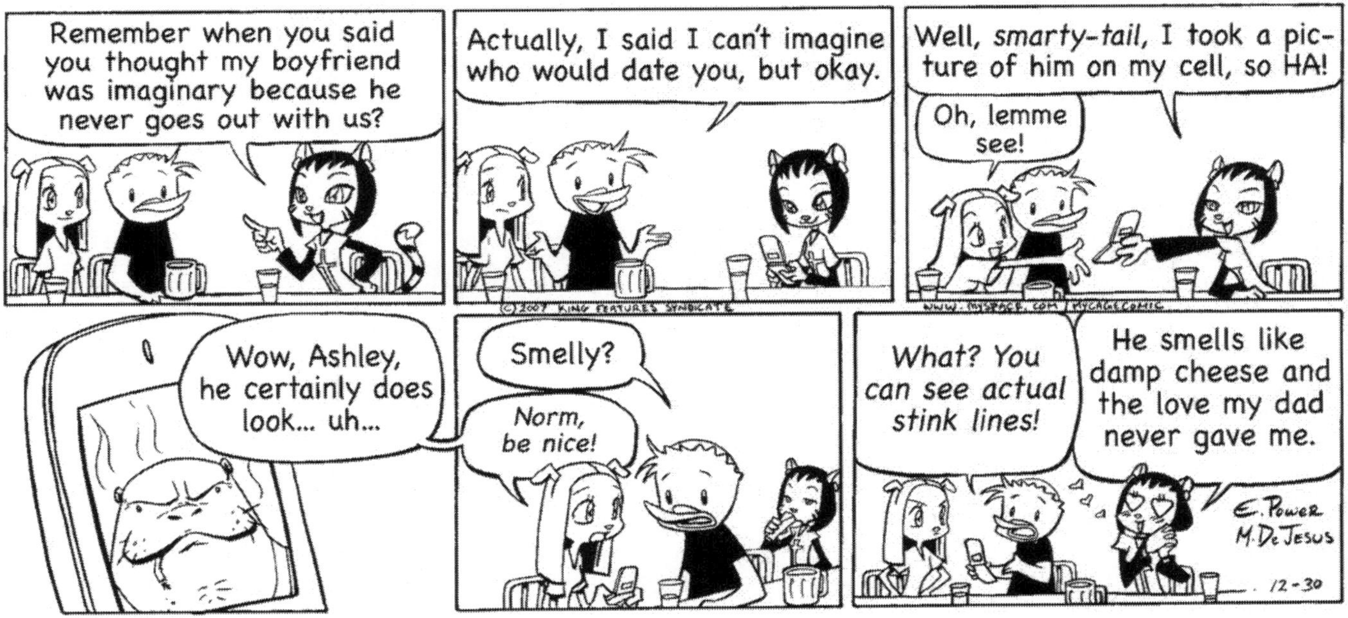
Remember when you said you thought my boyfriend was imaginary because he never goes out with us?
Actually, I said I can't imagine who would date you, but okay.
© 2007 KING FEATURES SYNDICATE
Well, *smarty-tail*, I took a picture of him on my cell, so HA!
Oh, lemme see!
WWW.MYSPACE.COM/MYCAGECOMIC
Wow, Ashley, he certainly does look... uh...
Smelly?
Norm, be nice!
What? You can see actual stink lines!
He smells like damp cheese and the love my dad never gave me.
E. Power
M. DeJesus
12-30

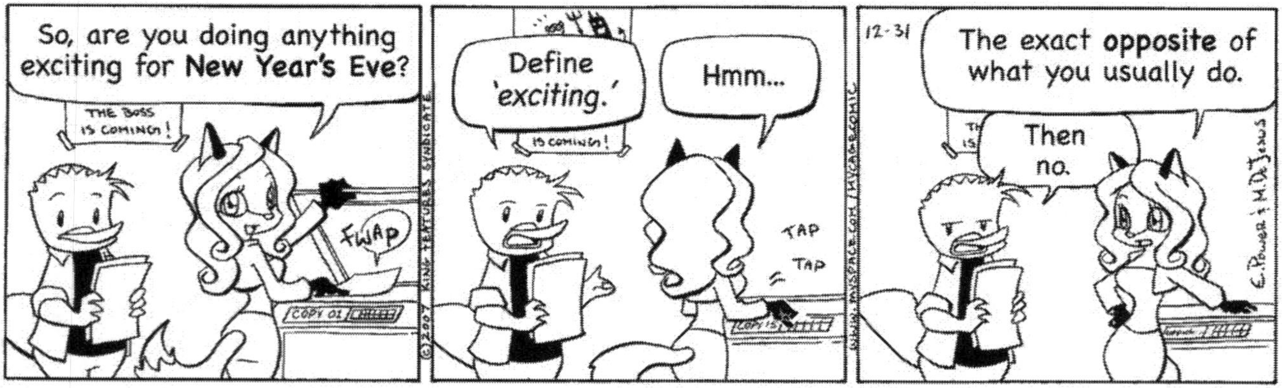
So, are you doing anything exciting for **New Year's Eve**?
THE BOSS IS COMING!
FWAP
COPY 01
©2007 KING FEATURES SYNDICATE
Define *'exciting.'*
Hmm...
TAP
TAP
WWW.MYSPACE.COM/MYCAGECOMIC
12-31
The exact **opposite** of what you usually do.
Then no.
E. Power & M. DeJesus

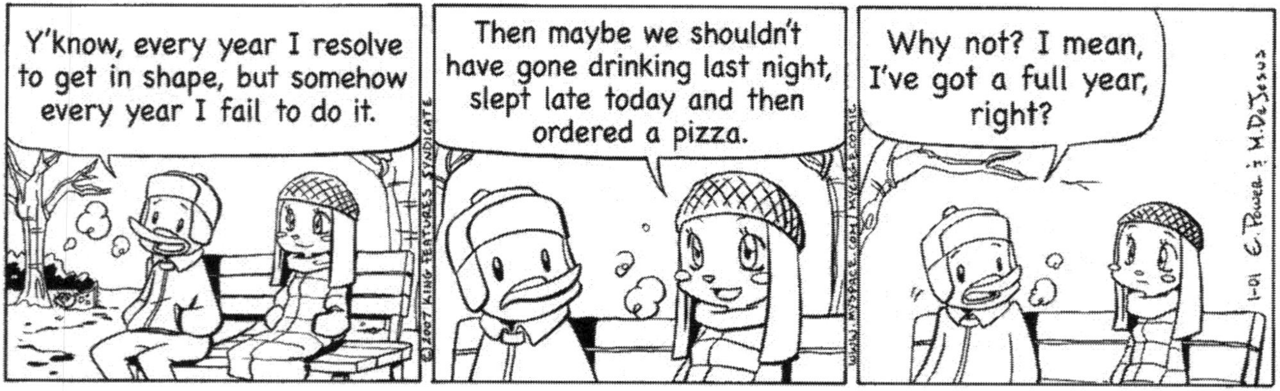
Y'know, every year I resolve to get in shape, but somehow every year I fail to do it.
©2007 KING FEATURES SYNDICATE
Then maybe we shouldn't have gone drinking last night, slept late today and then ordered a pizza.
WWW.MYSPACE.COM/MYCAGECOMIC
Why not? I mean, I've got a full year, right?
1-01
E. Power & M. DeJesus

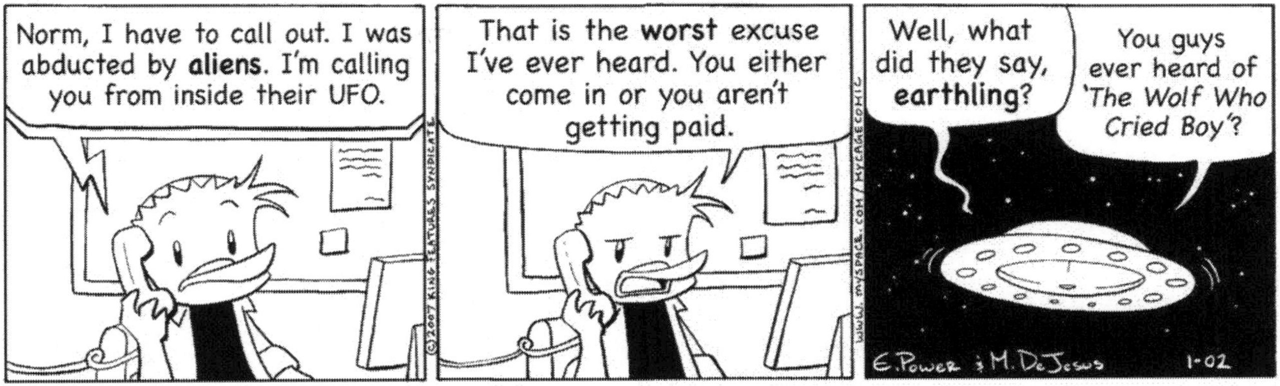
Norm, I have to call out. I was abducted by **aliens**. I'm calling you from inside their UFO.
©2007 KING FEATURES SYNDICATE
That is the **worst** excuse I've ever heard. You either come in or you aren't getting paid.
WWW.MYSPACE.COM/MYCAGECOMIC
Well, what did they say, **earthling**?
You guys ever heard of *'The Wolf Who Cried Boy'*?
E. Power & M. DeJesus
1-02

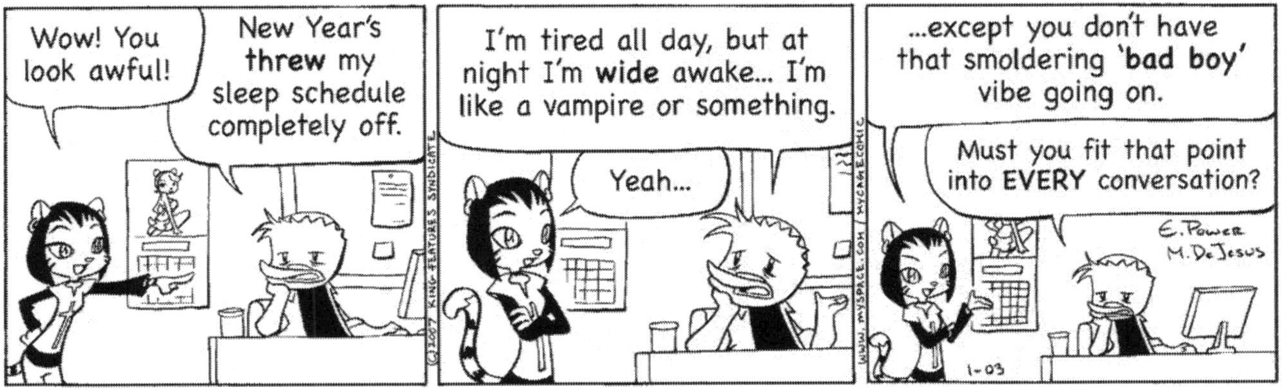
Wow! You look awful!
New Year's **threw** my sleep schedule completely off.
©2007 KING FEATURES SYNDICATE
I'm tired all day, but at night I'm **wide** awake... I'm like a vampire or something.
Yeah...
WWW.MYSPACE.COM/MYCAGECOMIC
...except you don't have that smoldering **'bad boy'** vibe going on.
Must you fit that point into **EVERY** conversation?
E. Power
M. DeJesus
1-03

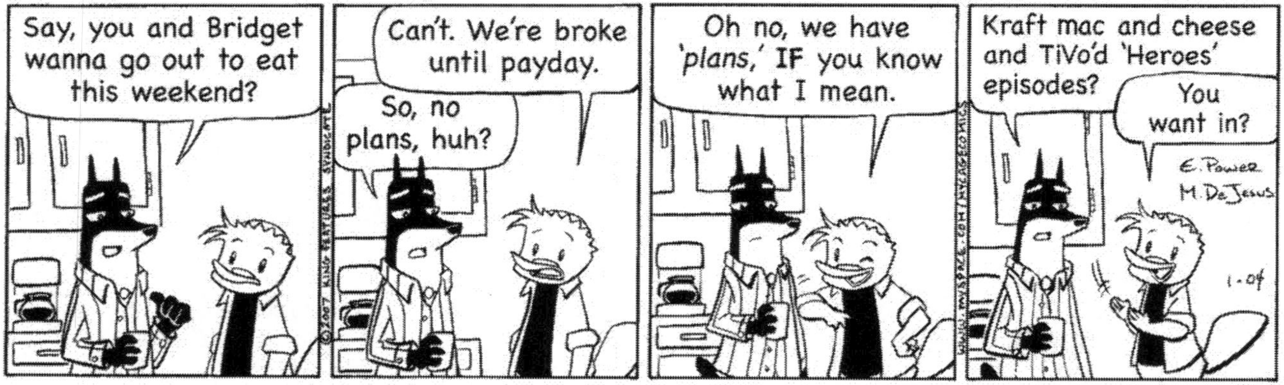
Say, you and Bridget wanna go out to eat this weekend?
Can't. We're broke until payday.
So, no plans, huh?
Oh no, we have *'plans,'* **IF** you know what I mean.
Kraft mac and cheese and TiVo'd 'Heroes' episodes?
You want in?
E. Power
M. DeJesus
1-04
© 2007 KING FEATURES SYNDICATE

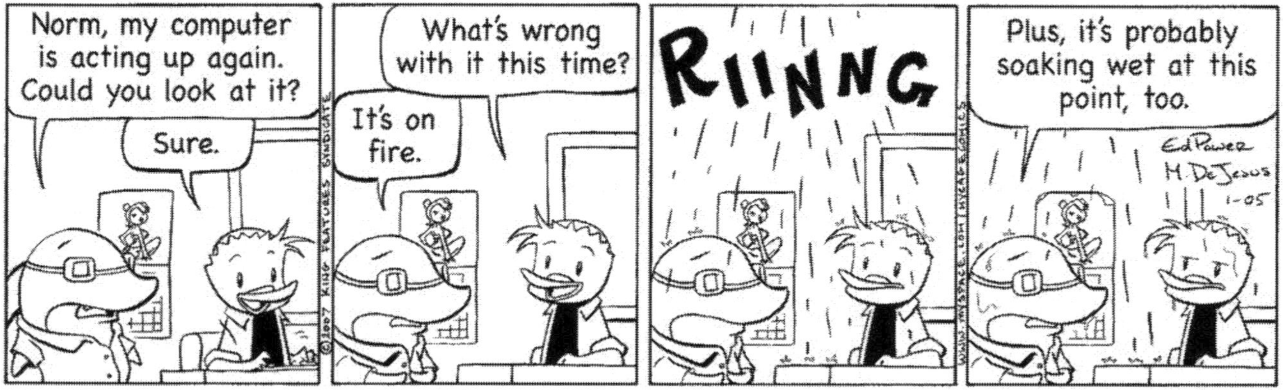
Norm, my computer is acting up again. Could you look at it?
Sure.
What's wrong with it this time?
It's on fire.
RIINNG
Plus, it's probably soaking wet at this point, too.
Ed Power
M. DeJesus
1-05
© 2007 KING FEATURES SYNDICATE

I've had it, Max! I'm done! No more covering for you with your wife or your boss!
© 2008 KING FEATURES SYNDICATE
Please. My wife is too sweet for you to tell her the truth about me, and Lenny thinks I run things here.
Meanwhile, I let you run the place however you want and pay you great, because I can't afford to lose you.
E. Power
M. DeJesus
1-6
WWW.MYSPACE.COM/MYCAGECOMIC
In a few years, I'll retire, tell Lenny the truth, you'll get my job, and you and Bridget will be set for life.
I like you, Norm. Stop being a yutz.
I think I sold my soul to a devil in tan Dockers for health care and a 401(k).
Pfft! At least you're manage-ment.

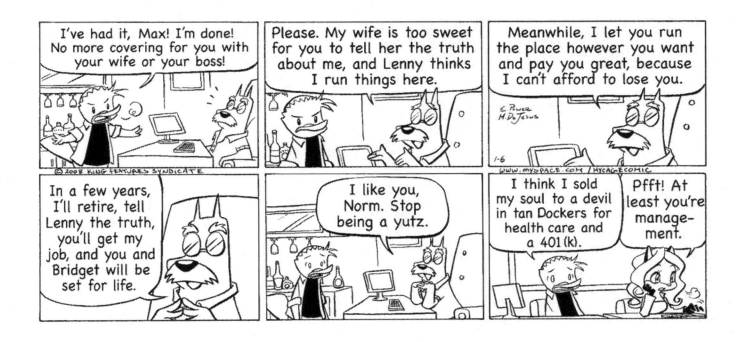

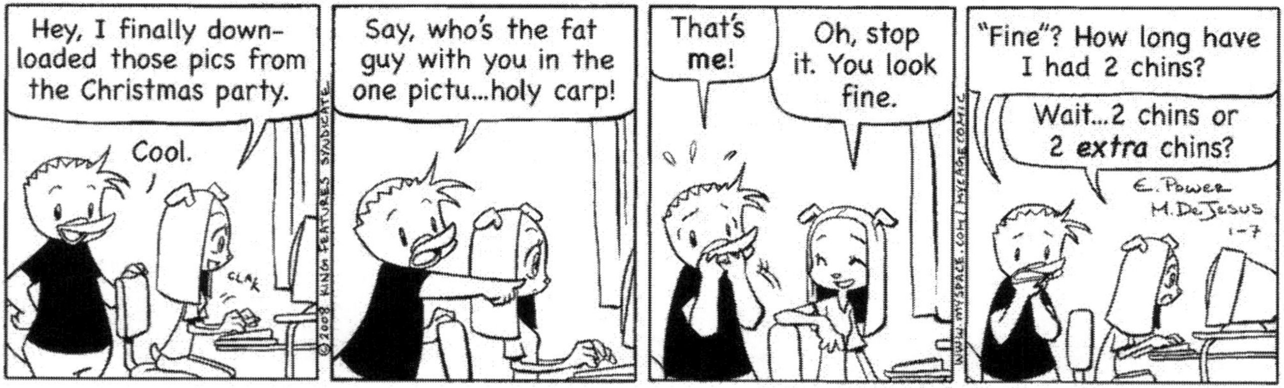
Hey, I finally down-loaded those pics from the Christmas party.
Cool.
CLAK
Say, who's the fat guy with you in the one pictu...holy carp!
That's **me**!
Oh, stop it. You look fine.
"Fine"? How long have I had 2 chins?
Wait...2 chins or 2 ***extra*** chins?
E. Power
M. DeJesus
1-7

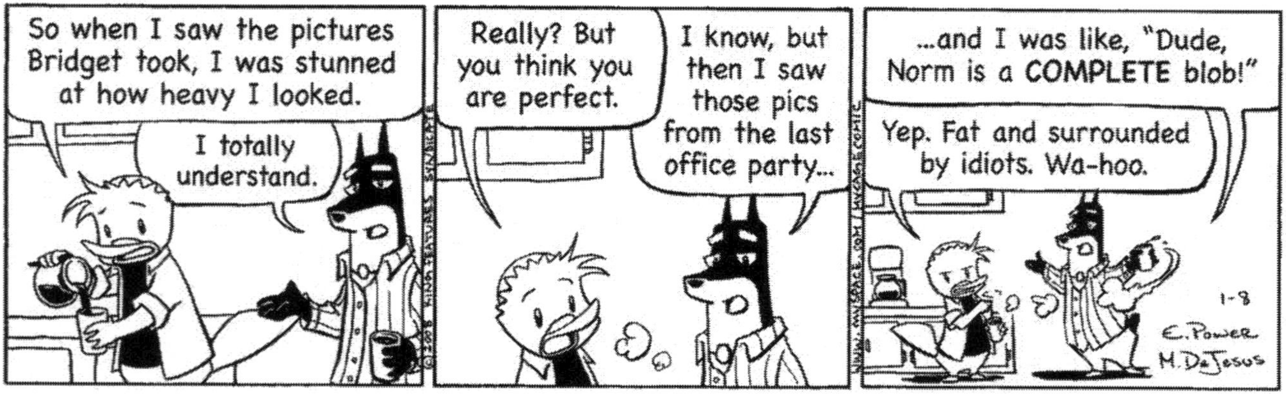
So when I saw the pictures Bridget took, I was stunned at how heavy I looked.
I totally understand.
Really? But you think you are perfect.
I know, but then I saw those pics from the last office party...
...and I was like, "Dude, Norm is a **COMPLETE** blob!"
Yep. Fat and surrounded by idiots. Wa-hoo.
1-8
E. Power
M. DeJesus

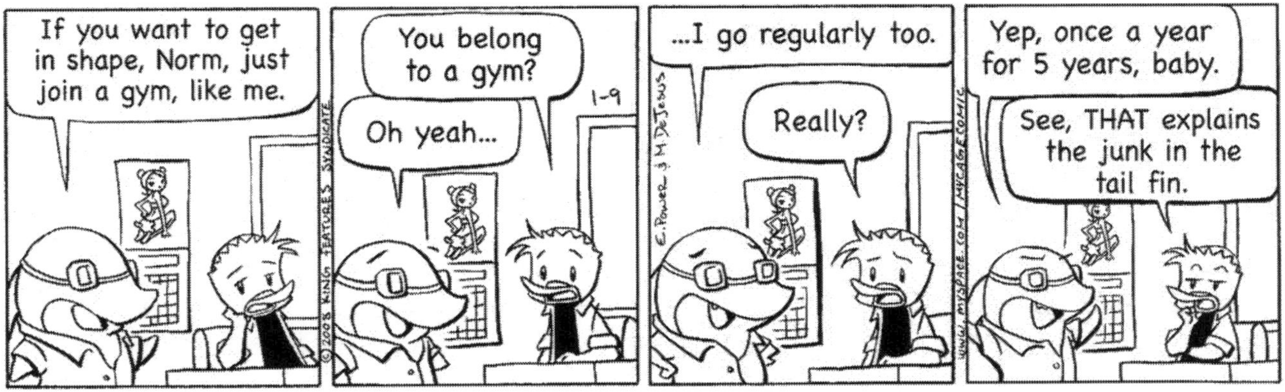
If you want to get in shape, Norm, just join a gym, like me.
You belong to a gym?
Oh yeah...
1-9
...I go regularly too.
Really?
Yep, once a year for 5 years, baby.
See, THAT explains the junk in the tail fin.
E. Power & M. DeJesus
www.myspace.com/mycagecomic

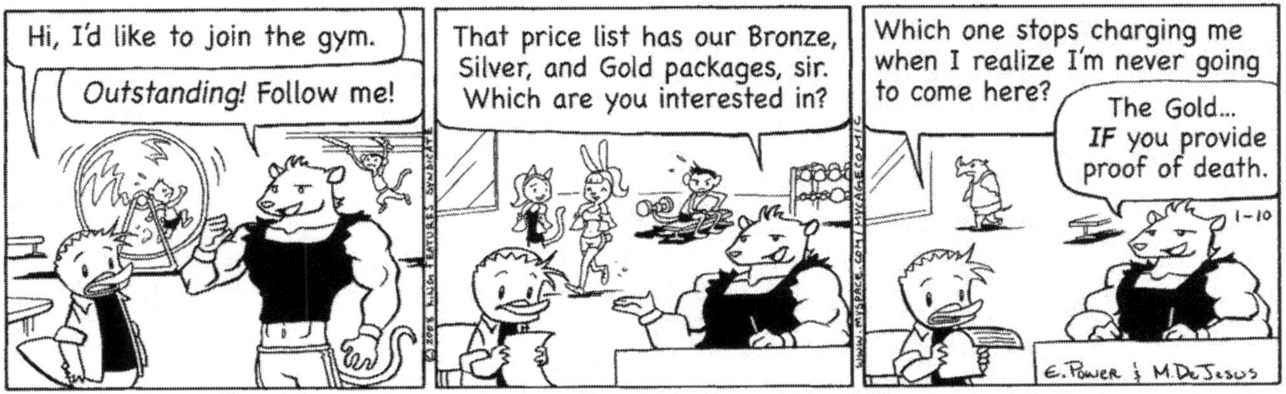
Hi, I'd like to join the gym.
Outstanding! Follow me!
That price list has our Bronze, Silver, and Gold packages, sir. Which are you interested in?
Which one stops charging me when I realize I'm never going to come here?
The Gold... *IF* you provide proof of death.
1-10
E. Power & M. DeJesus
www.myspace.com/mycagecomic

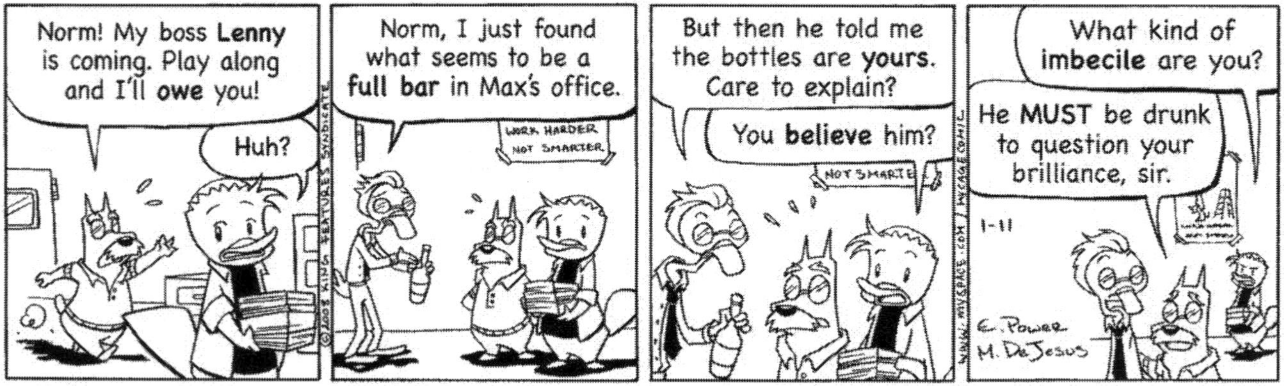
Norm! My boss **Lenny** is coming. Play along and I'll **owe** you!
Huh?
©2008 KING FEATURES SYNDICATE
Norm, I just found what seems to be a **full bar** in Max's office.
WORK HARDER NOT SMARTER
But then he told me the bottles are **yours**. Care to explain?
You **believe** him?
NOT SMARTE
WWW.MYSPACE.COM / MYCAGECOMIC
What kind of **imbecile** are you?
He **MUST** be drunk to question your brilliance, sir.
1-11
E. Power
M. DeJesus

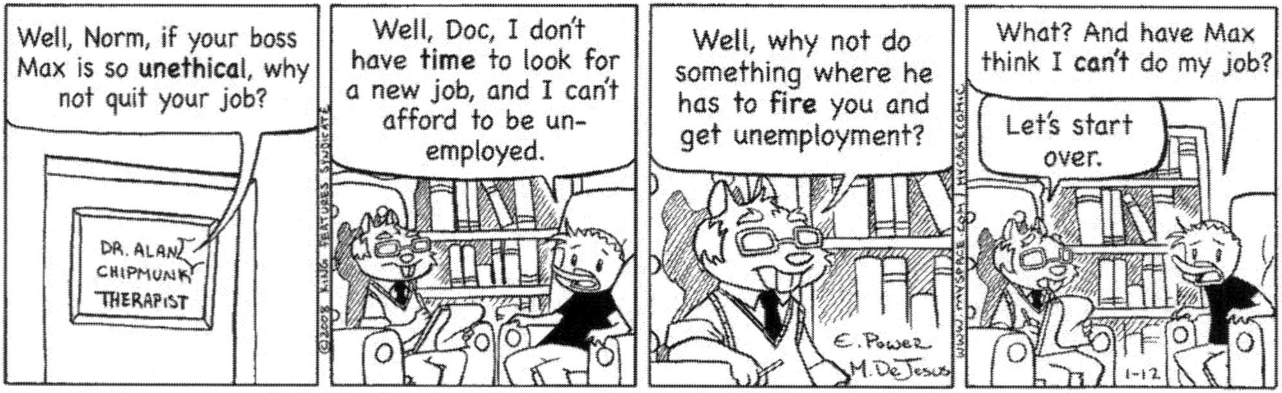
Well, Norm, if your boss Max is so **unethical**, why not quit your job?
DR. ALAN CHIPMUNK THERAPIST
©2008 KING FEATURES SYNDICATE
Well, Doc, I don't have **time** to look for a new job, and I can't afford to be un-employed.
Well, why not do something where he has to **fire** you and get unemployment?
E. Power
M. DeJesus
WWW.MYSPACE.COM / MYCAGECOMIC
What? And have Max think I **can't** do my job?
Let's start over.
1-12

Uh, hey, Bridget...sorry about the whole fight thing.
Uh-huh. Whatever.
©2008 KING FEATURES SYNDICATE
Inside Norm's head...
She's *still* mad at us?
Yeah, we need to do something **special** to apologize.
You know what that means.
Yep.
No way! You know what **he's** like these days.
WWW.MYSPACE.COM/MYCAGECOMIC
Doesn't matter. You're the boss.
Do it for Bridget.
FINE!
Recesses
Sigh
E. POWER
M. DEJESUS
Uh, hey, **Creativity**...sorry about the whole *'abandoning our dreams/corporate job'* thing.
Uh-huh. Whatever.
1-13

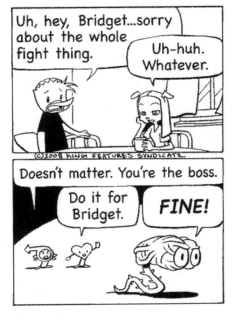

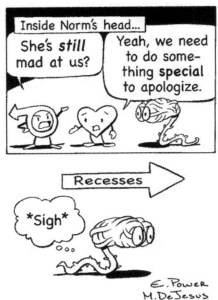

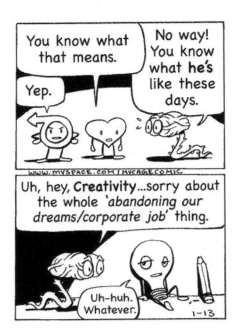

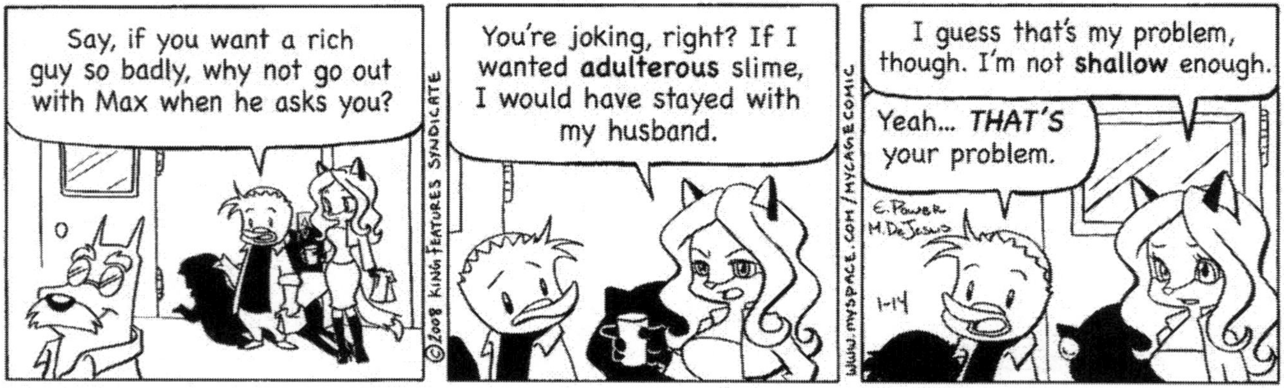
Say, if you want a rich guy so badly, why not go out with Max when he asks you?
©2008 King Features Syndicate
You're joking, right? If I wanted **adulterous** slime, I would have stayed with my husband.
www.myspace.com/mycagecomic
I guess that's my problem, though. I'm not **shallow** enough.
Yeah... ***THAT'S*** your problem.
E. Power
M. DeJesus
1-14

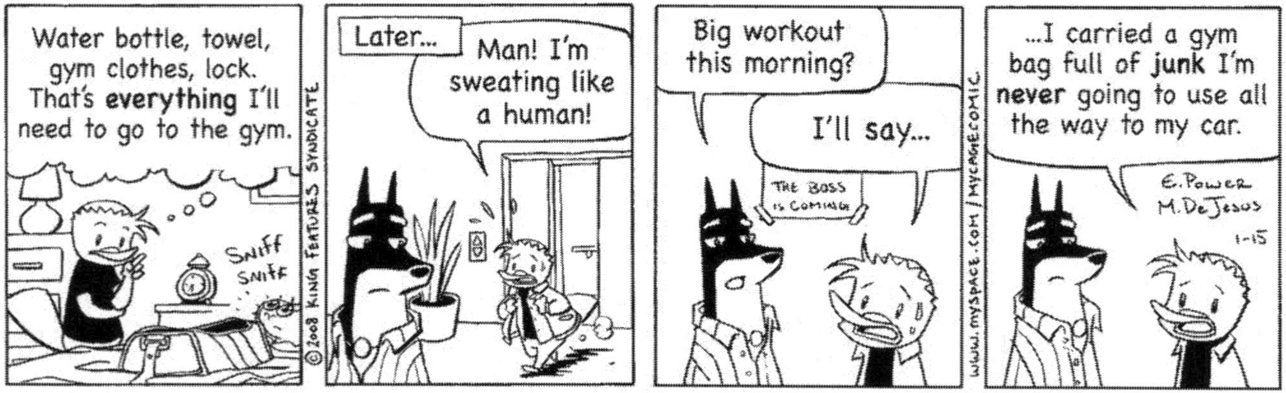
Water bottle, towel, gym clothes, lock. That's **everything** I'll need to go to the gym.
SNIFF SNIFF
©2008 King Features Syndicate
Later...
Man! I'm sweating like a human!
Big workout this morning?
I'll say...
THE BOSS IS COMING
www.myspace.com/mycagecomic
...I carried a gym bag full of **junk** I'm **never** going to use all the way to my car.
E. Power
M. DeJesus
1-15

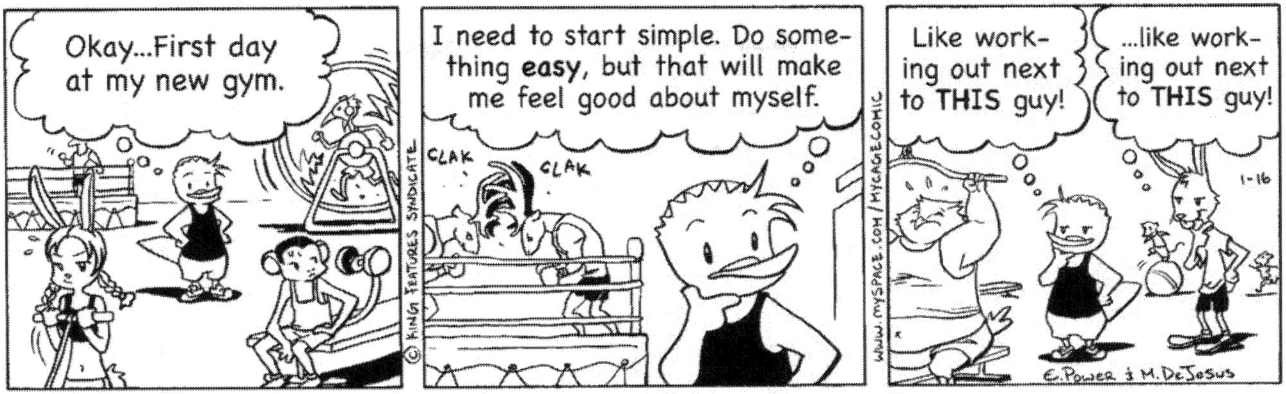
Okay...First day at my new gym.
CLAK
CLAK
I need to start simple. Do something **easy**, but that will make me feel good about myself.
Like working out next to **THIS** guy!
...like working out next to **THIS** guy!
1-16
© KING FEATURES SYNDICATE
WWW.MYSPACE.COM/MYCAGECOMIC
E. POWER & M. DEJESUS

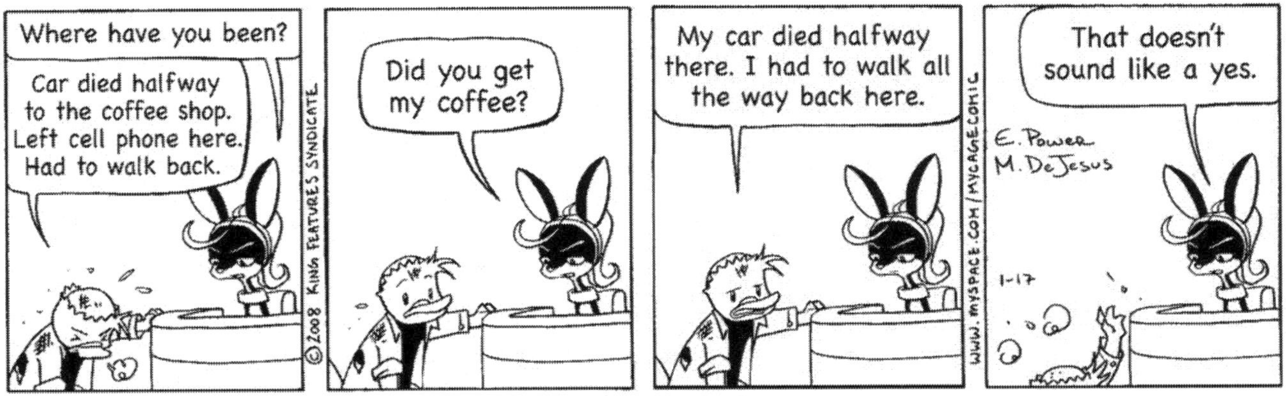
Where have you been?
Car died halfway to the coffee shop. Left cell phone here. Had to walk back.
© 2008 KING FEATURES SYNDICATE
Did you get my coffee?
My car died halfway there. I had to walk all the way back here.
WWW.MYSPACE.COM/MYCAGECOMIC
E. POWER
M. DEJESUS
1-17
That doesn't sound like a yes.

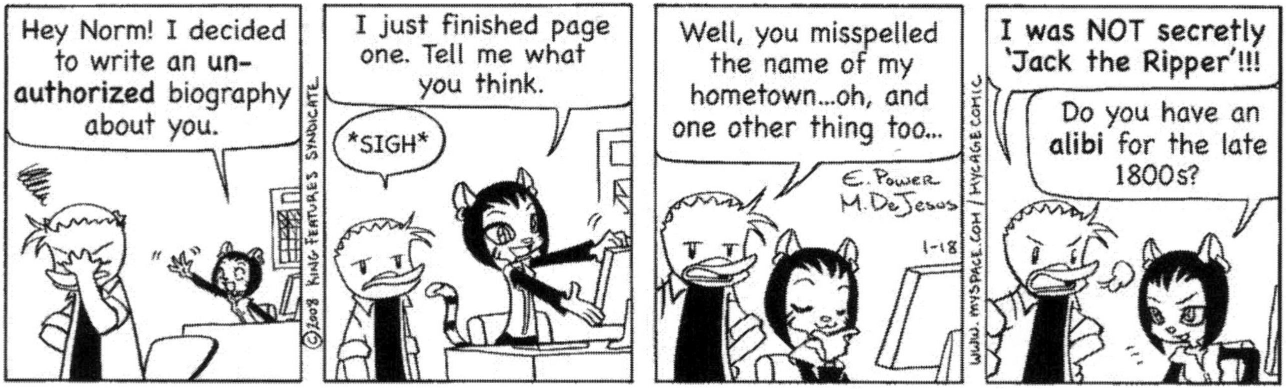
Hey Norm! I decided to write an **un-authorized** biography about you.
©2008 KING FEATURES SYNDICATE
I just finished page one. Tell me what you think.
SIGH
Well, you misspelled the name of my hometown...oh, and one other thing too...
E. POWER
M. DeJESUS
1-18
WWW.MYSPACE.COM/MYCAGECOMIC
I was NOT secretly 'Jack the Ripper'!!!
Do you have an **alibi** for the late 1800s?

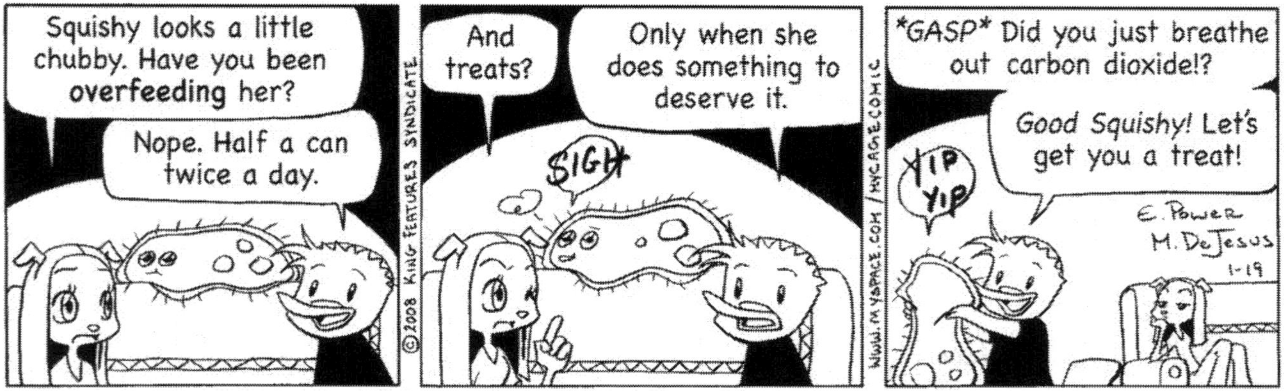
Squishy looks a little chubby. Have you been **overfeeding** her?
Nope. Half a can twice a day.
©2008 KING FEATURES SYNDICATE
And treats?
Only when she does something to deserve it.
SIGH
WWW.MYSPACE.COM/MYCAGECOMIC
GASP Did you just breathe out carbon dioxide!?
YIP YIP
Good Squishy! Let's get you a treat!
E. POWER
M. DeJESUS
1-19

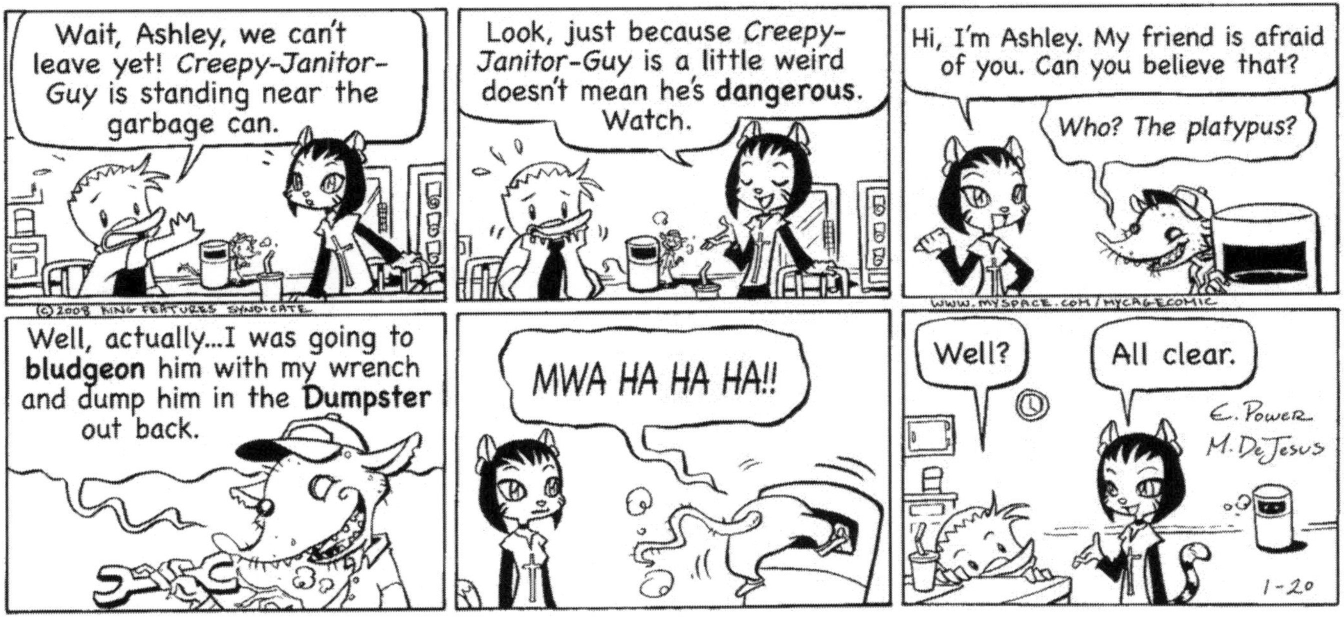
Wait, Ashley, we can't leave yet! *Creepy-Janitor-Guy* is standing near the garbage can.
Look, just because *Creepy-Janitor-Guy* is a little weird doesn't mean he's **dangerous**. Watch.
Hi, I'm Ashley. My friend is afraid of you. Can you believe that?
Who? The platypus?
© 2008 KING FEATURES SYNDICATE
WWW.MYSPACE.COM/MYCAGECOMIC
Well, actually...I was going to **bludgeon** him with my wrench and dump him in the **Dumpster** out back.
MWA HA HA HA!!
Well?
All clear.
E. Power
M. DeJesus
1-20

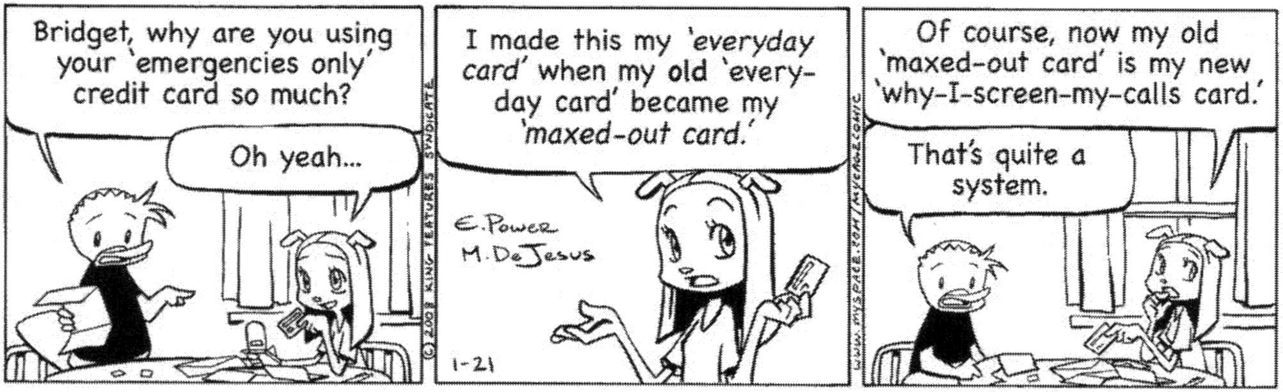
Bridget, why are you using your 'emergencies only' credit card so much?
Oh yeah...
I made this my *'everyday card'* when my **old** 'everyday card' became my *'maxed-out card.'*
E. Power
M. DeJesus
1-21
Of course, now my old 'maxed-out card' is my new 'why-I-screen-my-calls card.'
That's quite a system.
© 2008 KING FEATURES SYNDICATE
WWW.MYSPACE.COM/MYCAGECOMIC

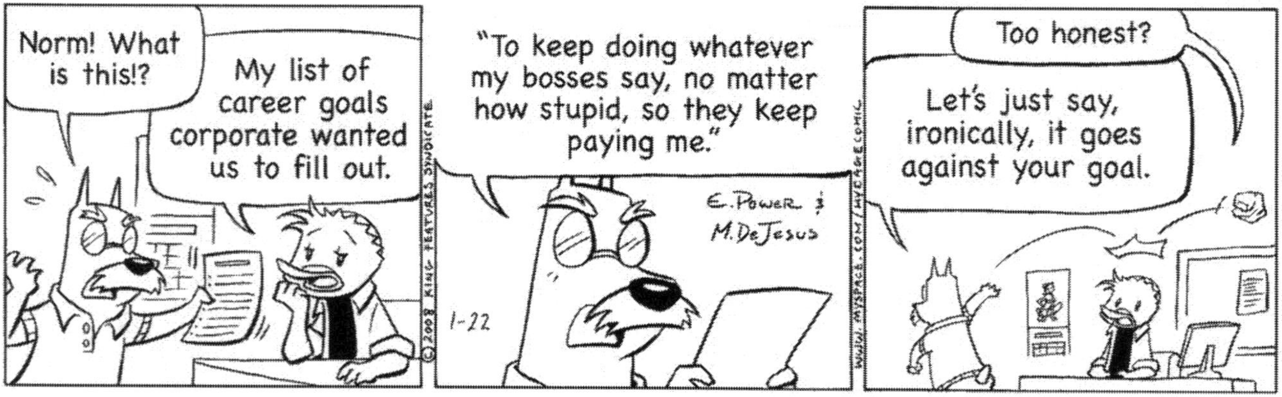
Norm! What is this!?
My list of career goals corporate wanted us to fill out.
"To keep doing whatever my bosses say, no matter how stupid, so they keep paying me."
E. Power &
M. DeJesus
1-22
Too honest?
Let's just say, ironically, it goes against your goal.
© 2008 KING FEATURES SYNDICATE
WWW.MYSPACE.COM/MYCAGECOMIC

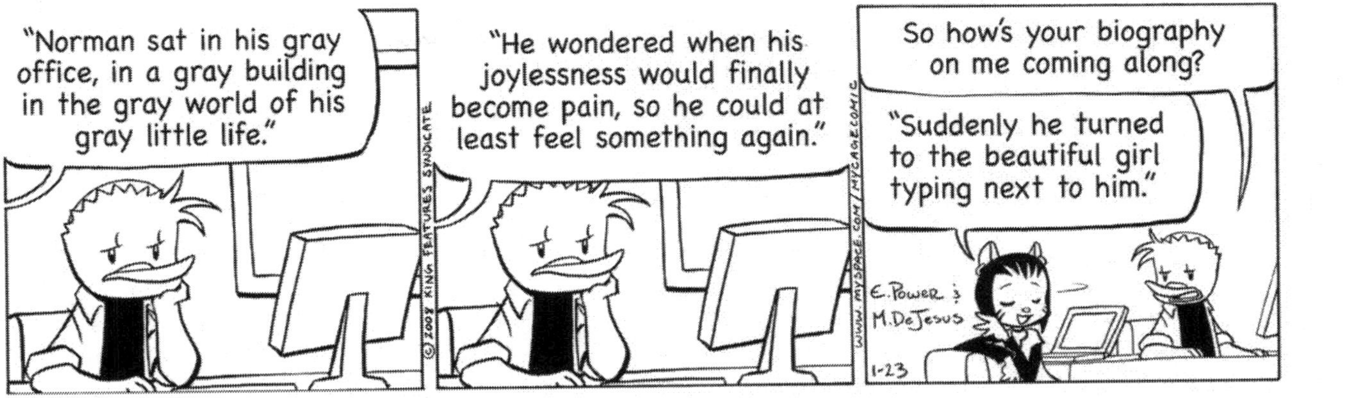
"Norman sat in his gray office, in a gray building in the gray world of his gray little life."
© 2008 KING FEATURES SYNDICATE
"He wondered when his joylessness would finally become pain, so he could at least feel something again."
WWW.MYSPACE.COM/MYCAGECOMIC
So how's your biography on me coming along?
"Suddenly he turned to the beautiful girl typing next to him."
E. Power & M. DeJesus
1-23

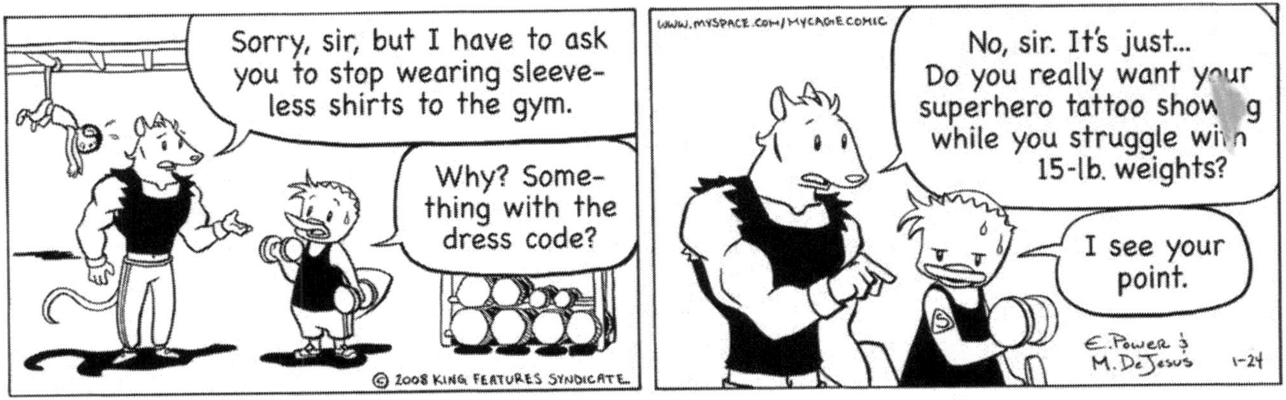
Sorry, sir, but I have to ask you to stop wearing sleeve-less shirts to the gym.
Why? Some-thing with the dress code?
© 2008 KING FEATURES SYNDICATE
WWW.MYSPACE.COM/MYCAGECOMIC
No, sir. It's just... Do you really want your superhero tattoo showing while you struggle with 15-lb. weights?
I see your point.
E. Power & M. DeJesus
1-24

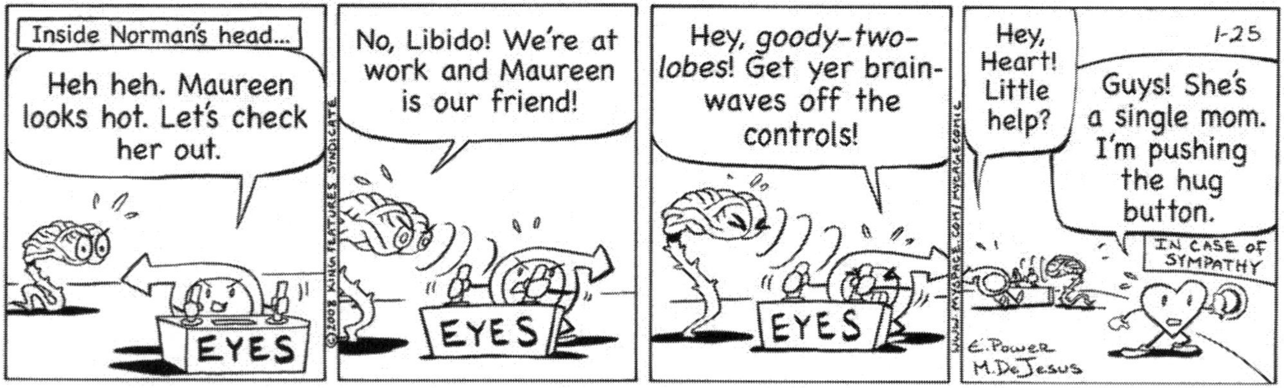
Inside Norman's head...
Heh heh. Maureen looks hot. Let's check her out.
EYES
No, Libido! We're at work and Maureen is our friend!
EYES
Hey, *goody-two-lobes*! Get yer brain-waves off the controls!
EYES
1-25
Hey, Heart! Little help?
Guys! She's a single mom. I'm pushing the hug button.
IN CASE OF SYMPATHY
E. Power
M. DeJesus

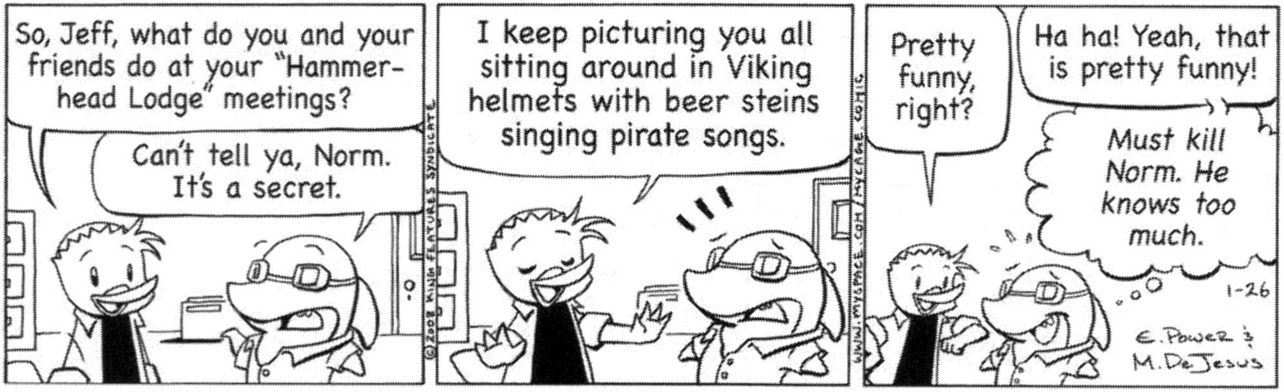
So, Jeff, what do you and your friends do at your "Hammer-head Lodge" meetings?
Can't tell ya, Norm. It's a secret.
I keep picturing you all sitting around in Viking helmets with beer steins singing pirate songs.
Pretty funny, right?
Ha ha! Yeah, that is pretty funny!
Must kill Norm. He knows too much.
1-26
E. Power &
M. DeJesus

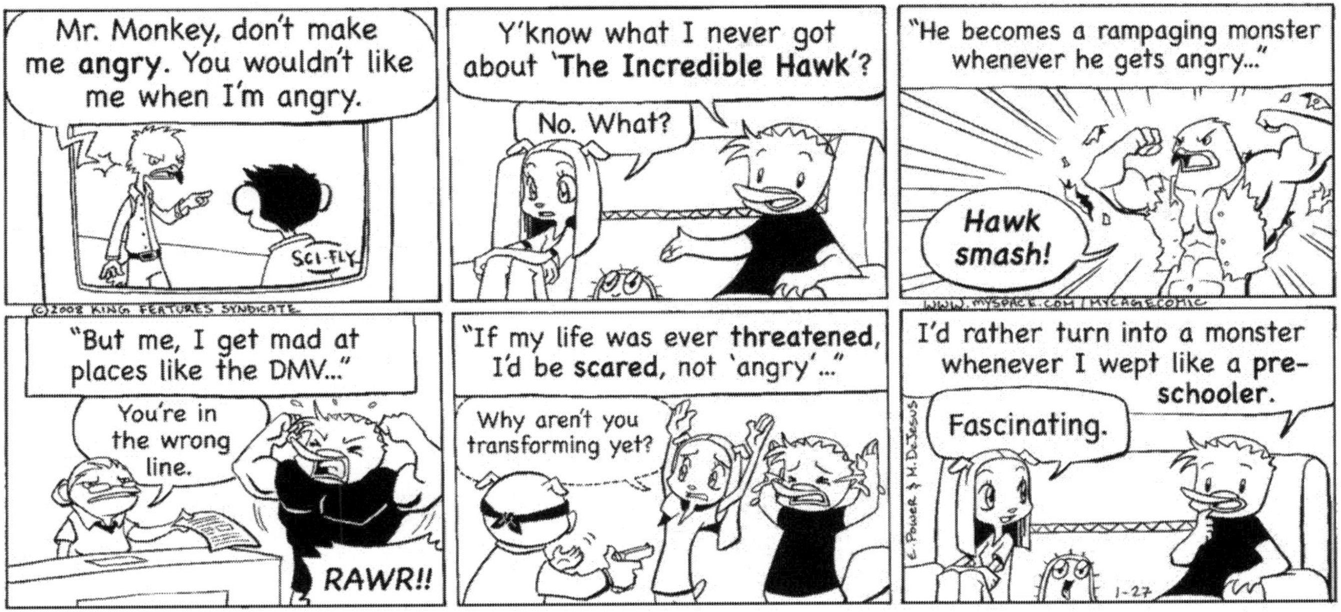
Mr. Monkey, don't make me **angry**. You wouldn't like me when I'm angry.
SCI-FLY
©2008 KING FEATURES SYNDICATE
Y'know what I never got about '**The Incredible Hawk**'?
No. What?
"He becomes a rampaging monster whenever he gets angry..."
Hawk smash!
WWW.MYSPACE.COM/MYCAGECOMIC
"But me, I get mad at places like the DMV..."
You're in the wrong line.
RAWR!!
"If my life was ever **threatened**, I'd be **scared**, not 'angry'..."
Why aren't you transforming yet?
I'd rather turn into a monster whenever I wept like a **pre-schooler**.
Fascinating.
E. Power & M. DeJesus
1-27

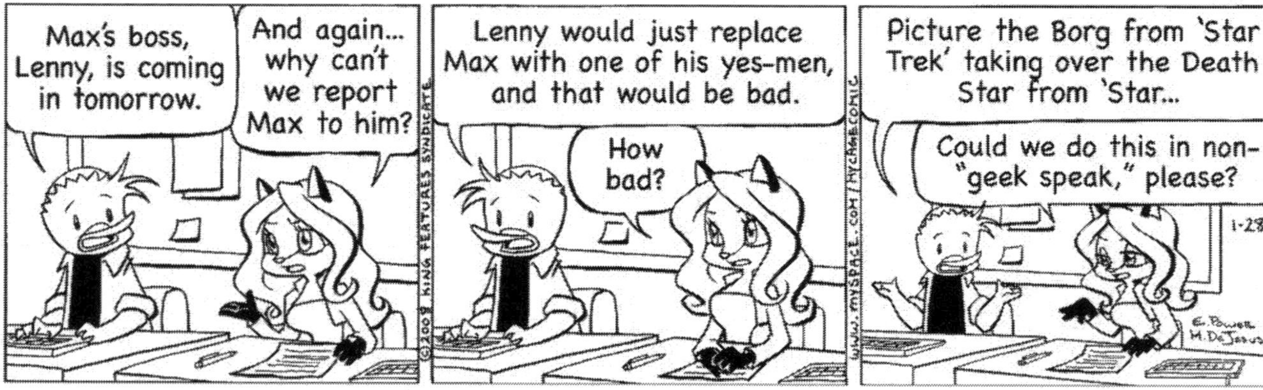
Max's boss, Lenny, is coming in tomorrow.
And again... why can't we report Max to him?
© 2008 KING FEATURES SYNDICATE
Lenny would just replace Max with one of his yes-men, and that would be bad.
How bad?
WWW.MYSPACE.COM/MYCAGECOMIC
Picture the Borg from 'Star Trek' taking over the Death Star from 'Star...
Could we do this in non-"geek speak," please?
1-28
E. POWER
M. DeJESUS

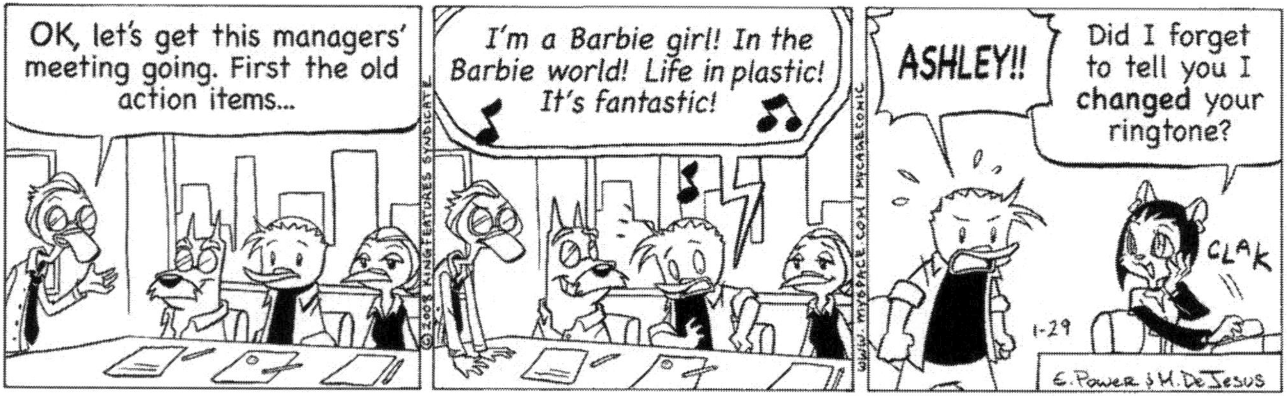
OK, let's get this managers' meeting going. First the old action items...
© 2008 KING FEATURES SYNDICATE
I'm a Barbie girl! In the Barbie world! Life in plastic! It's fantastic!
WWW.MYSPACE.COM/MYCAGECOMIC
ASHLEY!!
Did I forget to tell you I **changed** your ringtone?
CLAK
1-29
E. POWER & M. DeJESUS

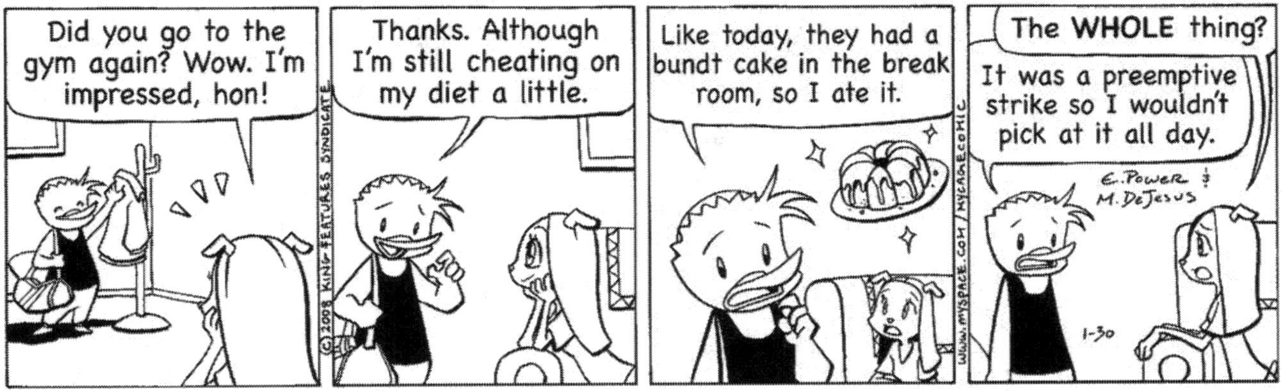

Did you go to the gym again? Wow. I'm impressed, hon!
Thanks. Although I'm still cheating on my diet a little.
© 2008 KING FEATURES SYNDICATE
Like today, they had a bundt cake in the break room, so I ate it.
WWW.MYSPACE.COM/MYCAGECOMIC
The **WHOLE** thing?
It was a preemptive strike so I wouldn't pick at it all day.
E. POWER & M. DEJESUS
1-30

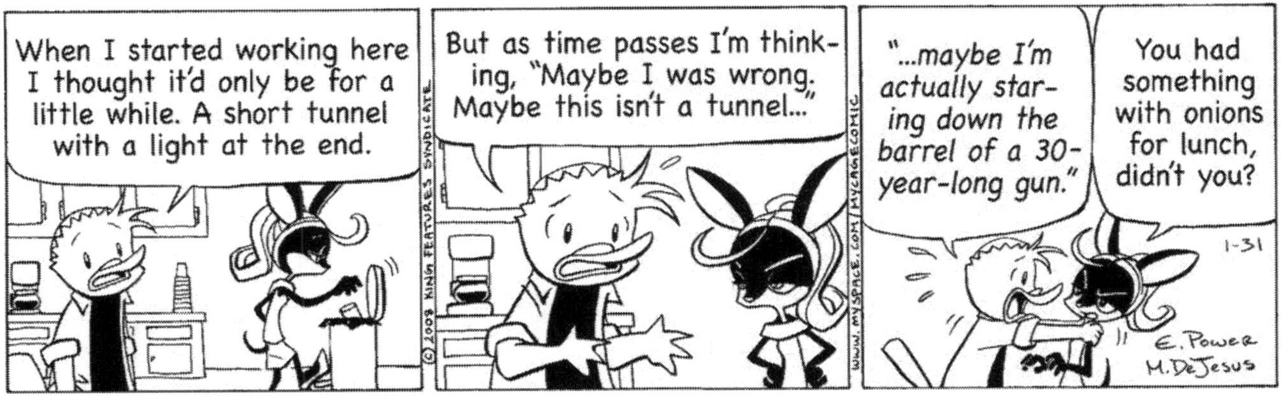

When I started working here I thought it'd only be for a little while. A short tunnel with a light at the end.
© 2008 KING FEATURES SYNDICATE
But as time passes I'm thinking, "Maybe I was wrong. Maybe this isn't a tunnel..."
WWW.MYSPACE.COM/MYCAGECOMIC
"...maybe I'm actually staring down the barrel of a 30-year-long gun."
You had something with onions for lunch, didn't you?
1-31
E. POWER
M. DEJESUS

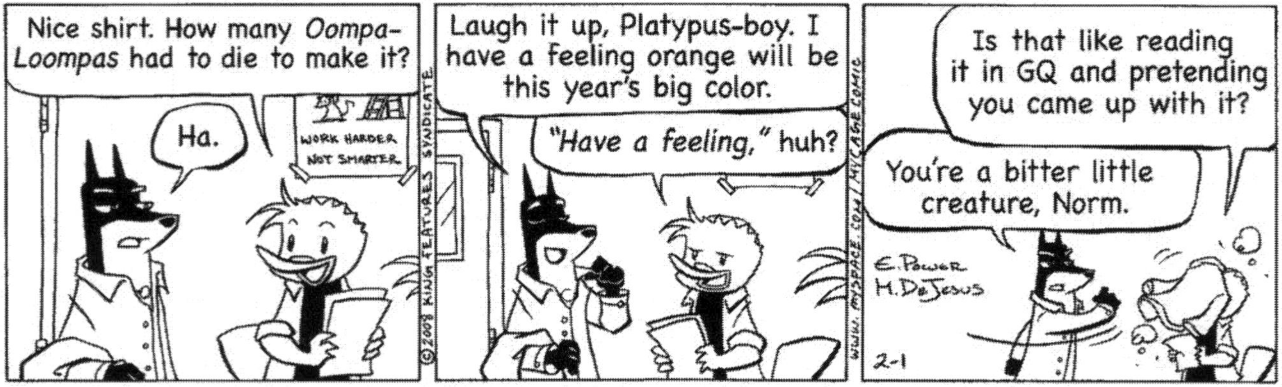
Nice shirt. How many *Oompa-Loompas* had to die to make it?
Ha.
WORK HARDER NOT SMARTER
©2008 KING FEATURES SYNDICATE
Laugh it up, Platypus-boy. I have a feeling orange will be this year's big color.
"Have a feeling," huh?
WWW.MYSPACE.COM/MYCAGECOMIC
Is that like reading it in GQ and pretending you came up with it?
You're a bitter little creature, Norm.
E. POWER
M. DEJESUS
2-1

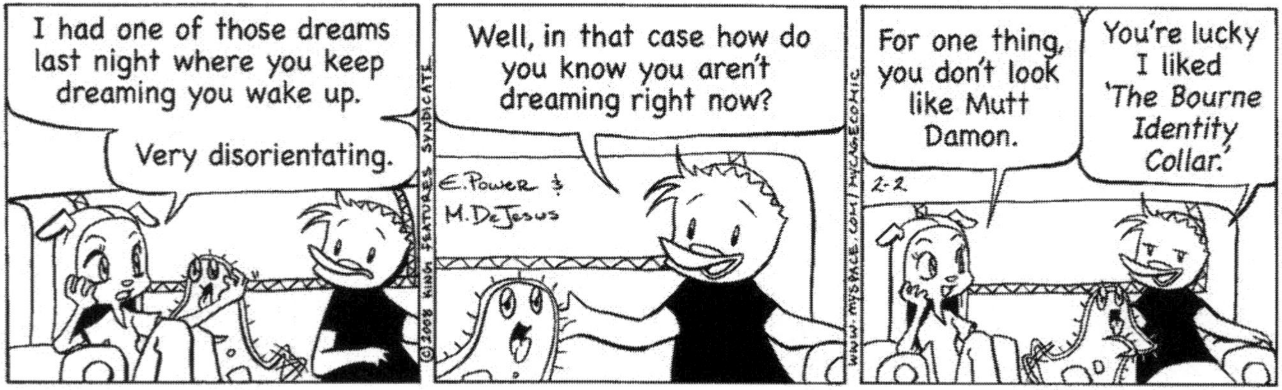
I had one of those dreams last night where you keep dreaming you wake up.
Very disorientating.
©2008 KING FEATURES SYNDICATE
Well, in that case how do you know you aren't dreaming right now?
E. POWER &
M. DEJESUS
WWW.MYSPACE.COM/MYCAGECOMIC
For one thing, you don't look like Mutt Damon.
You're lucky I liked *'The Bourne Identity Collar.'*
2-2

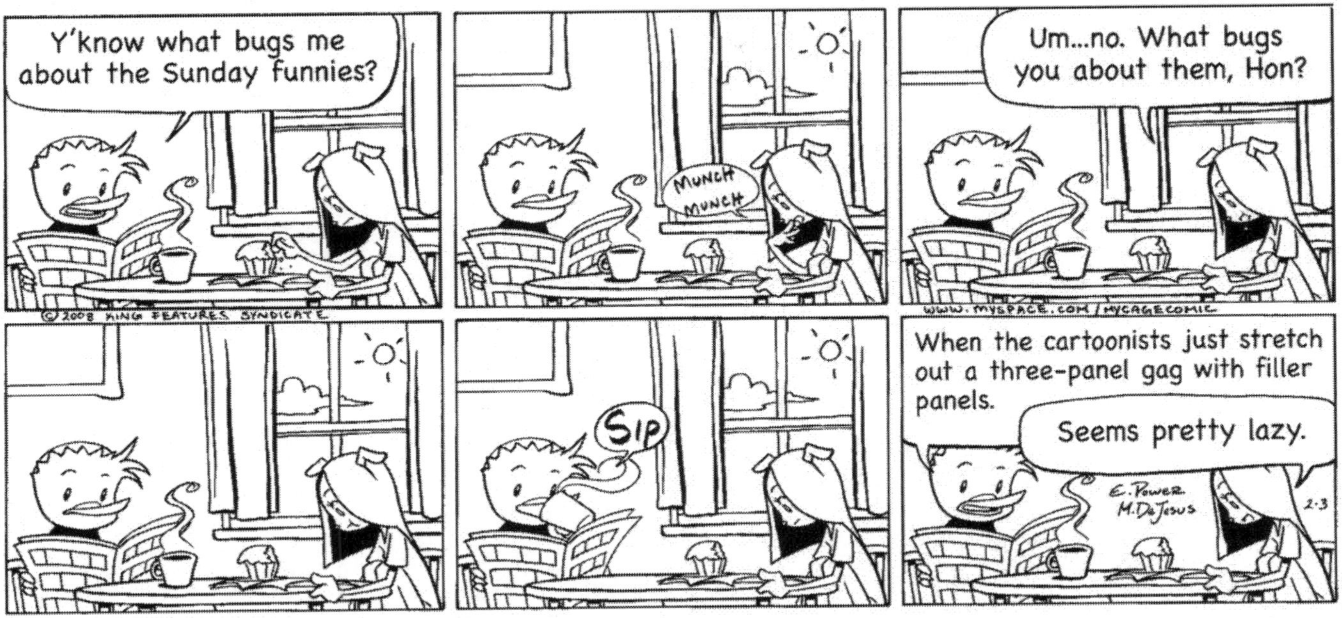

Y'know what bugs me about the Sunday funnies?
©2008 KING FEATURES SYNDICATE
MUNCH MUNCH
Um...no. What bugs you about them, Hon?
WWW.MYSPACE.COM/MYCAGECOMIC
SIP
When the cartoonists just stretch out a three-panel gag with filler panels.
Seems pretty lazy.
E. POWER
M. DeJESUS
2-3

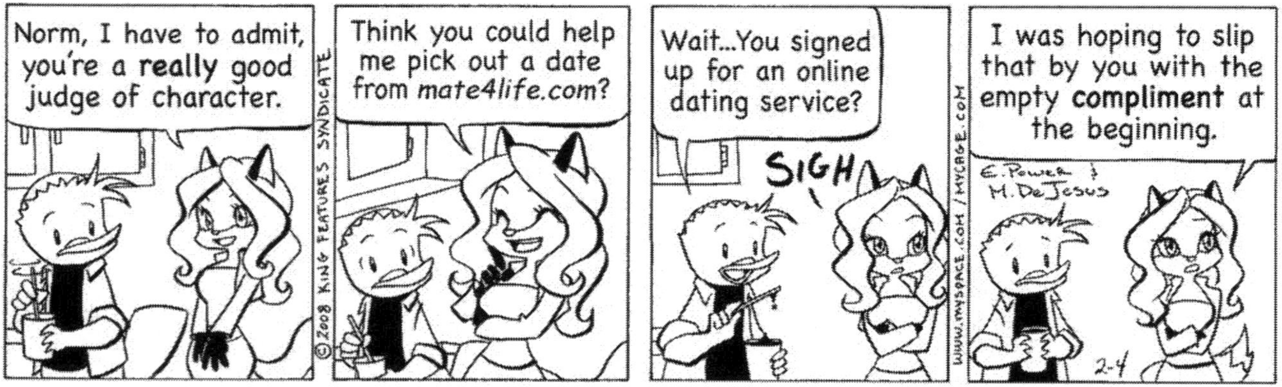
Norm, I have to admit, you're a **really** good judge of character.
© 2008 KING FEATURES SYNDICATE
Think you could help me pick out a date from *mate4life.com*?
Wait...You signed up for an online dating service?
SIGH
WWW.MYSPACE.COM / MYCAGE.COM
I was hoping to slip that by you with the empty **compliment** at the beginning.
E. Power & M. DeJesus
2-4

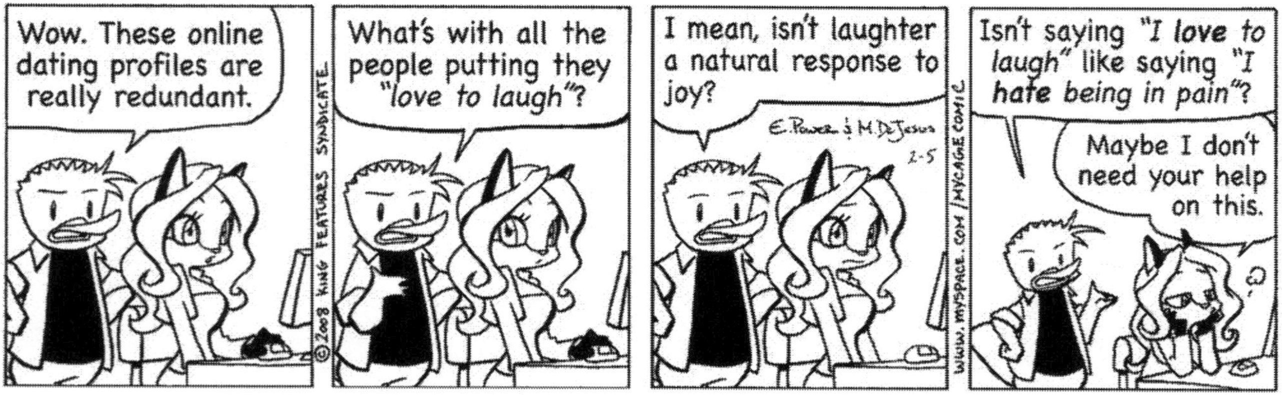
Wow. These online dating profiles are really redundant.
© 2008 KING FEATURES SYNDICATE
What's with all the people putting they *"love to laugh"*?
I mean, isn't laughter a natural response to joy?
E. Power & M. DeJesus
2-5
WWW.MYSPACE.COM / MYCAGE.COMIC
Isn't saying *"I love to laugh"* like saying *"I **hate** being in pain"*?
Maybe I don't need your help on this.

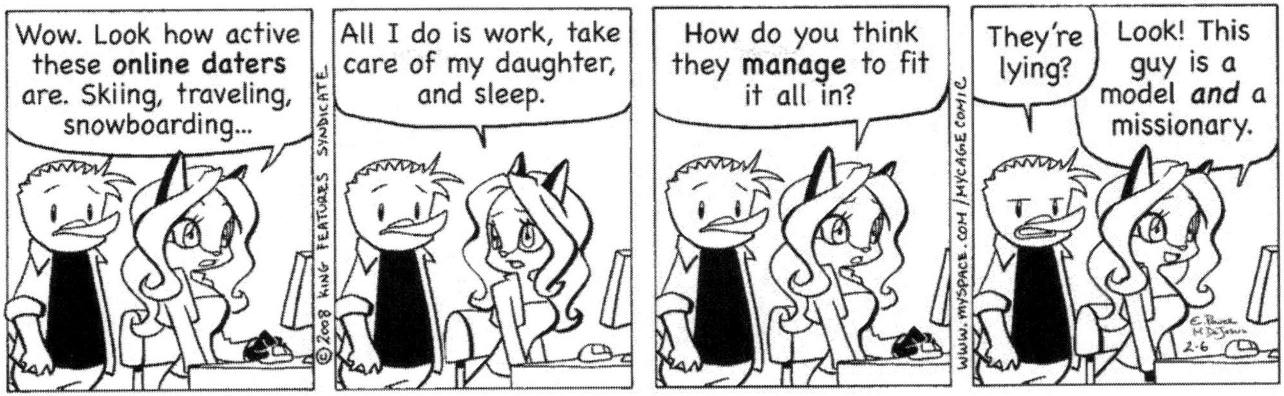
Wow. Look how active these **online daters** are. Skiing, traveling, snowboarding...
© 2008 King Features Syndicate
All I do is work, take care of my daughter, and sleep.
How do you think they **manage** to fit it all in?
www.myspace.com/mycagecomic
They're lying?
Look! This guy is a model ***and*** a missionary.
E. Power
M. DeJesus
2-6

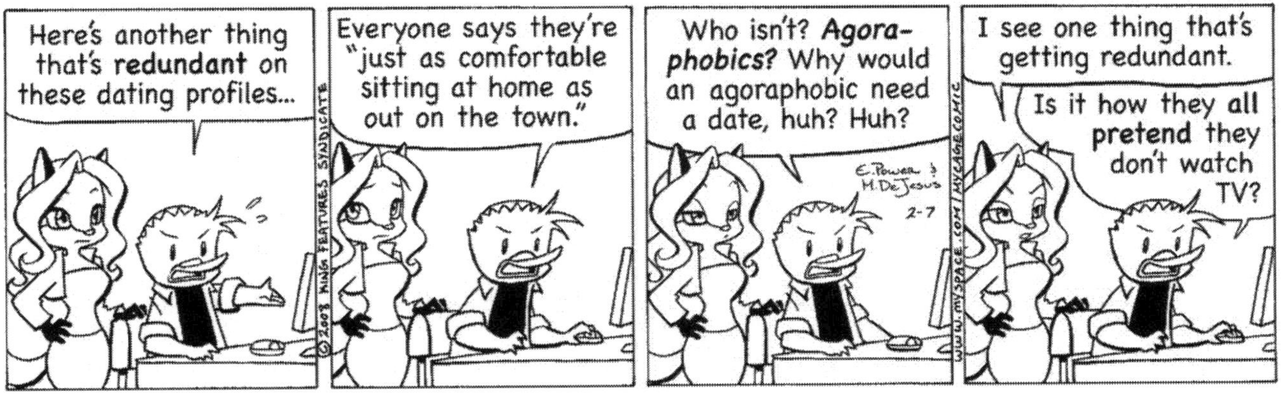
Here's another thing that's **redundant** on these dating profiles...
© 2008 King Features Syndicate
Everyone says they're "just as comfortable sitting at home as out on the town."
Who isn't? ***Agora-phobics?*** Why would an agoraphobic need a date, huh? Huh?
E. Power & M. DeJesus
2-7
www.myspace.com/mycagecomic
I see one thing that's getting redundant.
Is it how they **all pretend** they don't watch TV?

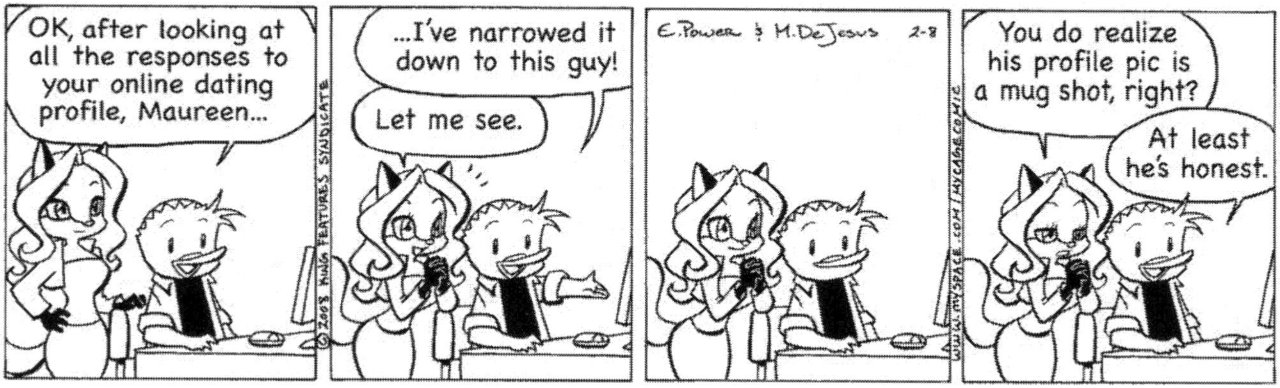
OK, after looking at all the responses to your online dating profile, Maureen...
© 2008 King Features Syndicate
...I've narrowed it down to this guy!
Let me see.
E. Power & M. DeJesus 2-8
You do realize his profile pic is a mug shot, right?
At least he's honest.
www.myspace.com/mycagecomic

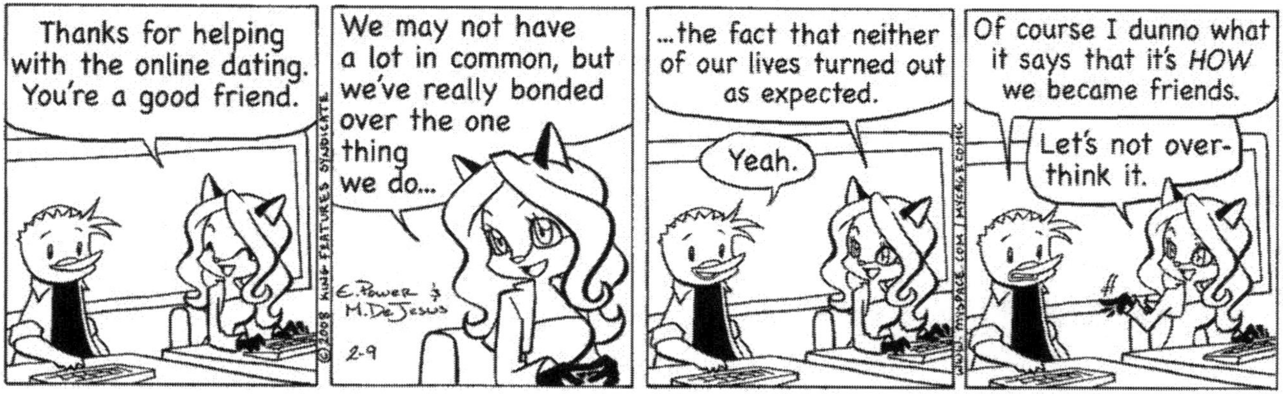
Thanks for helping with the online dating. You're a good friend.
© 2008 King Features Syndicate
We may not have a lot in common, but we've really bonded over the one thing we do...
E. Power & M. DeJesus
2-9
...the fact that neither of our lives turned out as expected.
Yeah.
www.myspace.com/mycagecomic
Of course I dunno what it says that it's *HOW* we became friends.
Let's not over-think it.

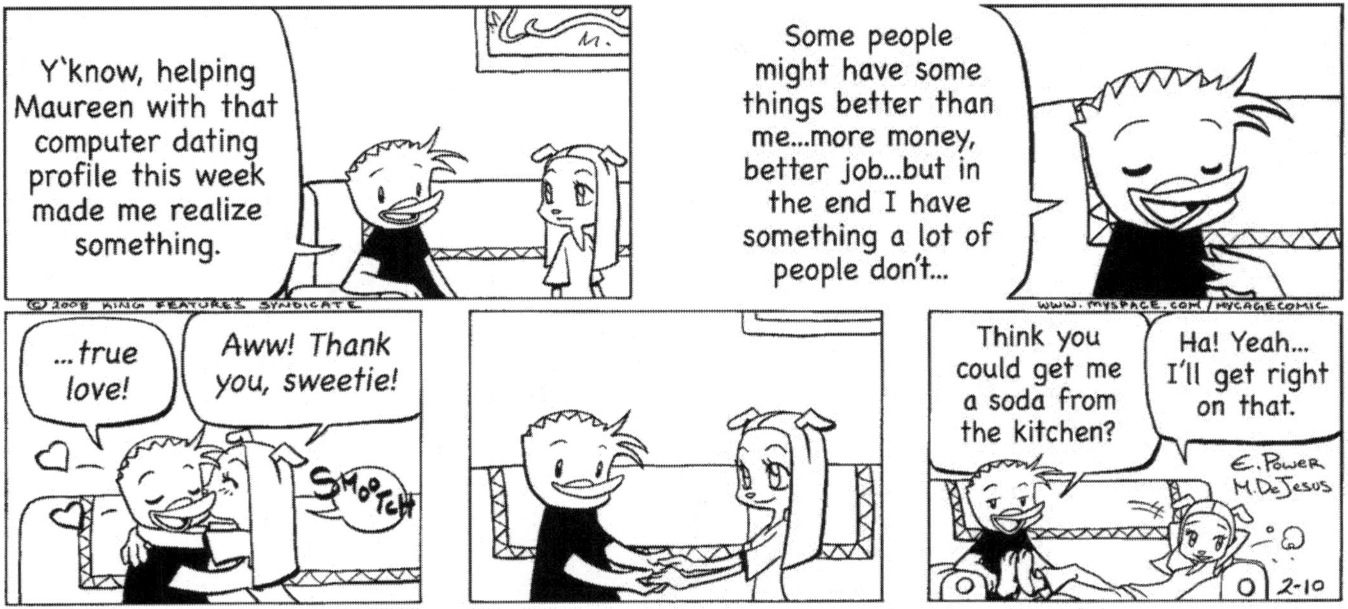

Y'know, helping Maureen with that computer dating profile this week made me realize something.
Some people might have some things better than me...more money, better job...but in the end I have something a lot of people don't...
© 2008 KING FEATURES SYNDICATE
WWW.MYSPACE.COM/MYCAGECOMIC
...true love!
Aww! Thank you, sweetie!
SMOOTCH
Think you could get me a soda from the kitchen?
Ha! Yeah... I'll get right on that.
E. Power
M. DeJesus
2-10

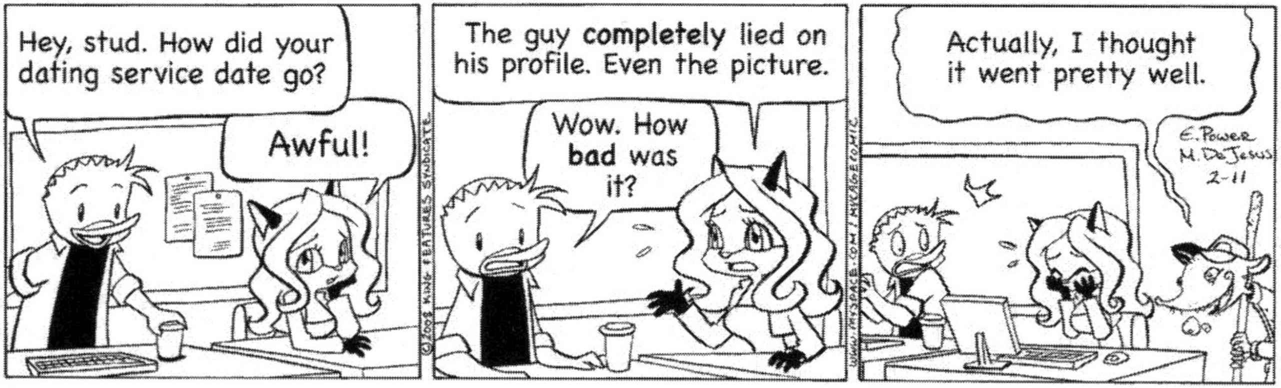
Hey, stud. How did your dating service date go?
Awful!
The guy **completely** lied on his profile. Even the picture.
Wow. How **bad** was it?
Actually, I thought it went pretty well.
E. Power
M. DeJesus
2-11

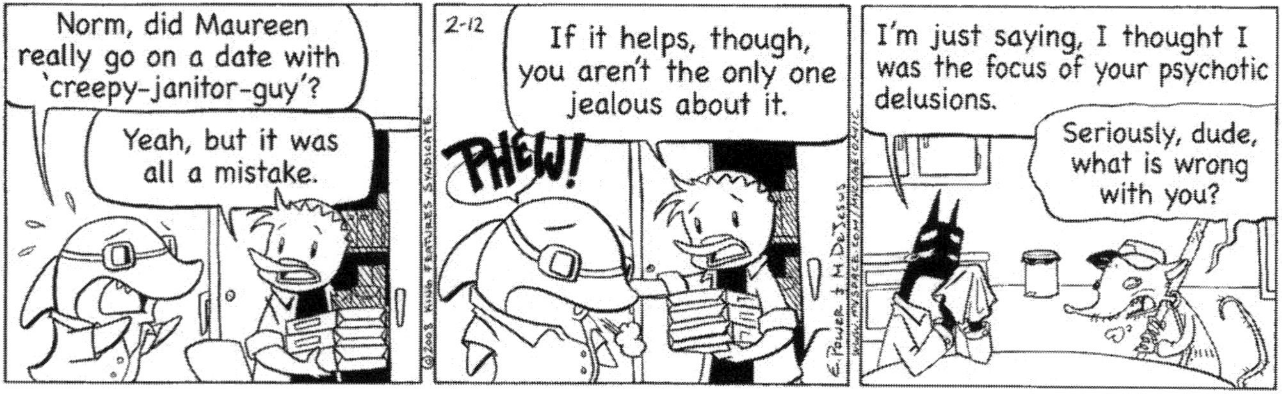
Norm, did Maureen really go on a date with 'creepy-janitor-guy'?
Yeah, but it was all a mistake.
2-12
If it helps, though, you aren't the only one jealous about it.
PHEW!
I'm just saying, I thought I was the focus of your psychotic delusions.
Seriously, dude, what is wrong with you?

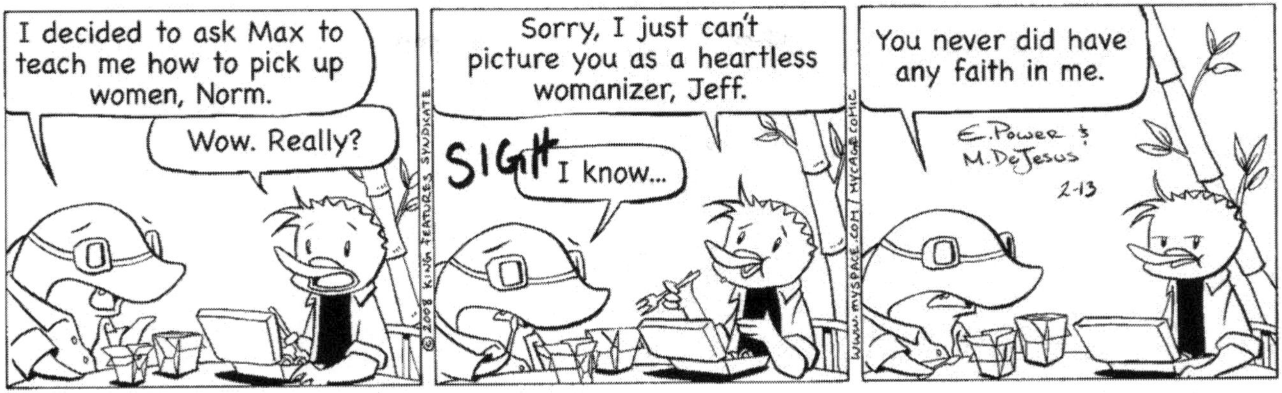
I decided to ask Max to teach me how to pick up women, Norm.
Wow. Really?
© 2008 King Features Syndicate
Sorry, I just can't picture you as a heartless womanizer, Jeff.
SIGH I know...
www.myspace.com/mycagecomic
You never did have any faith in me.
E. Power & M. DeJesus
2-13

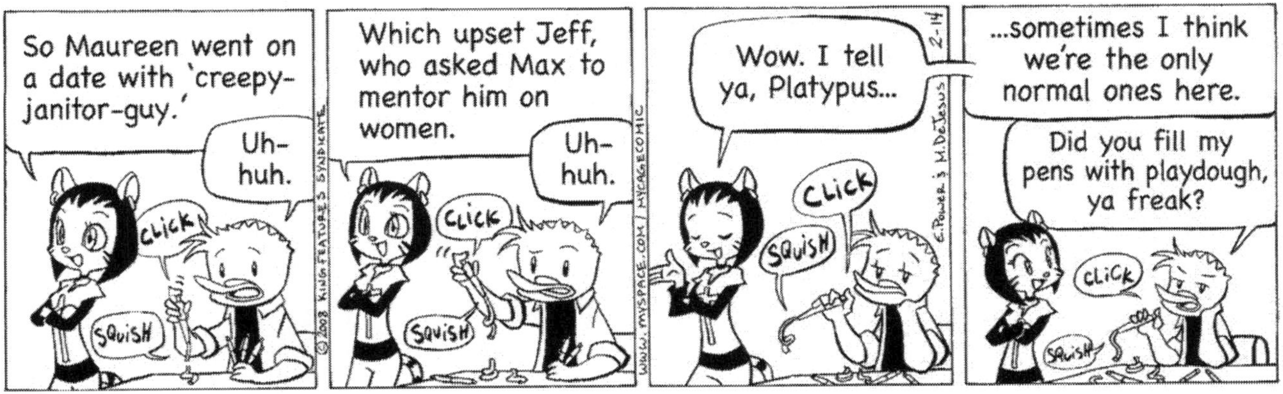
So Maureen went on a date with 'creepy-janitor-guy.'
Uh-huh.
CLICK
SQUISH
© 2008 King Features Syndicate
Which upset Jeff, who asked Max to mentor him on women.
Uh-huh.
CLICK
SQUISH
www.myspace.com/mycagecomic
Wow. I tell ya, Platypus...
CLICK
SQUISH
E. Power & M. DeJesus
2-14
...sometimes I think we're the only normal ones here.
Did you fill my pens with playdough, ya freak?
CLICK
SQUISH

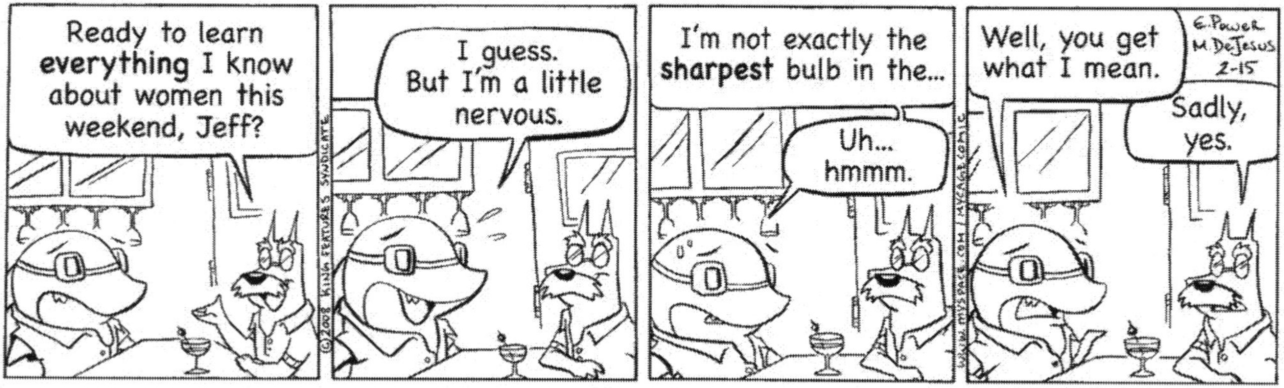
Ready to learn **everything** I know about women this weekend, Jeff?
I guess. But I'm a little nervous.
©2008 King Features Syndicate
I'm not exactly the **sharpest** bulb in the...
Uh... hmmm.
www.myspace.com/mycage.comic
Well, you get what I mean.
E. Power
M. DeJesus
2-15
Sadly, yes.

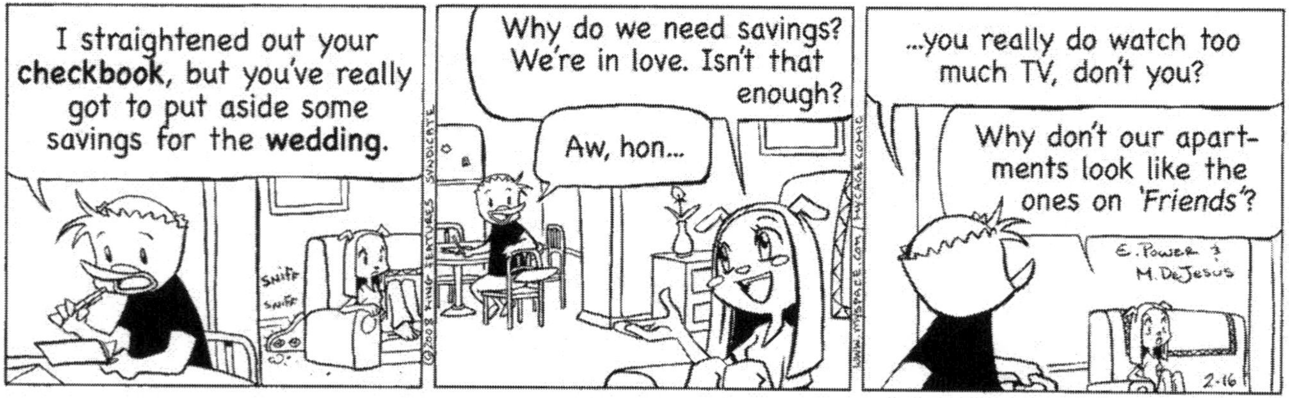
I straightened out your **checkbook**, but you've really got to put aside some savings for the **wedding**.
SNIFF
SNIFF
©2008 King Features Syndicate
Why do we need savings? We're in love. Isn't that enough?
Aw, hon...
www.myspace.com/mycage.comic
...you really do watch too much TV, don't you?
Why don't our apartments look like the ones on *'Friends'*?
E. Power &
M. DeJesus
2-16

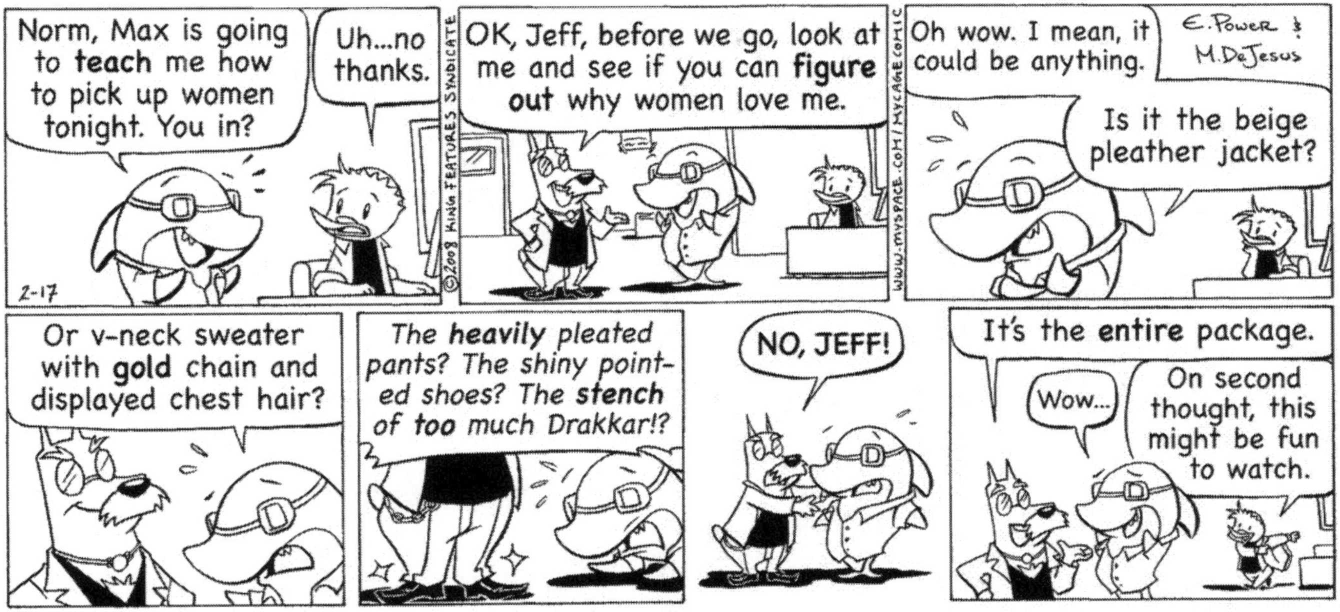
Norm, Max is going to **teach** me how to pick up women tonight. You in?
Uh...no thanks.
2-17
©2008 KING FEATURES SYNDICATE
OK, Jeff, before we go, look at me and see if you can **figure out** why women love me.
WWW.MYSPACE.COM/MYCAGECOMIC
Oh wow. I mean, it could be anything.
E. Power & M. DeJesus
Is it the beige pleather jacket?
Or v-neck sweater with **gold** chain and displayed chest hair?
*The **heavily** pleated pants? The shiny pointed shoes? The **stench** of **too** much Drakkar!?*
NO, JEFF!
It's the **entire** package.
Wow...
On second thought, this might be fun to watch.

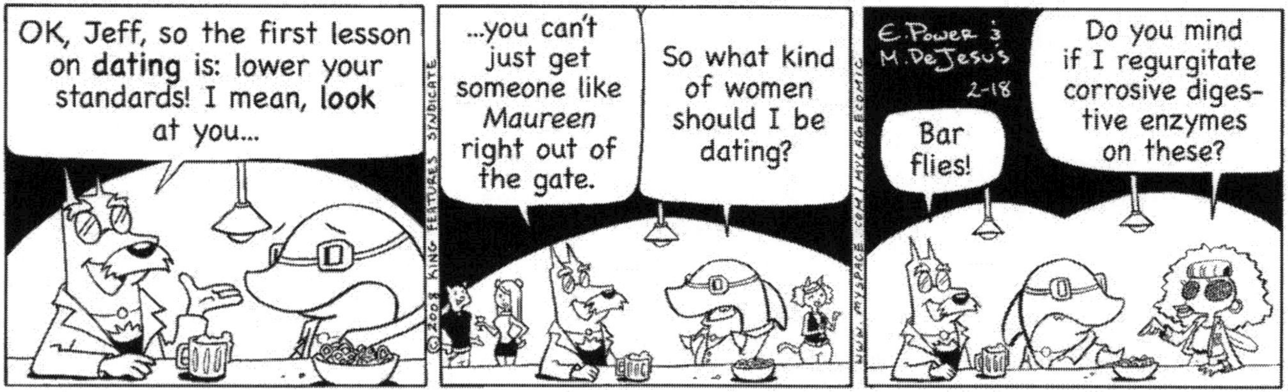
OK, Jeff, so the first lesson on **dating** is: lower your standards! I mean, **look** at you...
...you can't just get someone like *Maureen* right out of the gate.
So what kind of women should I be dating?
E. Power & M. DeJesus
2-18
Bar flies!
Do you mind if I regurgitate corrosive digestive enzymes on these?

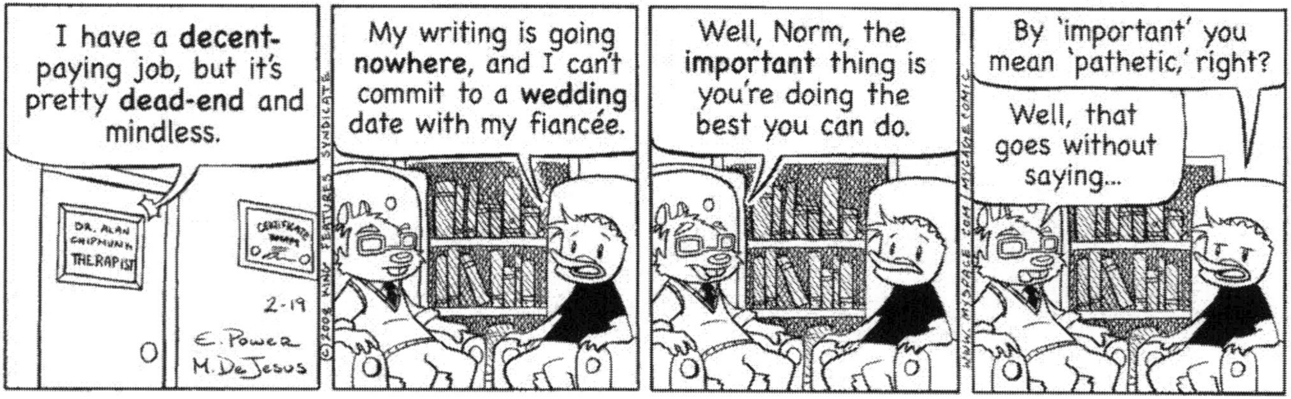
I have a **decent**-paying job, but it's pretty **dead-end** and mindless.
DR. ALAN CHIPMUNK THERAPIST
2-19
E. Power
M. DeJesus
My writing is going **nowhere**, and I can't commit to a **wedding** date with my fiancée.
Well, Norm, the **important** thing is you're doing the best you can do.
By 'important' you mean 'pathetic,' right?
Well, that goes without saying...

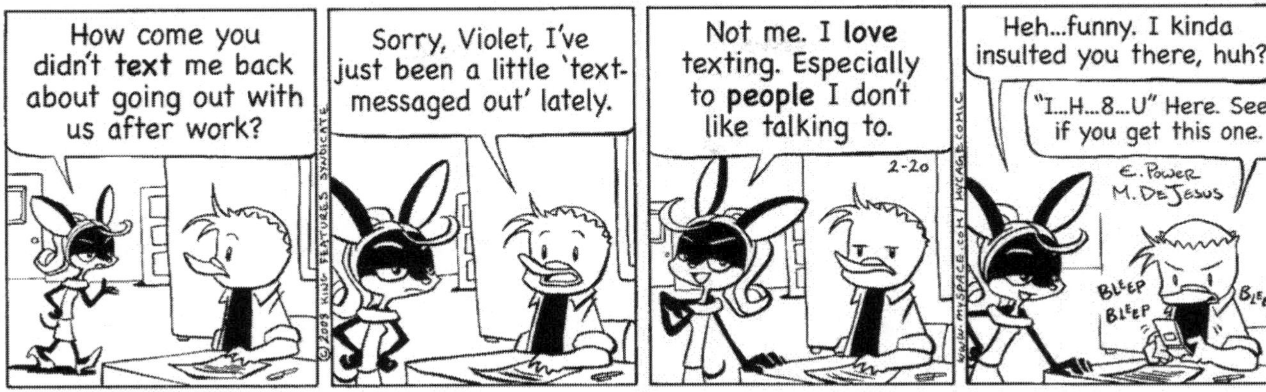
How come you didn't **text** me back about going out with us after work?
© 2009 King Features Syndicate
Sorry, Violet, I've just been a little 'text-messaged out' lately.
Not me. I **love** texting. Especially to **people** I don't like talking to.
2-20
Heh...funny. I kinda insulted you there, huh?
"I...H...8...U" Here. See if you get this one.
E. Power
M. DeJesus
BLEEP
BLEEP
BLEEP
www.myspace.com/mycage.comic

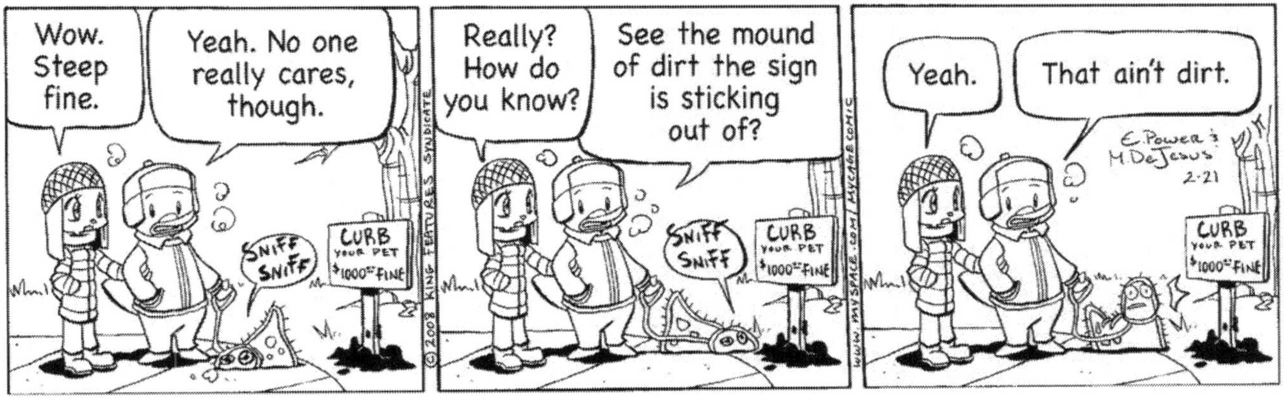
Wow. Steep fine.
Yeah. No one really cares, though.
SNIFF SNIFF
CURB YOUR PET $1000 FINE
© 2008 King Features Syndicate
Really? How do you know?
See the mound of dirt the sign is sticking out of?
SNIFF SNIFF
CURB YOUR PET $1000 FINE
www.myspace.com/mycage.comic
Yeah.
That ain't dirt.
E. Power & M. DeJesus
2-21
CURB YOUR PET $1000 FINE

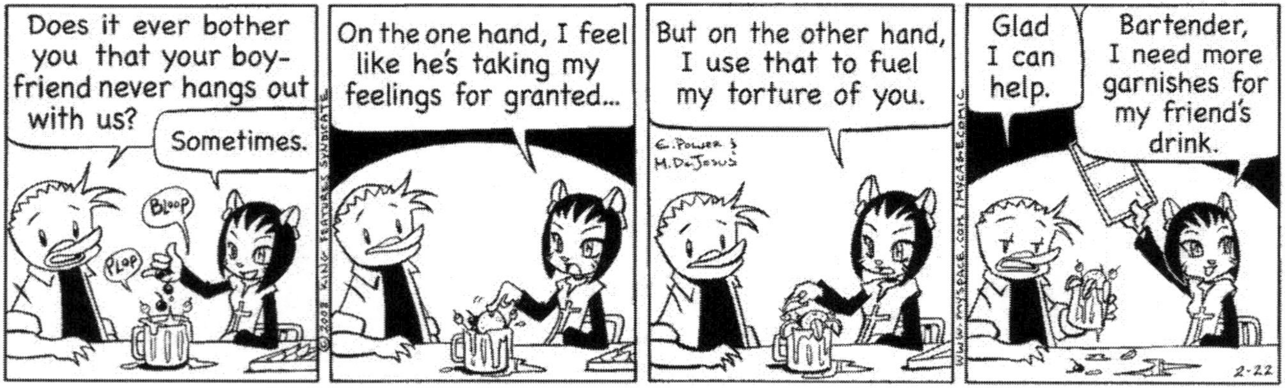
Does it ever bother you that your boy-friend never hangs out with us?
Sometimes.
BLOOP
PLOP
© 2008 KING FEATURES SYNDICATE
On the one hand, I feel like he's taking my feelings for granted...
But on the other hand, I use that to fuel my torture of you.
E. POWER & M. DEJESUS
WWW.MYSPACE.COM/MYCAGECOMIC
Glad I can help.
Bartender, I need more garnishes for my friend's drink.
2-22

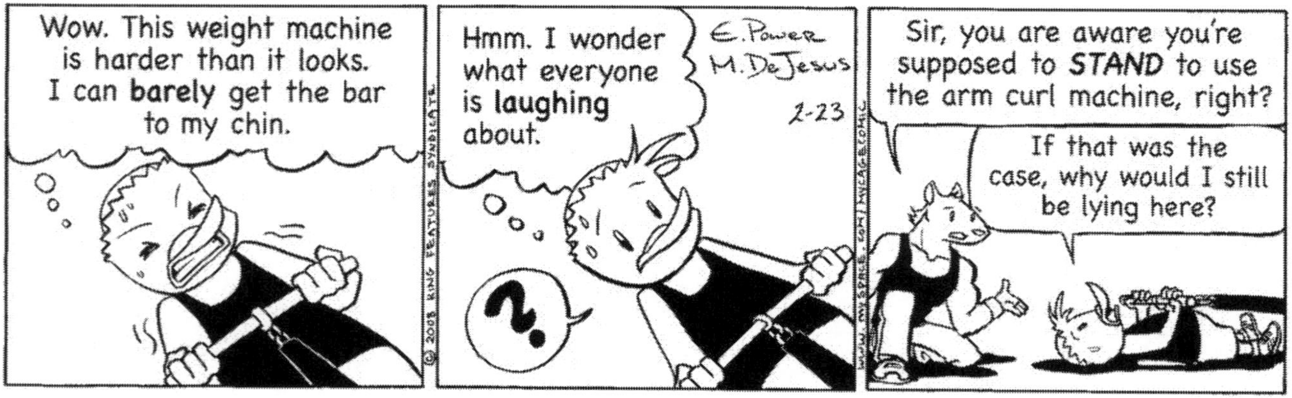
Wow. This weight machine is harder than it looks. I can **barely** get the bar to my chin.
© 2008 KING FEATURES SYNDICATE
Hmm. I wonder what everyone is **laughing** about.
?
E. POWER
M. DEJESUS
2-23
WWW.MYSPACE.COM/MYCAGECOMIC
Sir, you are aware you're supposed to ***STAND*** to use the arm curl machine, right?
If that was the case, why would I still be lying here?

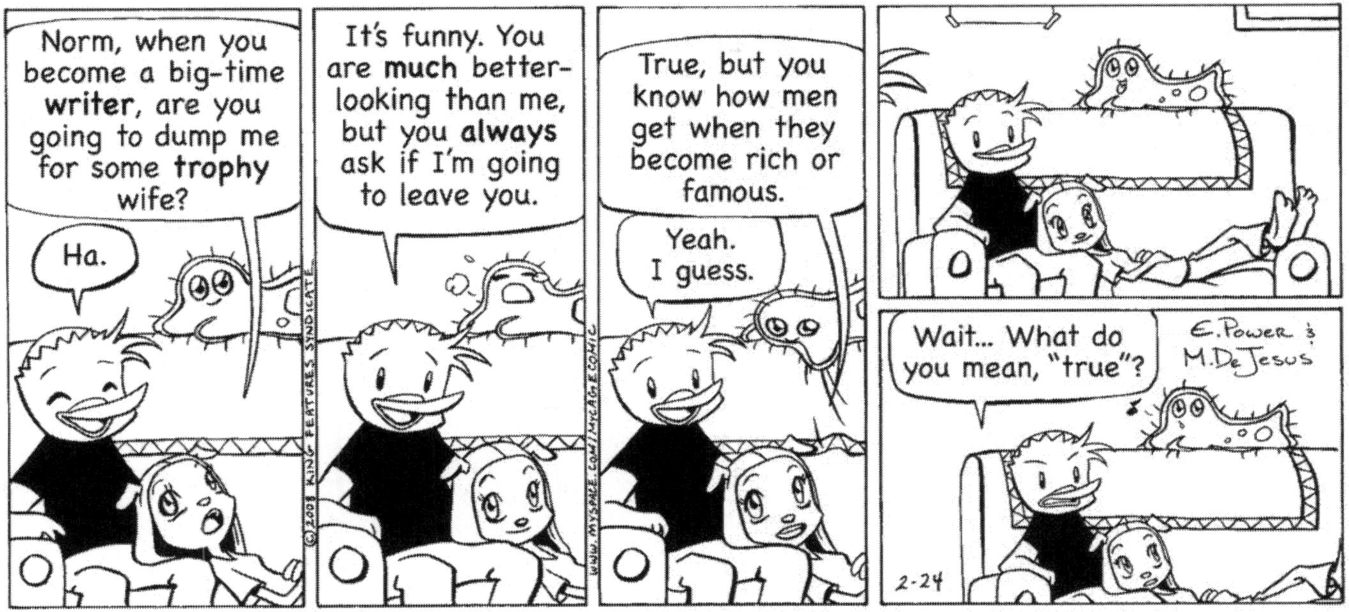
Norm, when you become a big-time **writer**, are you going to dump me for some **trophy** wife?
Ha.
©2008 KING FEATURES SYNDICATE
It's funny. You are **much** better-looking than me, but you **always** ask if I'm going to leave you.
WWW.MYSPACE.COM/MYCAGECOMIC
True, but you know how men get when they become rich or famous.
Yeah. I guess.
Wait... What do you mean, "true"?
E. Power & M. DeJesus
2-24

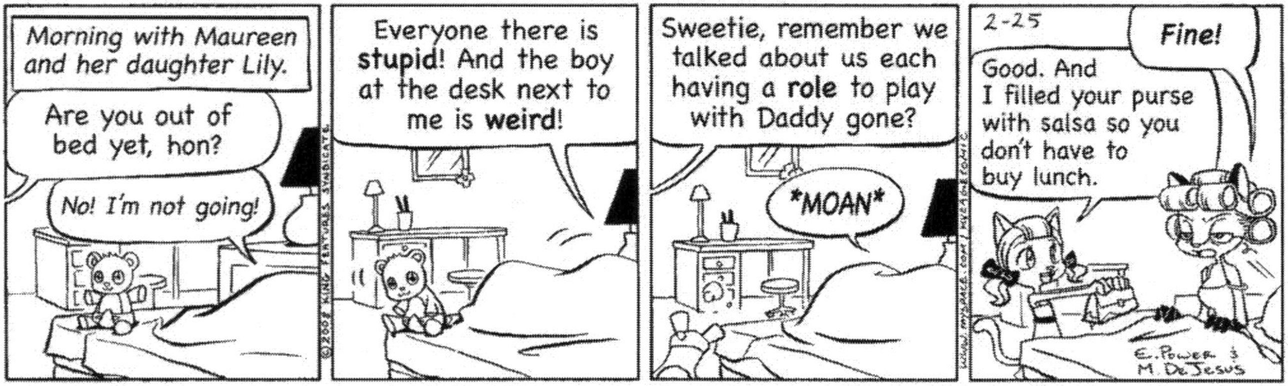
Morning with Maureen and her daughter Lily.
Are you out of bed yet, hon?
No! I'm not going!
Everyone there is **stupid**! And the boy at the desk next to me is **weird**!
Sweetie, remember we talked about us each having a **role** to play with Daddy gone?
MOAN
2-25
Good. And I filled your purse with salsa so you don't have to buy lunch.
Fine!
E. Power & M. DeJesus
©2008 King Features Syndicate
www.myspace.com/mycagecomic

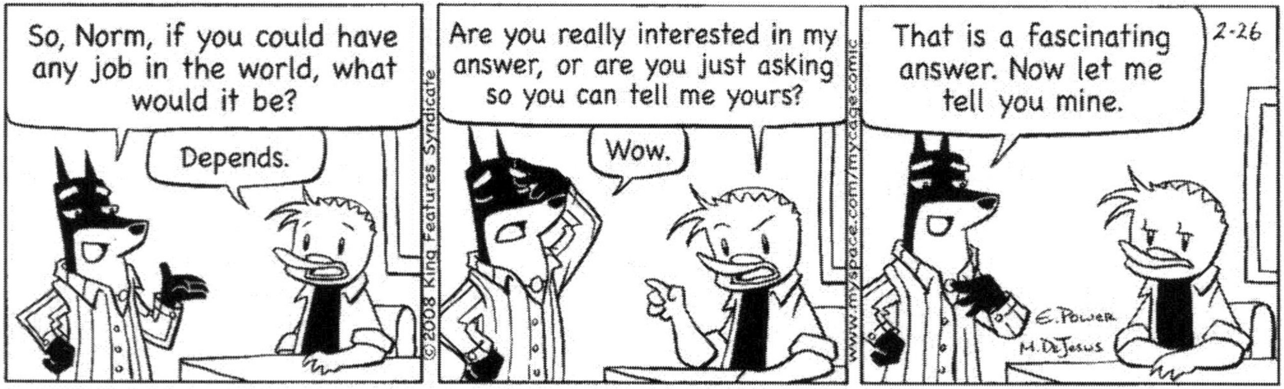
So, Norm, if you could have any job in the world, what would it be?
Depends.
Are you really interested in my answer, or are you just asking so you can tell me yours?
Wow.
That is a fascinating answer. Now let me tell you mine.
2-26
E. Power
M. DeJesus
©2008 King Features Syndicate
www.myspace.com/mycagecomic

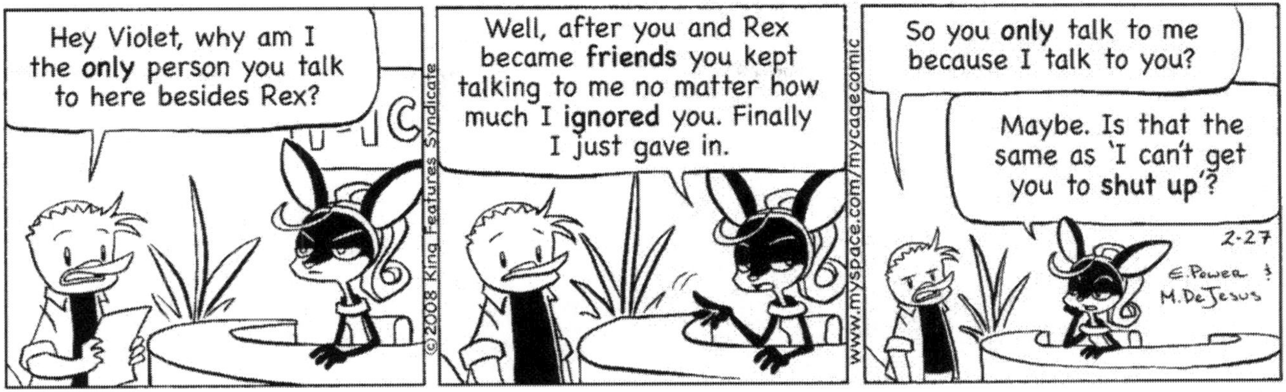
Hey Violet, why am I the **only** person you talk to here besides Rex?
Well, after you and Rex became **friends** you kept talking to me no matter how much I **ignored** you. Finally I just gave in.
So you **only** talk to me because I talk to you?
Maybe. Is that the same as 'I can't get you to **shut up**'?
2-27
E. Power & M. DeJesus
© 2008 King Features Syndicate
www.myspace.com/mycagecomic

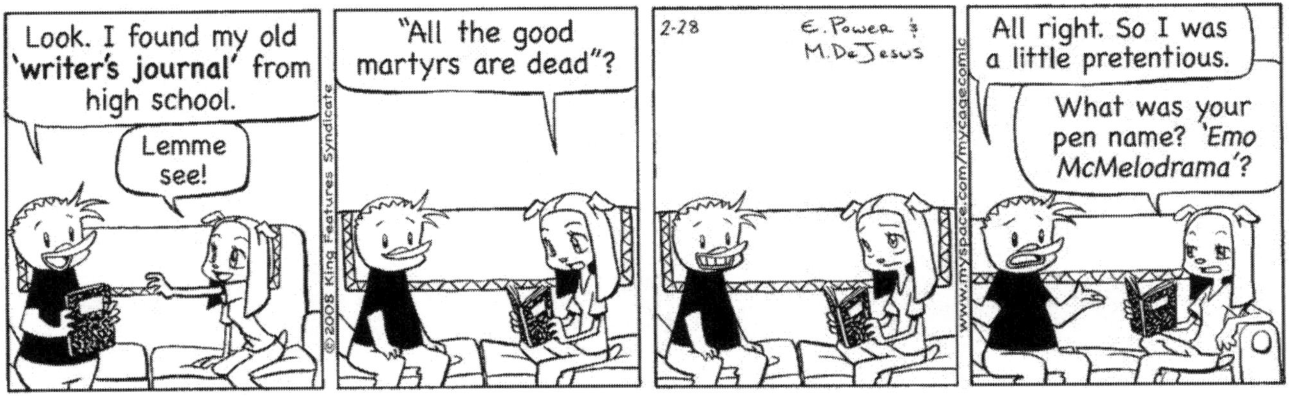
Look. I found my old **'writer's journal'** from high school.
Lemme see!
"All the good martyrs are dead"?
2-28
E. Power & M. DeJesus
All right. So I was a little pretentious.
What was your pen name? *'Emo McMelodrama'*?
© 2008 King Features Syndicate
www.myspace.com/mycagecomic

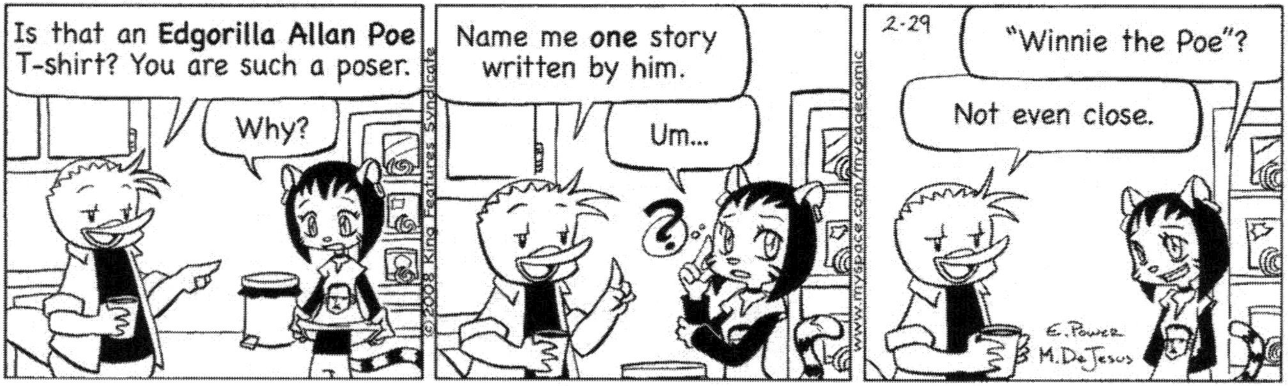
Is that an **Edgorilla Allan Poe** T-shirt? You are such a poser.
Why?
©2008 King Features Syndicate
Name me **one** story written by him.
Um...
?
www.myspace.com/mycagecomic
2-29
"Winnie the Poe"?
Not even close.
E. Power
M. DeJesus

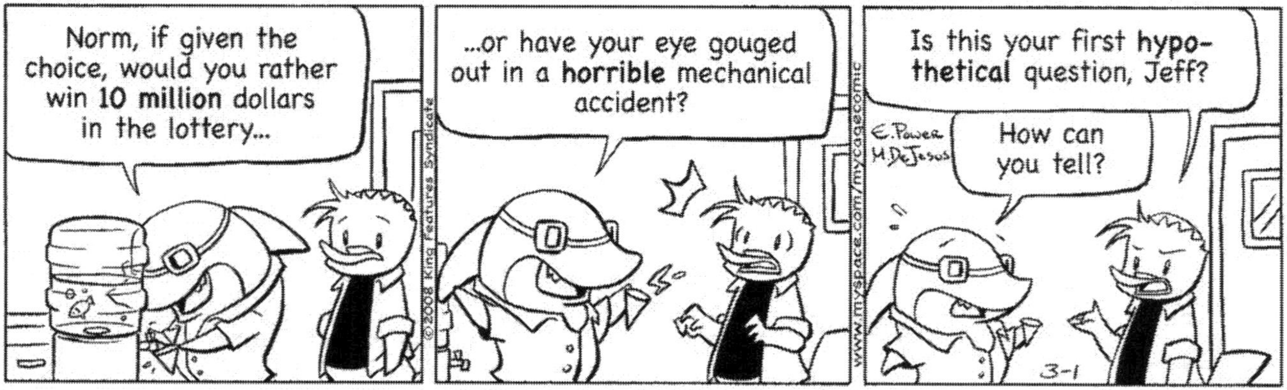
Norm, if given the choice, would you rather win **10 million** dollars in the lottery...
©2008 King Features Syndicate
...or have your eye gouged out in a **horrible** mechanical accident?
www.myspace.com/mycagecomic
Is this your first **hypo-thetical** question, Jeff?
E. Power
M. DeJesus
How can you tell?
3-1

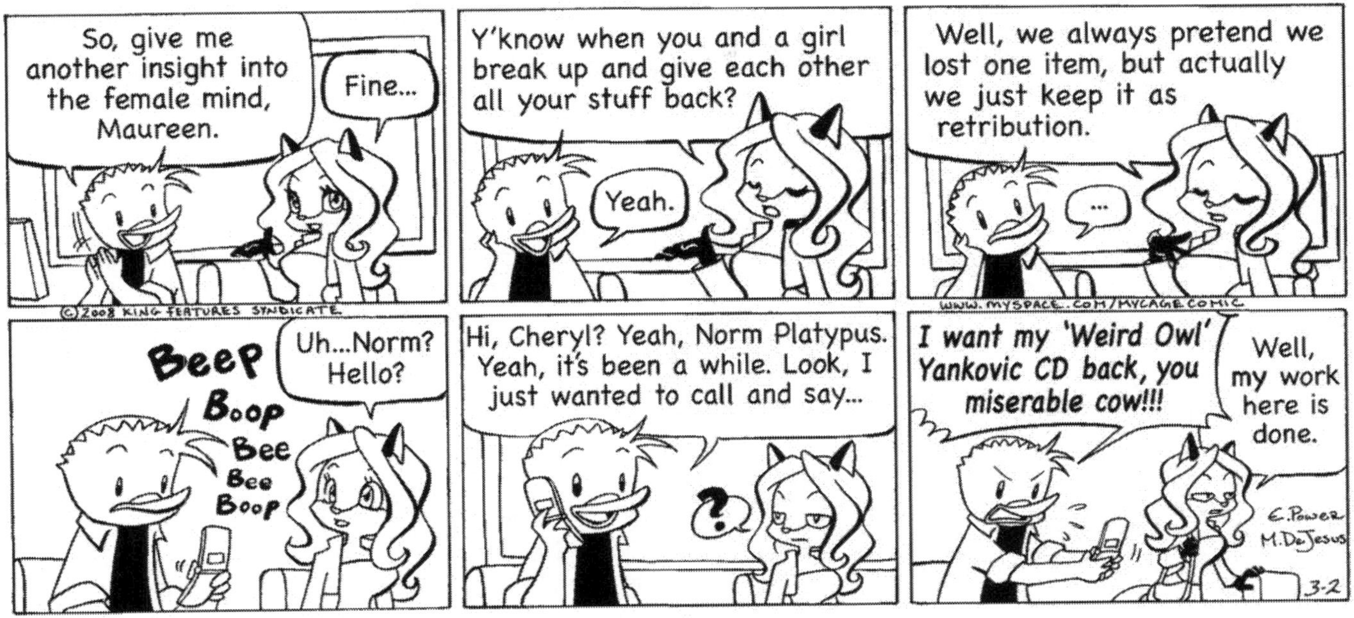
So, give me another insight into the female mind, Maureen.
Fine...
Y'know when you and a girl break up and give each other all your stuff back?
Yeah.
Well, we always pretend we lost one item, but actually we just keep it as retribution.
...
©2008 KING FEATURES SYNDICATE
WWW.MYSPACE.COM/MYCAGECOMIC
Beep Boop Bee Bee Boop
Uh...Norm? Hello?
Hi, Cheryl? Yeah, Norm Platypus. Yeah, it's been a while. Look, I just wanted to call and say...
?
I want my 'Weird Owl' Yankovic CD back, you miserable cow!!!
Well, my work here is done.
E.Power
M.DeJesus
3-2

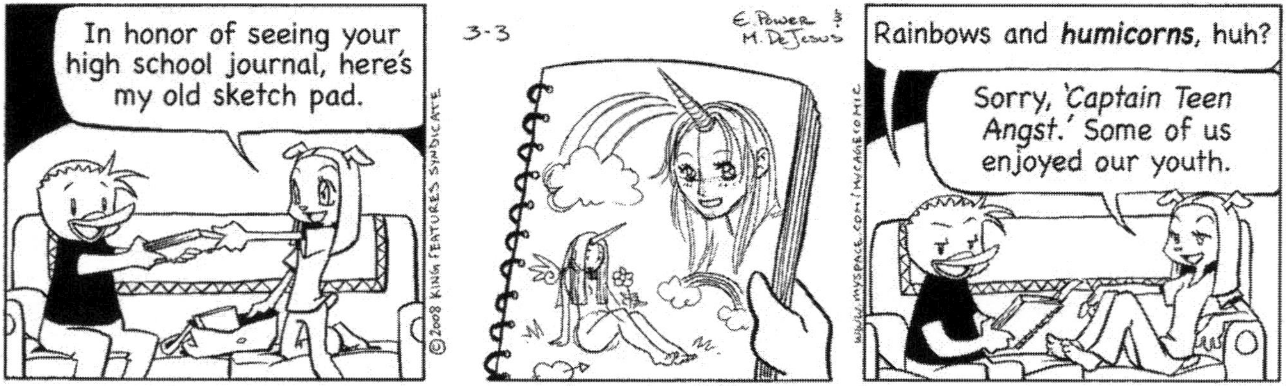
In honor of seeing your high school journal, here's my old sketch pad.
© 2008 King Features Syndicate
3-3
E. Power & M. DeJesus
www.myspace.com/mycagecomic
Rainbows and **humicorns**, huh?
Sorry, '*Captain Teen Angst*.' Some of us enjoyed our youth.

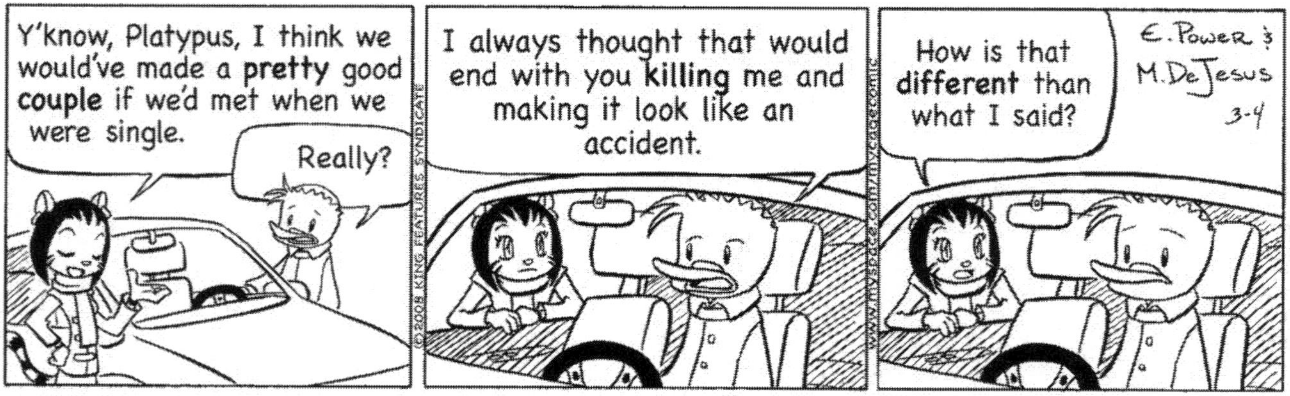
Y'know, Platypus, I think we would've made a **pretty** good **couple** if we'd met when we were single.
Really?
© 2008 King Features Syndicate
I always thought that would end with you **killing** me and making it look like an accident.
www.myspace.com/mycagecomic
How is that **different** than what I said?
E. Power & M. DeJesus
3-4

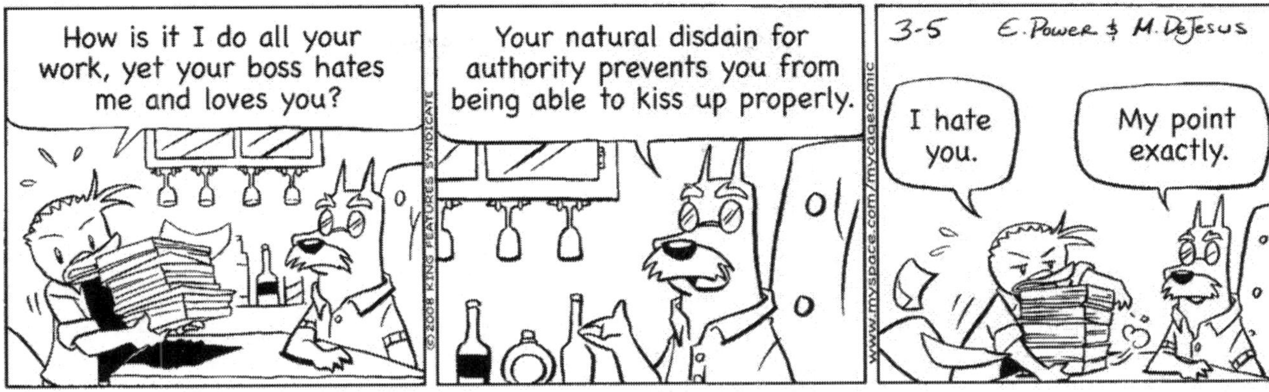
How is it I do all your work, yet your boss hates me and loves you?
©2008 KING FEATURES SYNDICATE
Your natural disdain for authority prevents you from being able to kiss up properly.
www.myspace.com/mycagecomic
3-5 E. Power & M. DeJesus
I hate you.
My point exactly.

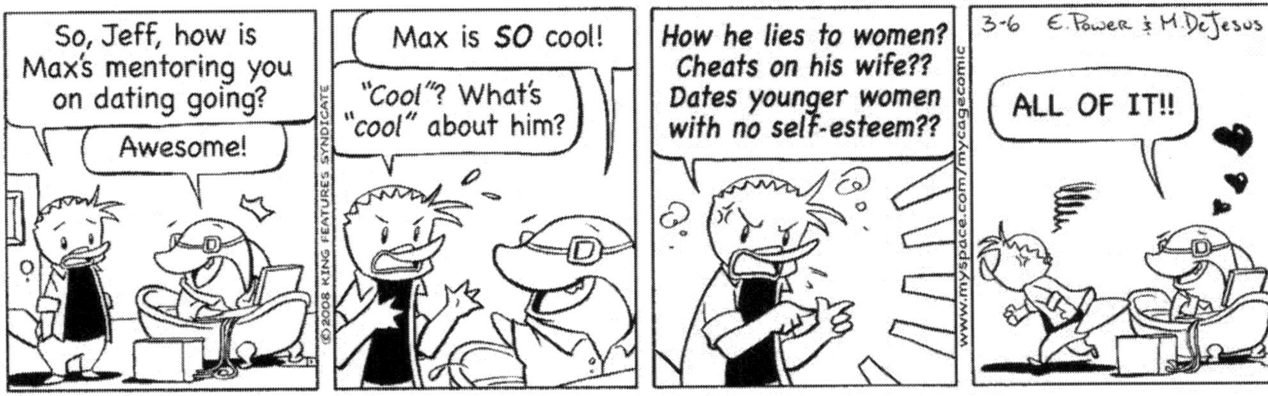
So, Jeff, how is Max's mentoring you on dating going?
Awesome!
©2008 KING FEATURES SYNDICATE
Max is *SO* cool!
"Cool"? What's "cool" about him?
How he lies to women? Cheats on his wife?? Dates younger women with no self-esteem??
www.myspace.com/mycagecomic
3-6 E. Power & M. DeJesus
ALL OF IT!!

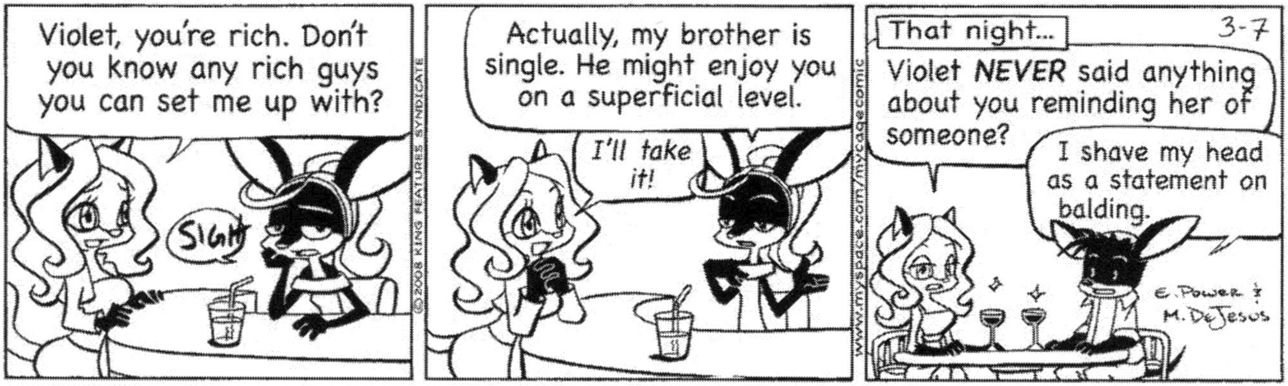
Violet, you're rich. Don't you know any rich guys you can set me up with?
SIGH
©2008 KING FEATURES SYNDICATE
Actually, my brother is single. He might enjoy you on a superficial level.
I'll take it!
www.myspace.com/mycagecomic
That night...
3-7
Violet **NEVER** said anything about you reminding her of someone?
I shave my head as a statement on balding.
E. Power & M. DeJesus

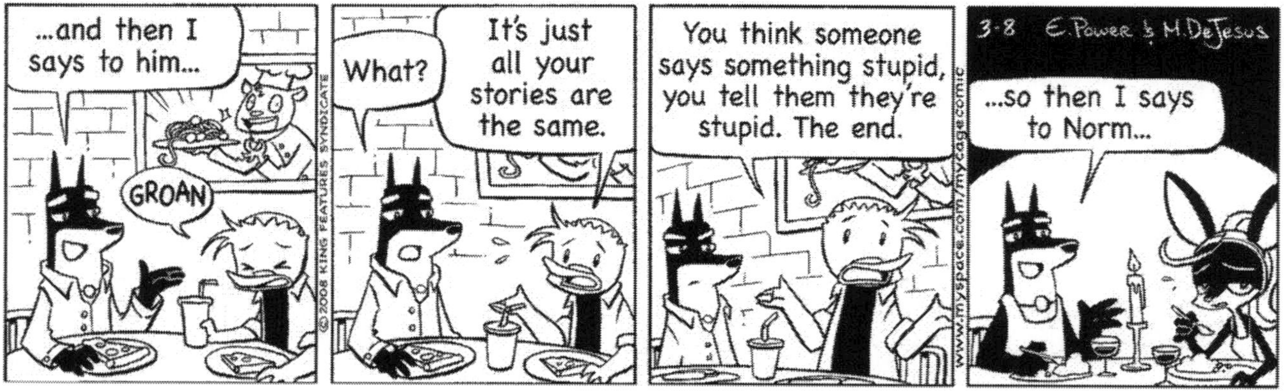
...and then I says to him...
GROAN
©2008 KING FEATURES SYNDICATE
What?
It's just all your stories are the same.
You think someone says something stupid, you tell them they're stupid. The end.
www.myspace.com/mycagecomic
3-8 E. Power & M. DeJesus
...so then I says to Norm...

As a boy, *Chuck Duckwing* saw his grandfather gunned down by a common criminal...

Noooooooo!

Vowing vengeance, he uses his grandfather's fortune to train his body and mind...

Wow. Working out is applied physics. Who knew?

© 2008 KING FEATURES SYNDICATE

...and designs an array of amazing weapons!

Humarangs

The Man-Ray

Man-cuffs

3-9

E. Power
H. DeJesus

WWW. MYSPACE. COM / MYCAGE COMIC

Now, dressed as the mythical hunter of animals, a "Human Being," he fights evil as... MAN-DUCK!!

...with his sidekick, SCOUT the boy-cub!!

Uh, hon, doesn't this seem a little like a certain other superhero?

Not in the slightest. Now, let me tell you about his arch-foe, FUNNY-RABBIT.

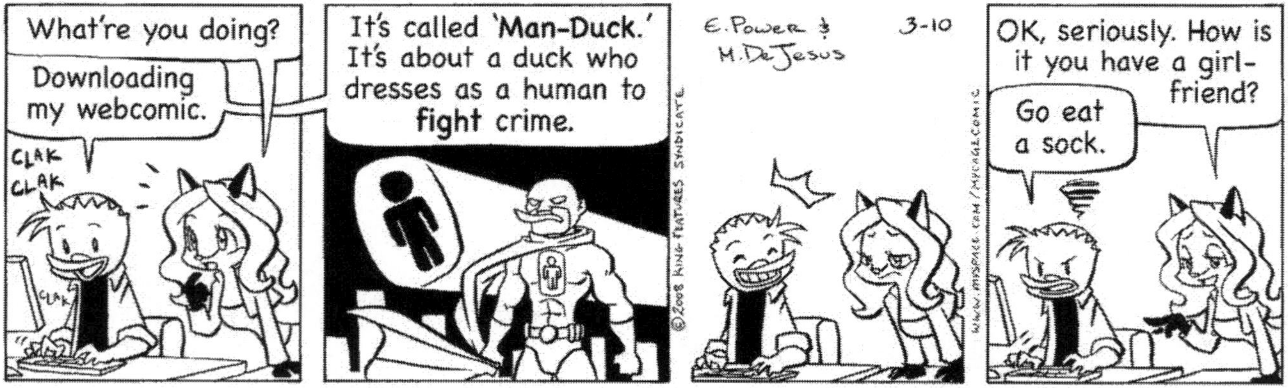
What're you doing?
Downloading my webcomic.
CLAK CLAK
CLAK
It's called **'Man-Duck.'** It's about a duck who dresses as a human to **fight** crime.
©2008 KING FEATURES SYNDICATE
E. Power & M. DeJesus
3-10
WWW.MYSPACE.COM/MYCAGECOMIC
OK, seriously. How is it you have a girl-friend?
Go eat a sock.

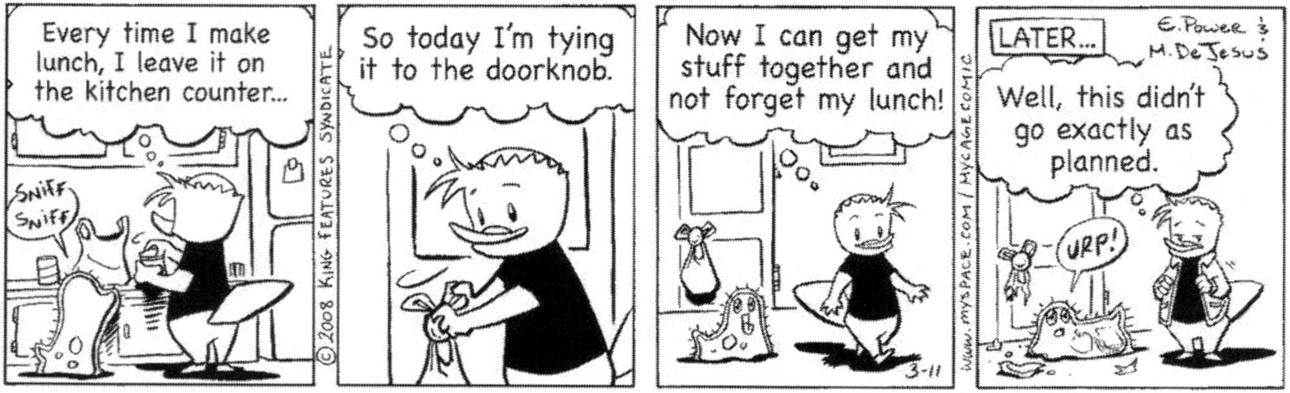
Every time I make lunch, I leave it on the kitchen counter...
SNIFF SNIFF
© 2008 KING FEATURES SYNDICATE
So today I'm tying it to the doorknob.
Now I can get my stuff together and not forget my lunch!
3-11
WWW.MYSPACE.COM / MYCAGECOMIC
LATER...
E. Power & M. DeJesus
Well, this didn't go exactly as planned.
URP!

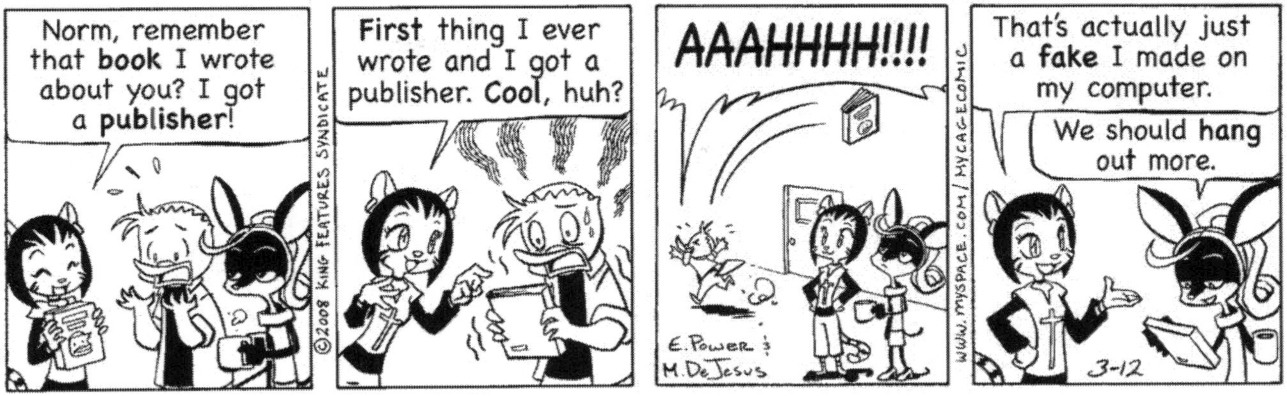
Norm, remember that **book** I wrote about you? I got a **publisher**!
©2008 KING FEATURES SYNDICATE
First thing I ever wrote and I got a publisher. **Cool**, huh?
AAAHHHH!!!!
E. Power & M. DeJesus
WWW.MYSPACE.COM/MYCAGECOMIC
That's actually just a **fake** I made on my computer.
We should **hang** out more.
3-12

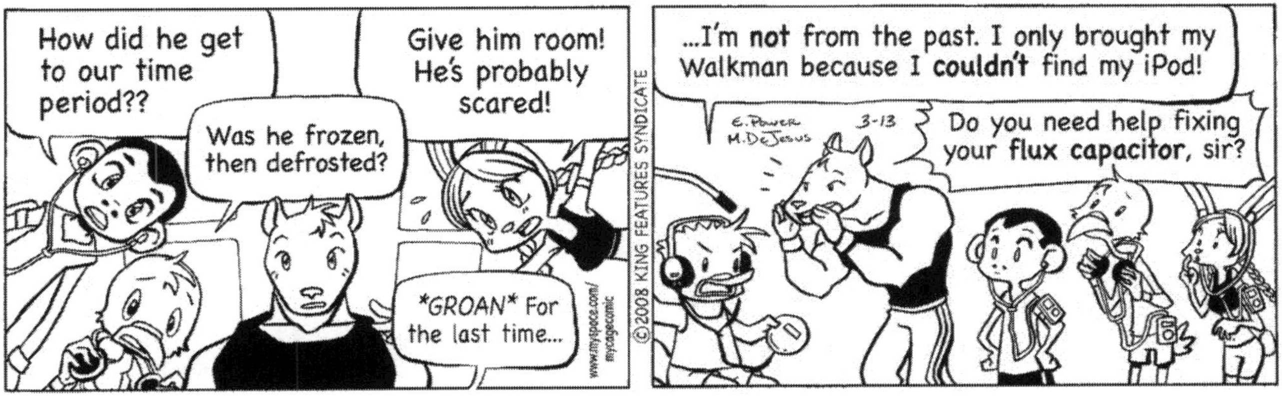
How did he get to our time period??
Was he frozen, then defrosted?
Give him room! He's probably scared!
GROAN For the last time...
www.myspace.com/mycagecomic
©2008 KING FEATURES SYNDICATE
...I'm **not** from the past. I only brought my Walkman because I **couldn't** find my iPod!
E. Power M. DeJesus
3-13
Do you need help fixing your **flux capacitor**, sir?

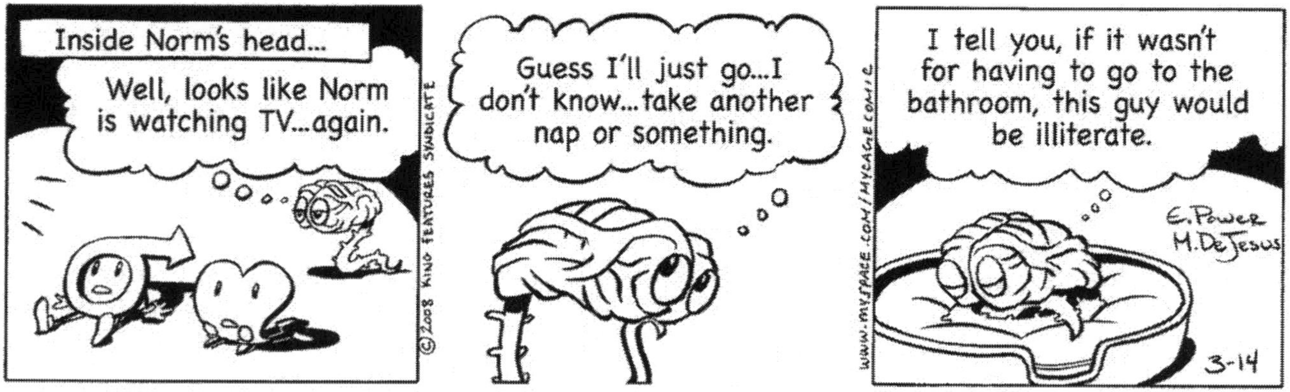
Inside Norm's head...
Well, looks like Norm is watching TV...again.
©2008 King Features Syndicate
Guess I'll just go...I don't know...take another nap or something.
www.myspace.com/mycagecomic
I tell you, if it wasn't for having to go to the bathroom, this guy would be illiterate.
E. Power M. DeJesus
3-14

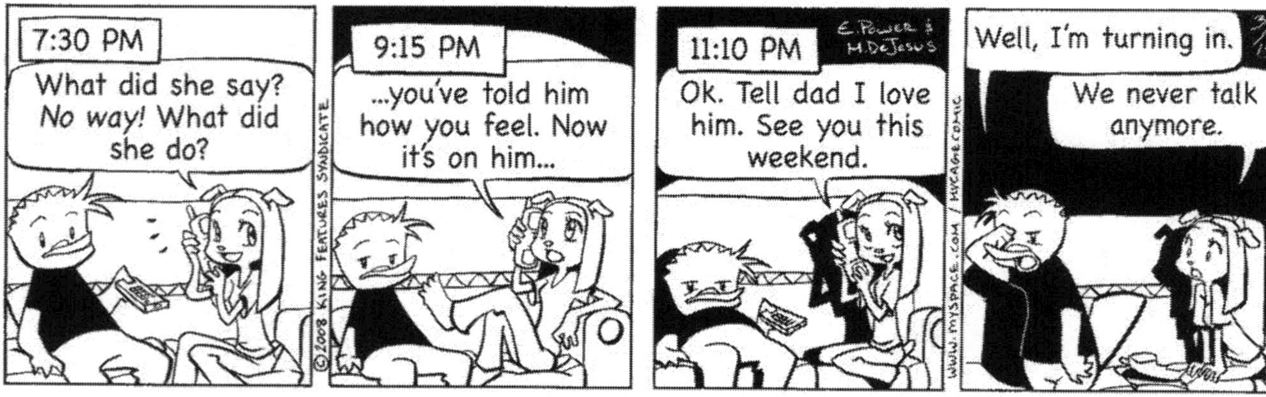
7:30 PM
What did she say? *No way!* What did she do?
©2008 King Features Syndicate
9:15 PM
...you've told him how you feel. Now it's on him...
11:10 PM
E. Power & M. DeJesus
Ok. Tell dad I love him. See you this weekend.
www.myspace.com/mycagecomic
Well, I'm turning in.
3/15
We never talk anymore.

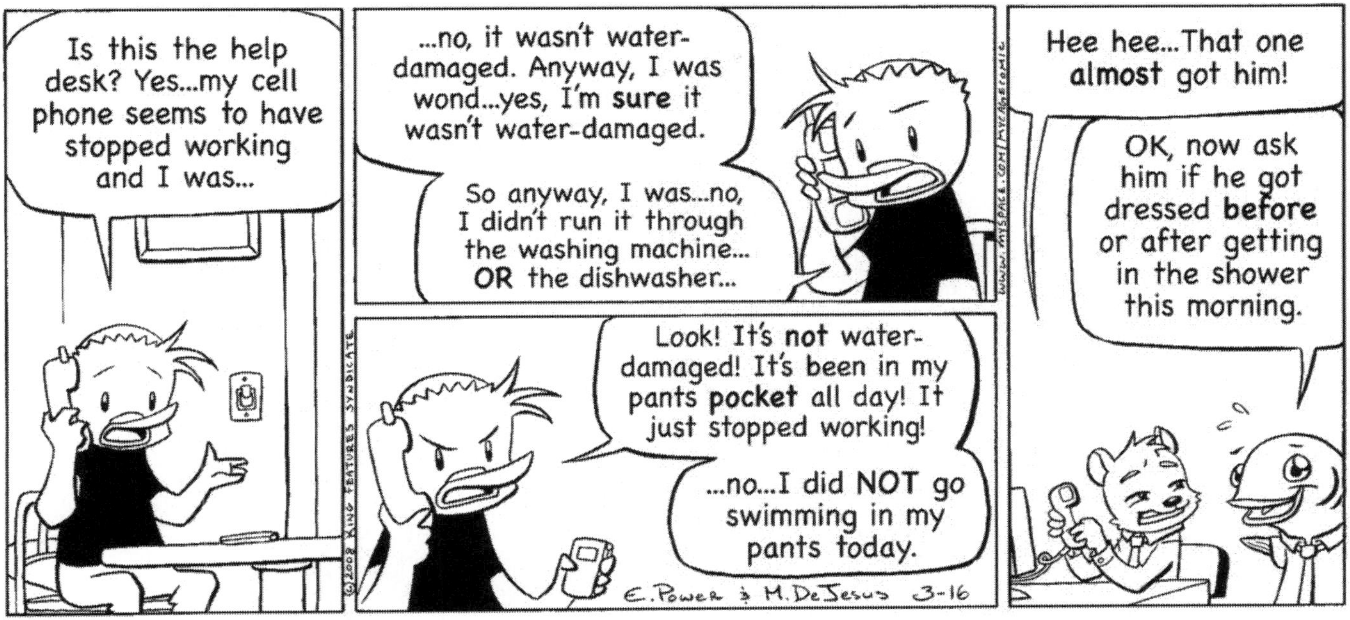
Is this the help desk? Yes...my cell phone seems to have stopped working and I was...
...no, it wasn't water-damaged. Anyway, I was wond...yes, I'm **sure** it wasn't water-damaged.
So anyway, I was...no, I didn't run it through the washing machine... **OR** the dishwasher...
Look! It's **not** water-damaged! It's been in my pants **pocket** all day! It just stopped working!
...no...I did **NOT** go swimming in my pants today.
E. Power & M. DeJesus 3-16
Hee hee...That one **almost** got him!
OK, now ask him if he got dressed **before** or after getting in the shower this morning.

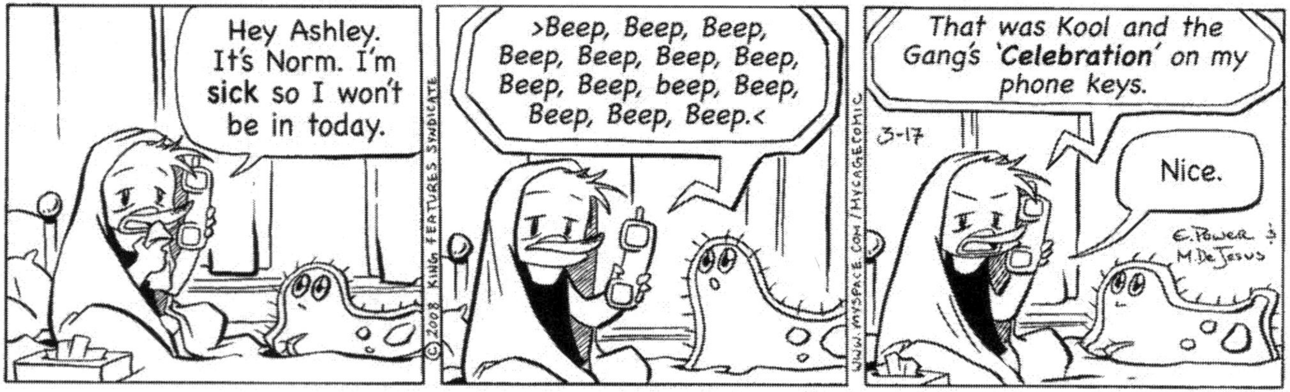
Hey Ashley. It's Norm. I'm **sick** so I won't be in today.
>Beep, Beep, Beep, Beep, Beep, Beep, Beep, Beep, Beep, beep, Beep, Beep, Beep, Beep.<
That was Kool and the Gang's '**Celebration**' on my phone keys.
Nice.
3-17
E. Power & M. DeJesus
© 2008 King Features Syndicate
www.myspace.com/mycagecomic

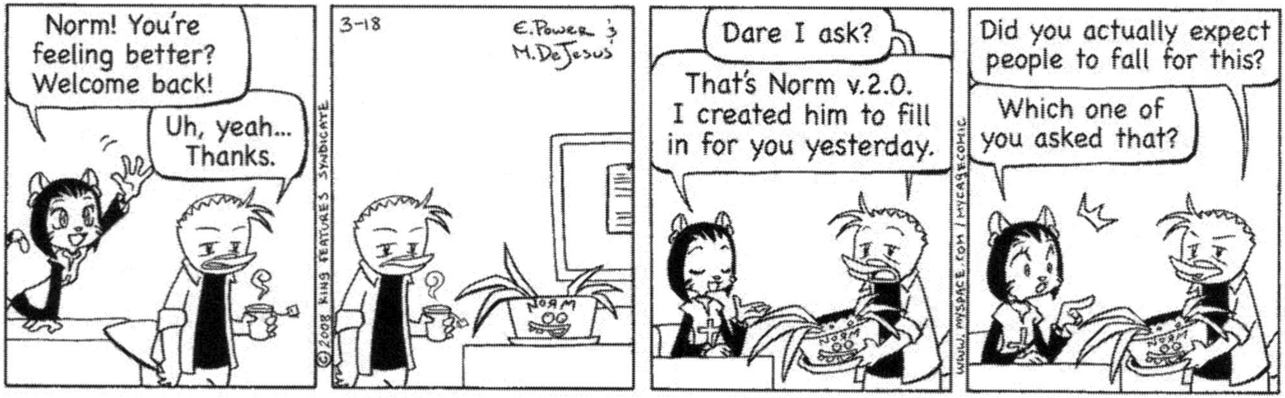
Norm! You're feeling better? Welcome back!
Uh, yeah... Thanks.
3-18
E. Power & M. DeJesus
NORM
Dare I ask?
That's Norm v.2.0. I created him to fill in for you yesterday.
Did you actually expect people to fall for this?
Which one of you asked that?
© 2008 King Features Syndicate
www.myspace.com/mycagecomic

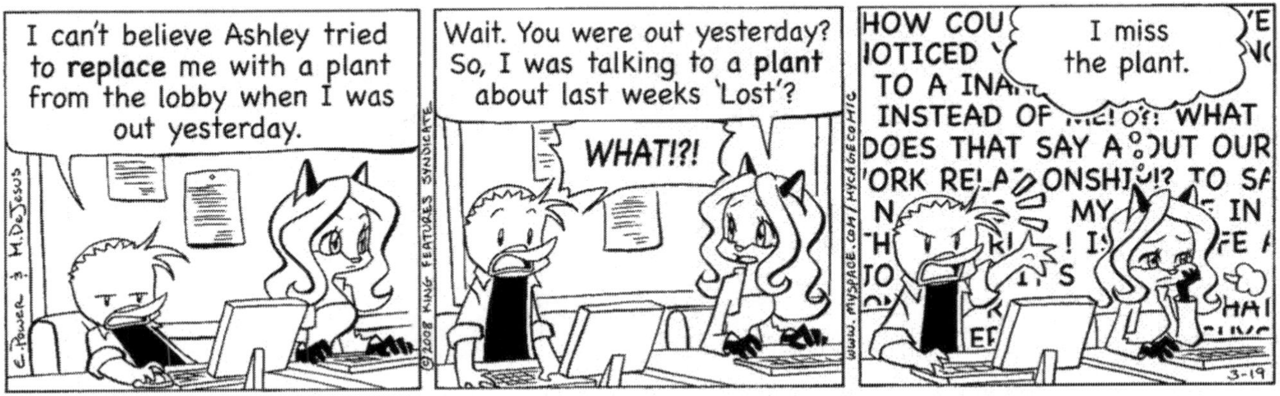
I can't believe Ashley tried to **replace** me with a plant from the lobby when I was out yesterday.
E. Power & M. DeJesus
© 2008 King Features Syndicate
Wait. You were out yesterday? So, I was talking to a **plant** about last weeks 'Lost'?
WHAT!?!
www.myspace.com/mycagecomic
I miss the plant.
3-19

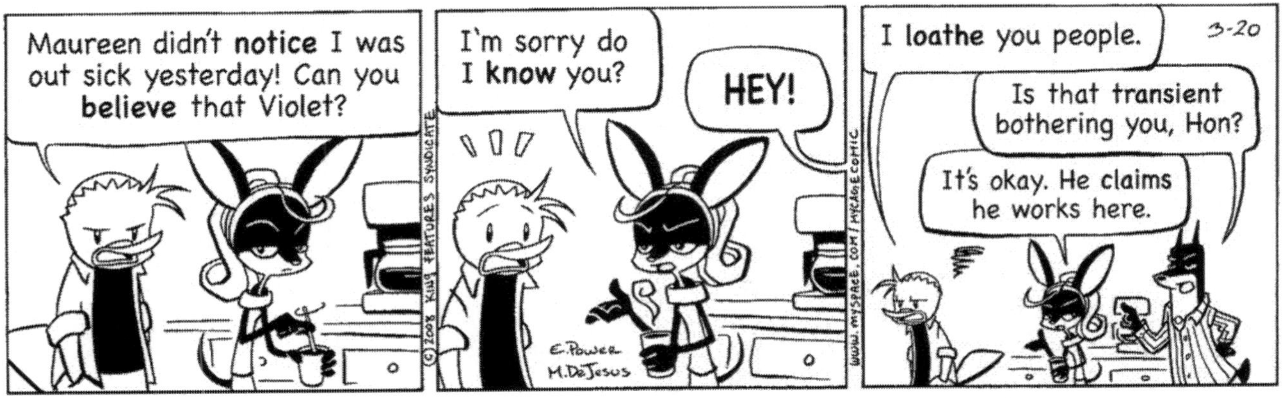
Maureen didn't **notice** I was out sick yesterday! Can you **believe** that Violet?
© 2008 King Features Syndicate
I'm sorry do I **know** you?
HEY!
E. Power
M. DeJesus
www.myspace.com/mycagecomic
I **loathe** you people.
3-20
Is that **transient** bothering you, Hon?
It's okay. He claims he works here.

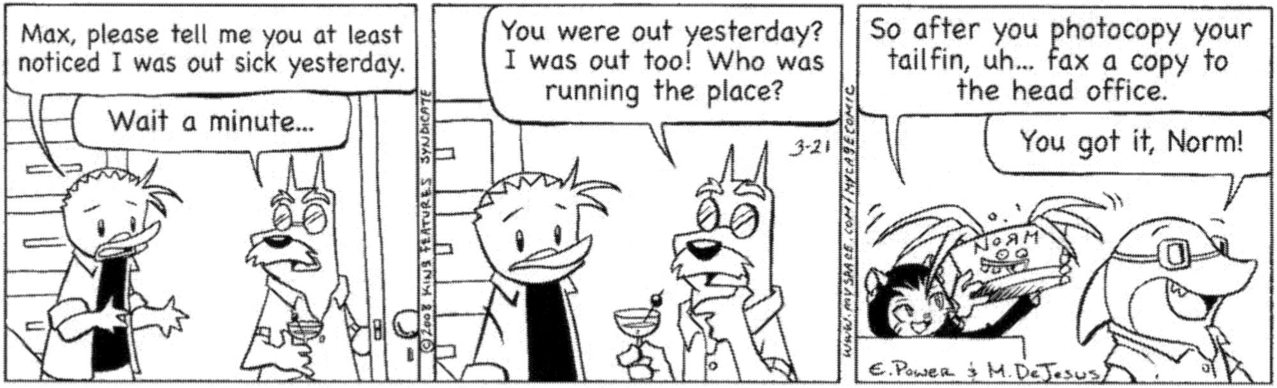
Max, please tell me you at least noticed I was out sick yesterday.
Wait a minute...
© 2008 King Features Syndicate
You were out yesterday? I was out too! Who was running the place?
3-21
www.myspace.com/mycagecomic
So after you photocopy your tailfin, uh... fax a copy to the head office.
You got it, Norm!
NORM
E. Power & M. DeJesus

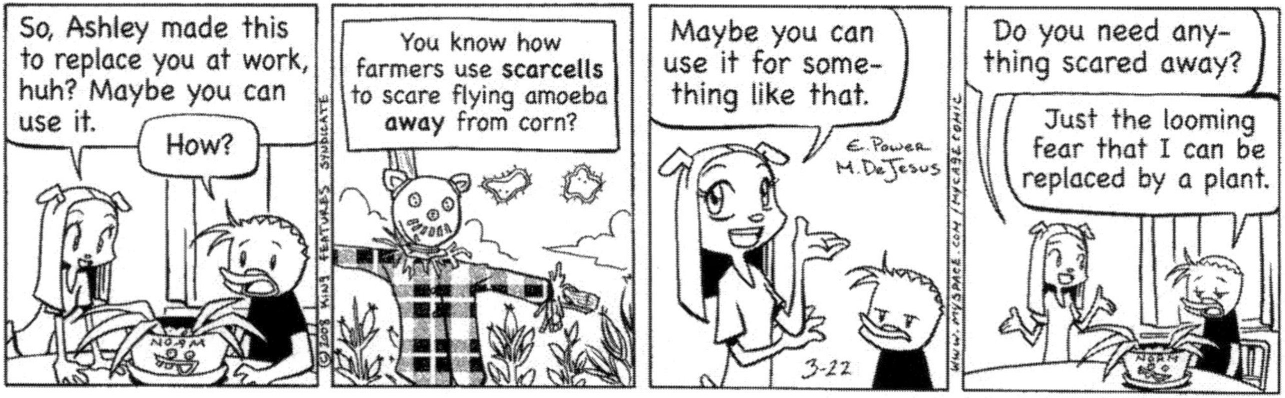
So, Ashley made this to replace you at work, huh? Maybe you can use it.
How?
NORM
© 2008 King Features Syndicate
You know how farmers use **scarcells** to scare flying amoeba **away** from corn?
Maybe you can use it for something like that.
E. Power
M. DeJesus
3-22
www.myspace.com/mycagecomic
Do you need anything scared away?
Just the looming fear that I can be replaced by a plant.
NORM

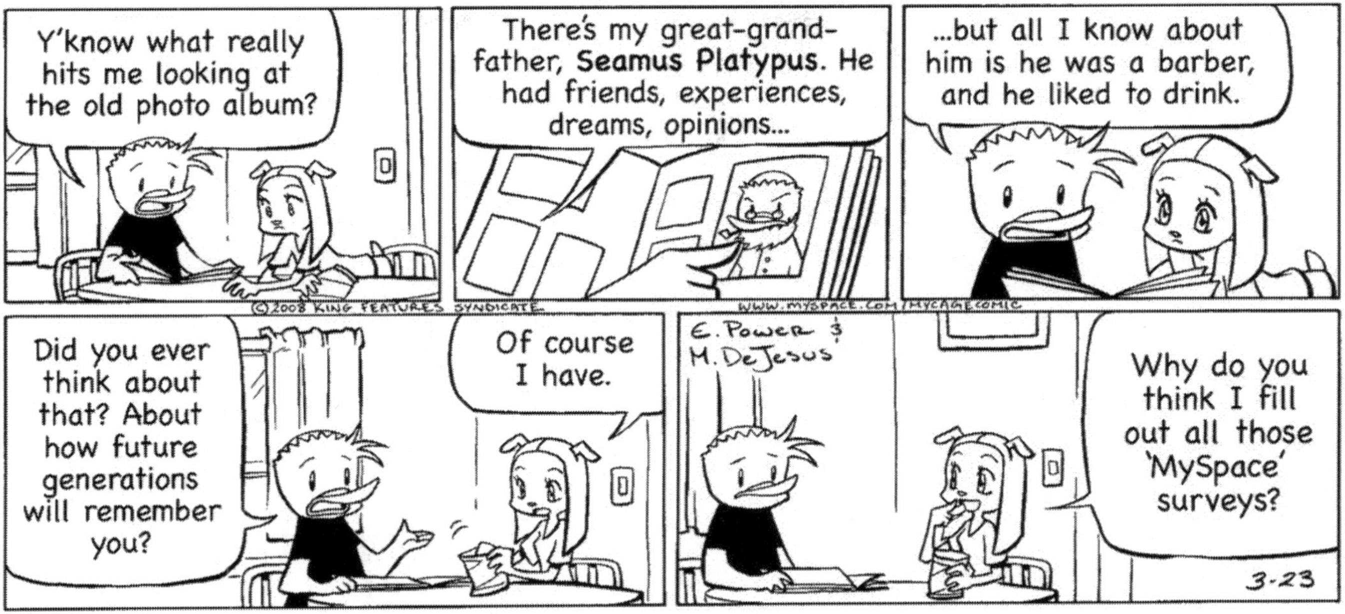
Y'know what really hits me looking at the old photo album?
There's my great-grand-father, **Seamus Platypus**. He had friends, experiences, dreams, opinions...
...but all I know about him is he was a barber, and he liked to drink.
©2008 KING FEATURES SYNDICATE
WWW.MYSPACE.COM/MYCAGECOMIC
Did you ever think about that? About how future generations will remember you?
Of course I have.
E. POWER & M. DEJESUS
Why do you think I fill out all those 'MySpace' surveys?
3-23

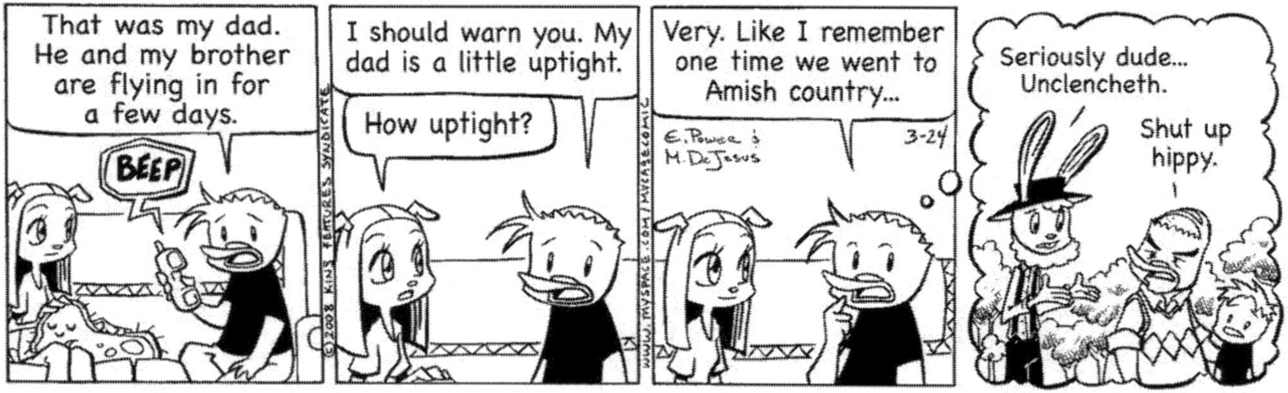
That was my dad. He and my brother are flying in for a few days.
BEEP
© 2008 KING FEATURES SYNDICATE
I should warn you. My dad is a little uptight.
How uptight?
WWW.MYSPACE.COM/MYCASECOMIC
Very. Like I remember one time we went to Amish country...
E. Power & M. DeJesus
3-24
Seriously dude... Unclencheth.
Shut up hippy.

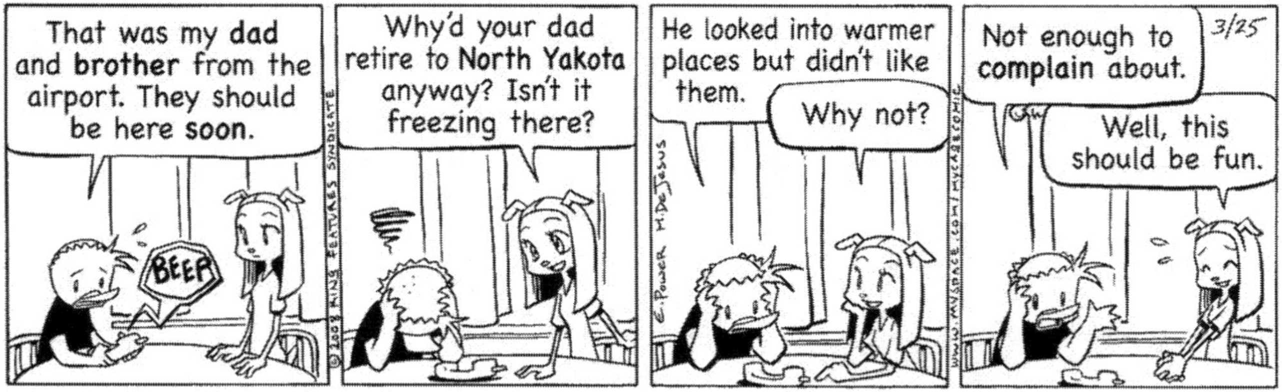
That was my dad and brother from the airport. They should be here soon.
BEEP
© 2008 KING FEATURES SYNDICATE
Why'd your dad retire to North Yakota anyway? Isn't it freezing there?
E. Power M. DeJesus
He looked into warmer places but didn't like them.
Why not?
WWW.MYSPACE.COM/MYCASECOMIC
Not enough to complain about.
3/25
Well, this should be fun.

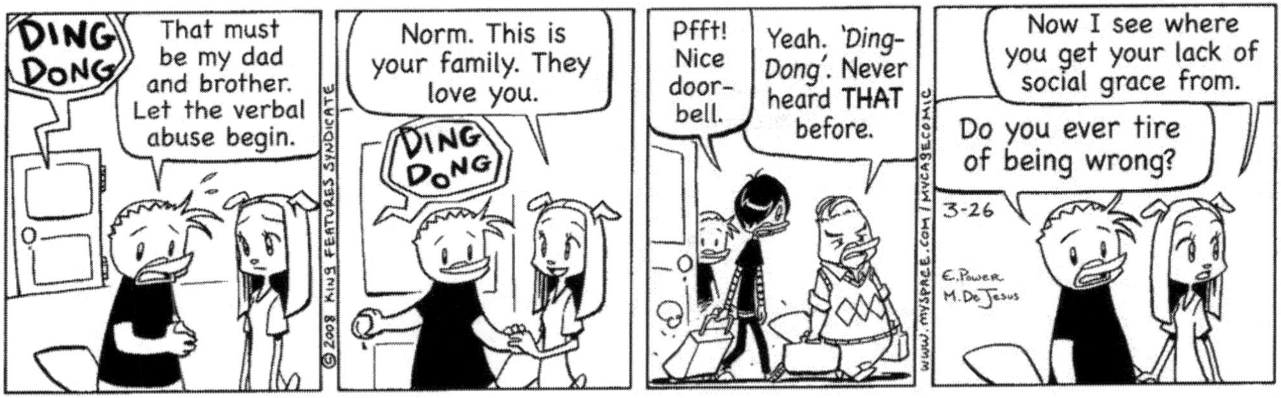
DING DONG
That must be my dad and brother. Let the verbal abuse begin.
© 2008 KING FEATURES SYNDICATE
Norm. This is your family. They love you.
DING DONG
Pfft! Nice door-bell.
Yeah. 'Ding-Dong'. Never heard THAT before.
WWW.MYSPACE.COM/MYCAGECOMIC
3-26
E. Power
M. DeJesus
Now I see where you get your lack of social grace from.
Do you ever tire of being wrong?

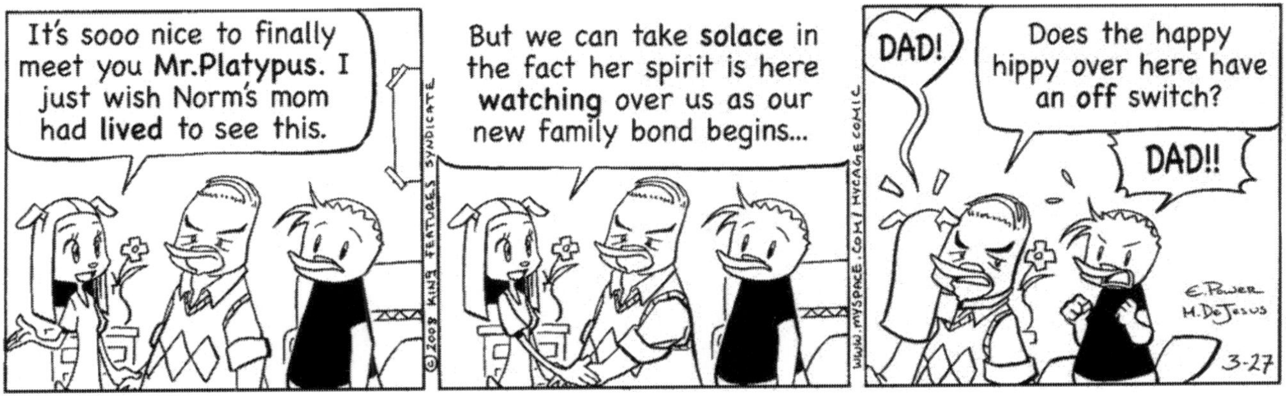
It's sooo nice to finally meet you Mr.Platypus. I just wish Norm's mom had lived to see this.
© 2008 KING FEATURES SYNDICATE
But we can take solace in the fact her spirit is here watching over us as our new family bond begins...
WWW.MYSPACE.COM/MYCAGECOMIC
DAD!
Does the happy hippy over here have an off switch?
DAD!!
E. Power
M. DeJesus
3-27

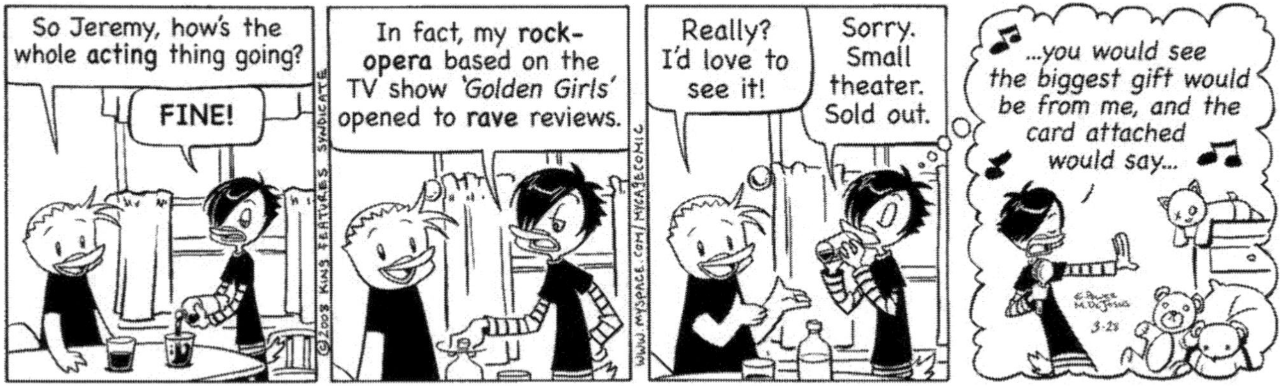
So Jeremy, how's the whole acting thing going?
FINE!
© 2008 KING FEATURES SYNDICATE
In fact, my rock-opera based on the TV show 'Golden Girls' opened to rave reviews.
WWW.MYSPACE.COM/MYCAGECOMIC
Really? I'd love to see it!
Sorry. Small theater. Sold out.
...you would see the biggest gift would be from me, and the card attached would say...
3-28

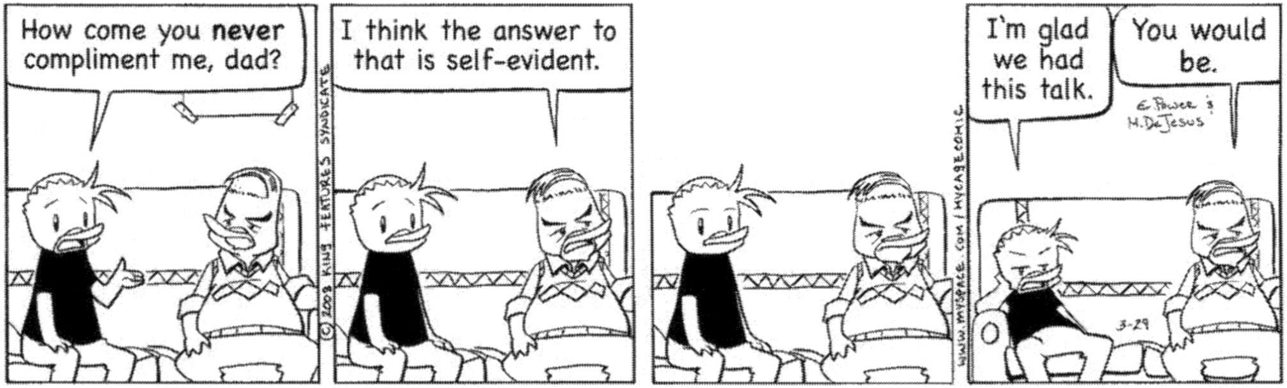
How come you never compliment me, dad?
© 2008 KING FEATURES SYNDICATE
I think the answer to that is self-evident.
WWW.MYSPACE.COM/MYCAGECOMIC
I'm glad we had this talk.
You would be.
3-29

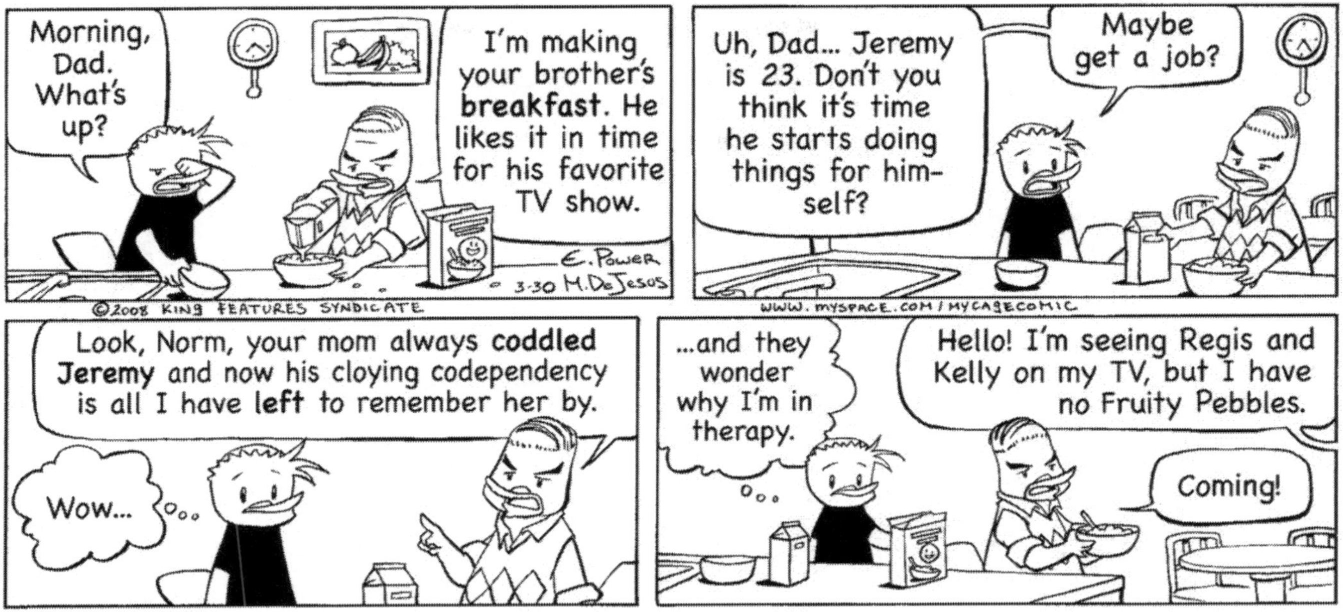
Morning, Dad. What's up?
I'm making your brother's breakfast. He likes it in time for his favorite TV show.
E. Power
3-30 M. DeJesus
©2008 King Features Syndicate
Uh, Dad... Jeremy is 23. Don't you think it's time he starts doing things for himself?
Maybe get a job?
www.myspace.com/mycagecomic
Look, Norm, your mom always coddled Jeremy and now his cloying codependency is all I have left to remember her by.
Wow...
...and they wonder why I'm in therapy.
Hello! I'm seeing Regis and Kelly on my TV, but I have no Fruity Pebbles.
Coming!

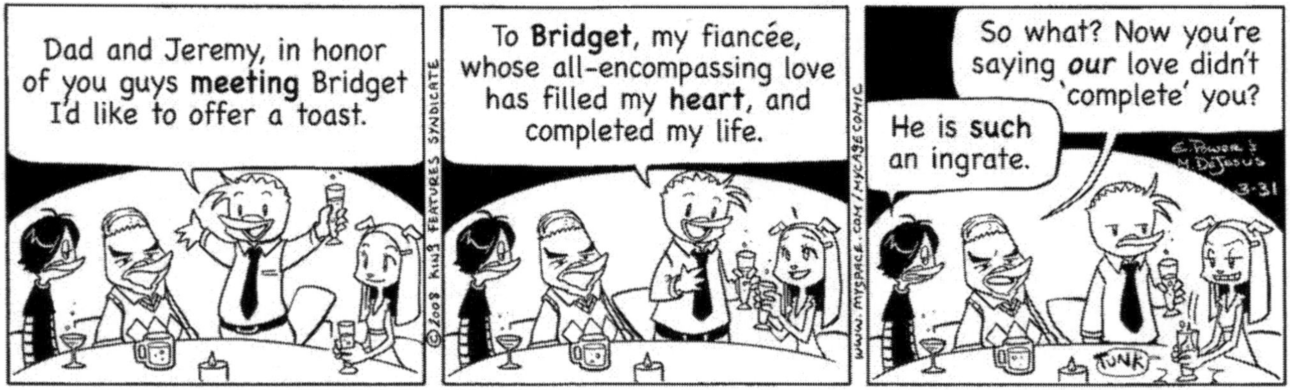
Dad and Jeremy, in honor of you guys **meeting** Bridget I'd like to offer a toast.
©2008 King Features Syndicate
To **Bridget**, my fiancée, whose all-encompassing love has filled my **heart**, and completed my life.
www.myspace.com/mycagecomic
So what? Now you're saying **our** love didn't 'complete' you?
He is **such** an ingrate.
TUNK
E. Power & M. DeJesus
3-31

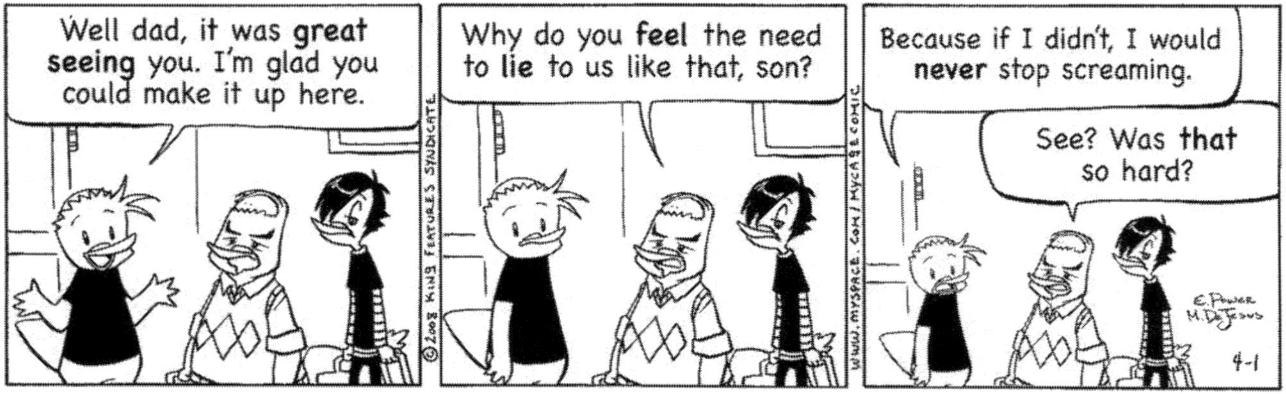
Well dad, it was **great seeing** you. I'm glad you could make it up here.
©2008 King Features Syndicate
Why do you **feel** the need to **lie** to us like that, son?
www.myspace.com/mycagecomic
Because if I didn't, I would **never** stop screaming.
See? Was **that** so hard?
E. Power M. DeJesus
4-1

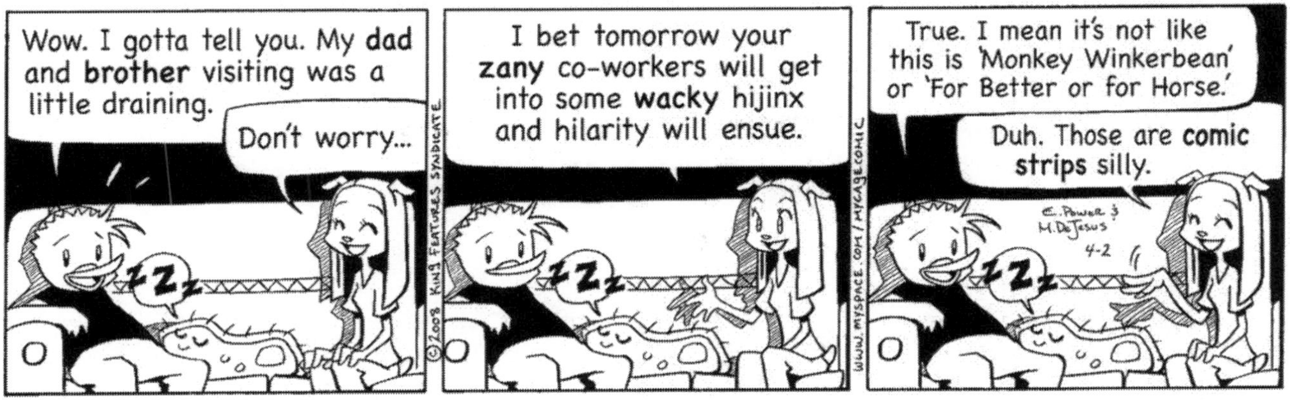
Wow. I gotta tell you. My **dad** and **brother** visiting was a little draining.
Don't worry...
I bet tomorrow your **zany** co-workers will get into some **wacky** hijinx and hilarity will ensue.
True. I mean it's not like this is 'Monkey Winkerbean' or 'For Better or for Horse.'
Duh. Those are **comic strips** silly.
©2008 King Features Syndicate
www.myspace.com/mycagecomic
E. Power & M. DeJesus
4-2

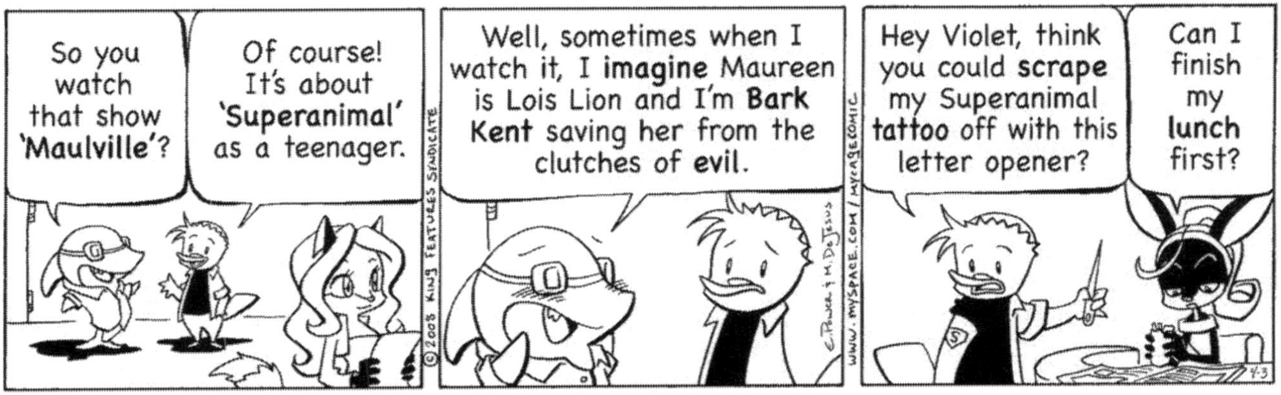
So you watch that show **'Maulville'**?
Of course! It's about **'Superanimal'** as a teenager.
Well, sometimes when I watch it, I **imagine** Maureen is Lois Lion and I'm **Bark Kent** saving her from the clutches of **evil**.
Hey Violet, think you could **scrape** my Superanimal **tattoo** off with this letter opener?
Can I finish my **lunch** first?
©2008 King Features Syndicate
www.myspace.com/mycagecomic
E. Power & M. DeJesus
4-3

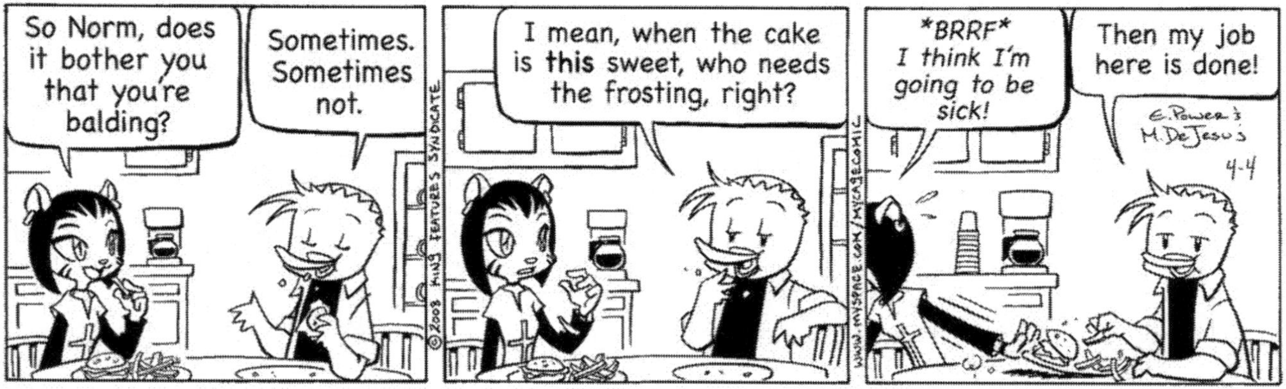
So Norm, does it bother you that you're balding?
Sometimes. Sometimes not.
©2008 KING FEATURES SYNDICATE
I mean, when the cake is **this** sweet, who needs the frosting, right?
WWW.MYSPACE.COM/MYCAGECOMIC
BRRF I think I'm going to be sick!
Then my job here is done!
E. Power & M. DeJesus
4-4

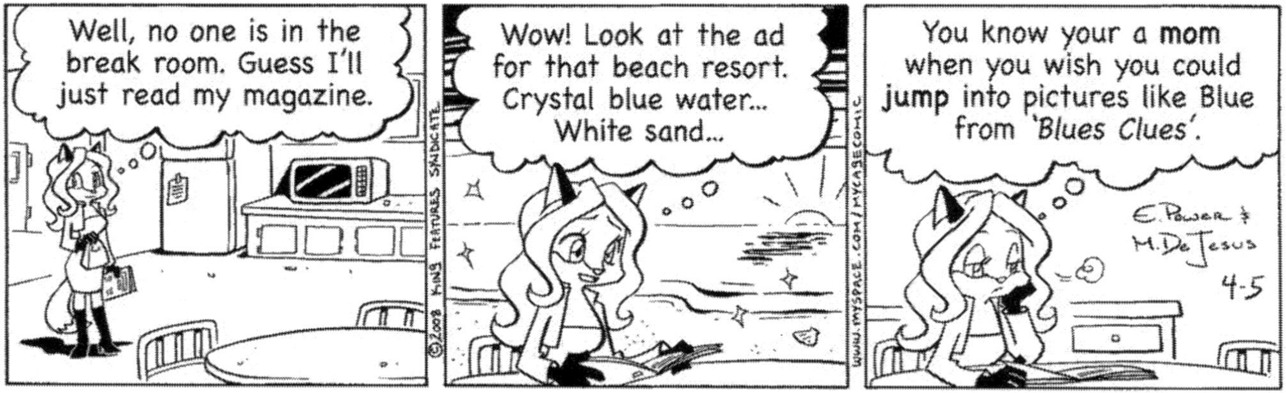
Well, no one is in the break room. Guess I'll just read my magazine.
©2008 KING FEATURES SYNDICATE
Wow! Look at the ad for that beach resort. Crystal blue water... White sand...
WWW.MYSPACE.COM/MYCAGECOMIC
You know your a **mom** when you wish you could **jump** into pictures like Blue from *'Blues Clues'*.
E. Power & M. DeJesus
4-5

Before going into his next song, **Norm Platypus** talks to the crowded arena...

Thank you, Zoo Jersey!!

© 2008 KING FEATURES SYNDICATE

This next song is a **cover** of the band known as *'Reel Pig Fish'*... it's called *'Sell Out'*!

The crowd goes **wild** as Norm **belts** out the lyrics with his emotion-filled **voice**...

Well, I know you can't work in fast food all your life...

www.myspace.com/mycagecomic

Norm goes into one of his **patented** guitar solos! The crowd is cheering **ravenously**!

All except for the girls in the front row, who seem to be—

—giggling?

E. Power & M. DeJesus

Sell out with me tonight!

Ha ha ha ha ha ha ha ha ha ha ha!!!

4-6

193

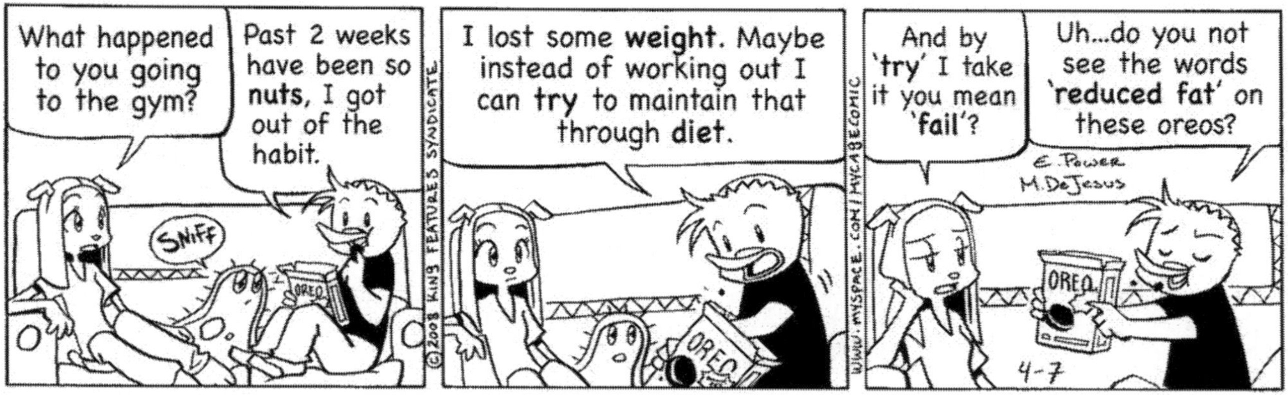
What happened to you going to the gym?
Past 2 weeks have been so **nuts**, I got out of the habit.
SNIFF
OREO
© 2008 KING FEATURES SYNDICATE
I lost some **weight**. Maybe instead of working out I can **try** to maintain that through **diet**.
OREO
And by '**try**' I take it you mean '**fail**'?
Uh...do you not see the words '**reduced fat**' on these oreos?
E. Power
M. DeJesus
OREO
4-7

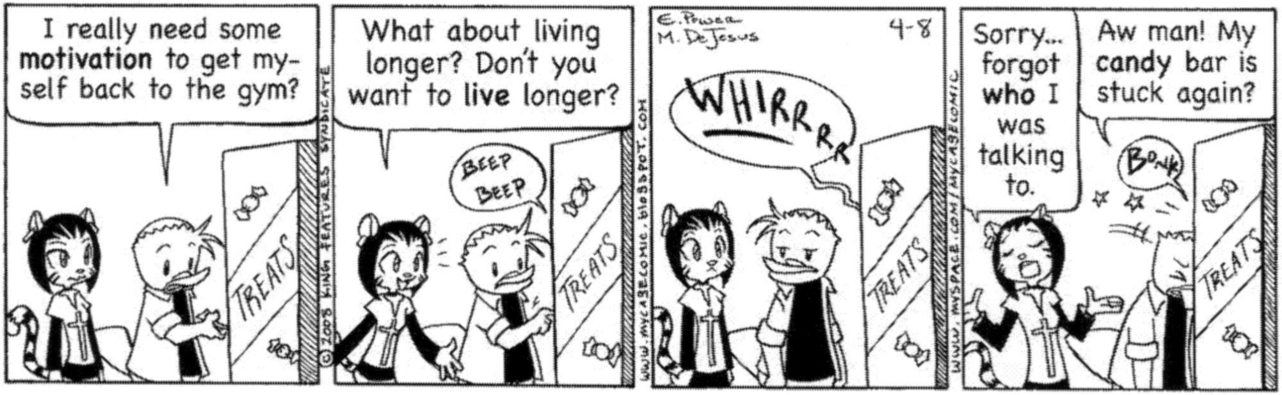
I really need some **motivation** to get my-self back to the gym?
TREATS
© 2008 KING FEATURES SYNDICATE
What about living longer? Don't you want to **live** longer?
BEEP BEEP
TREATS
E. Power
M. DeJesus
4-8
WHIRRRR
TREATS
Sorry... forgot **who** I was talking to.
Aw man! My **candy** bar is stuck again?
BONK
TREATS

C'mon...big bucks! No whammies! Big bucks! No whammies!

YAHOO!!

E. Power M. DeJesus

4-9

WHIRT

©2008 KING FEATURES SYNDICATE

Y'know, you could just **check** your balance before making a **withdrawl**.

And miss the thrill of **playing** my ATM like a slot machine? *NEVER!*

WWW.MYSPACE.COM/MYCAGECOMIC

ATM

Nice shirt, Rex. *giggle*

Yeah. Does Seinfeld know you borrowed his puffy shirt?

©2008 KING FEATURES SYNDICATE

Ha ha ha ha ha ha ha ha ha ha ha ha ha ha!!!

Go eat a sock!

WWW.MYSPACE.COM/MYCAGECOMIC

E. Power M. DeJesus

Wow. I think we hurt his feelings.

Yeah. Maybe under his big ego he's actually insecure.

4-10

WWW.MYCAGECOMIC.BLOGSPOT.COM

WA HA HA HAH HA HA HA HA HAHA HA HA HA HA HA HA HA HA HA HAHA HA HA HA HA HA HAH HA HA HA HA HAH

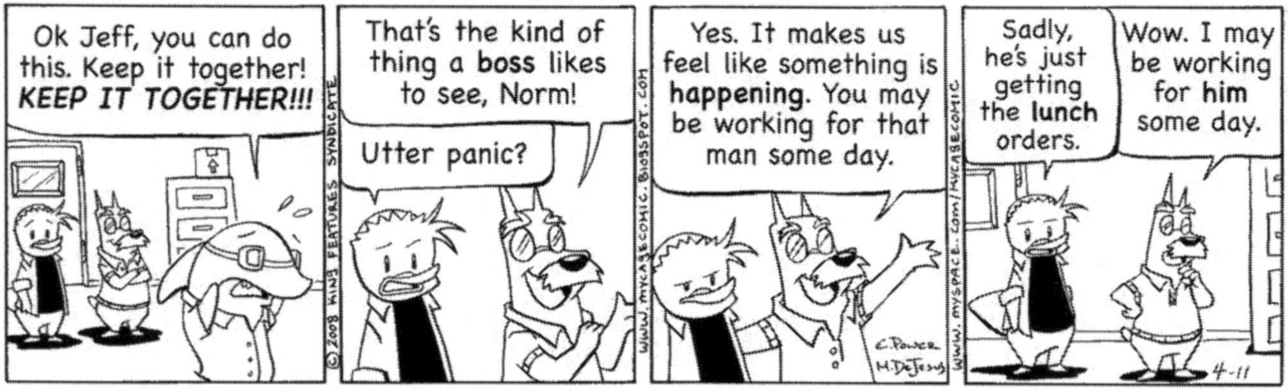
Ok Jeff, you can do this. Keep it together! *KEEP IT TOGETHER!!!*
© 2008 KING FEATURES SYNDICATE
That's the kind of thing a **boss** likes to see, Norm!
Utter panic?
WWW.MYCAGECOMIC.BLOGSPOT.COM
Yes. It makes us feel like something is **happening**. You may be working for that man some day.
E. Power
M. DeJesus
WWW.MYSPACE.COM/MYCAGECOMIC
Sadly, he's just getting the **lunch** orders.
Wow. I may be working for **him** some day.
4-11

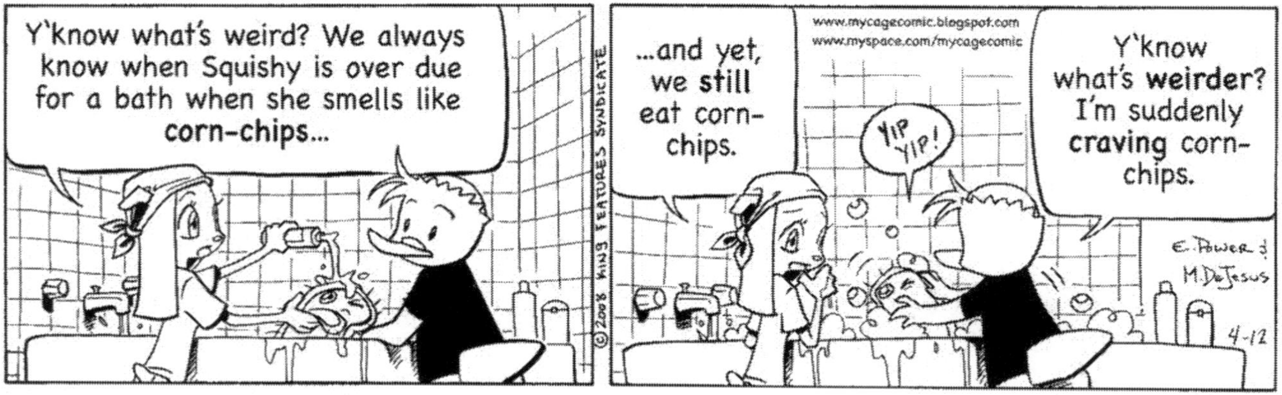
Y'know what's weird? We always know when Squishy is over due for a bath when she smells like **corn-chips**...
© 2008 KING FEATURES SYNDICATE
...and yet, we **still** eat corn-chips.
www.mycagecomic.blogspot.com
www.myspace.com/mycagecomic
YIP YIP!
Y'know what's **weirder**? I'm suddenly **craving** corn-chips.
E. Power &
M. DeJesus
4-12

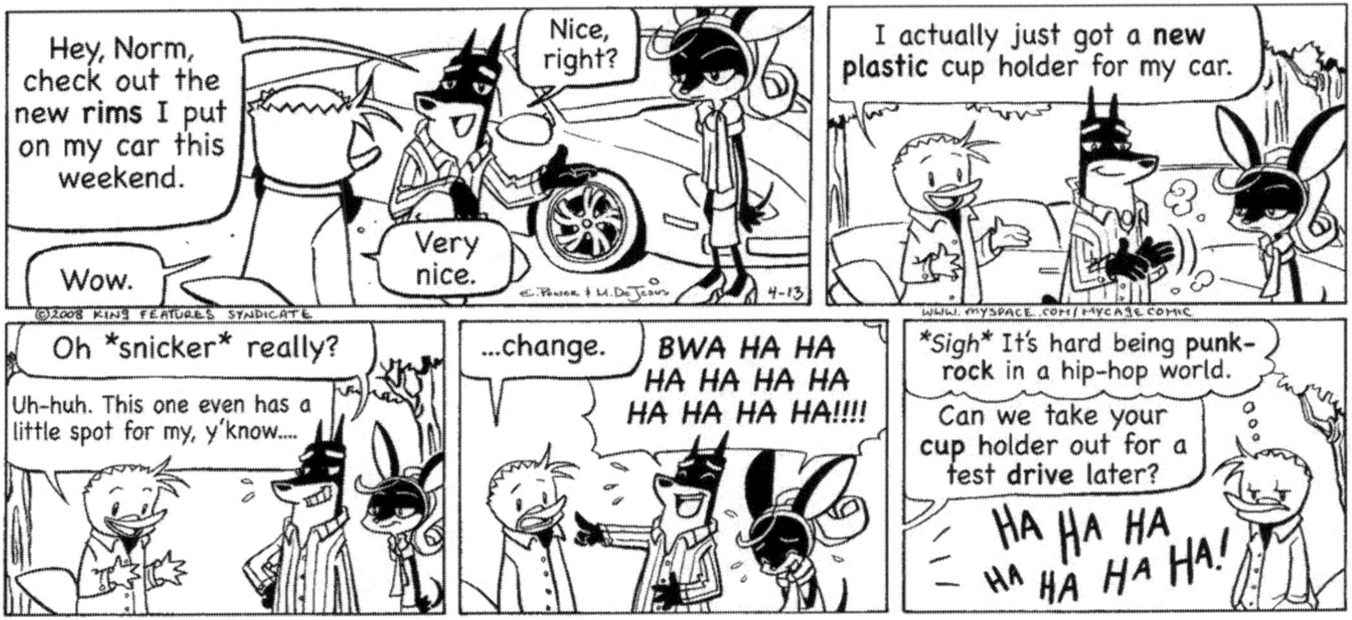
Hey, Norm, check out the new **rims** I put on my car this weekend.
Wow.
Very nice.
Nice, right?
E. Power + M. DeJesus
4-13
©2008 King Features Syndicate
I actually just got a **new plastic** cup holder for my car.
www.myspace.com/mycagecomic
Oh *snicker* really?
Uh-huh. This one even has a little spot for my, y'know....
...change.
BWA HA HA HA HA HA HA HA HA HA HA!!!!
Sigh It's hard being **punk-rock** in a hip-hop world.
Can we take your **cup** holder out for a test **drive** later?
HA HA HA HA HA HA HA!

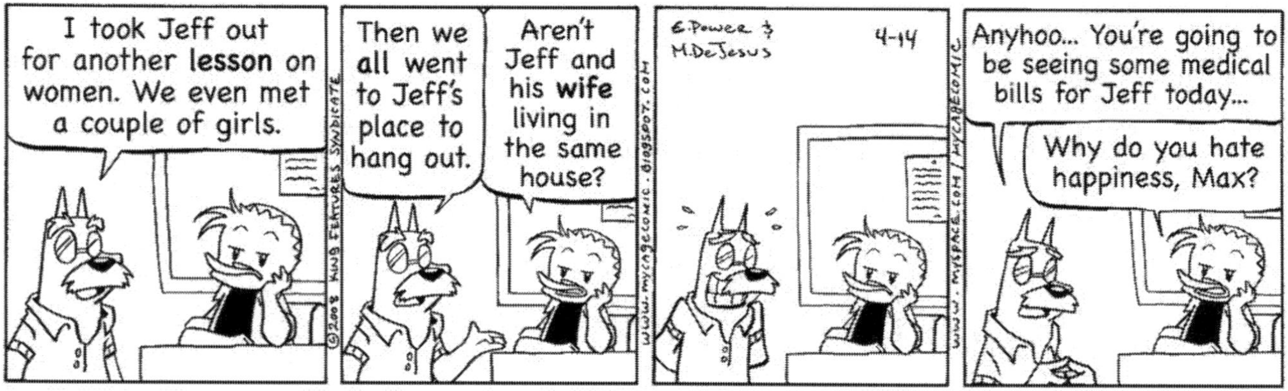
I took Jeff out for another **lesson** on women. We even met a couple of girls.
Then we **all** went to Jeff's place to hang out.
Aren't Jeff and his **wife** living in the same house?
E.Power & M.DeJesus 4-14
Anyhoo... You're going to be seeing some medical bills for Jeff today...
Why do you hate happiness, Max?
© 2008 KING FEATURES SYNDICATE
WWW.MYCAGECOMIC.BLOGSPOT.COM
WWW.MYSPACE.COM/MYCAGECOMIC

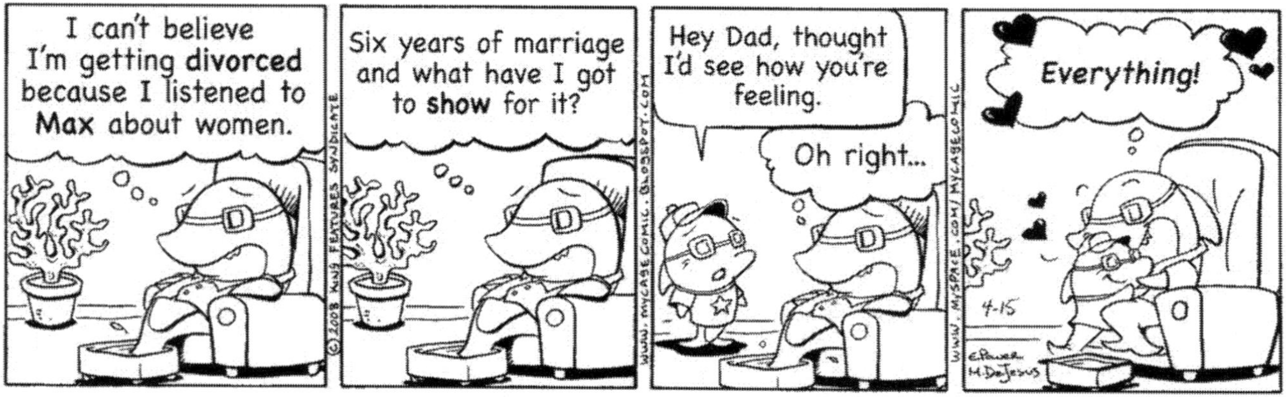
I can't believe I'm getting **divorced** because I listened to **Max** about women.
Six years of marriage and what have I got to **show** for it?
Hey Dad, thought I'd see how you're feeling.
Oh right...
Everything!
4-15
E.Power M.DeJesus
© 2008 KING FEATURES SYNDICATE
WWW.MYCAGECOMIC.BLOGSPOT.COM
WWW.MYSPACE.COM/MYCAGECOMIC

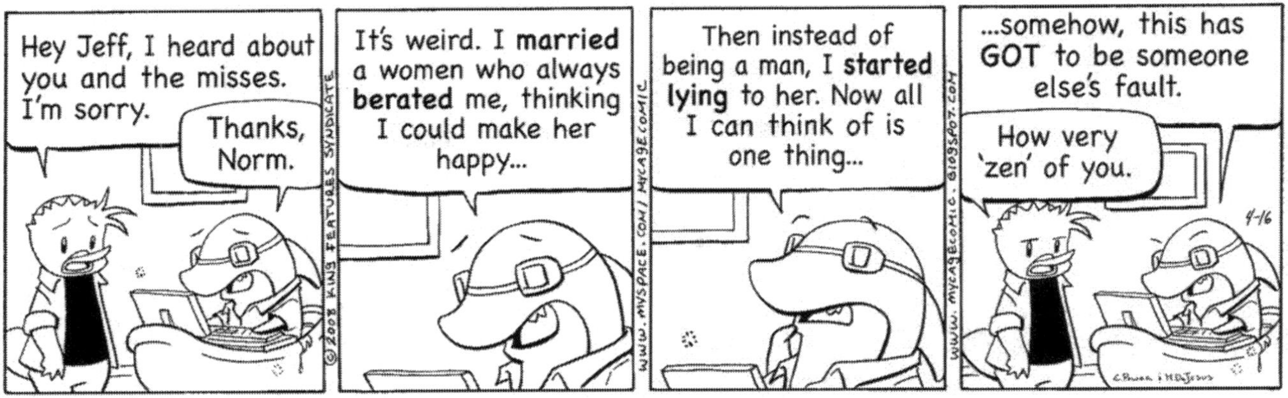
Hey Jeff, I heard about you and the misses. I'm sorry.
Thanks, Norm.
It's weird. I **married** a women who always **berated** me, thinking I could make her happy...
Then instead of being a man, I **started lying** to her. Now all I can think of is one thing...
...somehow, this has **GOT** to be someone else's fault.
How very 'zen' of you.
© 2008 KING FEATURES SYNDICATE
WWW.MYSPACE.COM/MYCAGECOMIC
WWW.MYCAGECOMIC.BLOGSPOT.COM
4-16

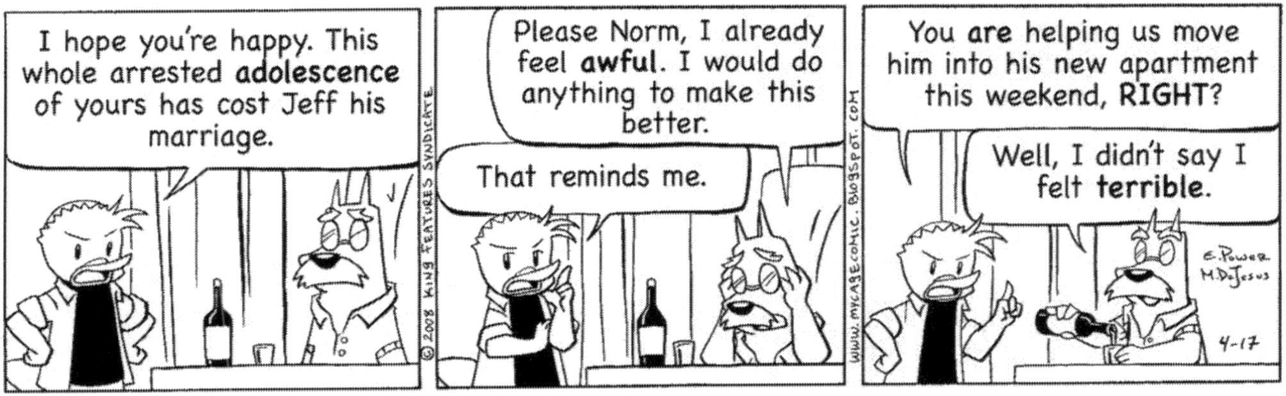
I hope you're happy. This whole arrested **adolescence** of yours has cost Jeff his marriage.
Please Norm, I already feel **awful**. I would do anything to make this better.
That reminds me.
You **are** helping us move him into his new apartment this weekend, **RIGHT**?
Well, I didn't say I felt **terrible**.
© 2008 KING FEATURES SYNDICATE
WWW.MYCAGECOMIC.BLOGSPOT.COM
E.POWER
M.DeJesus
4-17

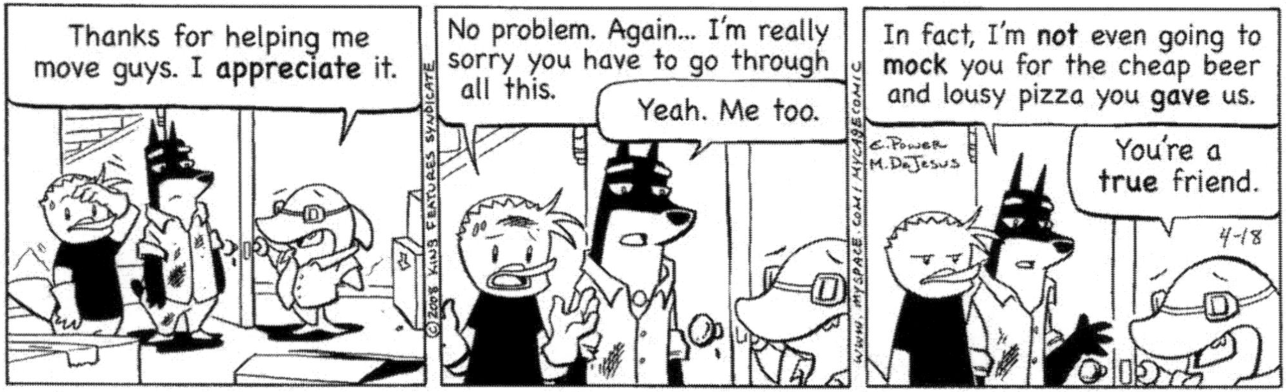
Thanks for helping me move guys. I **appreciate** it.
(c) 2008 KING FEATURES SYNDICATE
No problem. Again... I'm really sorry you have to go through all this.
Yeah. Me too.
WWW.MYSPACE.COM/MYCAGECOMIC
In fact, I'm **not** even going to **mock** you for the cheap beer and lousy pizza you **gave** us.
E.POWER M.DEJESUS
You're a **true** friend.
4-18

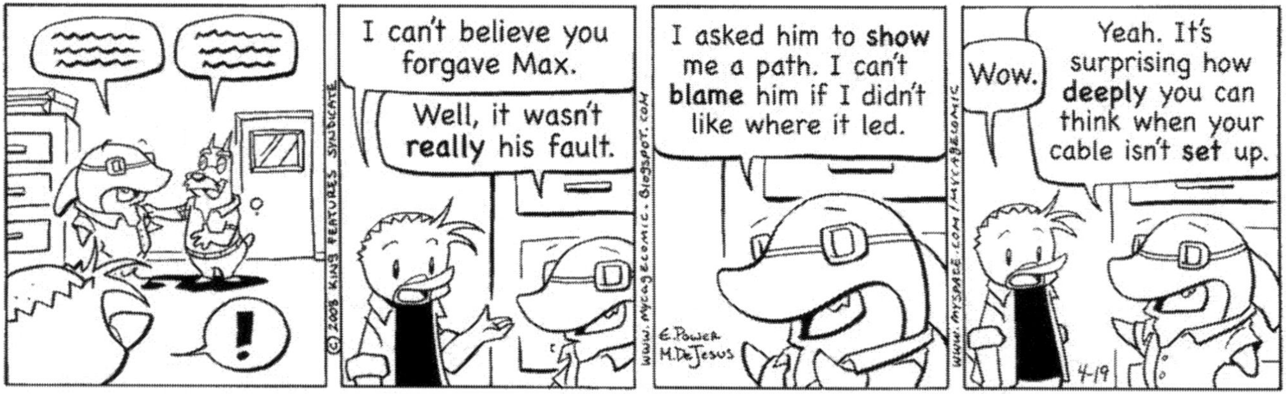
!
(c) 2008 KING FEATURES SYNDICATE
I can't believe you forgave Max.
Well, it wasn't **really** his fault.
WWW.MYCAGECOMIC.BLOGSPOT.COM
I asked him to **show** me a path. I can't **blame** him if I didn't like where it led.
E.POWER M.DEJESUS
WWW.MYSPACE.COM/MYCAGECOMIC
Wow.
Yeah. It's surprising how **deeply** you can think when your cable isn't **set** up.
4-19

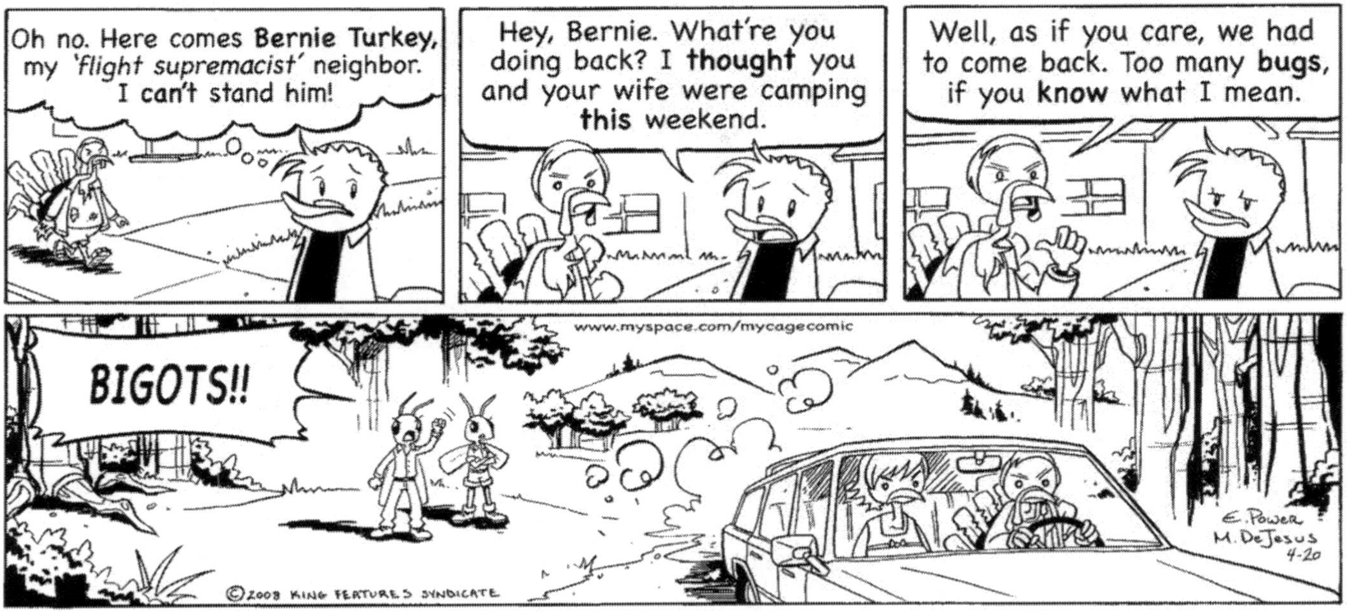
Oh no. Here comes **Bernie Turkey,** my *'flight supremacist'* neighbor. I **can't** stand him!
Hey, Bernie. What're you doing back? I **thought** you and your wife were camping **this** weekend.
Well, as if you care, we had to come back. Too many **bugs,** if you **know** what I mean.
www.myspace.com/mycagecomic
BIGOTS!!
E. POWER
M. DeJESUS
4-20
©2008 KING FEATURES SYNDICATE

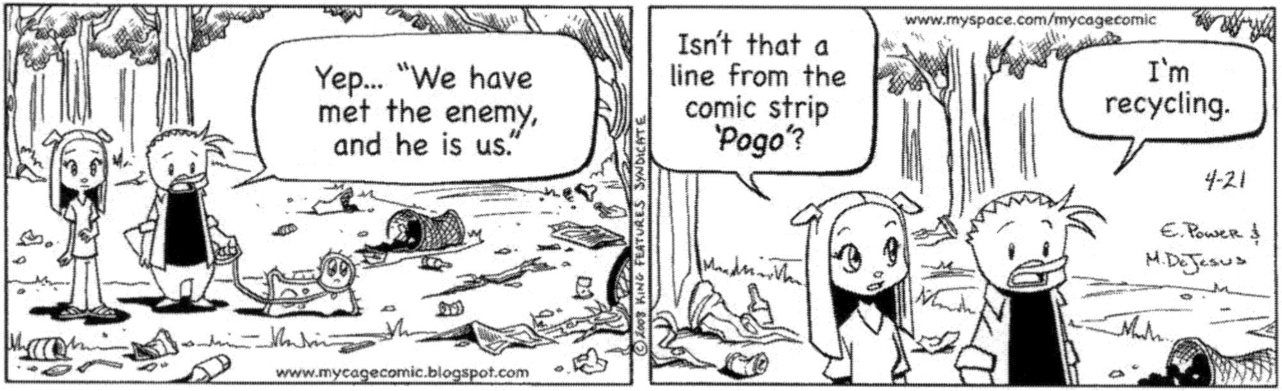
Yep... "We have met the enemy, and he is us."
www.mycagecomic.blogspot.com
© 2008 King Features Syndicate
www.myspace.com/mycagecomic
Isn't that a line from the comic strip 'Pogo'?
I'm recycling.
4-21
E. Power & M. DeJesus

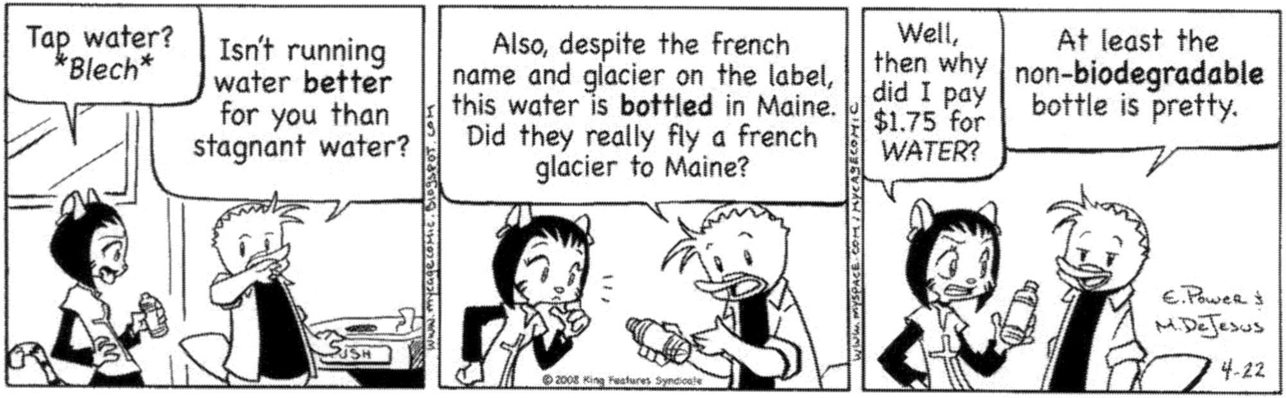
Tap water? *Blech*
Isn't running water better for you than stagnant water?
www.mycagecomic.blogspot.com
Also, despite the french name and glacier on the label, this water is bottled in Maine. Did they really fly a french glacier to Maine?
© 2008 King Features Syndicate
www.myspace.com/mycagecomic
Well, then why did I pay $1.75 for WATER?
At least the non-biodegradable bottle is pretty.
E. Power & M. DeJesus
4-22

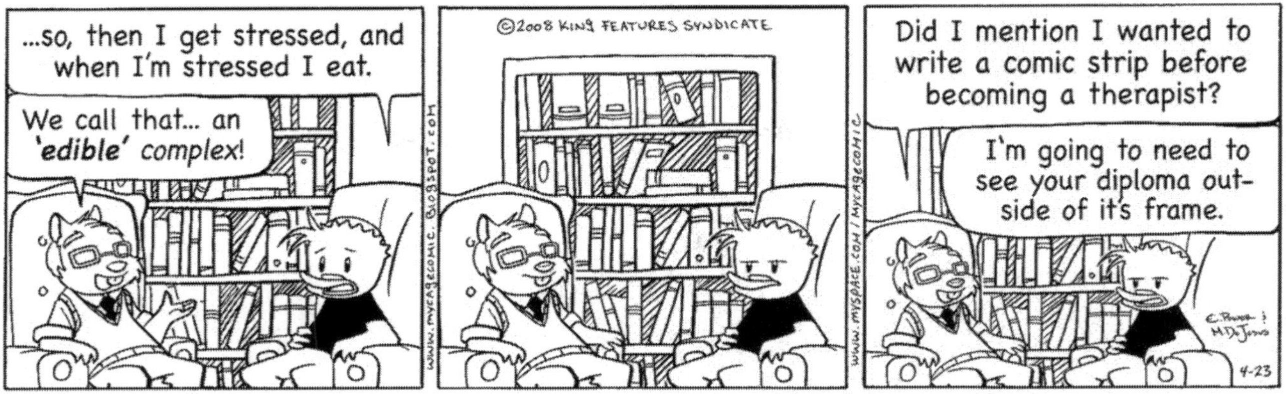

...so, then I get stressed, and when I'm stressed I eat.
We call that... an *'edible'* complex!
©2008 KING FEATURES SYNDICATE
WWW.MYCAGECOMIC.BLOGSPOT.COM
Did I mention I wanted to write a comic strip before becoming a therapist?
I'm going to need to see your diploma out-side of it's frame.
WWW.MYSPACE.COM/MYCAGECOMIC
4-23

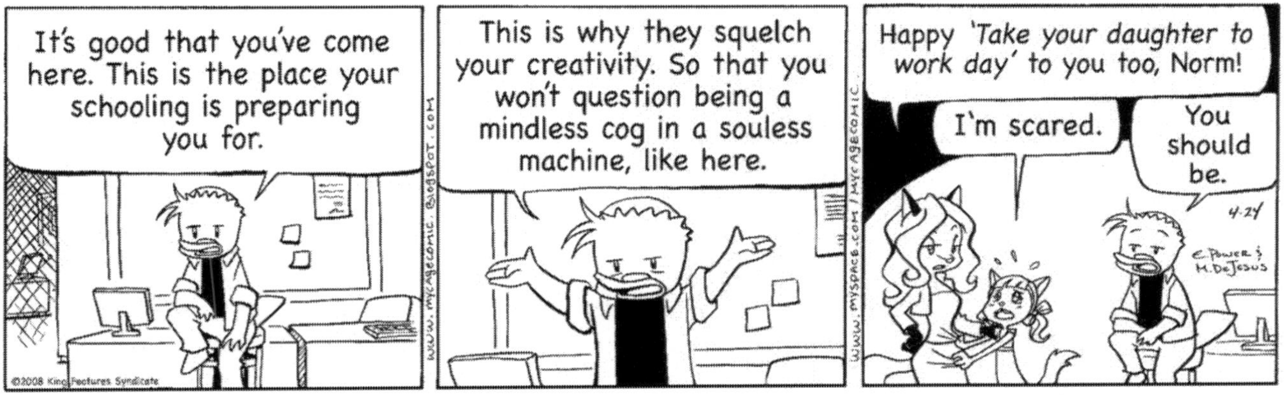

It's good that you've come here. This is the place your schooling is preparing you for.
©2008 King Features Syndicate
WWW.MYCAGECOMIC.BLOGSPOT.COM
This is why they squelch your creativity. So that you won't question being a mindless cog in a souless machine, like here.
WWW.MYSPACE.COM/MYCAGECOMIC
Happy *'Take your daughter to work day'* to you too, Norm!
I'm scared.
You should be.
4-24
E. Power & M. DeJesus

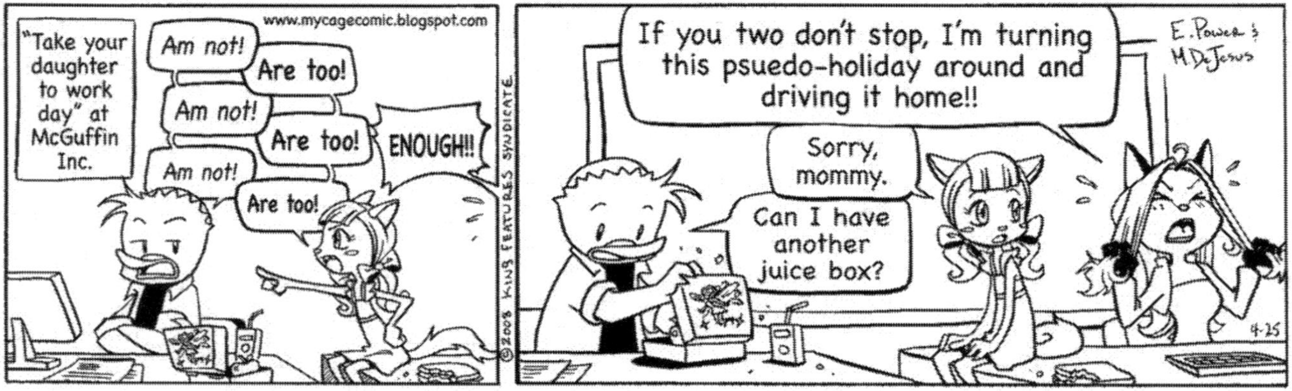
www.mycagecomic.blogspot.com
"Take your daughter to work day" at McGuffin Inc.
Am not!
Are too!
Am not!
Are too!
Am not!
Are too!
ENOUGH!!
© 2008 KING FEATURES SYNDICATE
If you two don't stop, I'm turning this psuedo-holiday around and driving it home!!
E. Power & M. DeJesus
Sorry, mommy.
Can I have another juice box?
4-25

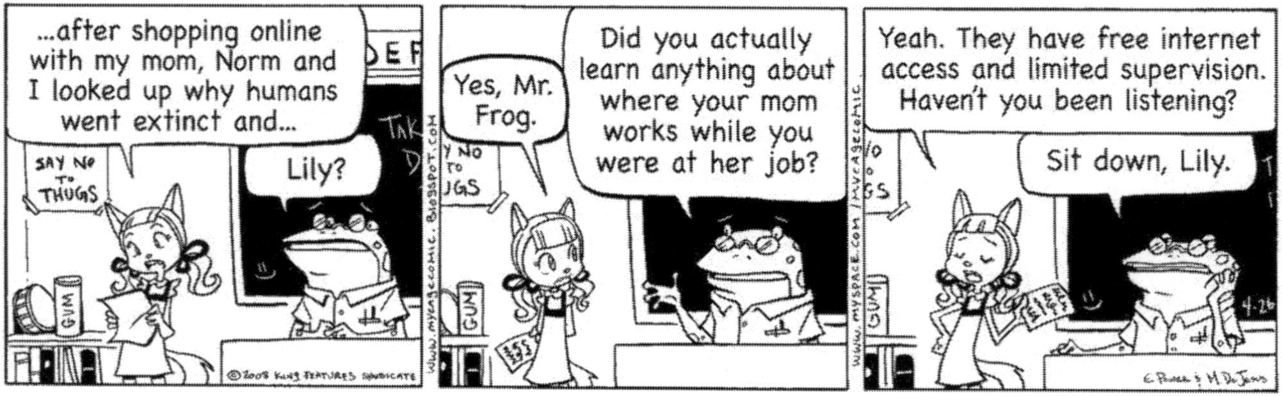
...after shopping online with my mom, Norm and I looked up why humans went extinct and...
SAY NO TO THUGS
GUM
Lily?
© 2008 KING FEATURES SYNDICATE
WWW.MYCAGECOMIC.BLOGSPOT.COM
Yes, Mr. Frog.
Did you actually learn anything about where your mom works while you were at her job?
WWW.MYSPACE.COM/MYCAGECOMIC
Yeah. They have free internet access and limited supervision. Haven't you been listening?
Sit down, Lily.
4-26
E. Power & M. DeJesus

I am *soooo* bored here with **Rex** out sick.
Guess I'll see what the conversation is at the **shallow** end of the gene pool.
BREAK ROOM
Hey Norm, **check** out the pic of that actress **Megan Fox** in this magazine.
Wow.
ALPHA MALE
© 2008 King Features Syndicate
She **really** is a fox.
Yeah *giggle* literally **AND** figuratively.
www.myspace.com/mycagecomic
www.mycagecomic.blogspot.com
snort Ha ha ha ha ha!!
Hee hee hee hee! *snort*
...or I could just **beat** myself in the head with my **key-board** for the next 5 hours.
What does **'figuratively'** mean?
4-27
E. Power
M. DeJesus

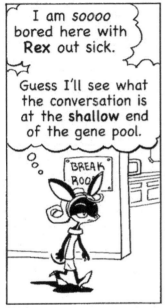

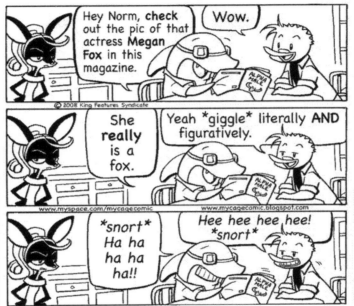

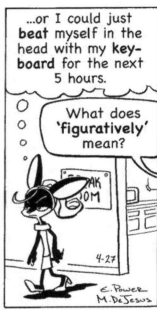

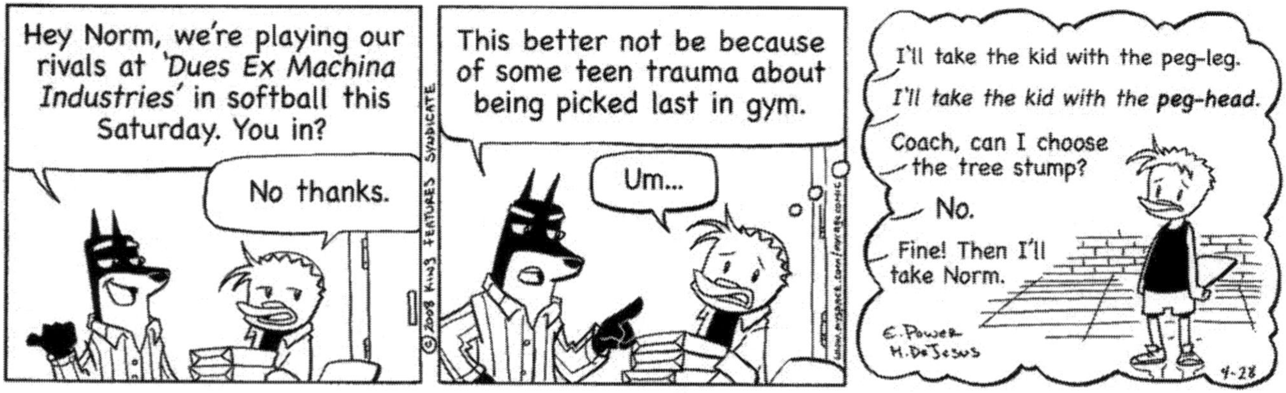

Hey Norm, we're playing our rivals at *'Dues Ex Machina Industries'* in softball this Saturday. You in?
No thanks.
© 2008 King Features Syndicate
This better not be because of some teen trauma about being picked last in gym.
Um...
I'll take the kid with the peg-leg.
*I'll take the kid with the **peg-head**.*
Coach, can I choose the tree stump?
No.
Fine! Then I'll take Norm.
E. Power
M. DeJesus
4-28

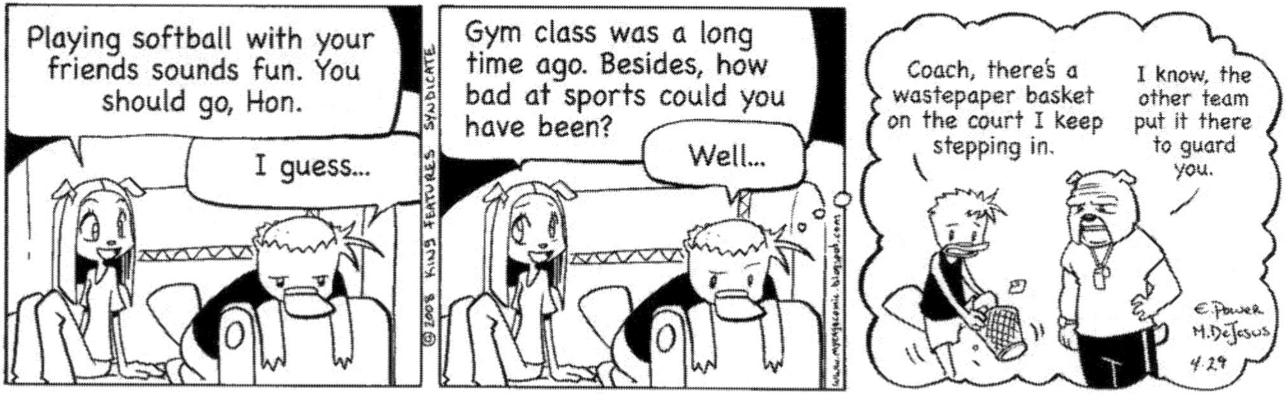

Playing softball with your friends sounds fun. You should go, Hon.
I guess...
© 2008 King Features Syndicate
Gym class was a long time ago. Besides, how bad at sports could you have been?
Well...
Coach, there's a wastepaper basket on the court I keep stepping in.
I know, the other team put it there to guard you.
E. Power
M. DeJesus
4-29

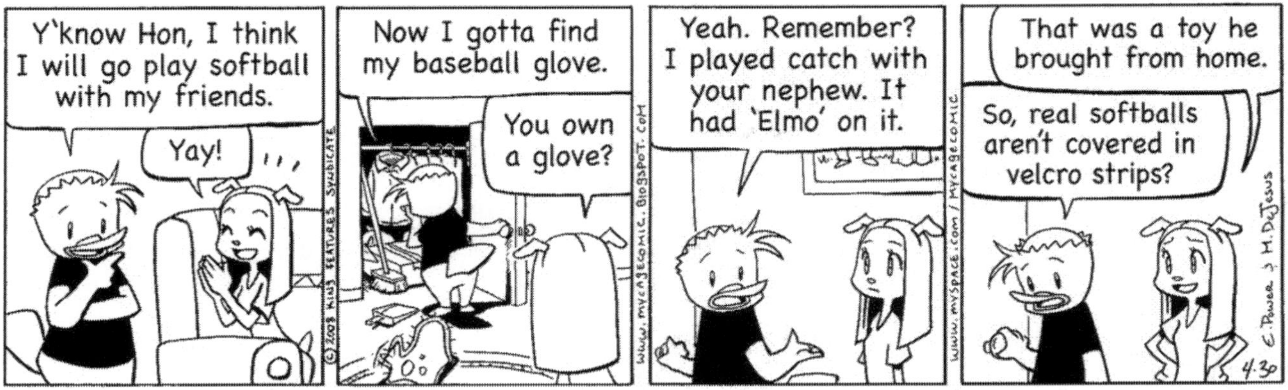
Y'know Hon, I think I will go play softball with my friends.
Yay!
©2008 King Features Syndicate
Now I gotta find my baseball glove.
You own a glove?
www.mycagecomic.blogspot.com
Yeah. Remember? I played catch with your nephew. It had 'Elmo' on it.
www.myspace.com/mycagecomic
That was a toy he brought from home.
So, real softballs aren't covered in velcro strips?
E. Power & M. DeJesus
4-30

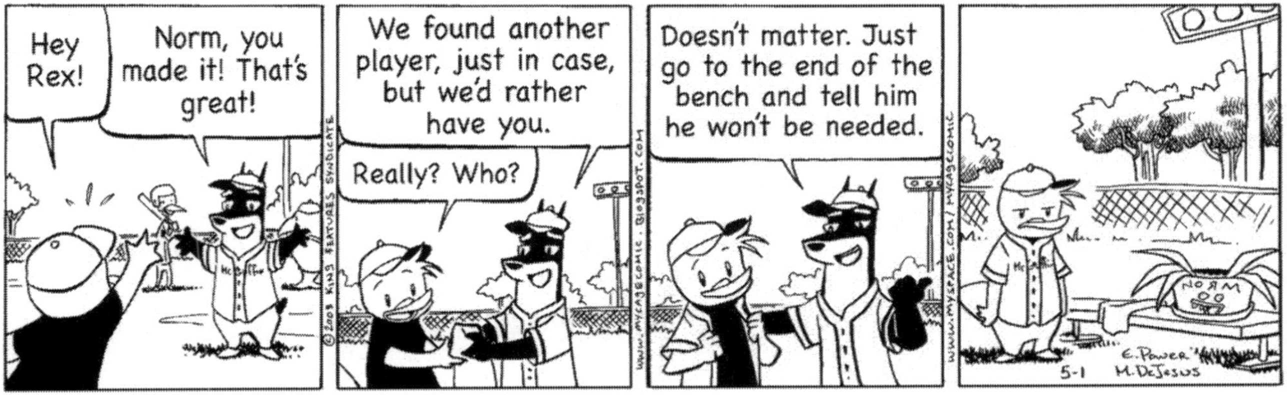
Hey Rex!
Norm, you made it! That's great!
©2008 King Features Syndicate
We found another player, just in case, but we'd rather have you.
Really? Who?
www.mycagecomic.blogspot.com
Doesn't matter. Just go to the end of the bench and tell him he won't be needed.
www.myspace.com/mycagecomic
NORM
E. Power
M. DeJesus
5-1

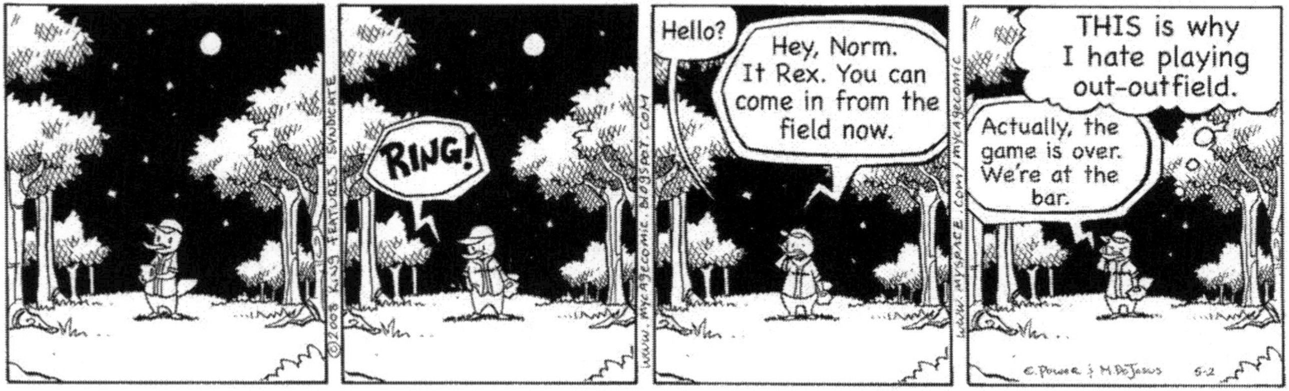
©2008 King Features Syndicate
RING!
Hello?
Hey, Norm. It Rex. You can come in from the field now.
www.mycagecomic.blogspot.com
www.myspace.com/mycagecomic
Actually, the game is over. We're at the bar.
THIS is why I hate playing out-outfield.
E. Power & M. DeJesus 5-2

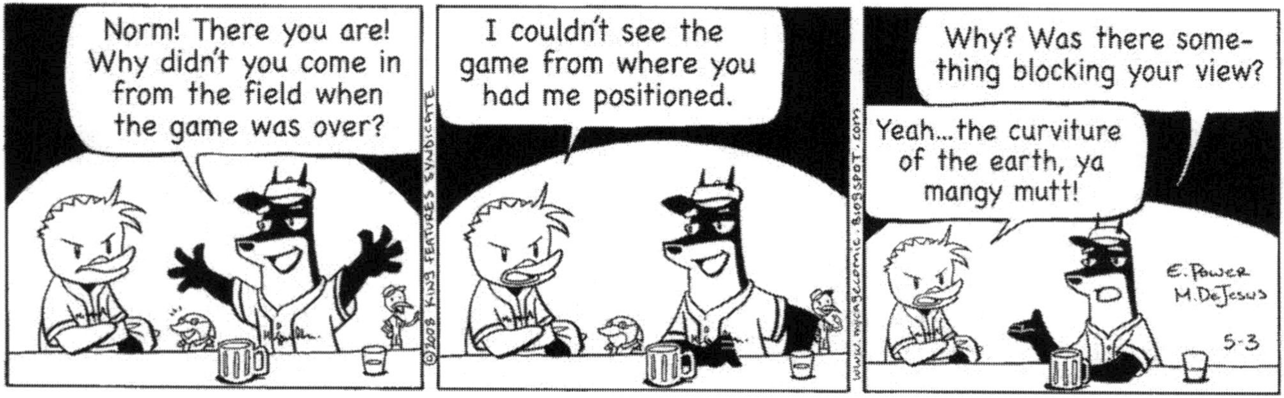
Norm! There you are! Why didn't you come in from the field when the game was over?
©2008 King Features Syndicate
I couldn't see the game from where you had me positioned.
www.mycagecomic.blogspot.com
Why? Was there something blocking your view?
Yeah...the curviture of the earth, ya mangy mutt!
E. Power
M. DeJesus
5-3

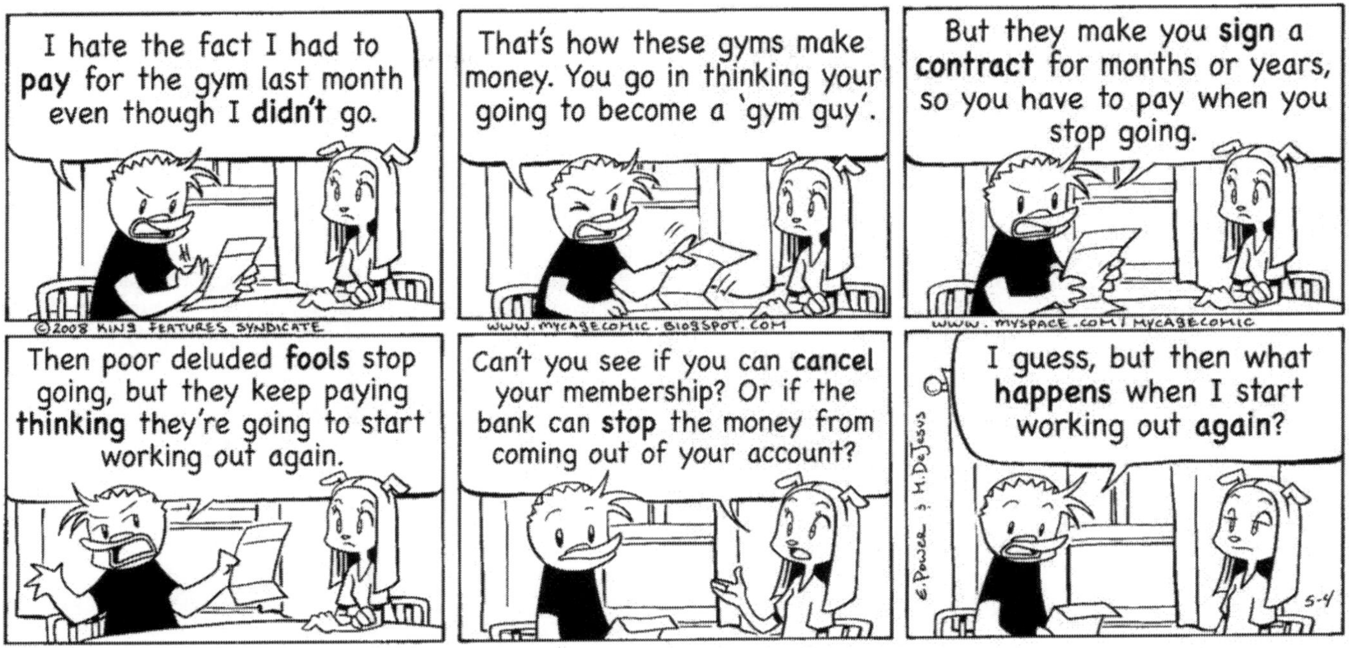
I hate the fact I had to pay for the gym last month even though I didn't go.
That's how these gyms make money. You go in thinking your going to become a 'gym guy'.
But they make you sign a contract for months or years, so you have to pay when you stop going.
©2008 KING FEATURES SYNDICATE
WWW.MYCAGECOMIC.BLOGSPOT.COM
WWW.MYSPACE.COM/MYCAGECOMIC
Then poor deluded fools stop going, but they keep paying thinking they're going to start working out again.
Can't you see if you can cancel your membership? Or if the bank can stop the money from coming out of your account?
E.POWER & M.DEJESUS
I guess, but then what happens when I start working out again?
5-4

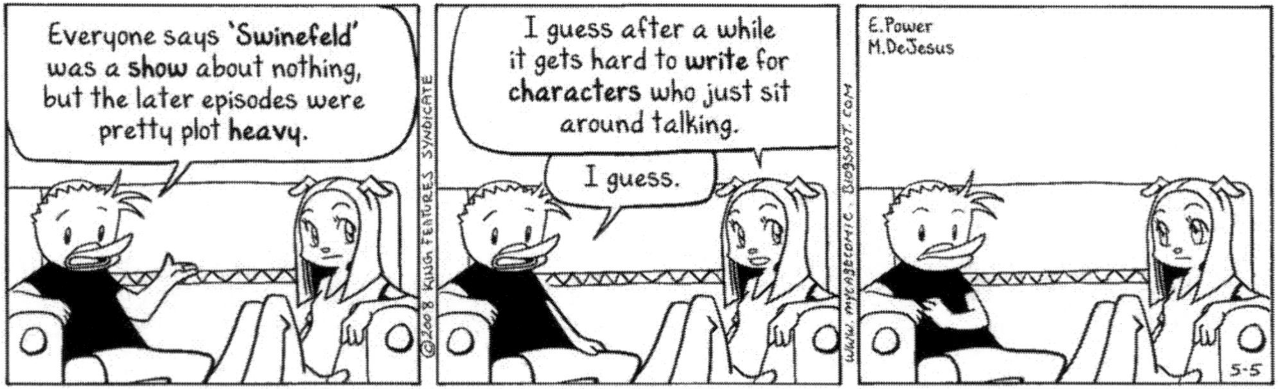
Everyone says 'Swinefeld' was a show about nothing, but the later episodes were pretty plot heavy.
©2008 KING FEATURES SYNDICATE
I guess after a while it gets hard to write for characters who just sit around talking.
I guess.
WWW.MYCAGECOMIC.BLOGSPOT.COM
E.Power
M.DeJesus
5-5

My Cage continues in newspapers
across the country. If it isn't in your local paper, and you would
like to support our strip, please write them and ask for My Cage.

For information and strips please visit us at
www.mycagecomic.com and www.mycagecomic.blogspot.com

Our online store can be found at www.cafepress.com/mycagecomic

Write us at mycagecomic@yahoo.com

Thank you!